Verification, Validation and Testing in Software Engineering

Aristides Dasso, Universidad Nacional de San Luis, Argentina

Ana Funes, Universidad Nacional de San Luis, Argentina

T0321964

IDEA GROUP PUBLISHING

Hershey • London • Melbourne • Singapore

Acquisitions Editor:	Michelle Potter
Development Editor:	Kristin Roth
Senior Managing Editor:	Jennifer Neidig
Managing Editor:	Sara Reed
Copy Editor:	Chuck Pizar
Typesetter:	Sharon Berger
Cover Design:	Lisa Tosheff
Printed at:	Integrated Book Technology

Published in the United States of America by
    Idea Group Publishing (an imprint of Idea Group Inc.)
    701 E. Chocolate Avenue
    Hershey PA 17033
    Tel: 717-533-8845
    Fax: 717-533-8661
    E-mail: cust@idea-group.com
    Web site: http://www.idea-group.com

and in the United Kingdom by
    Idea Group Publishing (an imprint of Idea Group Inc.)
    3 Henrietta Street
    Covent Garden
    London WC2E 8LU
    Tel: 44 20 7240 0856
    Fax: 44 20 7379 0609
    Web site: http://www.eurospanonline.com

Library of Congress Cataloging-in-Publication Data

Verification, validation and testing in software engineering / Aristides Dasso and Ana Funes, editors.
    p. cm.
  Summary: "This book explores different applications in V&V that spawn many areas of software development -including real time applications- where V&V techniques are required, providing in all cases examples of the applications"--Provided by publisher.
  ISBN 1-59140-851-2 (hardcover) -- ISBN 1-59140-852-0 (softcover) -- ISBN 1-59140-853-9 (ebook)
  1. Computer software--Validation. 2. Computer software--Verification. 3. Computer software--Testing. I. Dasso, Aristides, 1943- II. Funes, Ana, 1964-
  QA76.76.V47V488 2006
  005.14--dc22
                          2006013530

British Cataloguing in Publication Data
A Cataloguing in Publication record for this book is available from the British Library.

All work contributed to this book is new, previously-unpublished material. The views expressed in this book are those of the authors, but not necessarily of the publisher.

Verification, Validation and Testing in Software Engineering

Table of Contents

Preface vi

Chapter I
Fault-Based Testing 1
  Marisa Analía Sánchez, Universidad Nacional del Sur, Argentina

Chapter II
Validation and Verification of Software Systems Using Virtual Reality and
Coloured Petri Nets 24
  Hyggo Oliveira de Almeida, Federal University of Campina Grande, Brazil
  Leandro Silva, Federal University of Campina Grande, Brazil
  Glauber Ferreira, Federal University of Campina Grande, Brazil
  Emerson Loureiro, Federal University of Campina Grande, Brazil
  Angelo Perkusich, Federal University of Campina Grande, Brazil

Chapter III
Integrating Usability, Semiotic, and Software Engineering into a Method for
Evaluating User Interfaces 47
  Kenia Sousa, University of Fortaleza, Brazil
  Albert Schilling, University of Fortaleza, Brazil
  Elizabeth Furtado, University of Fortaleza, Brazil

Chapter IV
Automated Software Testing 71
  Paula Donegan, Instituto Atlântico, Brazil
  Liane Bandeira, Instituto Atlântico, Brazil
  Cristina Matos, Instituto Atlântico, Brazil
  Paula Luciana da Cunha, Instituto Atlântico, Brazil
  Camila Maia, Instituto Atlântico, Brazil

Chapter V
A Formal Verification and Validation Approach for Real-Time Databases 96
    Pedro Fernandes Ribeiro Neto, Universidade do Estado do Rio Grande do
      Norte, Brazil
    Maria Lígia Barbosa Perkusich, Católica de Pernambuco, Brazil
    Hyggo Oliveira de Almeida, Federal University of Campina Grande, Brazil
    Angelo Perkusich, Federal University of Campina Grande, Brazil

Chapter VI
Requirements for the Testable Specifications and Test Case Derivation in
Conformance Testing 118
    Tanja Toroi, University of Kuopio, Finland
    Anne Eerola, University of Kuopio, Finland

Chapter VII
Test-Case Mutation 136
    Macario Polo, University of Castilla - La Mancha, Spain
    Mario Piattini, University of Castilla - La Mancha, Spain

Chapter VIII
Discrete Event Simulation Process Validation, Verification,
and Testing 154
    Evon M. O. Abu-Taieh, The Arab Academy for Banking and
      Financial Sciences, Jordan
    Asim Abdel Rahman El Sheikh, The Arab Academy for Banking and
      Financial Sciences, Jordan

Chapter IX
The STECC Framework: An Architecture for Self-Testable Components 185
    Sami Beydeda, Federal Finance Office, Germany

Chapter X
Certifying Properties of Programs Using Theorem Provers 220
    J. Santiago Jorge, University of A Coruña, Spain
    Víctor M. Gulías, University of A Coruña, Spain
    David Cabrero, University of A Coruña, Spain

Chapter XI
Static Type Systems: From Specification to Implementation 268
    Pablo E. Martínez López, LIFIA, Facultad de Informática, UNLP, Argentina

Chapter XII
Generic Model of the Business Model and Its Formalization in Object-Z 317
    Marcela Daniele, Universidad Nacional de Río Cuarto, Argentina
    Paola Martellotto, Universidad Nacional de Río Cuarto, Argentina
    Gabriel Baum, Universidad Nacional de Río Cuarto, Argentina

Chapter XIII
Efficient Software Quality Assurance Approaches Oriented to
UML Models in Real Life 341
    Luis Fernández, Universidad Europea de Madrid, Spain
    Pedro J. Lara, Universidad Europea de Madrid, Spain
    Juan José Cuadrado, Universidad de Alcalá, Spain

Chapter XIV
Safecharts Model Checking for the Verification of Safety-Critical Systems 378
    Pao-Ann Hsiung, National Chung Cheng University, Taiwan
    Yen-Hung Lin, National Chung Cheng University, Taiwan
    Yean-Ru Chen, National Chung Cheng University, Taiwan

About the Authors 413

Index 421

Preface

Introduction

Validation and verification (V&V) — especially testing, probably one of its more well-known areas — is a sector of software engineering that has been around since the early days of program development.

We do V&V to assure that a software system meets the user's needs without defects. Bohem (1981) put it in a nutshell: You are doing validation when you are answering the question: "Are we building the right product?" You are doing verification when you are answering the question: "Are we building the product right?"

V&V both have static and dynamic techniques, and both are necessary to meet the normal quality requirements of every software project.

Validation is closely related to requirements specification. You can validate the user's requirements; this is where ambiguity reigns most of the time and where formal methods (Dasso & Funes, 2005) — through the use of specification languages — has made the biggest strides. There is still a wide gap between what the user wants and what the developer understands that the user wants. Very often this is where one of the causes of initial system failure can be found.

In most cases of system development, validation is left till nearly the end of the project when the user meets the system to give her or his final approval. Although, this is not always the case since there are development methodologies that require the involvement of the user thoughout the development process, for example, agile methods (Beck, 1999; Cockburn, 2001). However, validation could also come at the early stages of development if the user's requirements could be precisely defined and from them the rest of the development derived. This is where formal methods and their corresponding specification languages become involved. Then, it could be argued that validation would be a question of making sure that the formal specification is consistent with the user's requirements.

As mentioned, V&V included both dynamic and static techniques. One of the best known dynamic verification techniques is testing, and lately the use of formal techniques have revived this time-honoured technique. It is not only used to help develop automatic test-case generation but is also used in the area of fault tolerance and model checking (Holzmann, 1997). Although it can be argued as to whether or not model checking is really just a variation of a formal static technique.

In static verification, we recognize both semiformal and formal techniques. A walkthrough, or program inspection, is a more traditional form of semiformal static verification. This is a technical examination of the software code with the intention of finding and eventually removing defects as early as possible in the lifecycle of the product.

There are a number of techniques associated with program inspection. NASA has used this technique and has a manual for it called the "Software Formal Inspections Guidebook" (NASA, 1993). The word "formal" used in the manual's title might be misleading. We believe that the term formal should be reserved for those methods that use mathematics — and especially logics — as their foundation while techniques such as those described in the guidebook can be more appropriately called semiformal. However, the methodology of program inspections is a very effective technique and gives excellent results when properly applied.

Formal methods that use specification languages and automatic or semiautomatic provers are examples of the formal side of static verification. This implies reasoning with the requirements — written in some formal language — even before they are translated into executable code.

Probably the best-known and the more-used dynamic verification technique is testing. This technique has been used since the beginning of programming, but lately system-development techniques such as test-driven (Astels, 2003; Beck, 2002) methodology and the search for automatic derivation and production of test-cases has given testing a new impulse. In this book are chapters that deal with new testing techniques and ways of obtaining test cases.

This book also explores different applications in V&V that spawn many areas of software development — including real time applications — where V&V techniques are required. In all cases, examples of the applications are provided. So, the reader will find some useful techniques of V&V that can be used in different areas of software development.

There are many valuable formal and semiformal techniques of V&V that are not only illustrated with examples — some of them real-life examples — but also with thorough descriptions and a theoretical in-depth coverage.

Organization of This Book

This book has 14 chapters. The reader interested in further reading can find an abstract at the beginning of each chapter.

Chapter I, "Fault-Based Testing," reviews the art of fault-based testing — a technique where testers anticipate errors in a system in order to assess or generate test cases. The author also proposes and presents a new approach for fault-based testing. The approach consists of a set of steps, which are based on the application of (1) fault-tree analysis, (2) elaboration of the testing model using statecharts, (3) model reduction by slicing, and (4) test-sequence definition. The chapter presents an example of the approach for a Web application and finally a prototype of a tool that gives support to the proposed approach.

Chapter II, "Validation and Verification of Software Systems Using Virtual Reality and Coloured Petri Nets," presents a method for the V&V of software systems through the integration of coloured Petri nets and virtual reality. Coloured Petri nets are used to model and verify the correctness of software systems, while virtual reality modeling language (VRML) validates the software behavior while considering user acceptance. The authors also describe a software tool associated with the proposed method along with a case study for an embedded system.

Chapter III, "Integrating Usability, Semiotic, and Software Engineering into a Method for Evaluating User Interfaces," presents a lightweight development process — called UPi — for interactive systems. UPi is composed of activities that aim at designing user interfaces. These activities are based on rational unified process (RUP) activities, but they take into consideration usability aspects as well. The authors also describe an evaluation strategy that is based on UPi — called UPi-Test — for evaluating interactive systems. Finally, a case study using UPi-Test for the evaluation of the user interfaces for the electronic portal, insertion of texts application, and help of the Brazilian system for the digital television project is presented.

Chapter IV, "Automated Software Testing," provides the reader with the main aspects of test automation and gives relevant guidelines to assist him or her in its implementation. Some of the topics covered in this chapter include: different test stages where automation can be applied, analysis of benefits and risks of automated testing, a classification of automated test tools, and implantation of test automation into an organization.

Chapter V, "A Formal Verification and Validation Approach for Real-Time Databases," presents a formal V&V approach for real-time databases — databases where both data and transactions have timing restrictions. The approach comprises five steps where different models must be built, including an object model, a process model, an occurrence graph, message sequence charts, and a timing diagram. It uses hierarchical coloured Petri nets as formalism to describe the models. Also the design/CPN tool package is used to generate the models, verify the properties the models must satisfy, and generate graphs for user validation. The authors also present a case study for sensor networks.

Chapter VI, "Requirements for the Testable Specifications and Test Case Derivation in Conformance Testing," deals with how to produce specifications and test cases in the context of conformance testing, which is testing to determine if a software piece conforms to standards and specifications. The chapter is oriented to an area where conformance testing is particularly important and critical, namely the healthcare domain. The reader will find a testing environment described by the authors where test cases can be expressed in extensible markup language (XML) or clinical document architecture (CDA).

Chapter VII, "Test-Case Mutation," presents a technique to test test cases. Code mutation is a known testing technique that consists of producing changes in the program code to test test cases; however, as the authors of the chapter point out, it is an expensive technique. In this chapter, mutation operators are applied to test cases instead of code. The technique is illustrated and a tool built by the authors is described.

Chapter VIII, "Discrete Event Simulation Process Validation, Verification, and Testing," provides the reader with a good survey of how to apply different V&V techniques to simulation systems. The authors explore the different reasons why simulation process fails, analysing it in detail and then explaining the different V&V techniques used in simulation process.

Chapter IX, "The STECC Framework: An Architecture for Self-Testable Components," presents a strategy for improving testability of software components, particularly commercial off-the-shelf (COTS) components. The proposed strategy for self-testing COTS components — STECC — is based on the underlying idea of augmenting a component with the capabilities of testing tools to support testing tasks carried out by the component user. Specially, a STECC self-testable component is capable of generating test cases for program-based testing. Source code as the main input for this kind of testing thereby does not need to be disclosed to the tester. The chapter also explains in detail the STECC framework, which implements the necessary technical architecture to augment Java components with self-testability.

Chapter X, "Certifying Properties of Programs Using Theorem Provers," gives a detailed account of the use of formal methods — in this case, COQ and PVS — to assert the properties of programs. This chapter covers the area of static verification, and the authors give first a simple example so as to introduce the reader to the technique and then follow it with a more interesting and real-life problem. Recommended for those readers who want to have a hands-on experience with formal verification.

Chapter XI, "Static Type Systems: From Specification to Implementation," addresses the use of type systems in verification and discusses the effect that design decisions about type systems can have in relation to program verification. As the author remarks, it is not often that type systems are associated with V&V, although type systems have played and are playing a fundamental role in automatic and semiautomatic program verification. The chapter provides an informed discussion on type systems and their implementation that can help programmers to better understand this tool that is now built into most programming languages.

Chapter XII, "Generic Model of the Business Model and Its Formalization in Object-Z," presents a formalization in Object-Z of the unified software development process business model. Such formalization is obtained from an UML class diagram and is completed with the formalization of the business model rules in Object-Z. The chapter gives an introduction to the subject; discusses briefly different formalism to give formal semantics to UML; and then, after showing the generic model as a class diagram in UML, goes on to give its formalization. Finally, the authors apply the generic model to a credit card information service.

Chapter XIII, "Efficient Software Quality Assurance Approaches Oriented to UML Models in Real Life," deals with improving software quality assurance (SQA), striking a balance between quality and budget supported by risk analysis. The proposed process is described in detail and placed in context and also supported by a description of an algorithm as well as an ad hoc tool based on the Eclipse environment and a plug-in specially developed.

Chapter XIV, "Safecharts Model Checking for the Verification of Safety-Critical Systems," provides the reader with a lucid exposition of the use of model checking for safety-critical systems. The authors propose a formal technique that allows the use of safecharts — an extension of UML's statecharts — to bridge the gap between model checking and traditional testing and hazard analysis methods by mapping safecharts into timed automata. The reader will find an introduction to the subject and related work, as well as the formal definitions for safecharts, timed automata, and related techniques and languages. There are also some real-life application examples of the proposed method.

References

Astels, D. (2003). *Test driven development: A practical guide*. Prentice Hall PTR.

Beck, K. (1999). *Extreme programming explained: Embrace change*. Addison-Wesley.

Beck, K. (2002). *Test driven development: By example*. Addison Wesley Professional.

Boehm, B. (1981). *Software engineering economics*. Prentice Hall.

Cockburn, A. (2001). *Agile software development*. Addison-Wesley.

Dasso, A., & Funes, A. (2005). Formal methods in software engineering. In M. Khosrow-Pour (Ed.), *Encyclopedia of information science and technology* (pp. 1205-1211). Hershey, PA: Idea Group Reference.

Holzmann, G. J. (1997, May). The model checker SPIN. *IEEE transactions on software engineering, 23*(5).

NASA. (1993, August). *Software formal inspections guidebook* (NASA-GB-A302). Washington, DC.

Acknowledgments

In every project, there are a lot of people involved. We would like to thank everybody that has helped bring this book about, including the staff at Idea Group Inc., especially Kristin Roth, Jan Travers, and Mehdi Khosrow-Pour. Their guidance and enthusiasm have been a source of inspiration and a great support.

Of course, the book would not have come to life were it not for the authors, who also refereed chapters written by others. So, our heartfelt thanks to their inestimable collaboration that provided thorough, comprehensive, and constructive reviews.

We also thank the Departamento de Informática of the Universidad Nacional de San Luis, Argentina, for its support.

Aristides Dasso and Ana Funes
Editors

Chapter I

Fault-Based Testing

Marisa Analía Sánchez, Universidad Nacional del Sur, Argentina

Abstract

In this chapter, we review the state of the art and practice in fault-based testing. Based on the analysis and the reviews, we propose a comprehensive method for testing and present its main elements. Traditional fault-based testing is concerned with syntactic errors. These errors represent only a small portion of possible errors. Our testing approach is not restricted to these errors. We propose to use fault-tree analysis to determine how certain undesirable states can occur in a system. The results of the analysis expressed in terms of duration calculus formulas are integrated with statechart-based specifications. As a result, we obtain a testing model that provides a representation of the way the system behavior can be compromised by failures or abnormal conditions or interactions. In this way, we can automatically derive fault-based test cases. The example presented in this work illustrates the kinds of problems that arise in Web applications.

Introduction

Software-based systems incrementally provide critical services to users, including safety-critical software (e.g., avionics, medical, and industrial control), infrastructure-critical software (e.g., telephony and networks), and electronic commerce. Because of their complexity, software systems are prone to failure in many ways. However, systems are normally built considering the normal and expected pattern of behavior. Thus, **fault-based testing** approaches that consider the way the system behavior can be compromised by failures or abnormal conditions or interactions are desirable. Testing is fault-based when its motivation is to demonstrate the absence of pre-specified faults.

Furthermore, results of **reliability** theory show that partition testing is better than random testing, and this superiority is visible when the definition of partitions considers potential difficulties in design and implementation. This means that **specification-based testing** is inferior with respect to testing in which the refinement of partitions is more related with fault rates (Hamlet, 1992, 1994; Hamlet & Taylor, 1990). In particular, fault-based testing is more effective in finding errors.

To this date, no significant scientific advances have been made on fault-based testing. Previous works (Chen,Tse, & Zhou, 2003; Foster, 1980; Morell, 1990; Richardson & Thompson, 1993; Weyuker & Ostrand, 1980; White & Cohen, 1980) are intended for unit testing and are concerned with syntactic errors: errors in the use of relational or arithmetic operators, and incorrect variable references. These types of errors represent only a small portion of possible errors. In real applications, faults depend on a multiplicity of causal factors including technical, human, and institutional aspects. In this chapter, we propose a fault-based testing approach that is not restricted to syntactic errors. We generate test cases based on the system specification and fault-tree analysis results, thus overcoming the limitations of specification-based approaches that derive from the intrinsic incompleteness of the specification, and from the focus of specifications on correct behaviors, rather than potential faults. Hence, the objectives of this review are two fold: (1) reviewing the fault-based testing techniques, and (2) concluding on a method for testing that overcomes existing limitations.

The chapter is further structured as follows: The next section discusses related work and highlights the original aspects of our research. Then we give details of our approach to fault-based testing. Finally, we summarize the contribution of the chapter.

Background

Fault-Based Testing

Traditional **testing** has the objective of convincing that a program is correct with respect to a given function. Howden (1976) defines a reliable test set as the set that success implies program correctness. Suppose p is a program computing function f on domain D. A test set $T \subset D$ is reliable for p if $(\forall t \in T, p(t) = f(t)) \Rightarrow (\forall t \in D, p(t) = f(t))$. But there are some theoretical results that indicate that the general problem of defining a reliable test set is undecidible (Goodenough & Gerhart, 1975). Since reliable test sets of finite sizes are not attainable in general, testers need practical means of determining whether a test set is relatively sufficient.

Fault-based testing arises as an answer to the decidability problems derived from the objective of traditional testing to prove program correctness. Testing is fault-based when its motivation is to demonstrate the absence of pre-specified faults. From a traditional point of view, a test that does not reveal an error is not useful. Fault-based testing treats successful executions of a program as indications of the absence of some types of faults.

Budd and Angluin (1982) introduce the notion of correctness related with **mutation testing** that provides a formal model to fault-based testing. Mutation analysis induces faults into software by creating many versions of the software, each containing one fault. Test cases are used to execute these faulty programs with the goal of distinguishing the faulty programs from the original program. Faulty programs are mutants of the original, and a mutant is killed by distinguishing the output of the mutant from that of the original program. A test set that kills all the mutants is said to be adequate relative to the mutants. Mutation testing is a way to measure the quality of the test cases and the actual testing of the software is a side effect.

Mutation testing is computationally expensive, and hence has not become widely used. However, recent advances in reducing the cost of generating and running mutants could lead to a practical mutation testing (Chen et al., 2003; Offutt & Untch, 2000).

Fault-Based Testing Techniques

In this section, we describe some **fault-based testing** techniques. The following works consider syntactic errors. They assume the competent programmer hypothesis that restricts the set of potential faults to those that result from small modifications in program sentences. However, as we mentioned in the Introduction, faults depend on a multiplicity of causal factors. In the section entitled "A Fault-Based Testing Approach" we shall introduce our approach that emphasizes the semantic of the problem and considers combinations of faults.

Foster's work (1980) on error-sensitive test cases is an attempt to apply classical logic-hardware-testing techniques to the detection of software errors. In hardware testing it is possible to define test patterns that together would detect faults in any logic gate. Similarly, Foster proposes a set of heuristic rules to generate test data sensible to a type of error (e.g., reference to wrong variables, or incorrect relational or arithmetic operators). The limitation of the approach is that a complete set of rules that guarantee the detection of all code errors might be too complex to be useful. However, the work introduces the notion that an error has an effect over the final result only if it has been propagated. A set of data "sensitive to a type of error" allows propagation.

White and Cohen (1980) present a strategy that concentrates on the detection of domain errors. The input domain of a program is partitioned into subdomains based on the control flow. A domain error occurs when an input follows an incorrect path because of a control flow error. Domain errors are related with errors in predicates in the program. Thus the application of the strategy is limited by the difficulties caused by the rapid increase in the number of paths as the size of the program grows.

Weyuker and Ostrand (1980) introduce the concept of *revealing subdomains*. The input domain is partitioned into path domains. A path domain consists of a set of inputs where each follow the same path, or one of a family of related paths, through the program's flow graph. A second partition, the problem partition, is formed on the basis of common properties of the specification. These two partitions are then intersected to form classes that are the basis for test selection. The partition induced by the path domains separates the domain into classes of inputs which are treated the same way by the program, while the problem partition separates the domain into classes which should be treated the same by the program. The differences that result from the intersection are places where we should look for errors. The difficulty with their approach is that it does not provide a method to follow.

Richardson and Thompson (1993) present the RELAY model that describes criteria to select test data that guarantee the detection of certain classes of errors. The model describes in detail the necessary conditions to guarantee fault detection: origination of a potential fault, transfer of the fault through an assignment or a branch that evaluates an incorrect condition, until an oracle reveals the fault. For example, they define conditions for errors in the use of relational and arithmetic operators. They assume the competent programmer hypothesis, and that there is a single fault in the program or that multiple faults do not interact to mask each other.

Morell (1990) proposes a model of fault-based symbolic testing. In symbolic testing, he replaces program expressions with symbolic alternatives that represent classes of alternative expressions. The result is an expression in terms of the input and the symbolic alternative. Equating this with the output from the original program yields a propagation equation whose solutions determine those alternatives that are not differentiated by this test. Then, Morell proves the absence of infinitely many faults based on finitely many executions. Although the technique is applicable to demonstrating the absence of combinations of faults, combinatorial explosion quickly overtakes the process (Morell, 1990). Note that the **oracle** for symbolic output is required because testing involves symbolic execution and symbolic output. However, this work includes a description of the theoretical limitations of fault-based testing, and some of the results show the undecidable nature of the problem.

Chen et al. (2003) propose to enhance Morell's fault-based testing to alleviate the oracle problem. By integrating metamorphic testing (Chen et al.) with fault-based testing, alternate programs can be eliminated even if there is no oracle. When compared with other fault-based testing approaches, the approach requires additional effort in identifying metamorphic relations and running the program more than once (Chen, Feng, & Tse, 2002).

Fault Injection

Hamlet analyzes fault-based testing in relation with **reliability** theory (Hamlet, 1992, 1993). Reliability is the statistical study of failures, which occur because of some defect in the program. Reliability models indicate what confidence we can have in program's correctness. Hamlet argues that traditional Reliability theory is not satisfactory for software for the following reasons:

- It is based on an operational distribution that may not exist.

- Hypotheses about sample independence are not valid.

- Sampling over the input domain of the program is not appropriate to predict the direct relationship between defects and program size.

- The testing effort required to establish a certain mean time to failure (MTTF) with 90% confidence is at least twice that MTTF.

Hamlet observes that sampling over the state space of a program allows one to predict more precisely the failure rate with respect to program size. The base of this observation is that a failure is not more probable for one state than another. The problem is that, in general, the state space is larger than the input domain.

On the other hand, Voas, Morell, and Miller (1991) argue that points of the state space are themselves correlated. A set of inputs apparently independent can converge to the same state, and then they are not independent. Propagation of an incorrect state occurs when an error has an effect over the result. Then, correlated states are grouped into program computation and it is not necessary to sample the value of variables in a state if the final result does not depend on them.

In order to group correlated states, we need to determine control and data flow dependencies. Although there are some works that address this problem (Podgurski & Clarke, 1990), the general problem of determining such dependencies is unsolvable. Voas considers this problem in a different fashion: He directly perturbs a state (injecting a fault), and then monitors if the perturbation affects the results. In this way, he does not need to consider the input domain (he uses the state space), and he does not determine how to reach the perturbed states (i.e., there is no need for a dependency analysis). The works of Voas begin with the objective of providing a theory for why programs cannot fail (Voas & Miller, 1995; Voas et al., 1991).

Voas models the failure process of a fault localized to one program location, and identifies three necessary steps for an error to produce a software failure: The code location with an error should be executed; execution should affect the data state; and the incorrect data state should propagate (to affect the output). Then, Voas (1992) presents a technique, called propagation, infection, and execution analysis (PIE) that allows one to predict the probability that a program will fail if it contains an error. To summarize, the technique measures **software testability**, that is, the probability that software will not fail, even if it has defects. Related research has been conducted by Denaro, Morasca, and Pezzè (2002) who used logistic regression and cross-validation for deriving the correlation between software metrics and software fault-proneness.

Duration Calculus

The original **duration calculus** (DC) was introduced by Zhou, Hoare, and Ravn (1991) to formalize and reason about real-time requirements. The DC uses the integrated duration of states within a given interval of time to describe such requirements. A system is modeled by a number of functions from a temporal structure isomorphic to R^+ to a set of Boolean values. These functions are called the state variables of the system. The property that a state variable (or a Boolean combination of state variables) P holds throughout a nonpoint interval is defined by $\int P = \ell \wedge \ell = 0$ abbreviated $\lceil P \rceil$, where ℓ stands for the length of an interval. Subinterval properties are expressed by the binary "chop" operator (written ";") of interval logic.

Let for instance *ServerUnavailable* denote an undesirable but unavoidable state of some system, perhaps because it is busy. A system requirement may be that the server should not be unavailable for more than 10 seconds. To formalize this statement the following Boolean valued state is used:

$$ServerUnavailable:Time \rightarrow \{0,1\}$$

which expresses the unavailability of the server as a function of time. It is assumed that Boolean values are represented by 0 (*false*) and 1 (*true*). When a bounded time interval $[b,e]$ is considered, the duration of *ServerUnavailable* within the interval can be measured by $\int_b^e ServerUnavailable\ dt$. The requirement "The server should not be unavailable for more than 10 seconds" is thus written as: $\int ServerUnavailable < 10$.

In the following, we present the syntax and the semantics of propositional duration calculus based on the presentations given in Hansen and Zhou (1992).

Syntax

We assume a countable infinite set of logical variables V and a countable infinite set of state variables SV. Furthermore, like classical logic, we assume a finite set of function symbols and a finite set of predicate symbols.

- **State expressions:** The set of state expressions is defined by the following rules:
  1. 0, 1, and each $v \in SV$ are state expressions;
  2. if P and Q are state expressions, then $\neg P$ and $P \vee Q$ are state expressions, where $\neg$ and $\vee$ are propositional connectives on state expressions and semantically different from the connectives on formulas.

- **Terms:** The set of terms is defined by the following rules:

    1. if P is a state expression, then $\int P$ is a term;

    2. the special symbol ℓ, which stands for the length of an interval, is a term;

    3. if $r_1,...,r_n$ are terms and f_i^n is an n-ary function symbol, then $f_i^n(r_1,...,r_n)$ is a term.

    The term $\int P$ is called the duration of P.

- **Formulas:** The set of formulas is defined by the following rules:

    1. if A_i^n is an n-ary predicate symbol and $r_1,...,r_n$ are n terms then $A_i^n(r_1,...,r_n)$ is a formula;

    2. *true* is a formula;

    3. if δ is a formula, then $\neg\delta$ is a formula;

    4. if δ, σ are formulas, then $\delta\vee\sigma$ and $\delta;\sigma$ are formulas.

Semantics

In the following, we provide a brief introduction of DC semantics. The reader is referred to Hansen and Zhou (1992) for a complete description. The semantics of DC is based on an interpretation I that assigns a fixed meaning to each state name, type, and operator symbol of the language, and a time interval $[b,e]$. For a given I and $[b,e]$ the semantics defines what domain values, duration terms, and what truth values duration formulas denote. For example, $\int P$ denotes the $\int_b^e P(t)dt$.

A duration formula D holds in I and $[b,e]$, abbreviated $I,[b,e] \mapsto D$, if it denotes the truth value *true* for I and $[b,e]$. D is true in I, abbreviated $I \mapsto D$ if $I,[a,b] \mapsto D$ for every interval $[a,b]$. A model of D is satisfiable if there exists an interpretation I with $I \mapsto D$.

Fault-Tree Analysis

Fault-tree analysis (FTA) is a widely used technique in industrial developments, and allows one to describe how individual component failures or subsystems can combine to effect the system behavior (Leveson, 1995). The construction of a **fault-tree** provides a systematic method for analyzing and documenting the potential causes of a system failure.

The analyst begins with the failure scenario of interest and decomposes the failure symptom into its possible causes. Each possible cause is then further refined until the basic causes of the failure are understood.

A fault-tree consists of the undesired top state linked to more basic events by logic gates. Here we only consider *And, Or* gates, as fault-trees containing other gates may be expressed in terms of these. In general, fault-trees do not use the *Not* gate, because the

Figure 1. Fault-tree for the lever failure

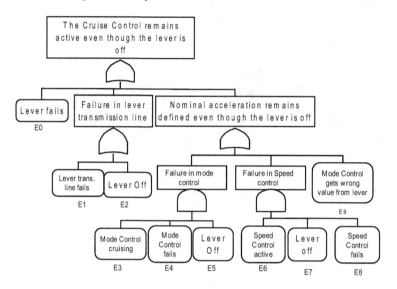

inclusion of inversion may lead to noncoherent fault-trees, which complicate analysis (Dugan & Doyle, 1996). Once the tree is constructed, it can be written as a Boolean expression and simplified to show the specific combinations of identified basic events sufficient to cause the undesired top state. The sets of basic events that will cause the root event are regarded as Minimal Cut Sets. The Minimal Cut Set representation of a tree corresponds to an *Or* gate with all the minimal cut sets as descendants.

Figure 1 is an example of a fault-tree that relates to a simplified automobile cruise control system. It states that if the cruise control remains active even though the lever is off then either the lever is off, or there is a failure in the lever transmission line, or the nominal acceleration remains defined even though the lever is off. Further the fault-tree states that if the mode control is cruising, and the mode control fails, and the lever is off, then there is a failure in the mode control. Also, if the speed control is active and fails, and the lever is off, then there is a failure in the speed control. There are five cut sets: $\{E_0\}$, $\{E_1, E_2\}$, $\{E_3, E_4 E_5\}$, $\{E_6, E_7 E_8\}$, and $\{E_9\}$.

Fault-Tree Semantics

In Hansen, Ravn, and Stavridou (1998), fault-trees have been given a formal semantics based on a real-time interval logic, the **duration calculus**.

The semantics of a **fault-tree** are determined by the semantics of the leaves, the edges, and the gates, such that the semantics of intermediate nodes are given by the semantics of the leaves, edges, and gates in the subtrees in which the intermediate nodes are roots. A leaf node is interpreted as a formula that may be the occurrence of a state P, that is, $\lceil P \rceil$; or the occurrence of a transition to state P, *that is,* $\lceil \neg P \rceil ; \lceil P \rceil$. The authors note that in safety-analysis terminology, the leaves in a fault-tree are called events, often meaning the occurrence of a specific system state, but also used in the software engineering sense, meaning a transition between two states (Hansen et al.). In particular, they define the occurrence of an event (i.e., a transition to state P), as $\lceil \neg P \rceil ; \lceil P \rceil$.

To formalize the first statement in Figure 1, that the lever fails, we use the following Boolean valued state:

$$LeverFails:Time \to \{0,1\}$$

which express the presence of a failure as a function of time. The property that a state, *LeverFails*, holds throughout a nonpoint interval is defined by $\int LeverFails = \ell \wedge \ell > 0$, abbreviated $\lceil LeverFails \rceil$. Finally, we define the occurrence of a transition to state *LeverFails*, as $\lceil \neg LeverFails \rceil ; \lceil LeverFails \rceil$.

Slicing

Program **slicing** is a technique for decomposing programs by analyzing their data flow and control flow. Starting from a subset of a program's behavior, slicing reduces that program to a minimal form that still produces that behavior. The original definition of slicing comes from Weiser (1984). Figure 2 illustrates the idea behind traditional slicing using the first example from Weiser's paper. The code in (b) is obtained from the code in (a) by including only those statements that could affect the value of the variable *Total* at line 12. The pair *(Total, 12)* is called a slicing criterion for this slice. A slicing criterion of a program P is a tuple *(i, V)* where i is a statement in P and V is a subset of the variables in P. A slicing criterion determines a projection which throws out of the trace of the program's execution all ordered pairs except those starting with i, and from the remaining pairs throws out everything except values of variables in V.

The traditional definition of slicing is concerned with slicing programs written in imperative programming languages. Therefore, it is assumed that programs contain variables and statements, and slices consist solely of statements. Sloane and Holdsworth (1996) extended the concept of slicing to a generalized marking of a program's abstract tree (Sloane, 1996). This generalization allows slicing based on criteria other than the use of a variable at a given statement. Based on this generalization, Heimdahl and Whalen (1997) proposed a reduction and slicing of hierarchical state machines, and exemplified their approach using requirements state machine language (RSML) specifications. For the best of our knowledge, Heimdahl and Whalen propose a slice based on data-flow and control-flow information to extract the parts of the specification effecting selected variables and transitions (The algorithm was not available for the authors). We also base our approach to slicing on a marking of the abstract syntax tree. In the following section, we describe our approach.

Figure 2. An example of traditional slicing: (a) original program, (b) a slice using criterion (Total, 12)

```
1  begin
2    Read(X,Y);
3    Total := 0.0;
4    Sum := 0.0;
5    if X <= 1
6      then Sum := Y
7      else begin
8          Read(Z);
9          Total := X*Y;
10    end;
11   Write(Total, Sum);
12 end
```

```
1  begin
2    Read(X,Y);
3    Total := 0.0;
4
5    if X <= 1
6      then Sum := Y
7      else begin
8
9          Total := X*Y;
10    end;
11
12 end
```

(a)   (b)

Slicing of Statecharts

The **slicing** algorithm for **statecharts** is based on a marking of an abstract syntax tree, and thus we need to define a formal grammar to describe correct syntax for statecharts. In the work in Sánchez and Felder (2001) we introduce a context-free grammar to specify syntax for statecharts. Given a statechart, an abstract syntax tree can be contructed according to the proposed grammar. A syntax tree is a graphical representation for derivations. This tree will serve as an input for the slicing algorithm.

A parser is an algorithm that determines whether a given input string is in a language and, as a side effect, usually produces a parse tree (or syntax tree) for the input. Recursive-descent parsing (Aho, Sethi, & Ullman, 1986) is one of the simplest parsing techniques that is used in practice. The basic idea of recursive-descent parsing is to associate each nonterminal with a procedure. The goal of each such procedure is to read a sequence of input characters that can be generated by the corresponding nonterminal, and return a pointer to the root of the parse tree for the nonterminal. The structure of the procedure is dictated by the productions for the corresponding nonterminal.

The procedure attempts to "match" the right hand side of some production for a nonterminal. To match a terminal symbol, the procedure compares the terminal symbol to the input; if they agree, then the procedure is successful, and it consumes the terminal symbol in the input. In our work we assume that the statechart is well formed. To match a nonterminal symbol, the procedure simply calls the corresponding procedure for that non-terminal symbol.

In order to implement a recursive-descent parser for a grammar, for each nonterminal in the grammar, it must be possible to determine which production to apply for that nonterminal by looking only at the current input symbol. We use a predictive parser to implement a recursive-descent parsing. In a predictive syntax analysis, the lexic component that is being analyzed determines unambiguously the production for each nonterminal. We include the algorithm for the parser in a previous work (Sánchez & Felder, 2001).

As mentioned previously, the slicing algorithm is based on a marking of the abstract syntax tree. A slicing criterion of a statechart is defined by a state. The criterion determines a projection on the sequences of the statechart that throws out all states and transitions that do not contribute to reach the state of interest.

The slicing algorithm traverses the syntax tree. The cost is lineal with respect to the depth of the tree, which is bounded by $O((p+q)*n)$ where n is the length of the largest sequence of the statechart (without cycles), and $(p+q)$ represent the number of levels that we add for each state and transition of the sequence. The variable p depends on the number of productions used to derive terminal symbols.

A Fault-Based Testing Approach

In this section, we introduce our approach to fault-based testing. We propose to generate test cases based on the specification and fault-tree analysis results. Fault-tree analysis results give insight into relevant combinations of faults.

However, we have to overcome the following issues:

1. For the case of **specification-based testing**, the number of possible behaviors is bounded by what is described in the specification. If we also consider the information outside the specification, the number of possible behaviors is incremented. Given the diversity of information that we have to consider to understand a system, it is not obvious how to define behaviors relevant to testing.

2. In general, information outside the specification is provided using different techniques and models. Then, we have to deal with specifications provided in different languages, with different levels of granularity and abstraction, and that they consider different views of the system.

To address the first point, we characterize possible behaviors and rank them by some criteria. Fault-tree analysis is used to determine how an undesirable state (failure state) can occur in the system. We propose to integrate Fault-tree analysis results with the specification statecharts of the desired behavior for the system. As a result, we obtain a statechart that provides a representation of the way the system behavior can be compromised by failures or abnormal conditions or interactions. Thus, we can automatically derive fault-based test cases from the model. Regarding the second point, we have to deal with information provided by fault-tree analysis and the system specification using statecharts. The integration is possible since the results of the analysis are expressed in terms of duration calculus formulas and we apply some conversion rules of a formula to a statechart.

The process of building a testing model has four basic steps:

1. Fault-trcc analysis
2. Elaboration of the testing model (using statecharts)
3. Model reduction (slicing)
4. Test sequence definition

We now describe an example. Then, we discuss the problems and our approach to solving them for each of the above steps of the testing process.

Running Example

A Web application is a program that runs in whole or in part on one or more Web servers and can be run by users through a Web site. Because of their complexity, Web applications are prone to failure in many ways. For example, a request that is satisfied under normal conditions can be unexpectedly rejected. That can be experienced in daily life when a Web server is not available because it is busy, when we cannot properly fill in an order form because we are not able to view information on a low resolution screen, or when we abandon a page because it makes heavy use of cookies and we have turned on alerts every time a cookie is activated. However, systems are normally built considering the normal and expected pattern of behavior. Thus, a fault-based testing approach that considers the way the system behavior can be compromised by failures or abnormal conditions or interactions is desirable.

As an example consider a typical Web application. We only include the views of the model necessary for our purpose. *Order* is one of the key concepts, and the behavior of the order is modeled in Figure 3 using a statechart diagram. An order has five states: *ReadingForm*, *AuthorizingCreditCardSale*, *Authorizing InvoiceSale*, *Placed*, and *Rejected*. If an invoice sale is not authorized because a customer has not enough credit, then he is asked to pay using a credit card.

Additionally, it is interesting to investigate if this normal pattern of behavior specified for the Order, can be corrupted by unexpected conditions. For example, it is typical that

Figure 3. Statechart of order

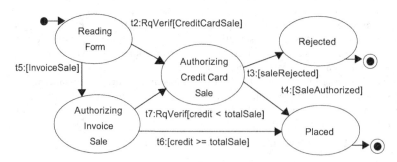

when a Web application is subject to unusual levels of activity, it may be unavailable for some time; and the applications that depend on it do not properly handle the error. In particular, consider the scenario in which an order is being processed and the credit card verification system is not available. It is necessary to test how the sales system behaves under this condition.

Steps of the Testing Approach

The process of building a testing model has four basic steps: (1) **fault-tree analysis**, (2) elaboration of the testing model (using statecharts), (3) model reduction, and (4) test sequence definition. Basically, these steps involve the tracing of duration calculus formulas describing cut sets to states or events of the specification statechart. In some cases, new states and transitions may be added to the initial statechart. This allows one to find out which states and transitions are relevant to the cut set, and then one has to work far enough back along paths to generate test sequences. Only relevant states and transitions are included in the testing model.

Step 1: Fault-Tree Analysis

A fault-tree describes the events that contribute to an undesirable system behavior, and also what components participate and which responsibilities they have. As an illustration of the use of fault-tree analysis, consider the running example and a fault-tree for the hazard *Order Rejected* in Figure 4. For reasons of space, we do not include a full description of nodes C_8, C_9, and C_{10}. There are nine cut sets: $\{C_8\}$, $\{C_9\}$, $\{C_{10}\}$, $\{C_1\}$, $\{C_2\}$, $\{C_3, C_4\}$, $\{C_3, C_5\}$, $\{C_3, C_6\}$, and $\{C_3, C_7\}$.

Step 2: Elaboration of the Testing Model

A thorough understanding of the system and its interrelationships is essential for this step. It is assumed that the system's intended behavior is specified using unified modeling language (UML) statecharts (Booch, Rumbauch, & Jacobson, 1998; Harel, 1987). Based on the cut sets expressed in terms of duration calculus formulas we build a testing model using statecharts. Given a cut set that contains n basic events E_i, $1 \leq i \leq n$, we define a state variable (or a combination of state variables) P_i to denote each E_i. Since each E_i refers to a state or transition of a system component, we should trace E_i to the respective statechart.

The integration is performed using conversion rules of a formula to a statechart. The rationale behind the rules is as follows. Given a duration calculus formula $C \equiv C_1; ...; C_n$, the analysis depends on the number of subintervals. Formula $C \equiv C_1$ may be the occurrence of a state. If $C_1 \equiv \lceil P \rceil$, and the state variable P denotes a state present in the specification statechart, then we "mark" the state to denote that it must be included in the final testing model. For any state variable that does not have a counterpart in the statechart, the analyst must decide upon the system state to be added in the testing

Figure 4. Fault-tree for order rejected

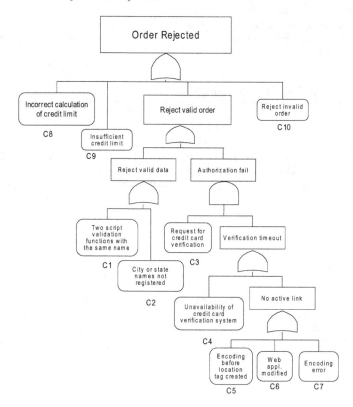

model. Most often, a new state is orthogonal to existing ones because it introduces a different view of the system behavior. We provide rules for formulas composed of one to four subintervals. These rules are the base cases. We also include a rule that considers formulas composed of *n* subintervals and whose definition is founded on the base cases. For a complete description of the conversion rules the reader is referred to Sánchez and Felder (2003). As an example, consider the following rules:

- **Rule I1:** Given a DC formula $\lceil D_1 \rceil$ (interval composed of a single subinterval):

  1. If D_1 denotes a state present in the statechart, do nothing.

  2. If D_1 denotes a state that does not exist in the statechart, add a new state labelled *S*. Human intervention is necessary to determine if the new state is orthogonal or not with respect to the states in the statechart. If the new state

is not orthogonal, add transitions from the existing states to this new state. The definitions of these transitions depend absolutely on the problem. If the new state represents an initial state, designate it as such.

- **Rule I2:** Given a DC formula $\lceil D_1 \rceil;\lceil D_2 \rceil$ (interval composed of two subintervals):

1. If D_1 and D_2 denote states (not orthogonal), there is a state transition:

    a. and none of the states are present in the statechart, create a new state S, include two substates D_1 and D_2, and add a transition from D_1 to D_2. Label this transition with the appropriate trigger event or a condition *true* to mean that the transition is always taken. If D_1 also represents an initial state, then designate it as such. Human intervention is necessary to determine if the new state S is orthogonal or not with respect to the states present in the statechart;

    b. and at least one of the states is present in the statechart, then, add the absent state, and a transition from the substate represented in the first subinterval, to the substate represented by the second subinterval. This transition is labeled with the appropriate trigger event or a condition *true* to mean that the transition is always taken.

2. If D_1 and D_2 denote orthogonal states:

    a. and none of these states are present in the statechart, create a new state S, include two orthogonal substates S_1 and S_2. In S_1 include two substates D_1 and D_1', add a transition from D_1 to D_1'. Label this transition with action $exitD_1 = true$. In S_2 include two substates D_2' and D_2, add a transition from D_1' to D_2. Label this transition with condition $exitD_1 = true$. Therefore, we synchronize the end of the duration of state D_1 with the start of D_2. Human intervention is necessary to determine if the new state S is orthogonal or not with respect to the states present in the statechart (see Figure 5);

    b. and D_1 does not exist in the statechart, then, include an orthogonal state S, with two substates D_1 and D_1', add a transition from D_1 to D_1'. Label this transition with action $exitD_1 = true$. For all transitions whose target state is D_2, add condition $exitD_1 = true$. Therefore, we synchronize the

Figure 5. Conversion of $\lceil D_1 \rceil;\lceil D_2 \rceil$ (Rule I2 (2a))

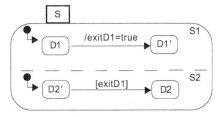

end of the duration of state D_1 with the beginning of state D_2;

c.   and D_2 is not present in the statechart, then, for all transitions whose source state is D_1, add action $exitD_1 = true$ in the label. Add an orthogonal state S_2 with two substates $D_2^{'}$ and D_2, and add a transition from $D_2^{'}$ to D_2 labeled with condition $exitD_1 = true$.

3.   If D_1 denotes a subinterval duration — for example, it is of the form ℓ op n, where $op \in \{<,>,=\}$ and n is a real number — add D_1 as a precondition of D_2 and apply Rule I1. This means that the occurrence of the state denoted by D_2 should satisfy the relation indicated by D_1.

In statecharts, external events are included as triggers of transitions. In duration calculus, we define the occurrence of an event as $\lceil\neg P\rceil;\lceil P\rceil$. This implies that given a formula $D \equiv D_1;D_2$, both D_1 and D_2 may be related to a single statechart event.

Subinterval formulas may also denote a sequence of (statechart) events. In this case, we should preserve the sequence order during conversion, and this can be solved using conditions that guard a transition from being taken unless it is true (see the following example).

The following example illustrates the result of the application of some of these rules. Consider the fault-tree in Figure 4. For the cut set $\{C_3, C_4\}$ ("Request for credit card verification" and "Unavailability of credit card verification system") we provide the following duration calculus formula:

$$\lceil\neg RqVerif\rceil;\lceil RqVerif\rceil;\lceil\neg SystemUnavailable\rceil;\lceil SystemUnavailable\rceil$$

The formula denotes the event of requesting credit card verification, and the unavailability of the credit card verification system. If there is not a statechart for the credit card verification system, we create a new one composed of two substates that are the source and target states of a new transition t_8 whose trigger event is encoded as *SystemUnavailable*. Multiple statecharts are treated as orthogonal components at the highest level of a single statechart.

If the subinterval $\lceil\neg RqVerif\rceil;\lceil RqVerif\rceil$ is related with the statechart event *RqVerif*, then we only "mark" transitions t_2 and t_7 to remember that it should be included in the testing model. To preserve the sequence order during conversion, we add action *preRqVerif=True* in transition t_2 and t_7; and *[preRqVerif==True]* as a condition for transition t_8 (see Figure 6).

Step 3: Model Reduction

During testing we may be interested in generating test sequences that reach some undesirable states. In Step 2 we explained that when we trace formulas to states or transitions, we should mark these states or transitions. We need a testing model that includes at least those states and transitions that have been marked. The slicing

Figure 6. Result of integration

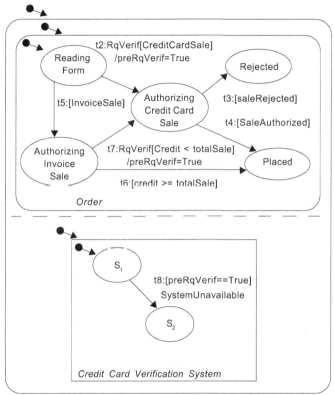

algorithm is performed by a traversal of the syntax tree, which begins at the node of interest, and then traverses and marks the branches that represent sequences that should be included in the slice. For the previous example, based on a marking for cut set $\{C_3, C_4\}$, we discard states *Rejected* and *Placed*; and transitions t_3, t_4, and t_6. Note that these states and transitions are not initially marked and do not contribute to reach the ones that have been marked.

Step 4: Test Sequence Definition

In Kim, Hong, Bae, and Cha (1999), the authors describe how to generate test cases based on UML state diagrams. These diagrams are based on statecharts. We consider their approach to generate test sequences from statecharts. The basic idea is to transform the state diagrams in extended finite state machines (EFSM). The hierarchical and concurrent

Figure 7. EFSM of the testing model

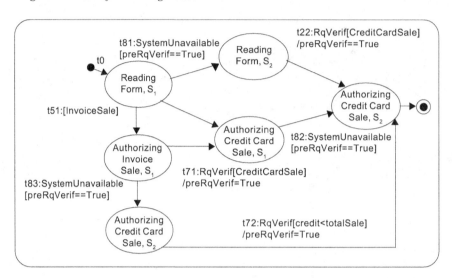

structure of states is flattened by (1) using the configurations of a statechart *Z* as the states of an EFSM *M*; and (2) using the possible steps of *Z* as the transitions of *M*. Control flow is identified in terms of the paths in the EFSMs. A configuration is a maximal set of states that a system can be in simultaneously. A step is a maximal set of enabled transitions that are triggered by an input and are mutually nonconflicting. The step is the central notion in the Statemate semantics (Harel, 1996).

Figure 7 depicts the EFSM obtained from the slice-based on cut set $\{C_3, C_4\}$. Using a transition-coverage criterion, we obtain test sequences (for example, (t_0, t_{21}, t_{82}), (t_0, t_{81}, t_{22}), $(t_0, t_{51}, t_{71}, t_{82})$, $(t_0, t_{51}, t_{83}, t_{72})$). Note that some of them are unfeasible.

The events that can contribute to a failure state may be hardware faults, software faults, or any other condition. In order to reproduce possible execution sequences based on this model, we need to generate or simulate each of these events. If the event refers to a software component, we can test the component to gain confidence on its quality. Also, we can use this information to inject software faults and quantify the effect of probable hidden errors.

Tool Support

We are developing a prototype tool, called FBTT, which supports our testing approach. From a user's perspective, the tool is very helpful in guiding the test-design phase. FBTT

Figure 8. FBTT architecture

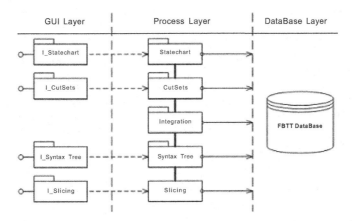

allows creating statecharts, describing the results of FTA expressed in terms of duration calculus formulas, integrating statecharts and formulas, and slicing statecharts.

The tool was implemented in Delphi 5.0 and runs under Windows XP and Windows 2000. We have concentrated on FBTT usability and scalability, as it is required for technology transfer. All the information related to a project is stored in Microsoft Access databases; this will allow users to produce customized reports. However, the tool is coded in a way that it can easily switch to another database engine. We have adopted a layered application architecture. The logical architecture provides separation between graphical user interface (GUI) and process algorithms and database management. The domain processes are organized using a pipe and filters architecture. The layered architecture is shown in Figure 8 with each of the three layers   GUI, process, and database consisting of one or more function blocks.

The FBTT tool has been used successfully on a number of small case studies. The algorithms used for integration are based on a data structure enabling the optimization of operations like searching.

FBTT supports the elaboration of fault-based testing models. However, when human assistance is needed during integration, it is sometimes difficult to see why. In the future we plan to extend the tool with a graphical interface that would allow the user to visualize the step-by-step results of the integration.

Conclusion

A review of the state of the art and practice in fault-based testing has been made. The capabilities and limitations of various strategies used have been presented and discussed. As a conclusion, we can say that the existing fault-based testing techniques are quite limited and our testing approach extends previous results on fault-based test case generation by including semantic errors and considering combinations of faults. If the fault-tree analysis is complete, then our testing approach assures that all conditions that enable a fault situation will show up as test cases.

Our approach can also be related to the concept of software testability. In our testing model, events that can contribute to a failure state may be hardware faults, software faults, or any other condition. An event representing a software fault indicates which faults can be injected to quantify the effects of probable hidden errors. Since injected faults arise from fault-tree analysis, we can focus on the faults related with our testing objective; and we do not assume single fault hypothesis, on the contrary, we consider combinations of faults.

It may be argued that a thorough understanding of the system is essential for the integration step. However, the analyst has to think about the system in great detail during tree construction. The most useful fault-trees require detailed knowledge of the design, construction and operation of the systems (Leveson, 1995).

The combination of fault-tree analysis and statecharts, poses another problem, such as the integration of heterogeneous specifications. We directed our efforts towards developing an approach that requires as little human intervention as possible. Most of the tasks involved — that is, the conversion of duration calculus formulas to statecharts and the slicing and generation of test sequences — can be automated.

One of the main problems of testing is the definition of an **oracle**. An oracle is a mechanism that specifies the expected outcome. In most testing proposals, the existence of an oracle is assumed. This is rather difficult to satisfy in practice since its creation is expensive and sometimes provides incorrect results. In our approach, since we do not aim to prove correctness, we do not need an oracle. Our objective is to demonstrate the absence of prespecified faults, and this is determined by observation if an undesirable state (given by the root node of a fault-tree) has been reached.

An assumption made in fault-based testing is the coupling-effect hypothesis. Research into the fault coupling effect demonstrated that test data sets that detect simple types of faults are sensitive enough to detect more complex types of faults (Offutt, 1992). The empirical investigations presented in Offutt consider mutation operators that describe syntactic changes on the programming language. Hence, the results cannot be interpreted in the context of our work in which we consider semantic information.

The testing method has been demonstrated by an example on a simple Web application. Most of the literature and tools on testing Web applications test nonfunctional aspects of the software (e.g., HTML validators, capture/playback tools, security-test tools, and load and stress tools). However, the different ways that pieces are connected in a Web application give rise to other problems. Andrews, Offutt, and Alexander (2005) categorize testing Web applications in terms of the type of connection: static links, dynamic links, user/time specific GUIs, operational transitions that the user introduces into the system outside of the control of the software, software connections among back-end software components, off-site software connections, and dynamic connections when Web components are installed during execution. The work of Andrews, et al. considers functional testing. They propose a system-level testing technique (regarded as FSMWeb) that combines test generation based on finite state machines (FSMs) with constraints. The approach builds hierarchies of FSMs that model subsystems of the Web applications and then generates sequences of actions labeled with parameters and constraints on parameters. The constraints are used to select a reduced set of inputs. The authors indicate that one limitation of the technique is that Web applications have low observability. Some of the output is sent back to the user as HTML documents, but Web applications also change state on the server and the database and send messages to other Web applications and services. In our approach, we alleviate this problem by avoiding the use of an oracle.

Another limitation in the FSMWeb technique is that it has limited support for unanticipated usercontrolled transitions (e.g., a user going directly to an internal Web page with a bookmark or use of the back button). The authors suggest modeling those transitions. However, this significantly increases the number of transitions. This problem is addressed in our approach by only generating test sequences that reach some prespecified undesirable states.

References

Aho, A., Sethi, R., & Ullman, J. (1986). *Compilers: Principles, techniques and tools*. Reading, MA: Addison Wesley.

Andrews, A., Offutt, J., & Alexander, R. (2005). Testing Web applications by modeling with FSMs. *Software Systems and Modeling, 4*(2), 326-345.

Booch, G., Rumbauch, J., & Jacobson, I. (1998). *The unified modeling language: User guide*. Reading, MA: Addison Wesley Longman.

Budd, T., & Angluin, D. (1982). Two notions of correctness and their relation to testing. *Acta Informatica, 18*(1), 31-45.

Chen, T. Y., Feng, J., & Tse, T. H. (2002). Metamorphic testing of programs on partial differential equations: A case study. In I. Sommersville (Ed.), *Proceedings of the 26th Annual International Computer Software and Applications Conference* (pp. 327-333). Los Alamitos, CA: IEEE Computer Society Press.

Chen, T. Y., Tse, T. H., & Zhou, Z. (2003). Fault-based testing without the need of oracles. *Information and Software Technology, 45*(1), 1-9.

Denaro, G., Morasca, S., & Pezzè, M. (2002). Deriving models of software fault-proneness. In G. Tórtora & S. Chang (Eds.), *Proceedings of the SEKE*. Ischia, Italy.

Dugan, J., & Doyle, S. (1996). Incorporating imperfect coverage into a BDD solution of a combinatorial model. *Journal of Automatic Control Production Systems, special issue on Binary Decision Diagrams for Reliability Analysis, 30*(8), 1073-1086.

Foster, K. (1980). Error sensitive test cases analysis (ESTCA). *IEEE Trans. on Software Eng., 6*(3), 258-264.

Goodenough, J., &. Gerhart, S. (1975). Toward a theory of test data selection. *IEEE Trans. on Software Eng., 1*(2), 156-173.

Hamlet, R. (1992). Are we testing for true reliability? *IEEE Software, 9*(4), 21-27.

Hamlet, R. (1994). Foundations of software testing: Dependability theory. In T. Ostrand (Ed.), *The 2nd ACM SIGSOFT Symposium on Foundations of Software Engineering* (pp. 128-139).

Hamlet, R., & Taylor, R. (1990). Partition testing does not inspire confidence. *IEEE Trans. on Software Eng., 16*(12), 1402-1411.

Hamlet, R., & Voas, J. (1993). Faults on its sleeve: Amplifying software reliability testing. In T. Ostrand & E. Weyuker (Eds.), *Proceedings of the International Symposium on Software Testing and Analysis* (pp. 89-98). USA: ACM Press.

Hansen, K. M., Ravn, A. P., & Stavridou, V. (1998). From safety analysis to software requirements. *IEEE Trans. on Software Eng., 24*(7), 573-584.

Hansen, M., & Zhou, C. (1992). Semantics and completeness of duration calculus. In J. W. de Bakker, C. Hizing, W. de Roever, & G. Rozenberg (Eds.), *Real-time: Theory in practice*, REX Workshop (LNCS 600, pp. 209-225). The Netherlands: Springer-Verlag.

Harel, D. (1987). Statecharts: A visual formalism for complex systems. *Science of Computer Programming, 8*, 231-274.

Harel, D. (1996). The statemate semantics of statecharts. *ACM Transactions on Software Engineering and Methodologies, 5*(4), 293-333.

Heimdahl, M., & Whalen, M. (1997). Reduction and slicing of hierarchical state machines. In R. Conradi (Eds.), *Proceedings of the Internationall Conference on Foundations of Software Engineering* (pp. 450-467). New York: Springer-Verlag, Inc.

Howden, W. (1976). Reliability of the path analysis testing strategy. *IEEE Transactions on Software Engineering, 2*(3), 208-214.

Kim, Y., Hong, H., Bae, D., & Cha, S. (1999). Test cases generation from UML state diagrams. *IEE Proceedings: Software, 146*(4), 187-192.

Leveson, N. G. (1995). *Safeware: System safety and computers*. Addison Wesley.

Morell, L. J. (1990). A theory of fault-based testing. *IEEE Transacions on Software Engineering, 16*(8), 844-857.

Offutt, J. (1992). Investigations of the software testing coupling effect. *ACM Trans. on Software Engineering and Methodology, 1*(1), 3-18.

Offutt, J., & Untch, R. (2000). Mutation 2000: Uniting the orthogonal. In *Proceedings of Mutation 2000: Mutation Testing in the Twentieth and the Twenty First Centuries*, San Jose, CA (pp. 45-55).

Podgurski, A., & Clarke, L. (1990). A formal model of program dependencies and its implications for software testing, debugging, and maintenance. *IEEE Transactions on Software Engineering, 16*(9), 965-979.

Richardson, D., & Thompson, M. (1993). An analysis of test data selection criteria using the RELAY model of fault detection. *IEEE Trans. on Software Eng., 19*(6), 533-553.

Sánchez, M., Augusto, J., & Felder, M. (2004). Fault-based testing of e-commerce applications. In J. Augusto & U. Ultes-Nitsche (Eds.), *ICEIS2004* (pp. 12-16). Porto, Portugal: INSTICC Press.

Sánchez, M., & Felder, M. (2001). Slicing of statecharts. In G. Fernandez & C. Pons (Eds.), *ASSE2001* (pp.177-190). SADIO.

Sánchez, M., & Felder, M. (2003). A systematic approach to generate test cases based on faults. In V. Braberman & A. Mendarouzqueta (Eds.), *Proceedings ASSE2003*, Buenos Aires, Argentina.

Sloane, A., & Holdsworth, J. (1996). Beyond traditional program slicing. In *Proceedings of the International Symposium on Software Testing and Analysis* (pp. 180-186). San Diego, CA: ACM Press.

Voas, J. (1992). PIE: A dynamic failure-based technique. *IEEE Transactions on Software Engineering, 18*(8), 717-727.

Voas, J., & Miller, K. (1995). Software testability: The new verification. *IEEE Software, 12*(3), 17-28.

Voas, J., Morell, L., & Miller, K. (1991). Predicting where faults can hide from testing. *IEEE Software, 8*(2), 41-48.

Weiser, M. (1984). Program slicing. *IEEE Transactions on Software Engineering, 10*(4), 352-357.

Weyuker, E., & Ostrand, T. (1980). Theories of program testing and the application of revealing subdomains. *IEEE Transactions on Software Engineering, 6*(3), 236-246.

White, L., & Cohen, E. (1980). A domain strategy for computer program testing. *IEEE Trans. on Software Eng., 6*(3), 247-257.

Zhou, C., Hoare, C., & Ravn, A. (1991). A calculus of durations. *Information Proc. Letters, 40*(5), 269-276.

Chapter II

Validation and Verification of Software Systems Using Virtual Reality and Coloured Petri Nets

Hyggo Oliveira de Almeida, Federal University of Campina Grande, Brazil

Leandro Silva, Federal University of Campina Grande, Brazil

Glauber Ferreira, Federal University of Campina Grande, Brazil

Emerson Loureiro, Federal University of Campina Grande, Brazil

Angelo Perkusich, Federal University of Campina Grande, Brazil

Abstract

Validation and verification techniques have been identified as suitable mechanisms to determine if the software meets the needs of the user and to verify if the software works correctly. However, the existing verification techniques do not support friendly visualization. Also, validation techniques with friendly visualization mechanisms do not allow the verification of the system's correctness. In this chapter, we present a method for the validation and verification of software systems through the integration of formal methods and virtual reality. Furthermore, a software tool associated with such a method is also described along with an embedded system case study.

Introduction

The complexity of software systems is increasing and, consequently, making it more difficult and necessary to determine if they work correctly. In the context of the currently applied development techniques and processes, tests are commonly used for validating software, but they cannot ensure that the software is in accordance with important behavioral properties, such as robustness or safety requirements.

Verification techniques aim to detect and aid the designer to correct mistakes during the software development, being useful when defining whether the software satisfies its requirements and specifications. Through formal modeling and verification methods, it is possible to determine if the system works correctly while considering all possible behaviors.

On the other hand, validation techniques determine if the software meets the needs of the user (Fuhrman, Djlive, & Palza, 2003). Thus, a graphical and friendly visualization of the system model is very useful in validating software in different domains. However, even though most of the formal modeling techniques have their own graphical representations, such as automata and Petri nets, they do not allow a friendly visualization and, subsequently, validation of the system's behavior. Without such friendly visualization, the final user needs to understand formal modeling concepts, which are not easily understood by nonengineers.

Coloured Petri nets (CPN) (Jensen, 1992) are used to model and verify the correctness of software systems, and virtual reality modeling language (VRML) (International Organization for Standardization, 1998) is applied to validate the software behavior considering the user acceptance.

We will present a software platform for managing the integration of CPN and VRML, easing the application of the proposed method. In order to illustrate the use of the method and the platform, an embedded software case study is presented. Finally, related approaches and concluding remarks are discussed.

Using the proposed method, it is possible to separate the formal verification and the validation activities of the system, allowing the verification of its correctness while still giving a friendly visualization for the final user. Moreover, the proposed tool aids the developers in integrating the CPN formal and the friendly VRML models, hiding the integration complexity.

Background

As we have said in the preceding section, the verification and validation phases of the approach we present here are based on coloured Petri nets and the VRML language. Therefore, in order to provide a better understanding of the next sections, it is desirable to present some background information.

Coloured Petri Nets

Petri nets are a formal method with a graphical representation used to model concurrent systems. With Petri nets, it is possible to specify and verify properties like precedence relation and deadlocks, among others. The graphical representation of a Petri net is a bipartite graph composed of places and transitions. Arcs connect places to transitions and transitions to places but never places to places or transitions to transitions. Each place can have zero or several tokens at a given moment. This is called the marking of the place. Therefore, the marking of a Petri net model is the set of markings of all places at a given moment. The transitions represent the actions that can take place.

Different extensions to the Petri nets formalism exist, such as timed Petri nets (Wang, 1998) and coloured Petri nets. In the context of this chapter, the hierarchical coloured Petri nets (HCPN), an extension of the coloured Petri nets, is the formalism we have used in our approach. The HCPN formalism has been used in the verification of many kinds of systems. Analysis of mobile distributed protocols (Zaslavsky, Yeo, Lai, & Mitelman, 1995), verification of multiagent plans (Almeida, Silva, Perkusich, & Costa, 2005) and embedded systems (Silva & Perkusich, 2005), and simulation of network management systems (Christensen & Jepsen, 1991) are some of the practical uses of HCPN.

Hierarchical coloured Petri nets incorporate data types and hierarchy concepts to ease the modeling task. In HCPN, a system is represented by a set of nonhierarchical CPN models, and each of these models is called a CPN page. Hierarchical characteristics are achieved due to the inclusion of two mechanisms: substitution transition and fusion places. The former is a transition that is replaced by a CPN page. The page to which the substitution transition belongs is called a superpage. The page represented by such a transition is called a subpage. Subpages and superpages are associated by means of sockets and ports. Fusion places are places that are graphically distinct but logically the same. Two or more fusion places form a fusion set and all the places in a fusion set always have the same marking.

Indeed, these two additional mechanisms, substitution transition and fusion places, are only graphical, helping in the organization and visualization of a CPN model. They favor the modeling of larger and more complex systems by giving the designer the ability to model by abstraction, specialization, or both. Moreover, the modeling activities in CPNs are supported by a set of computational tools named Design/CPN[1] (Christensen & Mortensen, 1996). These tools provide a graphical environment for the editing and syntax checking, as well as analysis methods like simulation and verification of CPN models.

Virtual Reality Modeling Technologies

Different virtual modeling technologies exist. In this section, we outline some of these technologies by exposing their main characteristics.

VRML[2] is a platform-independent language for modeling three-dimensional (3D) worlds. The intent of its creators was to allow 3D scenes to be visualized through the World Wide Web even over low-bandwidth connections. It became the *de facto* approach for providing 3D content on the web. Furthermore, as 3D modeling tools were able to export

Figure 1. The structure of a VRML world

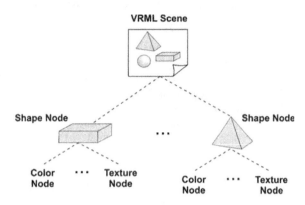

files to the VRML language, non-VRML experts, like architects and mechanical engineers, were able to build their 3D models and export them to the Web. This characteristic has allowed the usage of VRML in several branches of academy and industry, such as chemical-molecules validation (Casher, Leach, Page, & Rzepa, 1998), virtual buildings modeling (Ferreira, et al., 2004), mathematical functions visualization (Wang & Saunders, 2005), robot simulation (Rohrmeier, 2000), terrains representation (Reddy, Iverson, & Leclerc, 1999), and manufacturing systems (Krishnamurthy, Shewchuk, & McLean, 1998; Silva & Perkusich, 2003).

In a general way, VRML worlds are tree-like structures, as illustrated in Figure 1. Almost everything in VRML is viewed as a node. Cylinders, spheres, lights and even colors, are some examples of VRML nodes. However, these nodes have no behavior associated with them. It means that, 3D scenes composed only of VRML nodes are static. Therefore, in order to embed some dynamics in such scenes, three further mechanisms have been provided: *sensors*, *routes*, and *scripts*. A *sensor*, as its name indicates, senses the changes of a specific feature, such as time and mouse clicking. The information gathered by a *sensor* can be redirected to the other nodes in the 3D world through *routes*. These *routes*, therefore, act like event-dispatching mechanisms. Finally, *scripts*, also considered nodes, are the ways by which the developer manipulates the objects of a VRML scene.

Although VRML *scripts* are, most of the time, written in the JavaScript language (Goodman & Morrison, 2004), this is not the only option. It is also possible to implement such *scripts* by using the Java language. This can be performed through a mechanism called *external authoring interface* (EAI). EAI provides a set of Java classes that communicate with a VRML browser in order to manipulate a 3D world. The difference between these approaches is that in the second one the code of the script is separated from the VRML file. As we will show later in this chapter, this feature will be essential for the validation approach we are proposing.

The Java 3D[3] (Selman, 2002) API is part of Sun's JavaMedia suite and is devoted to the construction of Java applications and applets filled with 3D graphics. Like in VRML, Java 3D scenes are structured in a tree-like way. Therefore, each object in a scene is viewed as node of the tree. Through Java 3D, it is possible to control the shape, color, and transparency of objects. Furthermore, it allows the developer to define how such objects move, rotate, shrink, stretch, and morph as time goes by. Environmental manipulations are also possible, by defining background images, lighting modes, and even fog effects.

Internally, Java 3D uses the system native libraries, such as Direct3D and Open GL, to speed up performance. It provides applications with three different rendering modes: immediate, retained, and compiled-retained. The basic difference between these modes is concerned with performance, where the immediate mode is the slowest one and the compiled-retained is the fastest. Each of these modes has its own advantages, and therefore, the choice of which mode to use will depend on the application.

Extensible 3D graphics (X3D)[4] is both a language, based on extensible markup language (XML), and a format for creating and interchanging 3D content. As the X3D is compatible with the VRML specification, X3D files can be modeled using either X3D or VRML syntax.

Different from the previously presented technologies, X3D is embedded with the notion of *profiles*, each one providing a specific set of characteristics. The profiles are based on a componentized architecture, allowing the insertion of new components to support features not provided by the profile. This allows the definition of profiles targeted to specific fields, for example, medical and automobile visualizations.

The structure of a virtual world in X3D is similar to that of Java 3D and VRML, that is, a tree-like model. From the functional perspective, X3D provides many of the functionalities of VRML and Java 3D, such as scripts, lighting, materials, and animations. However, an interesting feature of X3D is the possibility of building virtual worlds by composing objects entirely from other scenes or locations on the Web.

Validation and Verification Method

In the context of our method for software verification and validation, we have defined three roles: *CPN Developer*, *VRML Developer*, and *Final User*. Based on these roles, some steps for verifying and validating the software have been defined. Figure 2 illustrates such separation of roles in a macro view of our method.

The *CPN Developer* knows how to model and verify the system according to its requirements using coloured Petri nets. The *CPN Developer* aims at proving that the specification is correct. In case of modeling, he or she must identify the global system behavior and model it using arcs, places, and transitions. In general, each transition represents an occurrence of a system execution (e.g., an event, a process, etc.). Therefore, firing a transition or a set of transitions simulates a system behavior. For example, the firing of a transition named "input" may simulate the fact that the user inputs data on the system. When verifying the system, the specification modeling is proved correct for all possible behaviors.

Figure 2. Separation of roles

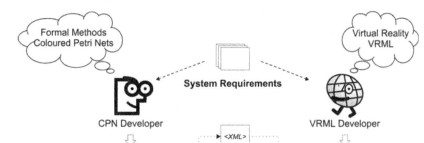

The *VRML Developer* knows how to model and validate the system. However, unlike the *CPN Developer*, the *VRML Developer* aims at final user validation. For that, he or she must model the system as simply as possible, yet still in accordance with the specification. The VRML modeling must be performed based on the events defined as transitions by the *CPN Developer*. Thus, the *VRML Developer* is responsible for correlating CPN and VRML events.

The *Final User* knows how the system works. He or she is responsible for specifying the system and validating if the system modeled is the one specified previously. For that, the *Final User* must describe the system requirements and visualize the VRML model in determining if it covers the requirements.

In what follows, we describe a set of steps for validating and verifying systems using CPNs and VRML. Each step is related to a specific role. In Figure 3, the phases of the method are depicted. A simple manufacturing system is used for illustrating the application of each phase (Silva & Perkusich, 2003).

System Specification (Final User)

The specification of the system is the first and main phase. Functional and nonfunctional requirements are described and, based on them, the modeling can be performed. A manufacturing system is a system organized into cells. Each cell has one or more related machines and a transport system. Two kinds of transport systems are considered: those inside cells and those outside cells. For simplicity, in this example the focus is on production and transport issues. In Figure 4, the architecture of the manufacturing system is illustrated.

Figure 3. Verification and validation method

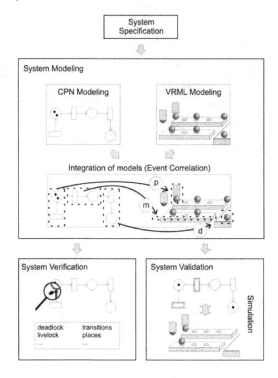

Figure 4. Simple manufacturing system

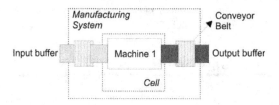

Figure 5. CPN modeling for the manufacturing system

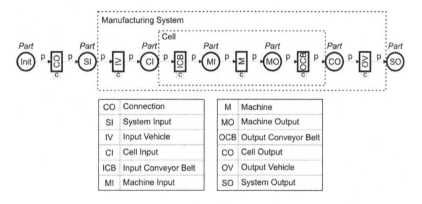

CO	Connection
SI	System Input
IV	Input Vehicle
CI	Cell Input
ICB	Input Conveyor Belt
MI	Machine Input

M	Machine
MO	Machine Output
OCB	Output Conveyor Belt
CO	Cell Output
OV	Output Vehicle
SO	System Output

CPN Modeling (CPN Developer)

The system is modeled using hierarchical coloured Petri nets. The Design/CPN tools set should be used in this phase. The result of this activity is a set of CPN models that can be simulated and later verified. Figure 5 illustrates the CPN modeling for the manufacturing system, presenting the places and transitions that are used to model the system specification.

VRML Modeling (VRML Developer)

In the third phase, the system is modeled using VRML. Any VRML modeling tool can be used to perform this activity. This modeling is usually simpler and friendlier than the CPN modeling, since the objective is to validate the system according to the user needs. Figure 6 illustrates the VRML modeling for the manufacturing system.

Integration of Models (VRML Developer)

The fourth step involves the correlation between the CPN and VRML events. The result of this activity is a map structure that represents the integration of the CPN and VRML models. For example, the event of firing a transition in the CPN model could represent a VRML event, such as a sphere moving. Figure 7 illustrates the correlation of events for the manufacturing systems. The correlated events are named CO, IV, OCB, and OV.

Figure 6. VRML modeling for the manufacturing system

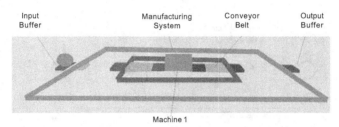

Figure 7. Correlating events for the manufacturing system models

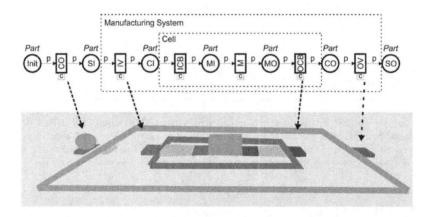

After the *system-modeling* phases, the system can be verified and validated. The generated models are used in the *system-verification* and the *system-validation* activities. Such activities are described below.

System Verification (CPN Developer)

In the fifth phase, the system is verified through the CPN models created during the *CPN-modeling* phase. Such models are passed to Design/CPN tools, in order to verify the correctness of the system according to behavioral properties using verification techniques such as model checking. Modeling and verification guidelines for CPNs using the Design/CPN tools and model checking can be found in Almeida et al. (2005).

System Validation (Final User)

In the last step, the system is validated through both the CPN and VRML models. A simulation of the system through the VRML models is performed based on the events generated by the simulation of the CPN models. Each event generated by the CPN model and defined as a "mapped event" in the *integration-of-models* activity can change the state of the VRML world. Thus, it is possible to visualize the behavior of the CPN-model simulation through the friendly VRML graphical animations.

A Software Platform for Integrating VRML and CPN

In order to make the application of the steps for the validation and verification of software systems easier, a software platform is described here.

The *CPN/VRML Software Platform* manages the integration of VRML and CPN models. For that, the Design/CPN tool is used for CPN modeling and simulation, and a Java-compliant VRML browser is used for the model visualization. The architecture of the software platform is presented in Figure 8, and the integration steps are described below, considering the event correlation performed in the *integration-of-models* phase.

1. The *CPN Module* is responsible for receiving event notifications from the Design/CPN simulation tools. During the simulation, each event is announced for the *CPN Module*. The communication is performed via sockets.

2. The *CPN Module* extracts the CPN model information using the Comms/CPN library (Gallasch & Kristensen, 2001) and forwards the event notifications to the mapping module.

3. The *Mapping Module* retrieves from the XML mapping files the VRML events that are related to the CPN event.

4. The *Mapping Module* forwards the identification of the VRML events that should be announced through a VRML-Java package.

5. Finally, the *VRML Module* updates the virtual world according to the CPN simulation events, allowing a friendly visualization of the CPN model. The *External Authoring Interface* mechanism, described in the "Background" section, is used to manipulate the VRML view.

Figure 8. Software-platform architecture

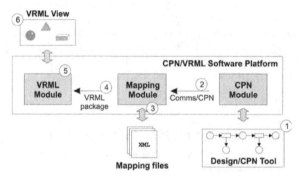

Case Study:
A Component-Based Embedded
Automation and Control System

In this section the application of the proposed method and software platform for validating and verifying a component-based embedded automation and control system is described.

System Specification

In Figure 9, the architecture of the embedded system, which is based on the framework structure introduced in Perkusich, Almeida, and Araújo (2003) is illustrated.

Figure 9. Architecture of the real-time embedded automation and control application

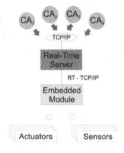

The entities shown in this figure are: sensors and actuators, client applications (CAs), the embedded module, and the real-time server. Sensors and actuators are not described since their roles in the architecture are clear. Client applications, in turn, represent application front-ends that access the services of the real-time server, like a Web application. Since Web-based software architectures are well-defined, a more detailed discussion about client applications is omitted from this chapter.

Embedded Module

The embedded module is a real-time system that interacts with the physical environment by means of the sensors and actuators, as well as distributed devices connected by a real-time TCP/IP network. The hardware components of the module receive events or alarms from sensors and write information in a shared-data area. Then, software components can read such alarm and event information, convert them to an adequate format, and send them to the real-time server.

On the other hand, the real-time server can request for an actuator through the software components that write the request in the shared-data area. Thus, hardware components can read the requests from a shared area and send them to the specific actuators. The internal architecture for the embedded module is shown in Figure 10.

Since the focus of this chapter is on the validation and verification of software systems, the software components that belong to such infrastructure are depicted in Figure 11 and are detailed in what follows.

- **I/O interpreter:** The I/O interpreter mediates the communication between software components and information in a shared area. It also interprets the information recovered from the shared area and instantiates objects that represent such information. On the other hand, the I/O interpreter receives information from the components as objects, translates them to the shared-data language, and then writes them in the shared area. The type of information present in the shared area may vary according to the sensor and actuators that are being used.

Figure 10. Internal architecture of the embedded module

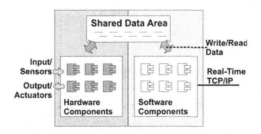

Figure 11. Software components infrastructure for the embedded module

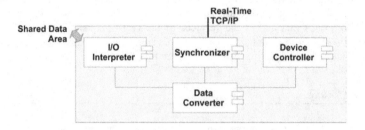

- **Data converter:** The data converter implements data conversion specific algorithms defined by the application. The data are converted from the I/O interpreter language to the specific application language. For example, when the I/O interpreter returns an object with a binary content, the data converter may transform it into an object with a decimal content, if this is the application format. The data conversion also depends on the type of information.

- **Synchronizer:** The synchronizer implements the synchronous communication among the software components of the embedded module and the software components of the real-time server. As said before, a real-time TCP/IP network is used. This component acts as a bridge between the two sides of the distributed application, and all the requests, or the response for the requests, issued between the real-time server and the embedded module occur through this component.

- **Device controller:** The device controller implements the initialization, tests, and liberation of devices connected to the interfaces of the embedded module. Such services are executed based on the requests submitted by the *Device Controller* to the shared area through the interpreter.

Real-Time Server

The real-time server can be a personal or industrial computer that manages the network. It runs the Linux/RT real-time operating system (Abbott, 2003). The internal architecture of the real-time server is shown in Figure 12. The software components that belong to the real-time-server infrastructure are briefly described as follows.

- **Synchronizer:** The synchronizer implements the communication on the real-time-server side. The implementation is similar to the embedded-module synchronizer.

- **Data controller:** The data controller provides data-flow control for the system (i.e., read, write, and parameter forwarding) based on the implementation of the services that are made available by the *UI Module*.

Figure 12. Software components infrastructure for the real-time server

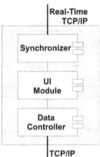

- **UI module:** The user-interface module provides an interface for the services implemented by the software components, so that they can be used by the application connected to the Internet.

CPN Modeling

In Figure 13, the CPN model for the embedded module is shown. The places, arcs, and transitions that model the *I/O-interpreter*, *Data-converter*, *Synchronizer*, and *Device-controller* modules are depicted in this figure. The complete description of the CPN modeling for this case study is presented in Silva and Perkusich (2005).

VRML Modeling

Figure 14 illustrates the VRML modeling of the real-time embedded automation and control application. The software components detailed earlier and the communication among them have been modeled using VRML nodes. Box nodes, with their names modeled with *Text* nodes, represent the software components; whereas *Cylinder* nodes represent the communication among the components.

The "System Validation" section will detail how the dynamic features (i.e., data exchange among the components and data processing) of the system are simulated in VRML.

Integration of Models

Some VRML events have been created in order to allow the integration between the CPN and VRML models. Such events are implemented in JavaScript and they are grouped into

Figure 13. CPN modeling for the embedded module

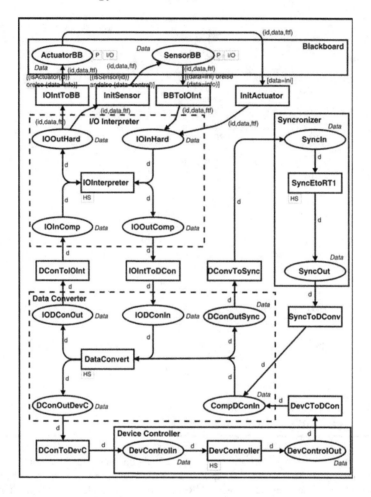

a *Script* node through VRML input events. In Listing 1, the JavaScript function that implements the VRML-event behavior correlated to the CPN transition *UIModule* is presented. Such an event simulates the data exchange between the *Data Controller* and the *UI Module* of the *Real-time Server*.

The *rtsDataControllerToUIModule* function forwards the received event *value* to the input event *communicateForward* of the *Cylinder* situated between the *Data Controller* and the *UI Module*. Besides, this function also forwards the value *true* to the input event *showDataExchange* of the *UI Module*.

Figure 14. VRML modeling for the real-time embedded automation and control application

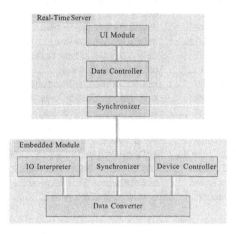

Listing 1. Function that implements the VRML event for the transition UIModule

```
function rtsDataControllerToUIModule(value, timestamp) {
        RTSDataControllerTOUIModuleCylinder.communicateForward = value;
        UIModuleComponent.showDataExchange = true;
}
```

The other VRML events are similarly implemented. The complete mapping between the CPN transitions and the correlated VRML events is presented in Table 1.

System Verification

Suppose that the sensors send an initial signal when the system is turned on or a new device is plugged in. Also, suppose that the system performs some task when it receives this kind of message and sends an acknowledgment, a calibration, or even an initialization message to the sensor. Such a scenario is illustrated in Figure 15.

When a sensor sends an initialization signal, the *Data Converter* sends it to the *Device Controller* to perform the associated control tasks. Since the simulation captures a single execution sequence or information flow in the model, the expected sequence or flow may

Table 1. Mapping between the CPN transitions and the correlated VRML events

CPN transition	VRML event
ToUiMod	rtsDataControllerToUIModule
UIModule	rtsUIModuleProcessing
BackToDCon	rtsUIModuleToDataController
DataControl	rtsDataControlProcessing
TORTSyncB	rtsDataControllerToSynchronizer
SyncOutRT	rtsSynchronizerProcessing
DConToIOInt	emDataConverterToIOInterpreter
IOIntToDCon	emIOInterpreterToDataConverter
DataConvert	emDataConverterProcessing
DConToDevC	emDataConverterToDeviceController
DevCToDCon	emDeviceControllerToDataConverter
DevController	emDeviceControllerProcessing
SyncToDConv	emSynchronizerToDataConverter
DConvToSync	emDataConverterToSynchronizer
IOInterpreter	emIOInterpreterProcessing

have been violated. Thus, we must verify the scenario for all possible situations based on model checking (Clarke, Emerson, & Sistla, 1986) to guarantee that the expected flow has always been satisfied. For that, the desired system properties should be described in a propositional temporal logic such as computation tree logic (CTL) (Clarke et al.). Its semantic is defined with respect to paths in a Kripke structure. A path on such a structure is an infinite sequence of states $(s_0; s_1; \ldots)$ such that s_{i+1} is reached from s_i for all $i \geq 0$. The CTL formula $AG\varphi$ means that for all paths starting from s_0, φ holds at every state along those paths. In other words, φ holds globally. The CTL formula $AF\varphi$ means that for all paths starting from s_0, φ holds at some state along the path. In other words, φ is inevitable.

Considering the scenario shown in Figure 15, we must prove that when some device sends an initialization message, the flow will be through the device controller. To prove this scenario, two atomic propositions *PA* and *PB* are used. The proposition *PA* is true if there is a token in place *IODConIn*, illustrated in Figure 13. The proposition *PB* is true if there is a token in place *DConOutDevC*, also illustrated in Figure 13. The CTL formula to prove this scenario is shown below:

$$AG \, (\, PA \rightarrow AF \, (\, PB \,) \,)$$

Therefore, the formula is true if *PA* is true and *PB* is true in the future. It means that if there is a token in the data converter input, this token is sent to device controller input, which is the component that implements control tasks such as initialization, calibration, and

Figure 15. Data converter flow to control signal

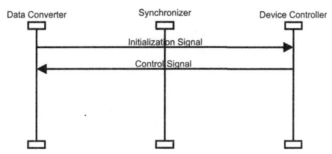

changing devices working parameters. The evaluation of this formula to true means that this part of the model behaves as expected for all possibilities of model execution. We can proceed with the same reasoning to prove that the flow of information back to the device also behaves as expected for all possibilities.

System Validation

The validation of the real-time embedded automation and control application is performed through the CPN and VRML models. The final user visualizes the interaction among the software components through the events generated by the CPN model and through a friendly user interface provided by the VRML model. The system validation becomes easier for the final user, since the VRML model entities are more abstract than the CPN model entities. In what follows, it is described how the dynamic features of the system are modeled in VRML.

The data exchange among the components is simulated through oriented *Cone* nodes (situated inside the *Cylinder* nodes), depending on the direction of the data flow. For example, in Figure 16, the data exchange between the *Data Controller* and the *UI Module* is presented: the *Cone* nodes are directed to the *UI Module* component, representing a data flow from the *Data Controller* to the *UI Module*. Besides, the *Sphere* node at the *UI Module* component represents the data that are sent from the *Data Controller* to the *UI Module*.

Another feature modeled for the system is data processing, which occurs within the software components. For that, a *Text* node with the word "Processing" is displayed at the bottom right of the current processing component and the letter "P" is displayed at the *Sphere* node, which represents the data being processed. In Figure 17, the data processing within the *Synchronizer* component of the *Real-time Server* is illustrated.

Figure 16. VRML modeling for data exchange among components

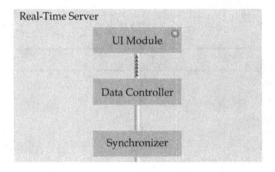

Figure 17. VRML modeling for data processing among components

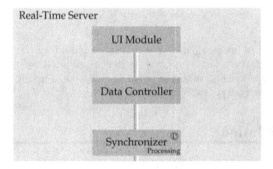

Related Approaches

Some related approaches are discussed in this section. A short description showing their features is presented along with some comparisons with our work.

Kindler and Páles (2004) present a prototype tool that allows the 3D visualization of Petri-net models, called PVNis. Such a tool is based on the Petri net kernel (PNK) (Weber & Kindler, 2003) and uses Java 3D for implementing the 3D-visualization. The approach used by this tool is based on the equipment of the Petri net with information on the physical objects used for 3D-visualization. The physical objects are included in the Petri-net model. A 3D model representing the shape of the object and an *animation function* representing the behavior of the object must be created for each place of the Petri net that corresponds to a physical object.

There is no method for validation and verification associated with this tool. Its purpose is only to provide the visualization of Petri net models in a 3D way. Therefore, there is also no effort to integrate the validation process through the 3D-visualization, with the verification process, or through the Petri net model. Such activities are realized separately.

Bardohl, Ermel, and Ribeiro (2000) introduce ideas towards visual specification and animation of Petri net-based models. In this work, the animation of algebraic high-level (AHL) nets (Padberg, Ehrig, & Ribeiro, 1995), which are a combination of place-transition nets and algebraic specifications (Ehrig & Mahr, 1985), is described. For that the animation, transformation rules are applied to the behavior rules (semantically equivalent to the transitions of the net) of an AHL net model, generating an animation view from the model. Such a view allows the visualization of the behavior of the system in a domain-specific layout.

In a Petri net Editor, the user defines the transformation rules from the Petri-net view to the animation view. In this way, there is no separation of the roles concerned with the use of this approach. Either the user that knows Petri nets must know the visual-modeling language or the visual modeler must know Petri nets. Finally, it seems the visual-modeling language is not as full-featured as VRML.

Conclusion and Future Trends

This chapter describes a method for the verification and validation of software systems using coloured Petri nets (CPN) and VRML. The method is defined over three separated roles: the *CPN Developer*, responsible for CPN issues; the *VRML Developer*, responsible for VRML issues; and the *Final User*, responsible for specifying and validating the system.

According to the proposed method, the system is modeled using CPN and VRML based on its requirements. Next, the CPN and VRML events are correlated in order to allow the CPN model simulation to control the VRML model simulation. For that, we propose a software tool that is used to correlate CPN and VRML events.

We describe the method as a set of phases for modeling and verification. The application of each phase is illustrated using a flexible manufacturing-system example. This makes it easier to understand the implementation of our method. As a real case study, we described the validation and verification of an embedded software system using the proposed method and platform.

The main future trend in the context of software verification and validation related to our work is to provide mechanisms for reducing the gap between validation and verification techniques. In this chapter, we propose a method and a tool that reduce such a gap, promoting the integration between VRML and CPN developers, still obtaining software verification and friendly software validation.

However, for some domains, the integration can be improved. For example, a VRML-component library for a specific domain may be created. Thus, when verifying and validating software for such domain, the integration tool could generate the VRML model based on the name of the component events. This automatic approach would reduce the effort on mapping CPN events to VRML ones.

On the other hand, verification tools could be improved in order to provide friendly mechanisms for visualizing what is being verified. It will be very important to the large-scale use of verification techniques in the context of industrial software engineering.

In this future, we plan to apply our method for validating and verifying software in other domains, focusing on complex interaction-centric ones (e.g., multiagent systems, as in Weiss, 2000, and workflow management systems, as in van der Aalst & van Hee, 2002). The validation of these systems through VRML may be primordial.

References

Abbott, D. (2003). *Linux for embedded and real-time applications*. Oxford, UK: Newnes.

Almeida, H., Silva, L., Perkusich, A., & Costa, E. (2005). A formal approach for the modelling and verification of multiagent plans based on model checking and Petri nets. In R. Choren, A. Garcia, C. Lucena, & A. Romanovsky (Eds.), *Software engineering for multi-agent systems III: Research issues and practical applications* (Vol. 3390, pp. 162-179). Berlin, Germany: Springer-Verlag.

Bardohl, R., Ermel, C., & Ribeiro, L. (2000). Towards visual specification and animation of Petri net based models. In *Proceedings of the Workshop on Graph Transformation Systems (GRATRA '00)* (pp. 22-31). Berlin, Germany.

Casher, O., Leach, C., Page, C. S., & Rzepa, H. S. (1998). Virtual reality modelling language (VRML) in chemistry. *Chemistry in Britain, 34*(9), 26.

Christensen, S., & Jepsen, L. O. (1991, June 17-19). Modelling and simulation of a network management system using hierarchical coloured Petri nets. In E. Moseklide (Ed.), *Modelling and Simulation, 1991: Proceedings of the 1991 European Simulation Multiconference, the Panum Institute Copenhagen, Denmark*. San Diego, CA: Society for Computer Simulation International.

Christensen, S., & Mortensen, K. H. (1996). *Design/CPN ASK-CTL manual*. Denmark: University of Aarhus.

Clarke, E. M., Emerson, E. A., & Sistla, A. P. (1986). Automatic verification of finite-state concurrent systems using temporal logic specifications. *ACM Transactions on Programming Languages and Systems, 2*(8), 244-263.

Ehrig, H., & Mahr, B. (1985). *Fundamentals of algebraic specification 1: Equations and initial semantics*. Berlin, Germany: Springer-Verlag.

Ferreira, G. V., Loureiro, E. C., Nogueira, W. A., Gomes, A. A., Almeida, H. O., & Frery, A. (2004). Uma abordagem baseada em componentes para a construção de edifícios virtuais (in Portuguese). In *Proceedings of VII Symposium on Virtual Reality-SVR 2004* (Vol. 7, pp. 279-290). Porto Alegre, Brazil: Sociedade Brasileira de Computação.

Fuhrman, C., Djlive, F., & Palza, E. (2003). Software verification and validation within the (rational) unified process. In *Proceedings of the Software Engineering Workshop, 2003, 28th Annual NASA Goddard* (pp. 216-220). Washington, DC: IEEE Computer Society.

Gallasch, G., & Kristensen, L. M. (2001). Comms/CPN: A communication infrastructure for external communication with Design/CPN. In K. Jensen (Ed.), *3rd Workshop and Tutorial on Practical Use of Coloured Petri Nets and the CPN Tools (CPN'01)* (pp. 75-90). Denmark: DAIMI PB-554, Aarhus University.

Goodman, D., & Morrison, M. (2004). *JavaScript bible.* Hoboken, NJ: John Wiley & Sons.

International Organization for Standardization. (1998). *ISO/IEC 14772-1:1998: Information technology — Computer graphics and image processing — The Virtual Reality Modeling Language — Part 1: Functional specification and UTF-8 encoding.* Geneva, Switzerland: International Organization for Standardization.

Jensen, K. (1992). *Coloured Petri nets. Basic concepts, analysis methods and practical use* (Vol. 1). Berlin, Germany: Springer-Verlag.

Kindler, E., & Páles, C. (2004, June 21-25). 3D-visualization of Petri net models: Concept and realization. In J. Cortadella & W. Reisig (Eds.), *Applications and Theory of Petri Nets 2004: Proceedings of the 25th International Conference, ICATPN 2004,* Bologna, Italy (Vol. 3099, pp. 464-473). Berlin, Germany: Springer-Verlag.

Krishnamurthy, K., Shewchuk, J., & McLean, C. (1998, May 18-20). Hybrid manufacturing system modeling environment using VRML. In J. J. Mills & F. Kimura (Eds.), *Information infrastructure systems for manufacturing II, IFIP TC5 WG5.3/5.7 Third International Working Conference on the Design of Information Infrastructure Systems for Manufacturing (DIISM '98),* Fort Worth, TX (Vol. 144, pp. 163-174). London: Kluwer.

Padberg, J., Ehrig, H., & Ribeiro, L. (1995). Algebraic high-level net transformation systems. *Mathematical Structures in Computer Science, 5*(2), 217-256.

Perkusich, A., Almeida, H., & Araújo, D. (2003). A software framework for real-time embedded automation and control systems. In *Proceedings of Emerging Technologies and Factory Automation, 2003 (ETFA '03) IEEE Conference* (Vol. 2, pp. 181-184). Washington, DC: IEEE Computer Society.

Reddy, M., Iverson, L., & Leclerc, Y. G. (1999). Enabling geographic support in virtual reality modeling with GeoVRML. *Cartography and Geographic Information Science, 26*(3), 180-182.

Rohrmeier, M. (2000). Web based robot simulation using VRML. In J. A. Joines, R. R. Barton, K. Kang, & P. A. Fishwick (Eds.), *Proceedings of the 32nd Winter Simulation Conference* (pp. 1525-1528). San Diego, CA: Society for Computer Simulation International.

Selman, D. (2002). *Java 3D programming.* Greenwich, UK: Manning Publications.

Silva, L., & Perkusich, A. (2003). Uso de realidade virtual para validação de modelos de sistemas flexíveis de manufatura (in Portuguese). *Anais do VI Simpósio Brasileiro de Automação Inteligente.* São Paulo, Brazil.

Silva, L., & Perkusich, A. (2005). A model-based approach to formal specification and verification of embedded systems using coloured Petri nets. In C. Atkinson, C. Bunse, H. G. Gross, & C. Peper (Eds.), *Component-based software development for embedded systems* (vol. 3778, pp. 35-58). Berlin, Germany: Springer-Verlag.

van der Aalst, W., & van Hee, K. (2002). *Workflow management: Models, methods, and systems: Cooperative information systems.* Cambridge, MA: MIT Press.

Wang, J. (1998). *Timed Petri nets: Theory and applications.* London: Kluwer Academic.

Wang, Q., & Saunders, B. (2005). Web-based 3D visualization in a digital library of mathematical functions. In *Proceedings of the Tenth International Conference on 3D Web Technology* (pp. 151-157). New York: ACM Press.

Weber, M., & Kindler, E. (2003). The Petri net kernel. In H. Ehrig, W. Reisig, G. Rozenberg, & H. Weber (Eds.), *Petri net technology for communication-based systems: Advances in Petri nets* (Vol. 2472, pp. 109-124). Berlin, Germany: Springer-Verlag.

Weiss, G. (Ed.). (2000). *Multiagent systems — A modern approach to distributed artificial intelligence.* Cambridge, MA: MIT Press.

Zaslavsky, A., Yeo, L., Lai, S., & Mitelman, B. (1995). Petri nets analysis of transaction and submitter management protocols in mobile distributed computing environment. In *Proceedings of the 4th International Conference on Computer Communications and Networks (ICCCN '95)* (pp. 292-299). Washington, DC: IEEE Computer Society.

Endnotes

[1]   Design/CPN can be downloaded at http://www.daimi.au.dk/designCPN/

[2]   VRML resources such as editors and browsers are available at http://www.vrmlsite.com/

[3]   The official site of Java 3D is available at https://java3d.dev.java.net

[4]   The official site of X3D is available at http://www.web3d.org

Chapter III

Integrating Usability, Semiotic, and Software Engineering into a Method for Evaluating User Interfaces

Kenia Sousa, University of Fortaleza, Brazil

Albert Schilling, University of Fortaleza, Brazil

Elizabeth Furtado, University of Fortaleza, Brazil

Abstract

We present artifacts and techniques used for user interface (UI) design and evaluation, performed by professionals from the human-computer interaction (HCI) area of study, covering usability engineering and semiotic engineering, which can assist software engineering (SE) to perform usability tests starting earlier in the process. Tests of various interaction alternatives, produced from these artifacts, are useful to verify if these alternatives are in accordance with users' preferences and constraints, and usability patterns, and can enhance the probability of achieving a more usable and reliable product.

Introduction

In a software development process (SDP), it is crucial for developers, customers, and users to interact in order to specify, generate, and evaluate the software. From software specification to its delivery, various kinds of tests must be performed, involving aspects such as: functionality, portability, performance, and usability. This work focuses on the context of usability, communicability, and functionality tests (e.g., appropriateness of a chosen interface design alternative to user preferences, consistency to a visual pattern, efficient execution of interactive tasks on interface objects, etc.).

Through our researches on tests in HCI and SE, and through our experiments on their integration in a SDP, we verified that HCI concepts facilitate the UI evaluation work performed by the test team of an interactive system under development. More specifically, by means of UI generation based on HCI models (e.g., task model), it is possible to evaluate the UI earlier (e.g., its functionality), independent of having the entire noninteractive specification ready. Prototypes, for instance, can represent UI design alternatives that may be tested early by HCI experts to verify if they are in accordance with user preferences, usability patterns, and so on.

This work presents a SDP to design and evaluate UIs, based on the integration of concepts, models, and activities of usability, semiotic, and software engineering.

This chapter is structured as follows: The "User-Interface Evaluation" section shows the contribution of each engineering area to UI evaluation; "The Process" section describes the UI design process; "The Evaluation Strategy" section describes the UI evaluation process, showing which concepts are used to perform tests and when they are performed; the "Case Study" section describes the case study in which we designed and evaluated UIs for the Brazilian System for the Digital Television (SBTVD); and, finally, the "Findings and Future Works" section describes findings and future works, and the "Conclusion" section concludes this work.

User-Interface Evaluation

In this section, we present concepts and evaluation techniques from usability engineering, software engineering, and semiotic engineering.

Usability Engineering

Usability engineering is a set of activities that ideally take place throughout the lifecycle of the product, with significant activity at the early stages even before the UI has been designed. The need to have multiple usability engineering stages supplementing each other was recognized early in the field, though not always followed in development projects (Gould & Lewis, 1985).

In usability engineering, techniques and methods are defined aiming to assure a high usability level of the interactive UIs. Among them, we emphasize the application of ergonomic criteria in the UI design. Verification of these criteria in designed UIs is called heuristic evaluation, performed by usability experts without user participation. Evaluators examine the IS searching for problems that violate general principles of good UI design, diagnosing problems, obstacles or barriers that users will probably encounter during their interaction. In addition, methods to capture usability requirements attend to user preferences, restrictions, and use-context. A usability requirement can be derived from an interaction restriction; such as if part of the system needs to be implemented for palm-top devices.

The evaluation approaches from usability engineering suggests a structured sequence of evaluations based on "usability inspections methods" and on "usability tests".

Some inspection methods are: (1) heuristic evaluation, verification of usability heuristics (Nielsen, 1993); (2) review of guidelines, verification if the UI is according to a list of usability guidelines (Baranauskas & Rocha, 2003); (3) consistency inspection, verification of the consistency among the UIs related to terminology, color, layout, input and output format, and so on; and (4) cognitive walkthrough, simulation of the user "walking" through the UI to execute typical tasks.

Some usability test methods are: (1) thinking out loud, we request the user to verbalize everything he or she thinks while using the system, and we expect that their thoughts demonstrate how the user interprets each UI item (Lewis, 1982); and (2) performance measures, quantification of some evaluated items to make future comparisons.

Software Engineering

Software engineering is composed of technologies and practices that are used in the development of software products, enhancing software productivity and quality, by providing a more systematic and controlled SDP (Sommerville, 2001).

In software engineering, there are various types of tests to be performed in each test stage, such as: usability tests to ensure that access and navigation through functionalities are appropriate for users; UI tests, to ensure a good functionality of the UI components and verify conformity to corporate patterns; and functionality tests, which are responsible for verifying if the generated software achieves all the proposed functionalities according to the customer's requests. Test cases (Myers, 2004) are normally generated and comprise procedures to be followed in test activities in order to deal with all possible situations when using the software, including basic flows, as well as error treatment and invalid data verification.

According to Pressman (1995), the main goal of test cases is to derive a set of tests that will probably reveal errors in the software. To achieve this goal, software engineering basically proposes two test categories: white-box and black-box tests.

For Pressman (1995), the white=box test must verify the internal part of the product, tests can be performed to guarantee that the components are integrated, and the internal operation achieves the performance level as specified in the requirements.

Functional tests, or black box tests, represent a test approach in which tests are derived from specifications of the system. In this kind of test, the evaluator is concerned with the functionality, not with the software implementation (Sommerville, 2001).

In these two test categories, software engineering defines four main types of tests: unit tests that are generally white-box tests; acceptance and regression tests that are usually black-box tests, and integration tests that blend this two categories.

Semiotic Engineering

Semiotic engineering is an HCI theory that emphasizes aspects related to the metacommunication designer user(s) via user-system communication, which passes through the UIs of interactive applications. The system is considered to be the "deputy" or a representative of the system designer (Souza, Barbosa, & Silva, 2001). The content of messages is the application usability model. Its expression is formed by the set of all interaction messages sent through the UI during the interaction process. The user plays a double role: interacting with the system and interpreting messages sent by the designer.

Semiotic engineering is essentially involved in test procedures with final users (empiric evaluation), aiming at system communicability analysis — based on qualitative evaluation, in which there are four phases: test preparation; labeling; interpretation, and formatting — and elaboration of the semiotic profile of the application to be evaluated. The techniques used in theses phases are: system-user observations, questionnaires, (somative-evaluation) inspections, interviews, filming,and so on.

Semiotic engineering is essentially present in tests with final users (e.g., empiric evaluation), aiming at analyzing the system communicability. A UI has a good level of communicability when it is able to successfully transmit the designer message to the user, allowing him or her to understand the system goal, the advantages of using it, how it works, and the basic UI interaction principles.

Evaluation

After studying about evaluation techniques, artifacts and approaches from software, usability, and semiotic engineering we are able to conclude that an evaluation process can be seen under various perspectives.

Concerning software engineering, we noticed the importance of software quality concerning functionality, performance, portability, and other nonfunctional requirements. Its artifacts and techniques include the evaluation of these aspects in an objective manner.

Usability engineering focuses in providing more ease of use, ease of learning, and efficiency to interactive systems.

Semiotic engineering includes procedures that allow the evaluation of the quality of the interactivity of systems by observing the communication through messages of the user to the system.

Based on these perspectives, we believe that an approach for UI evaluation of interactive systems that integrates these approaches is able to guarantee a system with quality concerning functionality, usability, and interactivity, derived from software, usability, and semiotic engineering, respectively.

Next, we will describe a lightweight development process for interactive systems, called UPi (Sousa & Furtado, 2004), which integrates HCI and SE activities, artifacts, and professionals.

The Process

UPi can serve as a guide, providing useful steps and artifacts that can be tailored and customized when organizations intend to develop usable interactive systems. One of the best advantages of UPi is the idea to focus on activities, artifacts and guidelines that add value to the UI generation. With this approach, it can be integrated with any other process and inherit activities that are vital to the entire process, but that are better defined and solidified in other processes. For instance, project management, configuration and change management, implementation, and deployment activities are very well detailed in the RUP (Kruchten, Ahlqvist, & Bylund, 2001). Besides the RUP, UPi can also be applied in conjunction with ISO 13407 (ISO 13407, 1999), which already has other activities defined and validated, such as project planning, testing, and so on.

UPi is composed of activities that aim at designing UIs. These activities are based on RUP activities, but they follow different guidelines that take into consideration usability aspects.

In this work, we are integrating UPi with UPi-Test (to be presented in the next section) in order to guide professionals that are developing interactive systems to evaluate them throughout the entire development process.

Phase I: Inception

The main goal in this phase is to elicit requirements from users in order to develop an interactive system that best suits their needs through the execution of some activities (presented as follows). These requirements are documented through certain artifacts: use-case models, task models, usability requirements, and paper sketches.

Use-case models represent a well-established manner to define the system functionality, while *task models* can be used to detail use cases by breaking them down into tasks. *Usability requirements* represent users' preferences or constraints that can be part of a usable interactive system. *Paper sketches* focus on the interaction, UI components, and on the overall system structure, keeping the style guide secondary, without being too abstract.

The purpose of the *Elicit Stakeholder Needs* activity is to understand users, their personal characteristics, and information on the environment where they are located that have a direct influence on the system definition, and to collect special nonfunctional requirements that the system must fulfill, such as performance, cost, and device requests.

The purpose of the *Find Actors and Use Cases* and *Structure the Use-case Model* activities is to define the actors (users or other systems) that will interact with the system and the functionality of the system that directly attend to users' needs and support the execution of their work productively.

The purpose of the *Detail a Use Case* activity is to describe the use case's tasks using the task model, to describe any usability requirements related to the use case, to define the system navigation based on the task model hierarchical structure, and to create paper sketches.

The purpose of the *Review Requirements* activity is to verify, with usability experts, if the paper sketches are in accordance to the task model and validate, with users, if the requirements are in conformance with their needs by showing them the elaborated paper sketches.

Phase II: Elaboration

The main goal in this phase is to transform the requirements in a representation that can be understood by UI designers and programmers. These representations are provided by the following artifacts: system architecture, UI Definition Plan, and drawing prototypes.

System Architecture is composed of smaller components that represent the main functionality of the entire system. The *UI Definition Plan* is a new artifact that aims to define which visual objects should be part of the UI. *Drawing prototypes* produce an accurate image of the system and they are useful to demonstrate patterns and style guides.

The purpose of the *Define and Refine the Architecture* activity is to (re)design the classes that represent the data that are handled by users while performing certain tasks.

The purpose of the *Define UI Plan* activity is to define which visual objects and which usability patterns can be part of the UI according to the nonfunctional requirements defined in the *Elicit Stakeholder Needs* activity.

The purpose of the UI Prototyping activity is to design a UI prototype in drawings following the description specified in the task models, in the UI definition plan and in the system architecture.

The purpose of the *Evaluate Prototype* activity is to verify if the UI prototypes are in accordance to usability principles and to validate with users if the UI prototypes are in conformance with their needs.

Phase III: Construction

The main goal of this phase is to implement and verify the accuracy of the components implemented and of the UI designed.

The purpose of the *Implement Components* activity is to develop the classes previously designed and implement the UI prototyped.

The purpose of the *Evaluate the Version of the System* activity is to verify if the functionality of the interactive system is in accordance with users' requirements.

Phase IV: Transition

The main goal of this phase is to deliver to the customer a system with high level of quality and usability.

The purpose of the *Deploy the System* activity is to make the system available for the customer.

The purpose of the *Evaluate the System* activity is to validate with users (by using the system in the deployment site) if the system conforms with their view of the system.

All of these phases are supported by processes concerning configuration and change management and project management, such as the RUP. This support is provided for the *Manage Change Requests* activity, which aims at evaluating the impact of change requests, deciding if they are to be included in the current iteration, and, if they are accepted, manage the changes in the appropriate artifacts.

Concerning the evaluation activities performed in each phase, they will be more thoroughly explained in the next section.

The Evaluation Strategy

The unified process for evaluating interactive systems "UPi-Test" (Schilling et al., 2005) has the same phases as the RUP (inception, elaboration, construction, and transition) (Kruchten, Ahlqvist, & Bylund, 2001). This process is based on the Unified Process for Interactive Systems, called UPi (Sousa & Furtado, 2004) and follows the approach to design UI prototypes dependent on the device (Coyette, Faulkner, Kolp, Limbourg, & Vanderdonckt, 2004).

Each phase is directly related to a specific area. This way, usability engineering supports the verification and validation in the inception and elaboration phases, software engineering supports verification in the construction phase, and semiotic engineering supports validation in the transition phase.

Figure 1 illustrates these four phases in the UPi-Test, each one with its flow of activities, artifacts, and techniques.

UPi-Test includes the verification and validation of usability and functionality of interactive systems UIs. Nonfunctional requirements are not in the scope of this work, such as aspects related to database (e.g., connection, integrity, etc.), security, and architecture. These aspects can be supported in future versions of this process.

Figure 1. Evaluation process of UIs

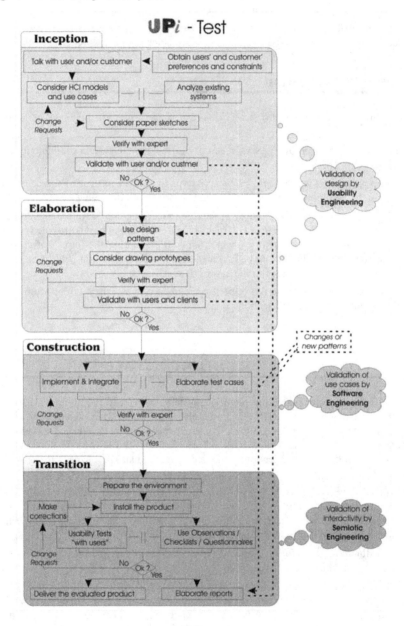

Phase I: Inception

The inception phase is important in guaranteeing that the following phases achieve results to attend to users' and customers' usability goals. This phase has the constant participation of users in order to understand their requests, which are verified and validated according to usability engineering to allow the development of these requests. The description of the activities and artifacts in this phase is presented as follows.

Talk with Users and/or Customers

This activity consists of the first contact with users or customers, in which system analysts understand their profiles, objectives, and the scenario where they are included. In this activity, it is necessary to use a technique to elicit requirements.

We propose an initial informal talk in order to better understand users' environment. Then, we suggest the performance of interviews, with the use of a questionnaire that aids in the identification of users and/or customers and their intended goals, preferences, and possible constraints.

Obtain Users' and Customers' Preferences and Constraints

In this activity, system analysts aim at eliciting users' and customers' preferences and constraints in order to design UIs that attend their needs and also to help usability experts during evaluation and to help UI designers during prototyping. Some examples of preferences are: design colors, font styles, navigation schemes. Some examples of constraints are: technology constraints, such as platform, device, and so on.

Consider HCI Models and Use Cases

Use cases represent an artifact from software engineering that identifies the functionality of interactive systems; users' interactions, expressed through users' tasks; and the system's responses to perform these interactions (system's tasks).

Task models detail a use case or a group of related use cases by specifying users' tasks and system's tasks. It is useful to support UI designers in the elaboration of prototypes because it is easy to identify the necessary views and objects in the prototype from the task model hierarchical structure.

Analyze Existing Systems

In this moment, it is important to analyze existing systems. This involves a comparative study of similar systems. These systems can be used as a reference in order for system analysts to propose new functionality or to choose design patterns, which are all useful for the design of UI prototypes.

Consider Paper Sketches

After talking with users and customers, the UI designer designs paper sketches. This prototype is verified and validated, as presented in the next activity.

Verify with Expert

This activity consists of the verification of paper sketches by the usability expert. The expert is concerned with verifying if users' goals, in terms of functionality, were included in the prototype, as well as if usability principles were used.

We propose that experts use the heuristic evaluation approach (Nielsen, 1993) as an inspection method. The usability heuristics will guide the usability expert in the process of verifying UIs' quality of use. We also suggest the use of the task model to verify if all the specified functionality was designed in the prototype.

When the expert notices that a functional requirement or any usability principle is missing, change requests can be made, which leads to changes in the models and new proposals of prototypes.

Validate with Users and Customers

After the verification with the expert, we propose a validation with users and customers so they can approve the generated artifacts. If the prototypes do not attend users' needs, change requests can be made, which leads to changes in the models (if new functionality is requested) and new proposals of prototypes (if changes in the navigation are requested). This process is repeated until the generated prototype attends users' preferences and needs.

This activity early in the process provides flexibility for users and customers to evaluate the evolution of the system, therefore, designers and users feel more confident with the UI design.

After the conclusion of the inception phase, the resulting artifacts are verified and validated as paper sketches.

Phase II: Elaboration

The elaboration phase is concerned with designing and evaluating drawing prototypes. In this phase, we use verification and validation techniques, such as heuristic evaluation and validations with users. After this phase, the resulting artifacts are drawing prototypes validated according to usability requirements and patterns. The description of the activities and artifacts in this phase is presented as follows.

Use Design Patterns

In order to guarantee the quality of the product and efficiency of the project, we suggest the use of design patterns for graphical UIs. These patterns will guarantee that we elaborate and develop UIs following already verified and validated parameters, which can be incremented by the reports generated in the end of the transition phase.

Consider Drawing Prototypes

UI designers are responsible for designing drawing prototypes based on paper sketches previously validated, and on usability patterns. These prototypes are verified and validated by the following two activities.

Verify with Expert

This activity consists of verifying the usability of drawing prototypes by experts. We propose that experts use the heuristic evaluation approach (Nielsen, 1993) as an inspection method to verify whether or not certain usability principles are present in the prototype.

When the expert notices that any usability principle is missing, change requests can be made, which leads to new proposals of prototypes. At this moment, it is not necessary to make changes in the models because this approach evaluates the quality of use, not functionality aspects, which were evaluated in the previous phase.

Validate with Users and Customers

After verification with the expert, a validation is proposed to users and customers so they can approve the generated prototypes. At this moment, users and customers evaluate the used usability patterns and the style guide. This process is repeated until the generated prototype attends users' preferences and constraints. If the prototypes do not attend users' needs, change requests can be made, which leads to new proposals of prototypes.

After the conclusion of the elaboration phase, the resulting artifacts are verified and validated drawing prototypes, which support development, tests, and deployment activities.

Phase III: Construction

In this phase, the UI is developed and the application is integrated with it. Considering software engineering, we propose functionality tests of an executable prototype (i.e., a product with some functionality) or the final product (i.e., a product with all the functionality), using functional test cases.

The activities and artifacts in this phase are presented as follows.

Implement and Integrate

These activities consist of developing the UI and integrating it with the application. The integrated product, either a prototype or the final system, can be useful for evaluating the navigation, interactivity, and functionality aspects.

Elaborate Test Cases

Test cases can be elaborated starting in the inception phase, using paper sketches, they can then be updated in the elaboration phase, using drawing prototypes, and finished in this activity. This artifact focuses on the system functionality, not on nonfunctional aspects.

The technique used to define test cases includes the following topics: association to a use case, specification of the item to be tested, preconditions to execute before testing, identification of valid and invalid inputs, and the expected outputs. The actual outputs are compared with the expected outputs described in the test cases and this comparison is used as validation of the use case.

Verify with Expert

This activity consists of the verification of the functionality of the product by usability experts and developers. Examples of aspects that are verified are: consistency of the outputs, navigation, existence of error messages, results after clicking on objects, as well as other aspects identified in the test cases.

After this verification, developers and experts can generate change requests to correct the errors; which leads to the repetition of the implementation and integration activities.

After the conclusion of the construction phase, the resulting artifact is the integrated product, which is tested with consideration to usability aspects in the transition phase.

Phase IV: Transition

This phase comprehends, in general terms, the preparation of the test environment, which can be a test laboratory or the environment where the system is used. With consideration to semiotic engineering, we use some validation techniques and artifacts. The description of the activities and artifacts in this phase is presented as follows.

Prepare the Environment

To prepare the environment, we suggest the installation of the system, software for capturing the system's use, and equipment, such as video cameras and necessary hardware devices. We also suggest the creation of questionnaires and checklists.

The test laboratory must be similar to the real user environment — with consideration to physical structure, climate, sound aspects, and equipment — in order to allow users to live the same conditions of the real environment. There should be a room where the test takes place and another one for observation.

Install the Product

In this activity, the product is installed, either a partial version or the final version of the system, in order to allow users to use the system in their real environment. This installation allows the tests to be performed.

Usability Tests "with Users"

This evaluation is performed with users. In it, evaluation techniques, proposed by semiotic engineering, are used, such as: recording, observation, questionnaires, and so on.

Before starting the tests, the usability expert talks with the user in order to: clarify that the system is under evaluation, not him/her; present the scenario used for the test; and make the user feel comfortable; which are aspects that influence the final results.

Observers that are in the observation room should fill out the questionnaires and checklists.

This activity can be divided in two moments, the first one, when the user interacts with the system to perform a task of his/her own interest; the second one, when the expert requires the user to perform a specific task.

In this activity, navigability, interactivity, and acceptability will be evaluated.

Use Observations/Checklist/Questionnaires

Observations, questionnaires, and checklists are artifacts and techniques proposed by the semiotic engineering in order to verify the user-system interactivity and communicability. Experts and observers will use these artifacts during the tests, which result in the definition of the quality of the interactive system. These results can lead to change requests for developers to correct the detected mistakes.

Users' comments and the actual execution of the tests will be recorded to help in the analysis of the results of the questionnaires and of users' observations.

Make Corrections

In this activity, developers make corrections proposed by experts after the tests. After the changes are made, users validate the product.

Deliver the Evaluated Product

As a result of the process, we have the results of evaluations, which are useful for future versions; and we also have a verified and evaluated product according to a set of techniques proposed by usability, software, and semiotic engineering.

If the product is a final version of the system, it is ready to be delivered for use. If it is a partial version (e.g., executable prototype), the professionals need to perform the activities in the construction phase, then in the transition phase, until the product reaches its final version.

Elaborate Reports

The results obtained will be used as a basis for the elaboration of evaluation reports, which propose adaptations in the used patterns and in the creation of new patterns that can be used in future iterations.

Case Study

In this chapter, we describe the case study of this research work, which is concerned with the evaluation of UIs for the SBTVD project, focusing on the applications: electronic portal, insertion of texts, and help.

Introduction

The digital TV represents digital and social inclusion for a great part of the Brazilian population, especially for people less privileged, who do not have access to computers, and therefore, cannot access the Internet.

The SBTVD must be adapted to the socioeconomic conditions of the country, as well as allow the use of conventional TV sets already in large use in the country in order to decrease risks and costs for the society.

The digital TV creates various possibilities of interaction between the TV and the user, such as: exchange of text or voice messages, virtual chats, searches for a favorite show, access to information about the government, and so on. These possibilities are different from the characteristics of the conventional TV, in which the user plays a passive role.

In the following section, we describe the performance of the activities proposed by UPi and UPi-Test. It is important to point out that the SBTVD is still under development. That is the reason why we cannot demonstrate all the activities of the process.

Phase I: Inception

Talk with Users and/or Customers

This activity was difficult to perform in this project because there is an almost unlimited number of users and/or customers. Fortunately, there were specific and clear specifications, established by the Brazilian government. Such specifications were used as requests from users and customers.

To define the scope of the application under our responsibility (access portal), we had meetings with representatives of the government and with other institutions that are participating in the project. These meetings were supported with brainstorming and the resulting decisions were analyzed and were shared with all the institutions through e-mails and discussion lists.

After these meetings, we decided that the portal will consist of a main application that allows the access to all other applications in the SBTVD, which can be: electronic mail, electronic commerce, EPG, help, electronic government, and so on.

Obtain Users' and Customers' Preferences and Constraints

The SBTVD project is concerned with various users' profiles, including the ones who are and those who are not used to technology, but not including the ones with any kind of disabilities.

In order to identify their possible preferences and constraints, we studied existing systems; we had many meetings and workshops. The opinions of all the participants in the project were taken into consideration because we can also be considered to be potential users.

Our main goal in the usability workshops was to choose the best usability pattern for each requirement based on the evaluation of positive and negative aspects of each proposed usability pattern, as specified in the UPi activity define UI plan.

These proposed usability patterns were selected from a list, such as the one available in Welie (2005), which are organized in the following format: problem to be solved, solution, context in which it can be used, and graphical illustration.

For the participants to evaluate the usability patterns, we provided a set of guidelines. After they read the guidelines, each group evaluated the positive and negative aspects of each usability pattern suggested for the requirement. Then, the participants discussed and reached the final decision as to what was the best usability pattern for the requirement under discussion.

The personalization group considered the guidelines as they evaluated the positive and negative implications of each usability pattern, aiming at achieving Nielsen's usability goals. For demonstration purposes, we focus on presenting the personalization of colors.

As a result of the evaluation, the personalization group decided to use color templates because of the greater impact of positive implications over the negative ones. The result of this work was the generation of a document associating usability patterns with their positive and negative implications. For instance, the selected pattern with more positive implications was "Provide predefined color templates to change font/background colors" instead of the pattern "Offer a list of colors from where the font/background colors can be chosen" because of the following positive implications: efficiency of use, compatibility of the system with the real world, and clarity of information. The second option had more negative implications than the first one, such as difficulty in use by beginners and the constant need to resize the space reserved to the presentation of information.

We defined that the applications in the SBTVD need to have a high level of usability. There was a list of technology constraints, especially the ones related to memory and processing capacity. Besides that, graphical representations need to be simple because conventional TV sets do not support images as computer monitors do, and the TV luminosity is very different from the one in monitors; consequently, colors and texts appear differently.

Consider HCI Models and Use Cases

In this activity, analysts and usability experts elaborated use case and task models, and then changed them, when change requests were made after the evaluation of users in the end of the Inception phase. The requests resulted in changes in the models because they were changes in the functionality, such as: do not consider access to multiple applications simultaneously (technical constraint) and include personalized help. These changes reflected in the models and will be considered in the prototypes.

Analyze Existing Systems

In this activity, we researched on the Internet in order to find digital TV systems already in use. It was very difficult to find them because there are few systems available for access in the Internet.

This analysis was used to identify some UI design patterns for the digital TV, such as: upper and bottom options bar, menu on the left, navigation icons, interaction buttons, and so on.

Consider Paper Sketches

After the analysis of existing systems, UI designers elaborated paper sketches (Figure 2). However, they needed to be redesigned after the evaluation of users in the end of the inception phase, which resulted in change requests.

Some change requests resulted in the following changes in the prototypes: transfer the bar from the top to the bottom of the screen, include the "TV" button in the bar when accessing an application or in the portal; include the "Portal" button in the bar when accessing an application, take off activated icons (because of technical restrictions), and give a preview of the requested options of personalization. However, other requests resulted in changes in the models as well as in the prototypes, such as the ones mentioned in the activity "Consider HCI models and use cases."

Figure 2. Paper sketch: Personalization

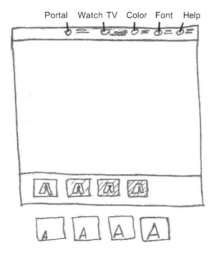

Verify with Expert

In this activity, we performed heuristic evaluations with three experts who considered the usability of the paper sketches. They observed aspects, such as: navigation between views and if usability principles were applied. Besides that, the experts verified if all users' goals, in terms of functionality (in the task models), were included in the prototypes.

Validate with Users and Customers

In meetings with the institutions participants of the project and with representatives of the Government users evaluated the elaborated prototypes.

Various change requests, as well as users' preferences were identified. These requests resulted in updates in the models and in redesign of the paper sketches.

As examples of preferences, we point out the following: Include the "TV" and "Portal" in the remote control; the bottom options bar should overpass the application; and make available a set of options for inserting text, such as the one used in computer keyboards, the one used in mobile phones, and in alphabetical order.

Phase II: Elaboration

Use Design Patterns

In this activity, the UI design patterns, identified while analyzing existing systems, were evaluated and the UI designers started to design drawing prototypes using the design patterns.

Consider Drawing Prototypes

The UI designers used image editors, such as Photoshopâ and Corel Drawâ, in order to design the drawing prototypes (Figure 3), which followed the selected patterns, the updated task models, and paper sketches. In this prototype, the small view on the right shows the preview of the required personalization about the color of the screen before applying it.

Verify with Expert

The drawing prototypes were evaluated by experts (Figure 4), who observed various aspects, such as: layout, colors and fonts, UI design patterns, and usability principles applied.

Figure 3. Drawing prototype: Personalization

Figure 4. Verification with expert

Validate with Users and Customers

This activity is yet to be fully performed in this project, currently; we have finished the document that specifies the SBTVD graphical UI, which is going to be evaluated by representatives of the Brazilian Government.

We scheduled a workshop with the other institutions participants of the project to evaluate the drawing prototypes (Figure 5). They requested us to elaborate other alternatives of UIs (including association of options in the UI with options on the remote control), increase the size of the options and fonts in the upper bar, and change the way to differentiate the selected option.

Figure 5. Validation with users

Phase III: Construction

Implement and Integrate

The implementation of the portal has not started yet. However, the developers have been studying and implementing simple applications for the digital TV, such as three possibilities of insertion of text (the one used in computer keyboards ('qwert'), the one used in mobile phones, and in alphabetical order).

Table 1. Test case: Personalization

Test case	Personalization
Test items	Changes in font and background color Changes in font size
Pre-conditions	The user must be accessing the portal
Inputs	The user must select a type of personalization: Font color The user selects green
Expected results	The portal must present the personalized content with a green background color

Elaborate Test Cases

The elaboration of functional test cases has started since the inception phase, when use cases and paper sketches were elaborated. Functional requirements were selected and the associated test cases were elaborated: structure applications, access applications, access help and personalization (Table 1).

Verify with Expert

In this activity, the programmers and the experts verify the applications using the test cases for guidance. Some of these evaluations were done in the small applications developed for insertion of text.

Phase IV: Transition

The usability experts and the developers have prepared the test environment. For that, they have: prepared the physical structure (e.g., TV, video camera, couch, computer to simulate the set-top box, etc.) and installed the necessary software (i.e., software to capture the user interaction with the TV, Linux Operating System, Java Virtual Machine, and applications to be tested).

A group of three usability experts were responsible for performing the following activities before the tests started: First, they defined a questionnaire to apply with users in order to understand their characteristics and familiarity to the DTV technology. Second, they selected appropriate metrics (e.g., number of errors, number of access to the help, etc). Third, they created a checklist based on Nielsen's usability goals and on the metrics from the previous step. Fourth, they prepared the environment with a DTV, a couch, and a center table in order to make users feel at home. Fifth, they selected ten users with different profiles between the ages of 18 and 26.

When the users arrived, each one at a time was taken to the DTV room, where a usability expert explained the goals of the test; applied the questionnaire; and defined a specific goal to be achieved while interacting with the DTV. While the user interacted with the application, usability experts filled out the checklist in the visualization room, where we monitored the environment and the user with a camera and captured the interaction with the DTV using specific software.

Findings and Future Works

After the tests, we evaluated the checklists and generated reports with solutions to the problems encountered during the tests. These reports contain comments about the icons, the navigation, and the help module of the portal application.

Figure 6. The portal application

- No user realized the possibility of navigation through the numbers associated to each icon, which represents an interactive application (see Figure 6).
- When they were told about this, they used it and said it was very practical.
- For them, the icons were not a natural representation, but they did not want to give any opinion about possible solutions.
- Some users did not notice the application that was selected. They said it was better to have a big square around the icon instead of the current selection.
- When the users were confused and wanted some help, they did not look for it in the portal (the blue option in the bottom bar that activates the help module). Some users activated the menu button of the remote control and others waited for the evaluator to tell them what was necessary to do to obtain the help.
- As the bottom bar is used as a design pattern to put the navigation options, and as each option is different depending on the situation (the application being executed), the users got very confused. We realized they looked at this bar only once, and then they did not look at it any more. After memorizing the options, they wanted to use them all the time, but the color was different, so they made many navigation errors.

From the execution of these tests, we were able to quantify the results: 85% of the users found the system easy to use, easy to read, and easy to navigate, but on the other hand, 50% had difficulties in identifying that an option was selected and in getting out of an unexpected situation.

Our next step is to make the necessary changes that are related to improving the layout, color contrast, and icon selection. In addition, the next tests will be done with the elderly in order to investigate people who are not used to interaction devices.

Conclusion

In this chapter, we present a new method, which focuses on integrating different techniques of usability, semiotic and software engineering. The aims are to design usable UIs following a model-based UI design process and to facilitate the test process by using the evaluated HCI models. In this manner, we hope to contribute to the development of interactive systems that are easy for users to learn and use, and to help testers in performing their usability tests in an efficient manner.

As main contributions, we focus on evaluating the usability of UIs with the constant participation of users and customers. Besides that, the integration of various approaches results in positive outcomes for the prototypes, as well as for multidisciplinary team members, who are better integrated and can have their knowledge enhanced, since they are continuously exchanging information and experiences.

References

Baranauskas, M. C. C., & Rocha, H. V. da. (2003). Design e Avaliação de Interfaces Humano-Computador, NIED–Núcleo de Informática Aplicada à Educação, UNICAMP–Universidade Estadual de Campinas.

Coyette, A., Faulkner, S., Kolp, M., Limbourg, Q., & Vanderdonckt, J. (2004). SketchiXML: Towards a multi-agent design tool for sketching user interfaces based on UsiXML. In P. Palanque, P. Slavik, & M. Winckler (Eds.), *3rd Int. Workshop on Task Models and Diagrams for User Interface Design* (pp. 75-82). New York: ACM Press.

Gould, J. D., & Lewis, C. (1985). Designing for usability: Key principles and what designers think. *Communications of the ACM, 28*(3), 300-311.

ISO 13407. (1999). *Human-centred design processes for interactive system teams.*

Kruchten, P., Ahlqvist, S., & Bylund, S. (2001). User interface design in the rational unified process. In M. Van Harmelen (Ed.), *Object modeling and user interface design* (pp. 45-56). New York: Addison-Wesley.

Lewis, C. (1982). *Using the "thinking-aloud" method in cognitive interface design* (IBM Research Rep. No. RC9265, #40713). Yorktown Heights, NY: IBM Thomas J. Watson Research Center.

Myers, G. J. (2004). *The art of software testing.* New York: John Wiley & Sons.

Nielsen, J. (1993). *Usability engineering.* Boston: Academic Press.

Pressman, R. S. (1995). *Engenharia de Software.* São Paulo: Makron Books.

Schilling, A., Madeira, K., Donegan, P., Sousa, K., Furtado, E., & Furtado, V. (2005). An integrated method for designing user interfaces based on tests. In *Proceedings of the ICSE 2005 Workshop on Advances in Model-Based Software Testing,* (pp. 27-31). St. Louis, MO: ACM.

Sommerville, I. (2001). *Software engineering*. New York: Addison-Wesley.

Souza, C. S. de, Barbosa, S. D. J., & Silva, S. R. P da. (2001). Semiotic engineering principles for evaluating end-users programming environments. *Interacting with Computers, 13*(4), 467-495.

Sousa, K. S., & Furtado, E. (2004). UPi — A unified process for designing multiple UIs. In *IEEE Computer Society, Proceedings of the International Conference on Software Engineering*, Edinburgh, Scotland (pp. 46-53). Edinburgh, Scotland: ACM.

Welie, M. van (2005). Retrieved September, 15, 2005, from http://www.welie.com

Chapter IV

Automated Software Testing

Paula Donegan, Instituto Atlântico, Brazil

Liane Bandeira, Instituto Atlântico, Brazil

Cristina Matos, Instituto Atlântico, Brazil

Paula Luciana da Cunha, Instituto Atlântico, Brazil

Camila Maia, Instituto Atlântico, Brazil

Abstract

This chapter approaches paramount aspects related to test automation, introducing the importance of implementation in the software market and essential bases, such as adjustment to the organizational reality and establishment of an efficient strategy. Types of tools and directives for a successful implantation are presented. Test automation has been considered the main measure taken to enhance test efficiency — fundamental in the software-development process. Responsible for verifying and/or validating the quality of the executable product compared to performed documentation and client requirements. Therefore, with the chapter content here provided, we aim to provide the reader with an understanding of test automation and grant relevant orientations to assist implementing it.

Introduction

Given the growing complexity of applications and new technologies, such as the advent of the client/server environment (in particular Web applications), the effort necessary for application testing has increased.

To assure that software conforms to requirements, various test stages may be identified: unit, integration, system, and acceptance. Bugs' impact increases with the evolution of the test stage in which they are found, in other words, the cost of detecting errors during unit test is less than integration and system tests.

Each use case has test objects that may need to be retested several times during the project, demanding resources. These retests normally are required when a new functionality is added or when a bug is corrected, because there is no guarantee that the changes made will impact negatively on other parts already constructed. Therefore, the assistance of a tool capable of repeating a test already executed in the past is quite interesting.

Besides, multiple execution paths and diversity of possible inputs and outputs of an application complicate the execution of manual tests, which may be simplified by automation. In addition, performance, load and volume tests are examples of tests that are difficult to be accomplished without the help of automated testing tools. There are also some types of tests that are almost impossible to be executed manually, for example, a test to verify a system's performance with thousands or millions of simultaneous accesses or having to use an enormous amount of data.

Automating software tests speeds development and reduces retesting effort spent in each stage, thus reducing time and cost. However, this reduction is normally noticed only after a while, because there are high investments in the implantation stage, such as organizational needs, training, and tools acquisition. Automation allows increase of amplitude and depth of developed tests.

Testing automation might or might not be helpful. It allows one to take advantage of idle machine time (i.e., the period in which the developer is not working) to execute tests. Therefore, test execution can be more effective and waste less resources.

Background

Automated software testing is an activity that seems to have obvious benefits: tests may be executed swiftly, are more consistent, and may be repeated various times without increasing cost. However, it is not a trivial activity and requires effective planning and elaborate test-case definition, as well as other characteristics, which will be explained in more detail later in this chapter. Benefits and risks, possible tools, an implantation methodology and directives for script generation are also described.

An automated test between different phases of the development process has the purpose of verifying if what was constructed from that stage backwards is correct and is adequate as an input for the next stage. An example would be a programmer testing a software component before doing the integration of components.

The generated test process is automated and capable of ensuring that the system logically operates according to the code by executing the functions through a series of test cases.

With a tool, you can expect the test script to conduct the verification processes and return results that verify whether the product under test meets code logic.

A test engineer usually follows a procedure to decide whether a problem found is a defect. However, an automated test tool makes decisions based on methods invocation, during which it detects errors and defects. Thus, the tool makes an effort to remind the developers of the importance of adopting a good error-handling technique.

But, can a tool verify that all test tasks have been performed? The answer is based on the requirements of your organization and on the architecture of the software project (Li & Wu, 2004).

Tests to validate a product against specified client requirements are more subjective and cannot always be automated. An example is a test executed by a user in a beta-program.

Manual Testing vs. Automated Testing

Software testing is necessary to guarantee the quality of a software product, may be performed during the whole software development process, in a manual, automated or hybrid manner, using different types of tests and tools.

Automated software testing simulates system behavior using tools. The test actions performed on the application are specified in code (scripts and test classes). In a context where required tests are not possible or viable to be executed manually, automated software testing is very important. As examples in which automated tests are indicated, one has Automated tests are used in regression, load, performance, and endurance tests and tests involving a vast amount of data.

Regression tests require testing all constructed functionalities after one of them is changed or a new one is inserted. Automation helps in this process, providing repetition of tasks already executed. Thus, functionality tests already recorded may be executed again, decreasing retest efforts.

For load tests, a high amount of users simultaneously accessing the application is necessary (e.g., in the order of 100; 1,000; and 10,000). How can such a test be performed? Automation is a resource that can easily simulate this scenario.

When using test performance, an automation test tool is used to capture time measurements each time they are executed. Performance degradations can be detected by collecting these measurements and reviewing them as time series (Karner, 1993).

Endurance testing requires automation. In this type of test, a specific application behavior is observed with the execution of its functionalities for a certain amount of time — weeks or months. This way, it is possible to detect problems like memory leaks, stack corruption and wild pointers.

Some specific tests — such as installation, configuration, and usability tests and specific hardware operations tests — require a strong human intervention, as well as a specific human evaluation and validation. Manual tests are recommended for these kinds of tests, being executed by at least one person, following a test procedure with application input and output data.

Test automation has a high cost. Training and scripts maintenance are necessary and, in case the tools used are not free, licenses are needed according to the number of users. However, automation has become essential given to systems' high complexity, need of performance and stress testing, resulting in increase of testing time and cost, reduction of software quality and, after the recognition of importance of software tests, pressure over project development teams has increased.

Test execution may also be performed with hybrid methods, characterized by applying jointly manual and automated techniques in the same project. The choice will depend on a thorough analysis of time and resources available and test complexity. The degree of maintenance and human intervention must be taken into consideration given to application modifications.

Many tests are not executed many times during a project life cycle. In these cases it is more advantageous to execute the tests manually, because efforts employed in their automation do not provide large returns. Therefore, it is not recommended to automate 100% of the tests.

Manual and automated tests should not be compared only in terms of time, effort, and cost, because the value of a test is especially in the information it provides. In the same way, manual and automated tests are not allowed to be compared in many cases, because they provide distinctive information, as seen before, for every type of test, one of them is normally indicated.

However, in certain situations it might be a reasonable goal to create the most extensive automated test suite, such as contractual or regulatory reasons, when it is necessary to prove that the final version passed a strong battery of tests; when tests will be delivered with the product so that customers can also run the tests themselves; when the product has stringent requirements for backwards compatibility, remaining for many versions, or when the only way to test some products is by writing programs to exercise them (Kaner, Bach, & Pettichord, 2002).

Overview of Automated Testing

Nowadays automated testing is considered the main resource to improve the efficiency of a test process (Rios & Moreira, 2003), using tools so that the computer is responsible for assistance, design achievement, execution or tests control. Information collection and their quick dissemination are assisted by automated tests to provide a faster feedback to the development team (Kaner, 2002).

Tools to execute automated tests normally simulate the use of an application by several users simultaneously, a high load of data processing, as well as repetition of tasks previously executed. Besides, automating regression tests is of great relevance for the maintenance phase, since tests executed during development may be repeated in new tests, when the system is already in production.

When the automation does not apply to the entire test process, it can be used to execute punctual tests. This occurs normally with some types of tests — such as load and performance tests — because they are truly difficult to be performed without the help of a tool, requiring big effort and many computational resources.

The preparation of automated tests takes more time than manual tests. This is mainly a consequence of high effort and cost necessary to generate and maintain automation code. Therefore, so that the investment may bring satisfactory return on investment, automation must help to achieve the specific tests mission (Kaner, 2002), providing a supply of functional and nonfunctional tests.

Automation must be introduced in a context where the test process is well performed, with well-defined activities and with a mature and experienced test team. Otherwise, automation will not assist the achievement of test objectives. For this reason, test processes must be fixed before automating them.

Specific management treatment is required, in other words, planning, execution, and control, because normally automation is characterized by its innovation and high investments, complexity, and risks. Without this management, the expected benefits may not be achieved, besides consuming resources and dispersing the team from their test objectives, consequently interfering on the quality of tested products. Moreover, previous strategies and planning definitions are necessary, so that risks are controlled, possibility of scripts reuse is increased and automation optimized.

Automated testing tools do not replace testers, nor will their work be simpler. Actually their effort will be redirected to essential activities of the test automation process. For this reason, it is of great relevance to prepare the group, because the success of automated testing depends predominantly on their skills.

Test-Stages Automation

Test automation may be applied to diverse stages: unit, integration, and systemic. Each one has peculiar characteristics and is implemented in a different way. Next, these aspects will be shown for each test stage.

Automated Unit Testing

Unit tests consist of testing components individually. The tester verifies the input domain only for the unit in question, ignoring the rest of the system. These tests require code construction executed during depuration mode.

The developer has the responsibility to ascertain that units are correctly constructed, analyzing code, comparing it with the system's specification and checking if any functionality is missing or was not completely developed.

Tests and error corrections may be made at any stage of the development cycle. Nevertheless, some authors like Boehm (1981), have shown that the cost of searching and finding errors increases while the development advances. It is cheaper to fix defects during the codification stage.

Procedure to implement unit testing:

1. Prepare test environment.
2. Define input domain based on requirements and use cases.
3. Define, for every input, expected output based on requirements and use cases.
4. Implement components to be tested.
5. Group unit tests in collections of components.
6. Implement unit tests.
7. Execute unit testing.
8. Fix component tested, if there is an error.
9. Execute step 8 while any error remains.

Unit testing consists basically of:

1. Variables initiation, including database population.
2. Business rules or input functions are applied.
3. Destruction of variables, including the cleaning up of data input to data base.
4. Comparison between results of applied function with expected results, failing in case they differ.

Grouping unit tests forms a tree, where the leaves consist of the unit tests and in the other nodes are the groupings of unit tests. This technique allows automating and executing all tests, a subset of them, or each one individually.

Unit test automation enables dynamic problem detection, generating automated reports, and facilitates execution of regression tests, which are necessary for every meaningful code update.

Automated Integrated Testing

Integrated tests are performed to test various parts of the system (components, modules, applications, etc.) that were separately developed in a set. Integration tests are executed after each of the system's parts has been tested individually, using unit tests or systemic tests, in case of applications that communicate (with each other).

Analyzing the time line, you can notice that integrated tests are mainly performed after a unit test and before systemic tests, normally are executed by developers that create their own builds and test integrates units or by a specialized testing team.

Procedure to implement integrated tests:

1. Prepare test environment, using test data and test server, which are configured to simulate the production environment.

2. Identify test cases based on requirements and architecture.

3. Detail procedures for each test case.

4. Implement integrated tests.

5. Execute integrated tests.

6. Analyze results. If errors are found, they must be registered in the problem reports tool and associated to responsibles for the corresponding corrections. If none are found codification may stop.

7. Fix problems encountered.

8. Execute tests again. After ending it, return to step 6.

Automated System Testing

System testing is the most misunderstood and most difficult testing process. System testing is not a process of testing the functions of the complete system or program, because this would be redundant with the process of function testing (Myers, 2004). System testing compares the system or program with its original objectives (requirements).

In this stage a test environment, compatible with the one in which the system or program will be used, is necessary.

Various test types are performed during this stage: usability, functionality, performance, stress, and so on. Some of these may be automated to make execution more agile, especially in case of regression tests.

Systemic tests may be automated in several ways, but a list follows with their basic activities:

1. Prepare test environment, installing and configuring necessary hardware and software.

2. Design test cases.

3. Define automation strategy.

4. Select project scope for automation.

5. Implement systemic test scripts for each test case.

6.   Execute systemic test.

7.   Analyze results. If errors are found, they must be registered in the problems report tool and associated to responsibles for the corresponding corrections.

8.   Fix problems found.

9.   Generate reports with tests status.

10.   Execute tests again, returning to step 6 after finishing them.

Automation Techniques

Automated functional test tools make use of some techniques that differentiate themselves basically because of the contents of the generated scripts: record & playback, scripts programming, data-driven and keyword-driven. These techniques will be explained as follows:

- **Record and playback:** Technique that consists of recording a test execution made on the application's interface and playing back this execution later. The generated scripts contain unalterable data, test procedures, and expected results. The advantage of this technique is the simplicity of generating scripts. However, there is a high sensibility to changes, which restricts a script's lifetime. For example, a simple change of an interface may lead to the necessity of recording again all the scripts, implying a high script maintenance cost.

- **Scripts programming:** Considering the components of the generated scripts, this technique is similar to the one above. However, this one allows updating generated scripts. With this resource, script programming has a higher rate of reuse, longer lifetime, and less difficulties to be maintained, compared to the technique of Record & Playback. Nevertheless, there is still a big volume of scripts and high-maintenance cost (Fantinato, Cunha, Dias, Mizuno, & Cunha, 2004).

- **Data-driven:** This is a technique that approaches test-data extraction through scripts, storing them in separate files. Therefore, scripts will only contain test procedures and actions for the application. This technique is useful for tests using different inputs and combinations of scripts with common test procedures (Kaner, 2002). This way, maintenance requires a reduced effort when it is necessary to include, update, or delete any test data. However, this technique depends on the test-execution logic, in other words, if any step is added to the procedure (or removed) the script needs to be generated again.

  Nevertheless, it allows automating in parallel: test data can be created while test procedures are being generated. The extraction of test data from scripts provides tests that are easy to understand and revise. Many test tools include direct support for the technique *data-driven* (Kaner, 2002).

- **Keyword-driven:** Based on retrieving test procedures from scripts, remaining only test data and specific test actions, which are identified by keywords. This resource's operation, being invoked by keywords and even receiving parameters, is similar to that of structured-program functions. An important enhancement of this technique is the reduction of script-maintenance effort if there is incorporation, removal, or modification of any step of a test-procedure execution (Fantinato et al., 2004).

In spite of tools existent in the market recommending a specific testing technique, the organization needs to establish the most adequate technique according to their own test context after analyzing all possibilities.

Good Practices for Automation

A list of relevant practices to improve systemic test-script implementation and reuse follows, which may be used according to the adopted technique:

- When recording a script for a test case, some necessary initialization may be necessary — such as database connection, variables, and functions — which can be shared between test cases of the same use case or even between many use cases.

- Each script may be recorded independently from the others, having its own variables, initialization, and so on, although it would be better to share common objects for test scripts, in other words, use the concept of modularity. For example, if it is necessary to clean up a database for a specific use case before executing any test script, or if there are common script steps, a text file to store these steps may be used and later on can be included at scripts execution time. If these steps change, only one place will have to be modified.

- Another practice is to define functions executing a common activity for many scripts, and only call it from those scripts.

- A clean and robust code must be implemented. Comments should be made for important lines or code blocks. While implementing, possible maintenance may not be discarded.

- When a flow alteration or verification point in a script is recorded again, there must be some care to update only script sections where there really must be a change.

- To delete any garbage shown in a form, before inserting any data, a combination of keys should be used ("HOME", "SHIFT+END" and "DELETE") when recording an action of data input.

- If test scripts are recorded initially from a prototype (in case the application is still not available), it is necessary to certify that names of fields and IDs of clickable icons on screen will not be altered. If they are changed, the script will need an update later.

- Dynamic data for test scripts should be used (test data separate of scripts). The immediate benefit is that, if additional data is needed, more records can simply be added; there is no need to modify the test script (Mosley & Posey, 2003).

Benefits and Risks

The benefits of automated tests are innumerable. Some of them will be described here, as well as risks that were considered most important.

A growing number of software versions to be tested exhausts the capacity of manual tests in terms of time, patience, input variation, attributes combination and, as consequence, cost. With advent of increasingly complex, integrated, and critical software, automated tests have become a necessity.

Benefits of test automation may be observed in any test stage, such as unit tests, integrated tests, and systemic tests.

Unit testing is a way of efficiently granting an applications quality. In this stage, a big quantity of errors can be detected and easier corrected. The manual execution of unit tests is a difficult process that consumes time and resources, being practically unviable since almost all system units must be tested, depending on the context, such as functions, subroutines, components, or classes.

Benefits of automated unit tests are easily noticed. During the project's life cycle unit tests, automation can decrease the costs of rewriting code, because more errors are found still in the codification stage. This test stage also grants more security when doing updates, since the entire set of tests are executed automatically. It is easier for program-mers to write test routines that retain their value in time and assure the correct functioning of units. Besides, automated unit testing provides test results immediately after their execution.

In *integrated tests*, where the focus is on systems architecture and integration between different units developed, it is also indispensable to execute them automatically. The integration between system units may occur daily during the development process and it is important to always test the relationships between those components using automatic mechanisms, like continuous integration.

Automation of *systemic tests* requires attention and planning, because in this stage the functionalities' behavior is verified according to specified requirements. System testing is conducted at a higher level. During systemic tests, an examination is made of integration of parts that make up the entire system (Dustin, Rashka, & Paul, 1999).

For each test stage, automation must take into consideration possible software changes. However, systemic test scripts have their execution recorded in an application interface, therefore, there must be a special care avoiding costs of rework. Flexible scripts (dependencies with interface are minimized) can assist scripts maintenance.

In general, test automation in any stage allows:

- **Test effort reduction:** Introduction of automated test tools will not immediately reduce the test effort. Experience has shown that a learning curve is associated with attempts to apply automated testing to a new project and to achieve effective use of automated testing.

While the testing effort will likely increase at first, a playback on test tool investment will appear after the first iteration of the tools' implementation, due to improved productivity of the test team.

Manual tests must still be performed on the project, while a learning curve may exist due to effort with familiarization and efficiency in the use of the tool (Dustin et al., 1999).

- **Schedule reduction:** As the testing effort may actually increase, the testing schedule will not experience an initial decrease but may instead become extended. Therefore, permission to increase the schedule is required when initially introducing an automated test tool. Once an automatic testing process is established and effectively implemented, the project can expect to experience gains in productivity and turnaround time, having a positive effect on schedule and cost (Dustin et al.,1999).

- **Improved regression testing:** An automated test tool provides simplified regression testing. Automated regression testing can verify in an expedient manner that no new bugs were introduced into a new build (Dustin et al., 1999).

- **Improved focus on advanced test issues:** Automated testing allows simple repeatable tests. A significant amount of tests are conducted on the basic user-interface operations of an application.

Besides delaying other tests, the tedium of these tests exacts a very high toll on manual testers. Manual testing can become stalled due to the repetition of these tests, at the expense of progress on other required tests. Automated testing presents the opportunity to move on more quickly and to perform a more comprehensive test within the schedule allowed. That is, automatic creation of user interface operability tests gets these tests out of the way rapidly and releases test resources, allowing test teams to turn their creativity and effort to more complicated problems and concerns.

- **Increased test coverage:** Automated testing may increase breadth and depth of test coverage, yet there will still not be enough time or resources to perform a 100% exhaustive test. Even with automation, testing every combination of a system exhaustively is impossible. Therefore, there must be strategies (equivalence partitioning) to select relevant test data.

- **Productivity increase:** Having increased test coverage, automation also increases productivity. Testers may verify more test cases in less time than when using manual tests.

- **Improved performance testing:** Many load-testing tools are available that allow one to automatically test the performance of a system's functionalities, producing timing numbers and graphs and thresholds of the system. There is no longer the necessity to sit with a stopwatch in hand. The objective of performance testing is to demonstrate that a system functions in accordance with its performance requirement specifications regarding acceptable response time, while processing the required transaction volumes on a production-size database (Dustin et al., 1999).

From these benefits, we can observe that automation is essential, because, even with an extremely experienced tester, it is almost impossible to know all the relations and combinations between attributes of medium- and large-sized applications.

Even so, the implementation of a solution for automated tests, even with excellent test tools available, is not trivial and can fail mainly due to:

- **Nonqualified test team:** An automated tool requires new skills for test analysts, therefore additional training is required. An efficient automation is not that simple. Test scripts automatically generated by the tool during recording must be modified manually, which requires scripting knowledge, so as to make the scripts robust, reusable, and maintainable. To be able to modify the scripts, the test engineer must be trained on the tool and the tool's built-in scripting language (Dustin et al., 1999).

- **Inadequate tools:** The automation tool must be in accordance to the company's business needs with the test process introduced. There are many tools that automate tests and a correct choice cooperates to fully use features offered. There is not a tool clearly superior to other tools for every situation. The choice of the most adequate tool depends on characteristics of applications, test stages to be automated, as well as the adopted organizational test policy.

  Simply using tools, by themselves, will not promote a significant quality enhancement of developed products, if not accompanied by an adoption of a work methodology.

  An incorrect choice may lead to automation failure, once the organizational testing needs will not be completely suppressed and resources and efforts addressed to manual tests deviated. Besides, given to the affected credibility, it may be difficult to obtain further investments of higher management to proceed with automation or even to reinforce manual tests.

- **Elevated cost with systemic test scripts maintenance:** This aspect may not compensate automation costs. Systemic test scripts have to be flexible enough to easily support various changes and insertion of new functionalities that appear during a project's life cycle.

  To create scripts easy maintainable, professionals with experience in software development are important. They are supposed to be capable of designing a modular script structure, in the same way as when doing a normal software design.

- **Automation of every test type:** As explained in this chapter, when tests require high human intervention it is not recommended to focus on automated tests.

- **Lack of planning and control of the automation process:** Test automation must be considered a separate project from the software development process. Cautions related to project management have to be taken, such as concerns with scope, time, cost, quality, integration, resources, and risks.

Execution of automated tests helps to provide reliable and stable applications. However, to reduce associated costs and risks, it is important to analyze factors mentioned earlier on. Thus automation benefits can be more evident in the organization and risks can be controlled by mitigation and/or contingency.

Automated Test Tools

The tools for automated testing are instruments to make the testing process easier, replacing and/or assisting manual tests performed by testers. Various tools exist to be used in the various test stages.

Many organizations have successfully chosen and purchased a test tool, but around half of those organizations have not achieved any benefit from their investment because their tools have ended up not being used (*shelfware*) (Fewster & Graham, 1999). A way of easing this risk is by knowing better the available market categories and types of automated tools.

Categories and Types

While GUI-testing tools (also called "capture/playback" tools or functional-testing tools) are much hyped in the testing industry, it is important to be aware of the other types of tools available to support the testing life cycle. This item provides an overview of the available tools, listed in Table 1, supporting the various test activities.

The existent divisions of types of test tools are not uniform. Therefore, to be more didactic and easier to understand the purpose of each test tool, they may be divided into categories, and those categories have many types of tools associated with them, according to their objectives:

- **Test-development tools:** Assist test plan elaboration and generation of test cases and input data. Test development is responsible for designing tests and test data, being the most important set of activities in a testing process. Tests must enclose all requirements, otherwise, they will be invalid.

- **Test execution tools:** Assist test case execution and results evaluation; include also the capture/programming of test scripts.

- **Test support tools:** Assists test-specific activities, not being considered particular for tests. Include tools to support revisions, inspections, walkthroughs, project management, as well as tools for defect tracking and database managing.

Following are some key points regarding some of the types of test tools, according to their categories.

Test-Development Tools

- **Test-procedure generators:** A requirements-management tool may be coupled with a specification-based test-procedure (case) generator. The requirements-management tool is used to capture requirements information, which is then processed by the test-procedure generator. The generator creates test procedures

Table 1. Tools by category and type

Tool Category	Type of Tool	Description	Example
Test Development	Test-procedure generator	Generates test procedures from requirements/design/object models	• TYX — Test Procedure Generation Wizards
	Test-data generator	Generates test data	• Tnsgen • DTM Data Generator
	Test-data extraction	Extraction and verification of test data	• Kapow Web Collector
Test Execution	Unit testing	Unit API testing and assertions verification	• PyUnit • JUnit • HttpUnit
	Memory-leak detection	Verify that an application is properly managing its memory resources	• JProbe • Pruify
	GUI-testing (capture/playback)	Automate GUI tests by recording user interactions with systems, so they may be replayed automatically	• Robot • WinRunner • QARun • Functional Tester
	Load, performance, and stress testing	Load/performance and stress testing	• Robot • LoadRunner • JMeter • JProbe
	Network testing	Monitoring, measuring, testing, and diagnosing performance across entire network	• CSSCheck • Bobby
Test Support	Test management	Provide such test-management functions as test-procedure documentation, storage, and traceability	• TestManager • TestDirector • QADirector
	Code-coverage analyzers and code instrumentors	Identify untested code and support dynamic testing	• Clover • NoUnit • Jtest
	Metrics reporting	Read source code and display metrics information, such as complexity of data flow, data structure, and control flow. Can provide metrics about code size in terms of numbers of modules, operands, operators, and lines of code.	• McCabe Visual Quality
	Usability measurement	User profiling, task analysis, prototyping, and user walkthroughs	• SUMI
	Defect tracking (bug tracking)	Manage data base with found defects	• ClearQuest • Bugzilla • Jira

by statistical, algorithmic, or heuristic means. In statistical test-procedure generation, the tool chooses input structures and values in a statistically random
distribution, or a distribution that matches the usage profile of the software under
test (Dustin, 2002).

Most often, test-procedure generators employ action-, data-, logic-, event-, and
state-driven strategies. Each of these strategies is employed to probe for a different
kind of software defect. When generating test procedures by heuristic- or failure-
directed means, the tool uses information provided by the test engineer. Failures
discovered frequently in the past by the test engineer are entered into the tool. The
tool then becomes knowledge-based, using the knowledge of historical failures to
generate test procedures.

- **Test-data generators:** Test-data generators aid the testing process by automatically generating test data. Many tools on the market support the generation of test
  data and populating databases. Test-data generators can quickly populate a
  database based on a set of rules, whether data is needed for functional testing, data-
  driven load testing, or performance and stress testing.

- **Test-data extraction tools:** Using production data for testing purposes increases
  the integrity of testing by allowing testing teams to establish test scenarios using
  real test cases rather than relying on fabricated testing environments.

  A test-data extraction tool minimizes time to create test data and maximizes integrity
  and usability of data.

Test-Execution Tools

- **Unit-testing tools:** This type of tool is used to program and execute tests in units
  of the developed application. The units are normally classes, methods, or flows.
  Generally a unit-testing tool supports only one development language.

- **Memory-leak detection tools:** These tools are used for a specific purpose: to verify
  that an application is properly using its memory resources. These tools ascertain
  whether an application is failing to release memory allocated to it, and provide
  runtime error detection. Since memory issues are involved in many program
  defects, including performance problems, it is worthwhile to test an application's
  memory usage frequently.

- **GUI-testing tools (capture/playback tools):** Many automated GUI testing tools are
  on the market. These tools usually include a record-and-playback feature, which
  allows the test engineer to create (record), modify, and run (playback) automated
  tests across many environments. Tools that record the GUI components at the user-
  interface control are most useful. The record activity captures the keystrokes
  entered by the test engineer, automatically creating a script in a high-level language
  in the background. This recording is a computer program, referred to as a test script.
  Using only the capture and playback features of such a tool uses only about one-
  tenth of its capacity, however. To get the best value from a capture/playback tool,
  engineers should take advantage of the tool's built-in scripting language.

To create a reusable and maintainable test procedure, the test engineer must modify the recorded script. The outcome of the script becomes the baseline test. The script can then be played back on a new software build to compare its results to the baseline. The results can be compared pixel-by-pixel, character-by-character, or property-by-property, depending on the test-comparison type, and the tool automatically pinpoints the difference between the expected and actual result (Dustin, 2002).

- **Load, performance, and stress testing tools:** Performance-testing tools allow the tester to examine the response time and load capabilities of a system or application. The tools can be programmed to run on a number of client machines simultaneously to measure a client-server system's response times when accessed by many users at once. Stress testing involves running the client machines in high-stress scenarios to determine whether and when they break.

- **Network-testing tools:** The popularity of applications operating in client/server or Web environments introduces new complexity to the testing effort. The test engineer no longer exercises a single, closed application operating on a single system, as in the past. Client-server architecture involves three separate components: the server, the client, and the network. Interplatform connectivity increases potential for errors. As a result, the testing process must cover the performance of the server and the network, the overall system performance, and functionality across the three components (Dustin, 2002). Many network test tools allow the test engineer to monitor, measure, test, and diagnose performance across an entire network.

Test-Support Tools

- **Test-management tools:** Test-management tools support the planning, management, and analysis of all aspects of the testing life cycle. Some test-management tools, such as IBM's Rational TestStudio, are integrated with requirement- and configuration-management and defect-tracking tools, in order to simplify the entire testing life cycle.

- **Code-coverage analyzers and code-instrumentors tools:** Measuring structural coverage enables the development and test teams to gain insight into the effectiveness of tests and test suites. They are able to quantify the design complexities, help produce the integration tests, and measure the number of integration tests that have not been executed. Some of them measure multiple levels of test coverage, including segment, branch, and conditional coverage.

- **Metrics reporting tools:** Tools responsible for reporting metrics analyze code complexity and identify application passages that offer a higher fault risk, reporting quality metrics. With these tools it is possible to know parts of code that have or have not been tested.

The usage of metrics-reporting tools assures higher product quality, because it is possible to have metrics showing the quality of what is being developed.

- **Usability-measurement tools:** Usability engineering is a discipline that includes user-interface design, ergonomic concerns, human factors, graphics design, and industrial and cognitive psychology. Usability testing is largely a manual process of determining the ease of use and other characteristics of a system's interface (Dustin, 2002). However, some automated tools can assist with this process, although they should never replace human verification of the interface.

- **Defect tracking (bug tracking):** Most of the existing commercial tools present a conjunction of tool types or even categories. It may be a big advantage to obtain these integrated tools. However in some cases not all functionalities are needed and the tools cost may be an inhibitor. Therefore, it is very important to analyze test tools' costs and benefits thoroughly.

Some test tools are intrusive, because it may be necessary to insert special code into the application program so that the automated tool may work correctly, interacting with the testing tool. Development engineers may be reluctant to incorporate this extra code. They may fear it will cause the system to operate improperly or require complicated adjustments to make it work properly. To avoid such conflicts, test engineers should involve the development staff in selecting an automated tool and if the tool requires code additions (not all tools do), developers need to know that well in advance.

Intrusive tools pose the risk that defects introduced by testing hooks (code inserted specifically to facilitate testing) and instrumentation could interfere with normal functioning of the system.

Besides, as with all technologies, test tools can be unpredictable. For example, repositories may become corrupt; baselines may not be restored, or may not always behave as expected. Often, much time must be spent tracking down a problem or restoring a back-up of a corrupted repository. Test tools are also complex applications in themselves, so they may have defects that interfere with the testing effort.

Programming Languages of Automated Test Tools

It has already been mentioned that there are a lot of test tools available on the market, and testing teams have used the tools and achieved great success. These test automation tools also include writing (i.e., coding) test scripts, which are software programs (Mosley & Posey, 2003). As such, they have their own programming languages and/or language extensions that are required to accommodate software-testing events, such as Java (JUnit and JProbe) or Visual Basic; in one of the standard scripting languages such as Perl, CGI, or VB Script; or in the operating system's command procedure language (Unix).

The scripting language is usually embedded in a capture/playback tool that has an accompanying source code editor. Some popular test tools write test scripts in Visual Basic 6.0 and execute the script in Visual Studio IDE. There is also literature that introduces how to write test scripts in Visual Basic 6.0 by hand. Some other tools are written in Java, such as JUnit, and JProbe and there are tools to write test scripts for software products run on Unix, Linux, and other platforms.

Test Tools Development

The usage of an automated tool will not always be adequate or provide necessary benefits. Diversified factors may lead to the necessity of building a tool:

- **Application incompatibility:** The application may contain an element that will cause compatibility problems with any capture/playback tool on the market. If a work-around cannot be created, it may not be possible to use the capture/playback tool. Even if a work-around can be created, it may not be worth the effort, being more beneficial to create a customized tool.

- **Operating system incompatibility:** If there is a market absence of a tool, compatible with the various operation systems in use, there is no other choice than to consider building a customized tool that will work in the specific environment under test.

- **Specialized testing needs:** In case the test tool cannot reach a critical/complex component, an enhancement to the tool may be developed.

In case the organization chooses to develop a testing tool, resources, cost and time need to be determined, as well as management permission. The tools development must be treated as development effort of the project that demanded the use of the tool (Fewster & Graham, 1999). Many books provide detailed explanations of how to proceed to develop a test tool inside an organization, such as Li and Wu (2004) and Fewster and Graham (1999).

Implantation of Test Automation

Many companies, certain of the advantages of test automation, want to define a process of test automation to enhance the software-testing process, but do not know how to do it. Next, some phases are described which may be used for the test-automation implantation.

Introduce Automated Test Ideas

In this stage, the expectations management related to test automation and explanation of its benefits are performed, introducing automated test ideas to the organization.

Some imagine that a lot of time is spent with automation and that it has high costs. Therefore it is important to study its applicability (Donegan et al., 2005), verifying management, financial and structural benefits and risks involved, because the advantages and disadvantages of automation are to be made clear for everyone. At this moment, those involved with the implantation, including internal investors, are supposed to be conscious that normally the return on investment will be obtained in a medium or long term, since test automation does not reduce testing time as soon as it is introduced. This occurs given to time spent with tools initial learning, adaptation to the new testing process, among other factors mentioned before.

Generally, introducing tests automation requires a lot of investment. That does not happen only with the acquisition of a tool, but also with professional preparation of stakeholders and with maintenance of existent hardware to support the one being installed. Those variables must be considered in the projects' budget.

In this stage, an open communication with high management is fundamental, being constantly informed of organizational risks already detected, as well as direct benefits of automation, so that they may support the entire automation process even being aware of the existent challenges.

It is important to form a team with specialized professionals to begin the implantation of tests automation. The team must have at least one representative with knowledge of the organizational culture. These professionals will also be responsible for conducting the next stage.

After taking into account all the factors mentioned, the organization might take the decision of beginning test automation, or may abort the idea, being aware of risks and benefits involved. In case the decision is positive, some of the initial automated test ideas above have to be detailed in a tests automation plan, defining tasks that will be executed.

Choose Test Tool

This stage guides the choice and evaluation of necessary tools for test automation.

Initially, the requirements of the tool are researched, according to organizational necessities: available resources, architecture of developed applications, platforms used, automation tool language, type and stage of desired test, and others. If possible, requirements should be prioritized conforming to the level of importance, making it possible to focus on key requirements in the evaluation process.

According to the requirements of highest importance, available tools in the market are selected. In case there is not any tool accessible to provide the organizational needs, the possibility of developing a homemade tool must be taken into account, which was seen earlier on in the chapter.

However, generally, a single test tool will not fulfill all the automated testing requirements for an organization, unless that organization works only with one type of operating system and one type of application. Expectations must be managed. It must be made clear that currently there is not a single tool on the market that is compatible with all operating systems and programming languages. This is only one reason why several tools are required to test the various technologies.

After preselecting the tools, there must be an assurance that the tools will fulfill the requirements and other points, like usability and performance. A way of doing this is using demo versions or doing hands-on. As a consequence, one or more tools are selected, according to company needs.

Refine Testing Process

This stage sketches the refinement of the organizational test process, including necessary activities for automated tests.

As an aftermath of the test tools choice, the process of implantation of automation begins. Now it is necessary to lay out objectives and strategies, by means of common architectures used in organizational projects. The strategy for automation in a company must contemplate directives that increase codification use and decrease their maintenance. See the "Good Practices" section.

After establishing these aspects, automation activities are defined. These activities are incorporated into the organizational testing process and stakeholders need to be properly trained. The mainly affected stakeholders are investigated, and a definition of the course goals (such as time and scope) is made.

A good way to consolidate the test process and chosen tools is to define a project to be automated and tested, called pilot project, applying the new test process and tools. It is necessary to monitor process planning, test-case elaboration, code creation, and tests execution and, especially, the results must be evaluated (Molinari, 2003).

All those involved in the test automation must participate, so that pertinent directives to the organizational context may be outlined and so that their commitment with the "Automation Product" is assured.

Develop Test Automation

Test Automation Planning

Conducting a common process of a Test Plan and designing test automation characterize the planning stage.

For the Test Plan, the scope of automation is defined and involved risks of the project in question are investigated, analyzed, and qualified. Besides, a test-automation strategy must be defined to orientate execution and monitoring, based on factors such as test scope, reuse of code, maintenance effort, and availability of time and resources.

Conventions of suites and code nomination may be established, as well as logical grouping relevant to worked scope. The most complex groups have to be identified and described in detail.

Test cases must have a well-defined design as they provide relevant information about the system to be tested without considering if tests are manual or automated. These test cases have to be analyzed, in order to identify the best automation possibilities. At this point, the test analyst must have a good understanding of how to raise valuable automation opportunities, in other words, opportunities that bring great aggregate value.

In case of automation of functional tests, another step consists of planning and designing useful test data, identifying the best way to communicate with code. See "Automation Techniques" section.

Test Automation Execution

Test execution approaches installation and configuration of tool and environment to initiate tests. This environment must also consider performance tests, which use various stations or virtual users. All necessary information concerning the environment must be contained in the test plan.

The preparation of a manual with instructions concerning chosen tools, test design information and adopted conventions is relevant.

The test team must develop test code based on the premises established during the planning stage and on the test projects already developed. The codes must be simple, robust, maintainable and, if possible, reusable.

After the test codes have been developed, unit, integrated and systemic tests can be performed. Generally, a different team of the one that executes systemic tests executes unit and integrated tests.

Each test team must report detected errors during test execution (integrated and systemic tests). A tool to report bugs facilitates this step.

Test Automation Management

Now that the tests are already planned and executed, they need to be managed. Control is essential for the test automation evolution analysis, with the perspective of analyzing if the new form of performing tests is acceptable and adaptable. Automation management is also fundamental to identify some points adopted during the planning stage that need to be adjusted, or even to reevaluate the tool with the purpose of certifying usability in the organization's context.

Tests codification must be constantly monitored, so that it can be a reflex of the application in such a way that modifications made in the product during its life cycle can also be contemplated in test code. This activity prevents reporting errors to the development team, caused by failure of test codification.

For systemic tests automation, when errors are found, it is necessary to do an analysis of them before sending the report to the development team, filtering duplicities and fake bugs, which are bugs caused by errors made during codification of tests.

Evaluate and Improve Test Automation

Automated test activities evaluation must be made during the whole test life cycle, so that improvements may be implanted. These enhancements can be observed along with execution of automated tests in organizational projects. Many of them are incorporated punctually into projects. The company is, therefore, responsible for collecting, evaluating, and incorporating the improvements to the organizational process, when it is the case. Afterwards, stakeholders must be informed of changes made to the process and, if necessary, be trained.

Another important point is the test tool performance evaluation and determining what can be done to enhance it in the next project or test cycle.

Related Works

There are many works related to test automation: reports and case studies of organizations that have implemented automated software tests; research projects published in diverse events and magazines, creating models for test automation, elaborating efficient techniques for different types of automated tests, as well as others.

Organizations that develop software are constantly automating their tests to improve process and product quality, there are many examples to be found nowadays, here are two specific organizations using automated tests: Instituto Atlântico and BMC Software.

Instituto Atlântico implanted automation of functional system tests initially in a pilot project and, nowadays, automated tests are being used in other projects of the organization. Time spent to develop automated use case tests sometimes is superior to the time necessary to test it manually. However, Instituto Atlântico uses regression tests and this economizes time to execute tests, recovering the amount of time already used with codification after some increments. The tools used are those from Rational IBM: Robot, Test Manager and, more recently, Functional Tester. More details can be read in Donegan et. al (2005).

BMC Software developed a system to automate tests of a products suite called BMC's MetaSuite — family of applications client/server. They formulated orientations to choose people to automate tests and what should be automated.

BMC uses the tool QA Partner. One of the main gains using this tool is the easy maintenance of test scripts. Test cases are implemented before the interface is completely ready, because the test cases are independent of implementation details. In a week, BMC executed around three times each test case of three suite products. And those tests could be amply repeated in a more consistent manner. More information can be found in Pettichord (2001).

There are some interesting publications following, related to test automation, providing new approaches to automation. They may be adopted by organizations, if they are in conformity with objectives and purposes of the organization or specific project using automated tests.

Interface-Driven Model-Based Test Automation

The paper describes an interface-driven approach that combines requirement modeling to support automated test case and test driver generation. It focuses on how test engineers can develop more reusable models by clarifying textual requirements as models in terms of component or system interfaces. The focus of interface-driven modeling has been recognized as an improvement over the process of requirement-driven model-based test automation (Blackburn, Chandramouli, Busser, & Nauman, 2002).

Model-Based Approach to Security Test Automation

The paper summarizes the results of applying a model-based approach to automate security functional testing. The approach involves developing models of security function specifications (SFS) as the basis for automatic test-vector and test-driver generation (Blackburn, Busser, & Nauman, 2002).

Further Reading

A very good place to do some further reading is in the Web site http://www.stickyminds.com. You can find every kind of papers related to software tests, including some very interesting related to automated software testing

In terms of tools to automate tests, if you are interested in more examples of existent tools, we advise you to access Brian Marick's website http://www.testingfaqs.org (Marick, 2005). He presents an extensive list of tools for some types of automated tests. To learn more about the development of a tool to automate tests, it is interesting to read "Effective Software Test Automation — Developing an Automated Software Testing Tool" (Li, 2004), a book that teaches how to build a fully automated testing tool and provides expert guidance on deploying it in ways reaching high benefits.

In the section "Implantation of Test Automation" we showed a brief methodology to automate tests in an organization, however if you desire some further readings, it is interesting to read about the automate testing life-cycle methodology (ATLM) by Dustin, Rashka, and Paul (1999).

Conclusion

Good planning, clear definition of roles of those involved with automated tests, adequate tools and implantation with strong management to control risks and costs are essential so that the automated tests are successful in an organization.

Risks and benefits involved with automation need to be researched and afterwards informed to all stakeholders involved, especially to the high management, so that there is an effective compromise. Nevertheless, results obtained during test automation also have to be disclosed.

Automated tests are capable of increasing test coverage; because of time gain, cost subsided by future problems, and increase of the application's stability and investors trust.

A methodology for implantation of test automation was explained in this chapter, suggesting test automation to be implanted in stages, beginning with the decision of automation until process improvement, facilitating an efficient management and control of the automation process. An important stage for test automation is the choice of tools to be used. To make the right choice it is important to know the organization's real needs, testing-process maturity, test-team experience, automation techniques, and advantages and disadvantages of available commercial tools.

When initiating test automation it is important to customize the organizational test process according to required activities necessary for automated tests, training professionals, preparing environment, among other aspects given along the chapter. Thus it is possible to perceive that test automation must be treated as a project, requiring a plan, activities execution, and results monitoring. Therefore, it is more likely to obtain a positive return for the organization.

References

Blackburn, M., Busser, R., & Nauman, A. (2002). *Interface-driven model-based test automation — Starwest 2002*. Retrieved September 2, 2005, from http://www.software.org/pub/externalpapers/starwest_2002.pdf

Blackburn, M., Chandramouli, R., Busser, R., & Nauman, A. (2002). *Interface-driven model-based test automation — Quality Week 2002*. Retrieved September 2, 2005, from http://www.software.org/pub/externalpapers/blackburn_issre_2002.pdf

Boehm, B. (1981). *Software engineering economics*. Englewood Cliffs, NJ: Prentice Hall.

Donegan, P., Bandeira, L., Matos, A., Cunha, P., Maia, C., & Pires, G. (2005) Aplicabilidade da automação de testes funcionais — a experiência no instituto atlântico. In *Simpósio brasileiro de qualidade de software* (pp. 447-454). Porto Alegre: Pontifícia Universidade Católica do Rio Grande do Sul.

Dustin, E. (2002). *Effective software testing: 50 specific ways to improve your testing*. Boston: Pearson Education.

Dustin, E., Rashka, J., & Paul, J. (1999). *Automated software testing: Introduction, management, and performance*. Boston: Addison Wesley.

Fantinato, M., Cunha, A., Dias, S., Mizuno, S., & Cunha, C. (2004). AutoTest — Um framework reutilizável para a automação de teste funcional de software. In Anais

SBQS — *Simpósio brasileiro de qualidade de software* (pp. 286-300). Brasília, Brazil: Universidade católica de Brasília.

Fewster, M., & Graham, D. (1999). *Software test automation: Effective use of test execution tools*. Boston: Addison Wesley.

Kaner, C., Bach, J., & Pettichord, B. (2002). *lessons learned in software testing: A context-driven approach*. New York: John Wiley & Sons.

Karner, G. (1993). *Metrics for objectory*. Unpublished diploma thesis, University of Linköping, Sweden.

Li, K., & Wu, M. (2004). *Effective software test automation: Developing an Automated software testing tool*. Alamdea, CA: Sybex.

Marick, B. (2005). *Testingfaqs.org — An information resource for software testers*. Retrieved September 2, 2005, from http://testingfaqs.org

McGraw, G., & Michael, C. (1996, July). Automatic generation of test-cases for software testing. In CogSci 1996, *Proceedings of the 18th Annual Conference of the Cognitive Science Society* (pp. 370-375). Mahwah, NJ: Lawrence Erlbaum.

Molinari, L. (2003). *Testes de software — produzindo sistemas melhores e mais confiáveis*. São Paulo, Brazil: Ed. Erica.

Mosley, D., & Posey, B. (2003). *Just enough software test automation*. New York: Yourdon Press Series, Prentice Hall.

Myers, G. (2004). *The art of software testing*. New York: John Wiley & Sons.

Pettichord, B. (2001). *Success with test automation*. Revised version of a Quality Week paper. San Francisco. Retrieved September 02, 2005, from http://www.io.com/~wazmo/succpap.htm

Rios, E., & Moreira, T. (2003). *Projeto & engenharia de software — testes de software*. Rio de Janeiro, Brazil: Atlas Book.

Chapter V

A Formal Verification and Validation Approach for Real-Time Databases

Pedro Fernandes Ribeiro Neto,
Universidade do Estado do Rio Grande do Norte, Brazil

Maria Lígia Barbosa Perkusich,
Universidade Católica de Pernambuco, Brazil

Hyggo Oliveira de Almeida,
Federal University of Campina Grande, Brazil

Angelo Perkusich,
Federal University of Campina Grande, Brazil

Abstract

Real-time database-management systems provide efficient support for applications with data and transactions that have temporal constraints, such as industrial automation, aviation, and sensor networks, among others. Many issues in real-time databases have brought interest to research in this area, such as: concurrence control mechanisms, scheduling policy, and quality of services management. However, considering the complexity of these applications, it is of fundamental importance to conceive formal verification and validation techniques for real-time database systems.

This chapter presents a formal verification and validation method for real-time databases. Such a method can be applied to database systems developed for computer integrated manufacturing, stock exchange, network-management, and command-and-control applications and multimedia systems. In this chapter, we describe a case study that considers sensor networks.

Introduction

Nowadays, the heterogeneity of platforms, distributed execution, real-time constraints, and other features are increasingly making software development a more complex activity. Besides, the amount of data to be managed is increasing as well. Taken together, complexity and data management are causing both risk and cost of software projects to get higher.

Database management systems are used to manage and store large amounts of data efficiently. However, when both data and transactions have timing restrictions, real-time databases (RTDB) are required to deal with real-time constraints (Ribeiro-Neto, Perkusich, & Perkusich, 2004). For an RTDB, the goal is to complete transactions on time, while maintaining logical and temporal consistency of the data. For real-time systems, correct system functionality depends on logical as well as on temporal correctness. Static analysis alone is not sufficient to verify the temporal behavior of real-time systems. To satisfy logical and temporal consistency, concurrency control techniques and time-cognizant transactions processing can be used, respectively. The last occurs by tailoring transaction management techniques to explicitly deal with time.

The real-time ability defines nonfunctional requirements of the system that must be considered during the software development. The quality assurance of real-time systems is necessary to assure that the real-time ability has been correctly specified. Imprecise computation is used as a technique for real-time systems where precise outputs are traded off for timely responses to system events. For that, formal models can be created to verify the requirement specifications, including the real-time specifications (Ribeiro-Neto, Perkusich, & Perkusich, 2003).

Validation as well as verification can be carried out by simulation model. With the simulation model, a random sample will be selected from the input domain of the test object, which is then simulated with these chosen input values. After that, the results obtained by this execution are compared with the expected values. Thus, a simulation model is as a dynamic technique, that is a technique that contains the execution of the test object. One major objective of simulation models is error detection (Herrmann, 2001).

The main motivation for this research is the fact that methods to describe conceptual models of conventional database systems cannot be directly applied to describe models of real-time database systems. It occurs because these models do not provide mechanisms to represent temporal restrictions that are inherent to real-time systems. Also, most of the available models focus on the representation of static properties of the data. On the other hand, complex systems, such as real-time databases, also require the modeling of dynamic properties for data and information. Therefore, the development of methods to design real-time databases with support for both static and dynamic modeling is an important issue.

In the literature, there are few works for real-time database modeling that allow a formal analysis, considering verification and validation characteristics. The existing tools for supporting modeling process especially do not present simulation capacity. The unified modeling language (UML) approach presents a number of favorable characteristics for modeling complex real-time systems, as described in Selic and Rumbaugh (1998) and Douglass (2004). UML also is used for modeling object-oriented database systems. However, the existing tools for UML modeling do not present simulation capacity.

This chapter describes a formal approach to verify and validate real-time database systems. The approach consists of the application of the five steps: (1) building an object model; (2) building a process model; (3) generating an occurrence graph; (4) generating a message-sequence chart; and (5) generating a timing diagram. The two first steps include static and dynamic analysis, respectively. The following steps allow the user to validate the model. Hierarchical coloured Petri nets (HCPNs) are used as the formal language to describe RTDB models (Jensen, 1998). The proposed approach can be applied to different domains, such as computer-integrated manufacturing, stock exchanges, network management, command-and-control applications, multimedia systems, sensor networks, and navigation systems. In this chapter, we describe a case study considering sensor networks. Sensor networks are used to control and to monitor the physical environment and sensor nodes may have different physical sensors and can be used for different application scenarios.

The remainder of this chapter is presented as follows. First, a background is presented, to ease the comprehension of approach. Concepts about RTDB, quality of services and HCPNs are defined. Second, the formal verification and validation approach for real-time databases is described as well as a sensor network case study. Third, future trends are presented. Finally, conclusions are presented.

Background

Real-Time Databases (RTDB)

The real-time database-management systems must provide the characteristics of conventional databases besides assuring that the real-time constraints are imposed on both the data and transactions. These constraints arise in applications where the transactions must meet deadlines.

The amount of applications that benefit from the utilization of RTDB is increasing as well. This increase is a consequence of the proliferation of embedded systems that includes both systems that are similar to those present in personal computers and smaller systems with a minimal memory and calculator capacity, such as those present in mobile devices.

An RTDB is required when: The volume of data is large; responses depend on multiple values; responses to aperiodic events are required; and there are constrained timing

Figure 1. Real-time database systems

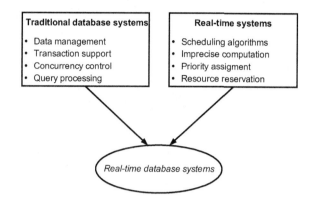

requirements. The correctness in real-time databases implies: satisfying all usual consistency constraints; executing transactions within timing constraints; and satisfying temporal consistency of the data. The real-time data and transactions are also defined. The data items reflect the state of the environment. The transactions are classified with respect to their deadlines, such as hard, soft, or firm; arrival-pattern — periodic, aperiodic, sporadic; and data-access-pattern — read-only, write-only and update. In Figure 1, a schema illustrating the properties of the RTDB is shown.

Data Properties

The data correctness in RTDB is assured by logical and temporal consistency. The real-time data can be classified into static and dynamic. The correctness of static data is guaranteed by the logical consistency, since is has not become outdated. The dynamic data may change continuously to reflect the real-world state, such as object positions, physic measure, stock market, and so on. Each dynamic datum has a timestamp of the latest update and the data can be divided into base data and derived data. A derived datum can be derived from various base data (Kang, 2001).

The external consistency of dynamic data is defined using validity intervals to assure the consistency between the state represented by the database content and the actual state of environment. The validity intervals are of two types as follows (Kang, 2001):

- **Absolute validity interval (*avi*)** is defined between the environment state and the value reflected in the database. The data x is considered temporally inconsistent if ($now - timestamp(x) > avi(x)$), where *now* is the actual time of system, *timestamp* is the time of the latest update of data.

- **Relative validity interval (*rvi*)** is defined among the data used to derive other data. Consider a data item y is derived from a data set $R=\{x_1,x_2,...,x_k\}$. y is temporally consistent if the if the data in R that the compose are temporally valid and the $|timestamp(x_i \bullet R) - timestamp(x_j \; 0 \; R)| \leq rvi(y)$. This measure arises to produce derived data from data with the approximate time.

The dynamic data are represented by x:(*value,avi,timestamp*) and will be temporally consistent. If both absolute and relative validity interval are satisfied. Consider the example where a data item t, with $avi(t)=5$, reflect the current temperature and the data item p represent the pressure with $avi(p)=10$. The data item y is derived from data set $R=\{t,p\}$ and have relative validity interval $rvi(y)=2$. If the actual time is 50, then (a) t:(25,5,45) and p:(40,10,47) are temporally consistent because as absolute validity interval as relative validity interval is valid. But, (b) t:(*25,5,45*) and p:(*40,10,42*) are not temporally consistent, because only the absolute validity interval is assured.

Transaction Properties

The real-time transactions are characterized along three dimensions based on the nature of transactions in real-time database systems: the nature of real-time constraints, the arrival pattern, and the data-access type.

- **Real-time constraints:** The real-time constraints of transactions are related to the effect of missing its deadline and can be categorized in hard, firm and soft. Hard deadlines are those that may result in a catastrophe if the deadline is missed. These are typically critical systems, such as a command delayed to stop a train causing a collision.

  To complete a transaction with a soft deadline after its time constraint is undesirable. However, soft deadlines missed can commit the system performance. The transactions with firm deadline will be aborted if its temporal constraints are lost.

- **Arrival pattern of transactions:** The arrival pattern of transactions refers to time interval of execution. Generally, the transactions are periodically executed in real-time databases, since they are used to record the device reading associated to the environment or to manipulate system events. The arrival pattern can be aperiodic, where there is not a regular time interval between the executions of transactions. The transactions also can execute in random time. However, there is a minimal time interval between the executions of transactions.

- **Data access type:** In relation to data access, the transactions are categorized as: write transactions (or sensors), update transactions, and read transactions. The *write transactions* obtain the state of the environment and write into the database. The *update transactions* derive new data and store them in the database. Finally, the read transactions read data from database and send them.

In the database, it is necessary to guarantee the same views, of the same data item, for different transactions. This property is called *internal consistency* and is assured by the ACID properties. ACID is an acronym for atomicity, consistency, isolation, and durability. These properties are defined for a real-time database as follows:

- **Atomicity:** Is applied for subtransactions, where a subtransaction must be whole executed or neither step must be considered of them.

- **Consistency:** The transaction execution must always change the consistent state of a database in another consistent state. An imprecision limited in the internal consistency can be permitted in order to meet the temporal constraints of transactions.

- **Isolation:** The actions of a transaction can be visible by other transactions before it commits.

- **Durability:** The actions of a transaction need not be persistent, since both data and transactions have temporal validity.

Concurrency Control

The negotiation between logical and temporal consistency, a concurrency-control technique should be capable of using knowledge about the application to determine which transactions can be executed concurrently. Such a technique, named semantic concurrency control, allows increasing the concurrent execution of transactions (method invocation). Based on the knowledge of the application the designer must define which transactions may be concurrently executed and when. Defining compatibilities between the executions of the transactions does this. Therefore, this technique allows relaxing the ACID properties.

Transactions in real-time do not need to be serialized, especially updated transactions that record information from the environment. However, the consequence of relaxing serialization is that some imprecision can be accumulated in the database, and in the vision of the database.

An object-oriented semantic concurrency control technique, described in DiPippo (1995), named *semantic-lock technique*, allows logical and temporal consistency of the data and transactions and allows the negotiation among them. The technique also allows the control of the imprecision resulting from the negotiation. The concurrency control is distributed among the objects, and a compatibility function, says CF for short, is defined for each pair of methods for database objects. *CF* is defined as follows:

$$CF(m_{ati}, m_{inv}) = Boolean\ Expression \rightarrow IA$$

where m_{ati} represents the method that is being executed and, m_{inv} represents the method that was invoked. The *Boolean Expression* can be defined based on predicates involving values of the arguments of the methods, the database attributes, and the system in general. *IA* is defined by an expression that evaluates the accumulated imprecision for the attributes of the database object and for the arguments of the methods.

The consequence of using such a concurrency control is that more flexible scheduling for transactions can be determined than those allowed by serialization. Besides, that technique can specify and limit some imprecision that may appear in the system due to relax of the serialization.

Quality of Service (QoS) Management

In a real-time database, the QoS management can help to verify both the correctness and performance of a system, through functions and performance metrics. This is necessary, since the real-time transactions have temporal constraints. Therefore, we consider transactions correct only if they finish within their deadlines using valid data.

The functions defined are the functions of *specification, mapping, negotiation,* and *monitoring.* The function specification defines which QoS parameters are available and determines their syntax and semantics. The mapping function has to be provided to translate the QoS requirements expressed.

The role of a QoS negotiation mechanism is to determine an agreement for the required values of the QoS parameters between the system and the users or applications. A QoS negotiation protocol is executed, every time a new user or application joins an active session, to verify whether the system has enough resources to accept the new user or application request without compromising the current performance. This function usually employs several QoS mechanisms to fulfill its task, such as: *admission control* is used to determine whether a new user can be served, while *resource reservation* has to be called as soon as the user is admitted, in order to guarantee the requested service quality. The negotiation function has the role of the compability function, described above.

We define two performance metrics to guarantee the RTDB performance. These metrics are shown as follows:

1. **Number of transactions that miss the deadline in relation to the amount of transactions that finish with success (*Pt*):** This metric set up the rate of missed deadline of transactions that can be allowed during a time interval. The metric is defined as:

$$Pt = 100 * \left(\frac{MissedDeadline}{FinishTransactions} \right)$$

where *Pt* is the amount of transactions that miss the deadline (*MissedDeadline*) in relation to the amount of transactions that finish with success (*FinishTransactions*).

2.   **Upper imprecision of data (*Impr*):** Is the threshold of imprecision admitted in the data item for it to be considered logically valid. *Impr* is defined as:

$$Impr = CurrentValue * \left(\frac{Imp}{100} \right)$$

where *CurrentValue* is the value of data item stored in database and *Imp* is the index of amount of imprecision admitted.

HCPN-Based Modeling

Hierarchical Coloured Petri Nets

Hierarchical coloured Petri nets (HCPNs) are an extension of coloured Petri nets (CPNs) (Jensen, 1998) and are a suitable modeling language for verifying systems, as they can express concurrency, parallelism, nondeterminism, and different levels of abstraction.

In Figure 2, a Petri net is illustrated, where hierarchical levels are allowed. These hierarchical levels are possible due to the inclusion of two mechanisms: substitution transitions and fusion places. A substitution transition is a transition that will be replaced by a CPN page. The page to which the substitution transition belongs is called a superpage and the page represented by the transition is called the subpage. The association between subpages and superpages is performed by means of sockets and ports.

Figure 2. Coloured Petri net

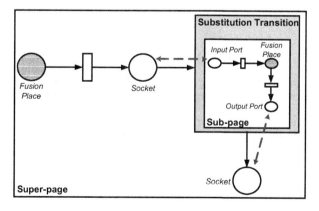

Sockets are all the input and output places of the transition in the superpage. Ports are the places in the subpage associated to the sockets. The ports can be input, output, or input-output. For simulation and state, space-generation sockets and ports are glued together and the resulting model is a flat CPN model. The fusion places are physically different but logically only one forming a fusion set. Therefore, all the places belonging to a fusion set have always the same marking. A marking of a place is the set of tokens in that place in a given moment. The marking of a net is the set of markings of all places in the net at a given moment (Jensen, 1998).

Indeed, these two additional mechanisms, substitution transitions and fusion places, are only graphical, helping in the organization and visualization of a CPN model. They favor the modeling of larger and more complex systems by giving the designer the ability to model by abstraction, specialization, or both.

Design/CPN Tools

Design/CPN (Jensen et al.,1999) is a tool package supporting the use of HCPN. The Design/CPN tool has four integrated parts:

1. The **CPN editor** supports construction, modification, and syntax check of CPN models.

2. The **CPN simulator** supports interactive and automatic simulation of CPN models.

3. The **occurrence graph tool** supports construction and analysis of occurrence graphs for CPN models (also known as state spaces or reachability graphs/trees).

4. The **perfomance tool** supports simulation=based performance analysis of CPN models.

The design/CPN package is one of the most used Petri net tools. Design/CPN supports CPN models with complex data types (colour sets) and complex data manipulations (arc expressions and guards), both specified in the functional programming language Standard ML(Jensen et al., 1999).

Real-Time Database Verification and Validation Method

The formal verification and validation method for real-time database systems consists of the application of the following steps, as illustrated in Figure 3, which are detailed in this section:

Figure 3. Real-time database verification and validation method

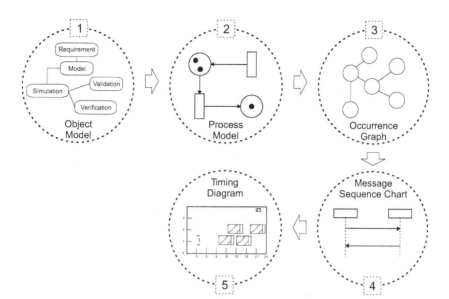

1. **Build an object model:** It is used to specify the requirements and identify the main components of the system. It is also used to model static properties of objects, such as attributes, operations, and logical and timing constraints. In any way, the object model defines the discourse universe to the process model.

2. **Build a process model:** It is used to model both functional and dynamic properties of objects. The functional properties define the object operations, while the dynamic property represents the temporal interactions of objects and its answers to the events. The process model is composed of the operations identified in the *object model*.

3. **Generate an occurrence graph:** It is a representation of the state space of the HCPN model.

4. **Generate a message sequence chart:** They are generated for each scenario, considering a possible execution sequence.

5. **Generate a timing diagram:** It is a diagram to show the timing constraints in time sample.

Build an Object Model

In the object model each *object* is a unique entity. Objects with the same data structure (attributes) and behavior (operations), in the context of the particular application environment are grouped into an object *class*. Classes can be grouped in a hierarchical structure. Classes may have attributes; the attributes are structural properties of classes that can have both logical and temporal constraints; the *relationships* are the links between the classes; the *operations* are functions or procedures applicable to the class attributes, and the *method* is the implementation of an *operation* (Rumbaugh, Blaha, Premerlani, Eddy, & Lorensen, 1991).

The object model consists of a set of: *class diagram*, *object diagram*, and *data dictionary*. The *class diagrams* have shown the general description of the system, while the *object diagrams* shown object instances. The data *dictionary* defines whole entities modeled (class, associations, attributes, operations).

The object model begins with the problem declaration analysis and has the following steps:

1.   **Identification of the objects:** The external actors and objects that interact with the system are identified as the problem context. Elements of the object model that emerge from the analysis of the real problem are directly mapped into logical objects. Each instance of an object is assumed to be unique. The objects in an object class have a unique identity that separates and identifies them from all other object instances.

2.   **Identification of relationships among objects:** A conceptual relationship among instances of classes. Associations have *cardinality* including one-to-one, one-to-many, and many-to-many. Most object-oriented texts do not address the *nature* of an association (i.e., mandatory or optional), except in the definition of the object behavior.

3.   **Addition of attributes to objects:** a data value that can be held by the objects in a class. Attributes may be assigned to different data types (e.g., integer).

4.   **Use of generalizations to observe similarities and differences:** the essential characteristics of an object or class, ignoring irrelevant features, providing crisply defined conceptual boundaries. This maintains a focus upon identifying common characteristics among what may initially appear to be different objects. Abstraction enhances reusability and inheritance.

5.   **Identification of operations:** the direct manipulation of an object, categorized as: *Constructor:* create an object and/or initialize. *Destructor:* free the state of an object and/or destroy the object. *Modifier:* alter the state of the object. *Selector:* access and read the state of an object. *Iterator:* access all parts of an object in a well-defined order.

6.   **Identification of concurrent operations:** In this step, the designer analyzes the system to discover which operations need to be executed concurrently and in that condition this occurs. In follow, it is defined the function that details the situations which the operations can be executed concurrently.

7.   **Identification of both logical and temporal constraints:** The designer must declare both logical and temporal constraints to objects. These constraints define the correct states of each object. Thus, the constraints are defined as predicates that

include the attributes value, time, and so on. For instance, the absolute validity interval defined to real-time data, in the Background section, expresses a temporal constraint to data objects.

Build a Process Model

The process model captures both functional and dynamic properties of objects. This model is used in the analysis, design, and implementation phases of the software-development life cycle. These phases can be tackled concurrently, using hierarchical coloured Petri nets. HCPNs are used to analyze the system behavior. In this model, the objects are described through HCPN modules (or pages) that are defined from object models. Then, for each object that contains operations identified in the model, a HCPN module is created, where the correspondent operations are modeled. We use the design/CPN tool package (Jensen et al., 1999) for HCPN modeling. For that, the following steps must be performed:

1. **Identification of the objects in HCPN:** In this step, all of the objects in the object model are identified, and for each object identified an HCPN module is constructed.

2. **Identification of functions for each object:** The operations that must be executed by each object are identified. What each object must execute is analyzed without considering its implementation.

3. **Definition of the interface for each object:** The interface of each object is declared, indicating the methods with its respective argument of input and output, the constraints defined to the classes, besides functions that describe the compatibility between methods.

4. **Definition of the internal structure of each object:** The methods detailed in the interface of objects are described, satisfying the requisites identified in the phase of identification of the objects.

Occurrence Graph (OG)

The occurrence graph tool is closely integrated with the design/CPN tool package (Jensen et al., 1999). The basic idea behind occurrence graphs is to make a directed graph with a node for each reachable marking and an arc for each occurring binding element. OGs are directed graphs that have a node for each reachable marking and an arc for each binding element. An arc binding the marking node that the binding element associated occurs at each marking node resultant of occurrence (Jensen, 1998).

The OG has a large number of built-in standard queries, such as *Reachable,* which determines whether there is an occurrence sequence between two specified markings, and *AllReachable,* which determines whether all the reachable markings are reachable from each other. These queries can be used to investigate all the standard properties of a HCPN. In addition to the standard queries, there are a number of powerful search facilities allowing formulating nonstandard queries. The standard queries require no programming at all. The nonstandard queries usually require that 2-5 programming lines of quite straightforward ML code.

Through an occurrence graph, it is possible to verify the properties inherent to the model. The occurrence graph tool allows obtaining reports with general properties about the model. These reports contain information about the graph and metaproperties that are utilities for comprehension of model behavior in HCPN. For instance: *boundness properties*, which supply the upper and lower limit of tokens that each net place can contain, besides marking limits for each place; *liveness properties,* which shown the markings and transitions that are dead (not precede none other marking) and which transitions are live (appear in some occurrence sequence started of the initial marking of the net). Occurrence graphs can be constructed with or without considering time or code segments.

When an occurrence graph has been constructed using the design/CPN it can be analyzed in different ways. The easiest approach is to use the *Save Report* command to generate a standard report providing information about all standard CPN properties:

- **Statistics:** Size of occurrence graph
- **Boundedness properties:** Integer and multiset bounds for place instances
- **Home properties:** Home markings
- **Liveness properties:** Dead markings, dead/live transition instances
- **Fairness properties:** Impartial/fair/just transition instances

To use the OG tool, the user simply enters the simulator and invokes the Enter Occ Graph command (in the file menu of design/CPN). This has a similar effect as Enter Simulator. It creates the occurrence graph code, that is, the ML code necessary to calculate, analyze, and draw occurrence graphs. Moreover, it creates a new menu, called Occ. This menu contains all the commands which are used to perform the calculation and drawing of occurrence graphs.

Generate a Message Sequence Chart (MSC)

MSC is a graphical and textual language for the description and specification of the interactions between system components. Message sequence charts may be used for requirement specification, simulation and validation, test-case specification and documentation of real-time systems.

As illustrated in Figure 4, the MSC comprises the QoS functions, the transactions with its operations, and the RTDB. In this method, the use of MSC is primordial, since it is possible to verify the properties of real-time database by representing the transactions properties and data properties, both with temporal constraints. Also, it is possible to validate the behavior of objects, its relationships, and the situations where concurrent access to the RTDB occurs through the object operations. To generate the MSC, we use the "*smc.sml*" library of the design/CPN tool package.

Figure 4. Description of message sequence chart

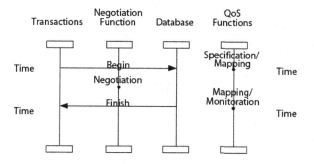

Generate a Timing Diagram (TD)

The design/CPN performance tool for facilitating simulation-based performance analysis of HCPN generates the timing diagram. In this context, performance analysis is based on the analysis of data extracted from a HCPN model during simulation. The Performance tool provides random number generators for a variety of probability distributions and high-level support for both data collection and for generating simulation output. The random number generators can be used to create more accurate models by modeling certain probability distribution aspects of a system, while the data collection facilities can extract relevant data from a CPN model.

Before data can be collected from a HCPN model, it is necessary to generate the *performance code*, that is, the ML code that is used to extract data from the HCPN model. The design/CPN performance tool can then be used to generate performance reports as a time diagram.

Case Study: Real-Time Database for Sensor Networks

Case Study Overview

A sensor network is considered as application domain to the case study, where the method proposed is applied. For this case study, a scenario where the environment monitored must have a steady temperature is described. The upper and lower bound for temperature is defined. Sensors are placed in the environment with the objective of acquiring and storing the temperature values.

Periodically, data stored in the sensors are sent to a real-time database server, through sensors transactions. The data obtained has temporal validity and the transactions have

Figure 5. Architecture of the sensor network case study

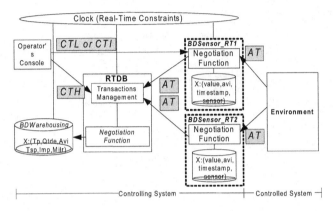

a deadline. The server is updated in order to allow historical queries. The architecture of the case study is illustrated in Figure 5.

Applying the Proposed Method

Building the Object Model

According to the steps defined to obtain the object model, we have:

1. **Identification of the objects:** The objects identified in the model are the sensors *BDSensor_RT1 and BDSensor_RT2,* and the real-time database server, called *BDWarehousing.*

2. **Identification of relationships among objects:** The sensors send data to the server through transactions. Each sensor updates the server, while the server is updated by various sensors.

3. **Addition of attributes to objects:** The data item X acquired by the sensor is composed of the following attributes: *Value* is the content of data item; *avi* is the absolute validate interval; *timestamp* is the late update time; and *sensor* identifies which sensor acquired the data. The attributes of the data item stored in the real-time database server has the fields: *Tp*, which is the data item processed; *Qtde,* which is the value that will be updated in the server; *Avi*, which is the absolute validate interval; *Tsp,* which is the late update time; *sensor*, which identifies the sensor that acquired the data; *Imp*, which is the accumulated imprecision; and *Milr*, which is the limit of *Imp.*

4. **Use of generalization to observe similarities and differences:** This step is unnecessary for this model, due to existence of only two objects.

Figure 6. Object model

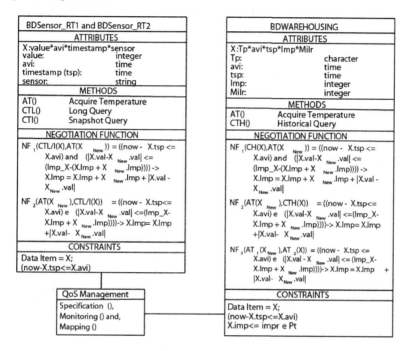

5. **Identification of operations:** The sensors aim at acquiring data of the external environment (method *AT*) and these data can be read by long and snapshot queries (method *CTL* and method *CTI*, respectively). Long queries are performed in a time interval, and snapshot queries are performed in an absolute time. The real-time database server has historical data obtained by sensors (method *AT*), and allows one to query this historical data (method *CTH*).

6. **Identification of concurrent operations:** The *BDSensor_RT1 and BDSensor_RT2* object has two negotiation functions that represent two different types of concurrency. The first situation is observed when the data item is being acquired and a query is invoked. The second situation of concurrency is possible when a query is running and an acquisition operation begins. In the *BDWarehousing*, three negotiation functions define the concurrence between the transactions. Besides the situations defined to the sensors, it is possible that two update operations try to access the same data item, where the sensor is updating the item and an applicative program is changing this data.

7. **Identification of both logical and temporal constraints:** In the sensor, the constraints defined to the data are: The type and the absolute validity interval of them.

The constraints defined to the server are: the type of data item and the performance metrics *Pt* and *Impr*, described in this chapter.

The QoS management is performed by the functions: specification, mapping, and monitoring, in addition to the negotiation function defined for the objects. Figure 6 illustrates the object model for the case study.

Building the Process Model

According to the steps defined to obtain the process model, we have:

1. **Identification of the objects in HCPN:** In this first step, the objects are identified from the object model for the the HCPN modules.

2. **Identification of functions for each object:** The sensor object implements the mechanisms of acquisition and stored data, besides reading the content stored. The real-time database server object implements the update and reading of the database.

3. **Definition of interface for each object:** In the HCPN module of sensor, the interface is defined by the methods: *AT*, *CTL,* and *CTI* and by attribute *X* that represents a record. The interface of the HCPN module to the server object indicates the methods *AT* and *CTH* and the attribute *DB* that represent a record with the fields defined to the data item stored in the server.

4. **Definition of internal structure for each object:** The internal structure is a hierarchical coloured Petri net to model the methods declared in the interface of the object.

The overview of the process model is illustrated in Figure 7. The HCPN modules are:

- **Declaration:** This represents the declarations, that is, the functions, types, and so on.
- **BDWarehousing:** It is the database server.
- **Negotiation1 and Negotiation:** This represents the negotiation functions.
- **Specification:** It is the module where the temporal parameters are specified.
- **Sensor1, Sensor2, and Sensor3:** This represents the modules for sensors.
- **UpdateS1, UpdateS2, and UpdateS3:** These are the sensors' transactions that update the server.
- **MonitoringS1, MonitoringS2, and MonitoringS3:** They are the monitoring functions related to each sensor transaction.
- **Update and MonitoringUp:** These modules are for the update transaction (only read) and the monitoring function defined for it.
- **Active and Performance:** These are control modules.

Figure 7. Process model

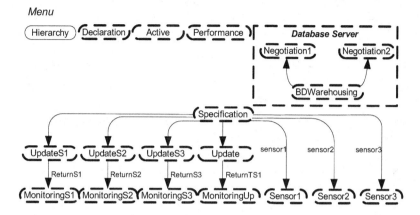

Generating the Occurrence Graph

For the real-time database modeled, the full standard report follows. According to the report, we have the full generation in 47 seconds, with 6,713 nodes and 22,867 arcs.

```
Statistics
--------------------------------------------------------------------
Occurrence Graph
  Nodes:  6,713
  Arcs:   22,867
  Secs:   47
  Status: Full
```

Some places are shown in the *boundedness properties*. The place ObjetoBD'ObjetoBDP represents the repository of data and it has the limit of 1 token. Two different combinations to the token in this place are represented in report.

```
Boundedness Properties
--------------------------------------------------------------------
Best Integers                   Bounds   Upper   Lower
  ObjetoBD'ObjetoBDP                1       1       1

Best Upper Multi-set Bounds
  ObjetoBD'ObjetoBDP              1  1`{nr = t1,vrr = 10,avir = 10,tsr = 33,impr = 1,milr =
8}++ 1`{nr = t1,vrr = 10,avir = 10,tsr = 39,impr = 1,milr = 8}
```

In *liveness properties*, we have 24 dead markings, that is, there are 24 different ways to the net stopping. In relation to dead transition, there is only one

FCObjetoBDLeAt'AvaliaFCLeAt. This transition is dead, since neither conflict occurred when a read transaction was executing and a write transaction was invocated.

```
Liveness Properties
--------------------------------------------------------------------------
Dead Markings:  24 [6713,6712,6711,6710,6703,...]
Dead Transitions Instances:  FCObjetoBDLeAt'AvaliaFCLeAt 1
```

Generating the Message Sequence Chart

In Figure 8, we have the MSC generated considering the scenario with two sensors acquiring the same data item.

- **Sensor1:** writes periodically in the local database, the release time is 1 time unit (t.u.) and the period is 3 t.u.
- **Sensor2:** writes periodically in the local database, the release time is 9 t.u., and the period is 9 t.u.

Moreover, there are two write transactions and one read transaction.

Figure 8. Message sequence chart

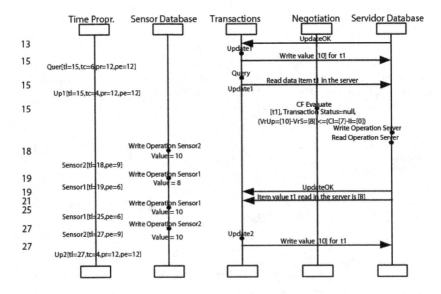

- **Update 1:** Periodically updates the database server object with respect to the data in *Sensor1*. The release time is 3 t.u., the computational time is 2 t.u., the deadline is 12 t.u., and the period is 12 t.u.

- **Update 2:** Periodically updates the database server object for sensor2. The release time is 9 t.u., the computational time is 4 t.u., the deadline is 18 t.u., and the period is 18 t.u.

- **Query:** Periodically queries the real-time database-server application. The release time is 3 t.u., the computational time is 6 t.u., the deadline is 12 t.u., and the period is 12 t.u.

The release time is the moment when all the necessary resources to the execution of the transaction and sensors are available. Starting from this moment the transaction will be ready to be executed. The computation time is the processing time necessary to execute it. The deadline defines the maximum transaction execution period. Finally, the period defines the periodicity of the transaction and sensor.

In the MSC, it is also possible to verify the QoS functions, where the negotiation between transactions conflicting and the time properties are visible during whole lifetime of a system.

Generating the Timing Diagram

In Figure 9, the timing diagram for the execution of transactions and sensors is presented. In this figure, it is possible to see a representation of the timing model execution for both transactions and sensors, where the execution is represented by rectangles.

In the vertical axis, the transactions and the sensors are represented. In the horizontal axis the release time and the periods for both, transactions and sensors, and computational times and deadline for transactions are represented. For each transaction, we consider three states: start; processing, and committing. The start of the execution of

Figure 9. Timing diagram

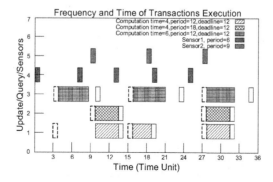

a transaction is illustrated by a dotted line rectangle. The processing is represented by a filled rectangle, and the committing by a continuous line rectangle. For the sensor, we only show the state processing.

In the vertical axis, the *Update 1* transaction is represented in 1. The *Update 2* transaction is represented in 2. The *Query* transaction is represented in 3. The *sensor1* is represented in 4, and the *sensor2* in 5.

Future Trends

As for future trends, we believe that our method should be applied to other application domains. Also, the method can be expanded in order to add more functionality and graphs. Depending on the application domain, the method could be customized and its phases adapted according to the domain features.

Moreover, automatic code generation could be considered. It would be useful to ensure that the programming code for the software is according to the verified and validated model. In this context, we are currently developing an automatic code generator from HCPN model to the Java programming language.

Conclusion

In this chapter we presented a method for real-time database verification and validation. The main objective of this method is to make possible the identification of whole components of a system for modeling, analyzing, verifying, and validating them.

The method is based on a model developed using hierarchical coloured Petri nets. The computational tool used to generate the model, verifying the properties and generating graphs for validation by users was the design/CPN tool package.

Using the proposed method, a real system can be studied without the danger, expense, or inconvenience of the manipulation of its elements. It is performed through the analysis of the system's conceptual model and the application of guidelines which drive the developer in the validation and verification activity.

When dealing with complex systems, the process of analysis, verification, and validation needs to be automated. However, the utilization of mathematical models is primordial, which allows automatic verification and validation. It makes it possible to identify various potential deficiencies in the conceptual model, such as contradictions, ambiguity, redundancy, so forth.

References

DiPippo, L. C. (1995). *Semantic real-time object-based concurrency control*. PhD thesis, Department of Computer Science and Statistics, University of Island, Kingston, RI.

Douglass, B. P. (2004). *Real time UML: Advances in the UML for real-time systems* (3rd ed.). Boston: Addison-Wesley.

Herrmann, J. (2001). *Guideline for validation & verification real-time embedded software systems*. Software Development Process for Real-Time Embedded Software Systems (DESS), D 1.6.2, V 01.

Jensen, K. (1998). An introduction to the practical use of coloured Petri nets. In W. Reisig & G. Rozenberg (Eds.), *Lectures on Petri nets II: Applications, Lecture Notes in Computer Science* (vol. 1, pp. 237-292). Berlin, Heidelberg, Germany: Springer-Verlag.

Jensen, K. (1999). *Design/CPN 4.0*. Meta Software Corporation and Department of Computer Science, University of Aarhus, Denmark. Retrieved May 19, 2006, from http://www.daimi.aau.dk/designCPN/

Kang, K. D. (2001). *qRTDB: QoS-sensitive real-time database*. PhD thesis, Department of Computer Science, University of Virginia, Charlottesville.

Ribeiro-Neto, P. F., Perkusich, M. L. B., & Perkusich, A. (2003). Real-time database modeling considering quality of service. In *Proceedings of the 5th International Conference on Enterprise Information Systems,* Angers, France (vol. 3, pp. 403-410).

Ribeiro-Neto, P. F., Perkusich, M. L. B., & Perkusich, A. (2004). Scheduling real-time transactions for sensor networks applications. In *Proceedings of the 10th International Conference on Real-Time Computing Systems and Applications (RTCSA),* Gothenburg, Sweden (pp. 181-200). Berlin, Heidelberg, Germany: Springer-Verlag.

Rumbaugh, J., Blaha, M., Premerlani, W., Eddy, F., & Lorensen, W. (1991). *Object-oriented modeling and design*. Upper Saddle River, NJ: Prentice-Hall.

Selic, B., & Rumbaugh, J. (1998). Using UML for modeling complex real-time systems. In *LCTES '98: Proceedings of the ACM SIGPLAN Workshop on Languages, Compilers, and Tools for Embedded Systems* (pp. 250-260). Berlin, Heidelberg, Germany: Springer-Verlag.

Chapter VI

Requirements for the Testable Specifications and Test Case Derivation in Conformance Testing

Tanja Toroi, University of Kuopio, Finland

Anne Eerola, University of Kuopio, Finland

Abstract

Interoperability of software systems is a critical, everincreasing requirement in software industry. Conformance testing is needed to assure conformance of software and interfaces to standards and other specifications. In this chapter we shortly refer to what has been done in conformance testing around the world and in Finland. Also, testability requirements for the specifications utilized in conformance testing are proposed and test-case derivation from different kinds of specifications is examined. Furthermore, we present a conformance-testing environment for the healthcare domain, developed in an OpenTE project, consisting of different service-specific and shared testing services. In our testing environment testing is performed against open interfaces, and test cases can, for example, be in XML (extensible markup language) or CDA R2 (clinical document architecture, Release 2) form.

Introduction

In many organizations, the number of information systems is large and hence so are integration needs between these systems. At the moment, new systems are integrated into existing ones by tailoring them separately often by point-to-point integration. This is extremely expensive and inefficient in the long run. Application integration and process integration between organisations have increased the need to agree about common standards and open interfaces. By application integration we mean integration between software systems, whereas by process integration we mean the integration of human activities inside or between organisations. Normal software testing with different variations is important to assure functionality and quality of software systems, and their interoperability. If systems have open, standard-based interfaces their interoperability improves, introduction and integration become easier and less local adaptation work is needed. Today standardisation and conformance testing of open interfaces have been emphasized nationwide and internationally. Normally, the target architecture is defined first and interface definitions are then derived based on it. However, the development is still in its infancy. Interface definitions are not enough, conformance testing is also needed to examine if the systems really conform to standards or other specifications. Conformance testing can be utilised by component developers, component integrators and software clients. Component developers can show conformity to the standards of clients. Component integrator checks conformance to standards and integrates components without a great amount of local tailoring. Clients benefit from implementations that conform to standards by getting better interoperability and quality of software. In addition, clients may only change some components when renewing the system, and a big-bang situation, in which the whole application must be renewed at the same time, can be avoided.

Standardisation and conformance testing have been studied quite a lot in the telecommunication domain (ITU-T Recommendation X.290, 1996) but the practice is not well-established in other domains. Some business processes are quite deterministic (e.g., order-delivery and referral-report), while others are nondeterministic (e.g., marketing and home care) and the execution order of the processes can not be predicted as easily as the order of manufacturing processes. In general, a great number of interfaces exist to other systems. For example, in Kuopio University Hospital in Finland there are more than 180 information systems, most of them with nonconsistent or nonexisting interfaces. Those information systems have to communicate inside and between different organisations. Local tailoring is needed, which, in turn, causes interoperability problems. Systems are handling patient data. This also partly increases the difficulty to standardise data. In addition, systems are safety critical. Thus, interfaces and systems are harder to standardise and conformance testing is more difficult to perform than in many other domains. Standards are needed to promote interoperability. However, it should be remembered that standards can also be contradictory, such as ISO 15745 and ISO 16100 standards for interoperability (Kosanke, 2005).

In the OpenTE project, our research problem is how to develop a reliable conformance-testing environment for healthcare applications. The environment should be applicable in the software industry and healthcare organisations. We use constructive and experimental research methods. At the moment, our prototype-testing environment consists of different service-specific and shared testing services (see Figure 2). We have 13 participants including research organisations, software companies, and healthcare districts in the OpenTE project. The OpenTE project continues the work done in the PlugIT project (from Oct 2001 to Aug 2004, see http://www.plugit.fi/english/), in which open interface specifications, such as common services, and context management, for healthcare application were developed. We noticed that conformance testing of open interfaces needs to be examined and elaborated upon. Thus, we developed a conformance-testing model to test applications' conformity to specifications. The model consists of four phases: an initial phase, testing performed by the developer, testing performed by the testing lab, and certificate issuing. Even though we have studied health information systems and their integration, similar integration needs can be found, and our model is applicable to other domains and integration models. Our conformance-testing model is discussed more in Toroi, Mykkänen, and Eerola (2005).

The objective of this chapter is to propose new requirements for the interface specifications from the testability point of view. The chapter strives to describe different kinds of specifications, evaluate how useable they are in the healthcare domain, and analyse how test cases can be derived from different specifications in conformance testing. The chapter presents a conformance-testing environment developed in the OpenTE project. Furthermore, the chapter clarifies the conformance-testing position among other testing phases, compares interoperability testing to conformance testing, and considers responsibility questions of conformance testing.

The rest of this chapter is organized as follows. First, we give background to conformance testing in general and in healthcare domain. Second, we consider common requirements for the specifications and conformance testing, propose new requirements for the interface specifications from the testability point of view, and analyse test-case derivation from different specifications. Third, the OpenTE approach to conformance testing in the healthcare domain is discussed. We present a conformance-testing environment developed in our project, and analyse how test cases can be derived from different specifications in conformance testing. Finally, we discuss future trends and conclude the chapter.

Background

Conformance Testing in General

Software testing is an important tool for improving software quality and reliability. Software testing covers many kinds of testing methods, such as module, integration, acceptance, performance, and conformance testing. Each of the methods improves testing, and strengthens each other's. Attention should be given to the quality of testing, such as coverage, as well. Nowadays, open interface specifications and information-exchange standards have become general, which in turn enables the improvement of testing.

Conformance is defined by ISO/IEC as the fulfilment of a product, process, or service of specified requirements (ISO/IEC Guide 2, 1996). A *conformance clause* is defined as a section of the specification that states all the requirements or criteria that must be satisfied to claim conformance. The term *interoperability* in software system point of view means that a system is capable of executing services for other systems and utilizing services from other systems (Herzum & Sims, 2000). Two common forms of testing for interoperability are called interoperability testing and conformance testing. *Interoperability testing* is defined as the assessment of a product to determine if it behaves as expected while interoperating with another product (Kindrick, Sauter, & Matthews, 1996). However, interoperability testing is not enough. It only tests that a set of systems are interoperating. It does not guarantee that other systems interoperate with these systems. Conformance testing is needed to achieve a higher level of confidence that these systems will successfully interoperate with other systems as well. *Conformance testing* is a way to verify implementations of the specification to determine whether or not deviations from the specifications exist (Rosenthal & Skall, 2002). In conformance testing, software implementations are black boxes; only the interfaces and their relationship to the specifications are examined. In other words, when an interface receives a request, it is tested if the interface can handle the request and respond to it correctly. Conformance testing is necessary, but not sufficient, for interoperability, because conformance clauses (or specifications) typically only cover some aspects of interoperability. For example, infrastructure and techniques are implementation-specific features not specified in the specification, thus influencing interoperability. Moseley, Randall, and Wiles (2004) assert that conformance testing is necessary in accomplishing effective and rigorous interoperability testing. Thus, both interoperability and conformance testing are needed.

There are many roles and activities involved in the conformance-testing process. Departments of government and legislation pass laws, decisions, recommendations, and reasons for specifications and conformance testing. It is good that oversight is the government's responsibility. However, government involvement in testing may also have dangerous features if government dictates what is being tested and how widely (Rada, 1996). Carnahan, Rosenthal, and Skall (1998) have introduced that interaction between roles, and activities can be illustrated by a diamond-shaped model, where each role (seller, certificate issuer, testing lab, and control board) is in the corner of the diamond. We have adapted the idea and compare the interaction to a triangle where the certificate issuer and testing lab are not in separate roles (Toroi et al., 2005). A buyer (client) requires from a seller (developer) that a product conforms to the specification. The developer develops an application with certain interface implementations and applies for the brand to the application. The testing lab/certificate issuer performs interface testing and issues the brand if the application successfully completes the conformance testing. The control board is answering queries and disputes related to the testing process. The developer is responsible for the product even if it had got the brand and passed the conformance testing.

Regardless of all the above advantages it should be noticed that conformance testing can not be used as verification. Conformance testing only increases the probability that applications are implemented according to the interface specification. The developer and the integrator must perform normal software inspections and testing phases before conformance testing. The conformance-testing phase depends on the level of the specification against which testing is performed. If the specification is at a detailed level, conformance testing is performed quite early in the implementation process. If the specification covers the whole system conformance testing is performed after the whole development phase.

Conformance Testing in Healthcare

Software companies and healthcare organizations strive to improve health information systems. Today, one of the most important goals is a seamless and flexible service chain for patients. This requires that doctors and nurses exchange information and use applications in an efficient, safe, and secure way. Personnel in a hospital do not work all the time with computers. Most of the communication is asynchronous and there is also a lot of manual work. In this situation users need an agreed mode of action and some software facilitating communication.

Integrating the healthcare enterprise (IHE) promotes the use of standards by developing integration profiles (HIMSS & RSNA, 2002). With the help of integration profiles, standards can be implemented to the implementations at a more accurate level.

Australian Healthcare Messaging Laboratory (AHML) is a part of the Collaborative Centre for eHealth (CCeH) at the University of Ballarat. AHML provides message testing, compliance and certification services for developers and vendors, system integrators and users within the healthcare industry. Clients can send electronic healthcare messages via the Internet to the AHML Message Testing Engine. Messages are tested against healthcare messaging standards. Test cases are built using messaging standards and client-specific requirements, if any. Message-based integration may lead to data-oriented integration, where data has been copied into several places. Thus we have investigated other possibilities — for example, API, service, and component based integration. Because people's work, in co-operation and communication, is often asynchronous, process integration and application integration are needed at the same time.

The Software Diagnostics and Conformance Testing Division (SDCT), part of NIST's (National Institute of Standards and Technology) Information Technology Laboratory is working with industry by providing guidance on conformance topics, helping to develop testable specifications, and developing conformance tests, methods and tools that improve software quality and conformance to standards. SDCT has especially focused on developing XML conformance test suites and has also written guidance on how to write better specifications. NIST, the World Wide Web Consortium (W3C) and the Organization for the Advancement of Structured Information Standards (OASIS) have given guidance on how specifications should be written. OASIS has published a document describing how to specify software conformance to a specification, and identifying conformance requirements to be included in specifications (Rosenthal & Skall, 2002). W3C has put effort on quality assurance and specification guidelines (W3C, 2005).

Health Level 7 (HL7) Conformance SIG (Special Interest Group) attempts to improve interoperability and certification processes. HL7 provides a mechanism to specify conformance for HL7 Version 2.X and HL7 Version 3 messages and provide a framework for facilitating interoperability using the HL7 standard. The problem with HL7 version 2.X standards is that they are difficult to use in practice, and users are unable to ascertain compliance with standards against their specific needs (TNT Global Systems, 2002). As a solution, HL7 has developed message profiles, which add specificity to existing messages and identify scenarios by providing a template for documenting particular uses of HL7 messages. In our research, the minimum-level specification was specified for CCOW, HL7 standard (Tuomainen, Mykkänen, Rannanheimo, Komulainen, & Korpela, 2004). CCOW was adapted to the minimum-level specification, and only the most essential parts of it have been included.

In our testing environment, testing is performed against open interfaces, and test cases can be, for example, in XML or CDA R2 forms. Furthermore, new requirements for specifications from the testability point of view have been proposed.

Requirements for the Testable Specifications

In this section, common requirements for the specifications are considered, new requirements for the interface specifications from the testability point of view are proposed, and test-case derivations from different specifications are analysed.

General Requirements for the Specifications

A specification can be in different states: draft, accepted, or publicly available specifications. At first, specifications are *drafts*. However, draft specifications are not testable. When a management group accepts a draft specification, it becomes an *accepted version* of the specification. If an accepted specification is published, it becomes a *publicly available* specification. If a specification is accepted or public, it is sufficiently testable and hopefully stable. Software compared to the specifications has three states, available, implemented, or conformable to specification. *Available* state means that the software exists but it does not necessarily have any implemented interfaces according to the specifications. An *implemented* state means that the specified interfaces have been implemented to software. When the developer has implemented interface implementations to the software, testing has to be performed to verify conformance to the specification. A testing lab performs conformance testing. If the software passes the tests, it moves to a *conformable-to-specification* state and the brand can be issued to the software. Specifications in the healthcare context are further discussed in the section "General Requirements in Healthcare Domain".

Testability of the Specifications

Binder (1994) has presented testability factors in object-oriented systems. Key testability factors are representation, implementation, built-in test, test suite, test tools, and test process. When considering testability of the interface specifications, representation, test suite, and test process can be used. Next, we adapt Binder's view and describe those in more detail.

Representation

The form of the specifications can range from formal specifications to natural-language statements. The more formal the specification is, the more testable it is. Governmental laws, decisions, and recommendations — as well as specifications — are mostly written in natural language. Actors in different organisations need to use specifications in invitation for tenders when ordering applications and they have to understand specifications. Natural language is used because it is easier to form and understand than formal languages. The specification has to be current, so that conformance testing is performed against the right version, and test cases test the right features. Models and diagrams help to understand the specification better, so they improve testability. Use case and scenario diagrams are especially useful. Permitted combinations of the parameters have to be restricted because, for example, if it is allowed to search anything with any key, the number of combinations explodes. However, it is the fact that everything cannot be tested anyway. Specification must be explicit, unambiguous, and consistent. Furthermore, it must contain only measurable, feasible, realistic, and necessary requirements.

Test Suite

It is advantageous to deliver a test suite with the specification. For example, NIST is delivering a test suite for ebXML messaging. This assists testing because certain issues can be discovered beforehand and more testing time can be devoted to one's own, situation-specific test cases. It is easier to follow specifications if test cases are ready-made. However, the official conformance test suite can also have errors (Garstecki, 2003).

Test Process

Reviews and inspections of the specification and prototyping are normal quality-assurance practices. Reference implementations can be made to help developing specifications and test cases (Mykkänen et al., 2004). In an ideal situation specifications, test cases, and reference implementations are developed simultaneously. This guarantees that when the final version of the specification is ready, it is more mature, and there is no need to change it immediately afterward. Further, we propose that conformance testing should allow those deviations from specifications which are not significant and which do not harm the purpose and semantics — for example, resilience of tagged data in XML (solved with dispatchers).

New Proposed Requirements for the Specifications

The specifications have to be defined so that testability and conformance are taken into consideration early in the specification lifecycle. In that case requirements in the specification will be testable and definite. Otherwise, it could happen that implementations are even impossible to test against specifications. W3C and OASIS have given guidance on how specifications should be written (Rosenthal & Skall, 2002; W3C, 2005). According to the guidelines, a specification must contain a conformance clause and use key words to specify conformance requirements. In the conformance clause all the requirements or criteria that must be satisfied to claim conformance are defined (ISO/IEC Guide 2, 1996). The conformance clause shall address the following issues: what needs to be conformed, modularity, profile and levels, extensions, discretionary items, deprecated features, languages, and characters coding. We have adapted and extended the OASIS and W3C guidelines for the conformance specifications. We propose the following additional aspects that the specification must address:

- **Architecture:** A target architecture description is utilized to show principle decisions and visions in the domain. The architecture description will help users of the conformance clause to understand why given specifications are needed. Thus, it assists in conforming. Specifications should be modular. If needed, they are divided into subspecifications. Further, the specification must be possible to be composed to other specifications not known beforehand. Relationships and dependencies between specifications should be clearly defined and minimized (cohesion, coupling).

- **Specification levels:** Domain-related specifications should be distinguished from technical specifications. Thus, it is good to divide the specification into levels, for example, functional-, conceptual-, and technical-level specifications, where each of the levels contains only certain issues. Different actors can view different documents and do not have to look for features they are interested in among all the other features. Functional level specifications include all the user actions with execution order and exceptions. The specification has to define execution order of the deterministic actions with scenario diagrams. Conceptual-level specification contains all the used concepts and relationships to the other specifications. Software clients can use functional and conceptual level specifications when adding specifications to the call for tenders, and requiring standard-based software. Technical-level specification contains all the technical details needed to implement specifications, such as interfaces, methods, parameters, infrastructure descriptions, and usage examples. Furthermore, the specification has to specify pre- and post-conditions for all the methods. Pre- and post-conditions improve testability.

- **Interoperability:** Everything concerning software interoperability has to be mentioned in the specification. The specification has to define how implementations have to handle distribution, data security, encryption, and transactions. Also, the quality requirements are indicated in the specification if they are essential for the situation. Useful quality requirements are, for example, continuous operating time (7 days a week/24 hours a day), execution time, robustness, usability, memory requirements, and response time. Requirements depending on the situation are included in the specification only if needed.

- **Extensions in the future:** In order to be prepared for the future, a specification has to list all the possible extensions and new features that the implementations have. For example, the specification should be simple enough at first and features discovered advantageous in practice are added to it later on. However, the specification has to be reasonable, so that implementations conforming to it have an acceptable cost level. Extensions can harm the interoperability and cause troubles in the future. When the extended implementation is delivered to several clients and the specification later undergoes changes that influence the extended part conflictingly, the implementation may be costly or even impossible to update consistently with the specification. Further, if deprecated features are documented they can stay better in mind, and can be mixed with supported features. Thus, one must consider carefully whether a description of deprecation is more trouble than it is worth.

- **Re-evaluation:** In the specification, we must describe how different versions of implementations, specifications, and test suites affect conformance, that is, in what situations conformance remains and when conformance has to be re-evaluated. Normally, if a new version of the specification is released, the old conformance holds, but retesting is needed against the new version of the specification. If a new version of the implementation is released conformance always has to be retested for the new version of the implementation. Implementations tested with different test-suite versions can conform to the specification but are not necessarily interoperable, for example, because of the extended features.

- **Key words:** Key words are used to specify requirements in the specification. Requirements can be mandatory, conditional, optional, or suggested (Rosenthal & Skall, 2002). We have noticed in workshops with software and healthcare organisations that conditional, that is, the key word SHOULD, must be avoided because it is confusing and causes interoperability problems. It is recommended that requirements are either obligatory (conformance testing is needed) or completely optional (conformance testing is not needed). Requirements have to be prioritized and conflicts solved in the requirement-specification phase, not left to the implementers. However, when eliciting requirements, the key word SHOULD is useful in getting comments and ideas from the developers to those who define specifications.

Test-Case Derivation from the Specifications

The ease of test case derivation from the specifications influences testability of the specifications. Specifications can be grouped from the most formal to the least formal specifications: formal, semiformal, and natural-language specifications. In the following, specifications and test-case generation from them are presented in more detail.

- **Formal languages:** If the specification is given in formal language, for example, Z-language (Barden, Stepney, & Cooper, 1994), the specification is exact, and test cases can be derived automatically from it. For the use of formal languages there are tools, for example, PROBE, and ClawZ. However, formal languages are quite complex to formulate, even for experts. In order to utilise specifications software clients have to understand them properly but formal languages are difficult to interpret. They are suitable for situations where exact mathematics is needed and sufficient expertise is available, such as in radiotherapy.

  Logical expressions can be also thought of as formal languages. If the specification is already in axiomatic form, test cases are derived from logical expressions. If the specification has been written in natural language it is translated into logical expressions at first, and then test cases are derived from them (Rosenthal, Skall, Brady, Kass, & Montanez-Rivere, 1997). The method can be used when the specification is already in axiomatic form, for example, when deciding detrimental side effects of medication. However, if the specification has to be translated into logical expressions, at first, we think that translation is quite troublesome, and too many interpretations and ambiguity remain. In addition, conformance to the specification cannot be proved. It can only be proved that the implementation is not conformable to the specification.

  The test suite can also be defined in formal language. One method is to describe test suite in formal Tree and tabular combined notation (TTCN), which is based on ISO 9646-3 (X.292) standard. Test cases are derived automatically from the abstract test suite, for example, with the help of Open TTCN, Telelogic TAU TTCN Suite, or Clarinet-TTCN ATM ETS tools. TTCN language is in extensive use in telecommunication applications but it may not be equally applicable to other domains. To be used efficiently, for example, in healthcare domain the notation should be modified. However, the editing is quite inconvenient. Furthermore, the order of the operations is not always as predetermined as in the telecommunication domain.

- **Semiformal languages:** Useful semiformal languages are, for example, UML state diagrams, use cases, and scenario diagrams. They are well-known methods, and quite easy to use and understand. If the specification is defined with UML state-diagram, test cases can be derived from it (Gnesi, Latella, & Massink, 2004). Gnesi, Latella, and Massink have developed a theoretical background to generate test cases automatically in a conformance testing setting. However, proper test- and regression-test-selection techniques are still needed to use this method in practice. This method is suited for situations in which actions have clear execution order, and are deterministic, that is, a certain input causes transition to a certain state. However, it is not very useful in nondeterministic situations, in which the order of the activities is not known beforehand, such as communication in organisational networks and expert organisations.

El-Fakih, Yevtushenko, and Bochmann (2004) have presented the conformance specification in the form of a finite state machine (FSM). Implementation is also presented in the form of FSM. Test cases are derived from it. By comparing FSMs it can be observed if the implementation is conformable to the specification. El-Fakih et al. assume that the parts of the implementation that correspond to the unmodified parts of the specification have not been changed. However, in regression testing the parts in which the change might have been influenced also have to be retested. There is a chance that the kind of FSM cannot be formed from the implementation, which defines exactly the implementation and not what should have been done. This method is useful in the situations where interoperability between components or systems is tested, as long as interoperability is defined with FSM. However, usually, interaction between information systems is not fixed in the specifications. If COTS components are tested, the source code is not available, so the method cannot be used.

If the specification is in the form of use cases, test cases are derived from them. However, there exists a gap between an implementation and a specification. Test cases cannot be derived automatically from use cases; however, there is a big interest to that direction. For example, Binder (1999) has presented extended use cases. The problem with extended use cases is that use cases are not used to specify performance or fault tolerance. Kirner et al. (1999) have proposed that the use cases can be extended into behaviour cases, which are implementation-specific descriptions of a specific use case. Then, the behaviour cases can be extended into test cases. Alexander (2003) has proposed misuse cases as a tool for finding security requirements and decreasing risks.

The semiformal specification can also be XML-based. XML-format helps to understand specification in technical level and clarifies it. Bhatti, Bertino, Ghafoor, and Joshi (2004) have proposed XML-based specification language for security models. It incorporates content- and context-based dynamic-security requirements for documents in XML-based Web services.

- **Natural language:** If the specification has been generated in natural language, test cases can be derived by hand and, for example, by using reference implementations. Natural-language specification can be used when official certified implementations are not the main goal. They are more suitable for informal conformance reviews. More formal specifications are needed to avoid inconsistencies and inaccuracies. If semiformal specifications are not available in testing, testers can form needed diagrams and confirm their validity from the developer and client organisations.

OpenTE Approach
to Testing Environment

In this section, general requirements for the specifications in the healthcare domain are presented. After that, OpenTE approach to testing environment is proposed. Finally, test-case derivation methods in a healthcare context are analysed.

General Requirements in the Healthcare Domain

In healthcare, governmental laws and recommendations supervise the defining of specifications and standards concerning, for example, secure communication, authentication and authorization, and permission to exchange personal data. Further, software organisations develop their software according to the client's requirements and new ideas of software engineers. Thus, specifications have different levels and they can be

Figure 1. Features influencing the specification and conformance testing (Adapted from Toroi et al., 2005)

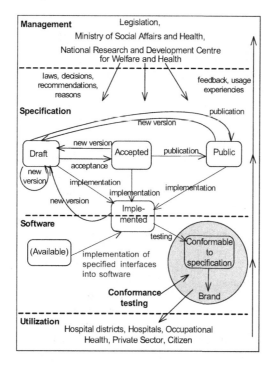

more or less official. The more official the specification is the more critical it is and the more testing that is needed.

In Finland, laws, decisions, recommendations, and reasons for specifications and conformance testing are given by legislation, the Ministry of Social Affairs and Health, and the National Research and Development Centre for Welfare and Health (see Figure 1). Specifications have three different states: drafts, accepted, or publicly available specifications. At first, specifications are drafts. When management group accepts a draft specification, it becomes an accepted version of the specification. If an accepted specification is published, it becomes a publicly available specification. Software has three states, available, implemented or conformable to specification. Available state means that there exists the software but it does not necessarily have any implemented interfaces according to the specifications. Implemented state means that the specified interfaces have been implemented to software. When the developer has implemented interface implementations to the software, testing has to be performed to verify conformance to the specification. A testing lab performs conformance testing and if the software passes the tests the software becomes conformable to specification state and the brand can be issued to the software.

Hospital districts, hospitals, occupational health, private sector, and citizens utilize software conformable to specifications. They also give feedback and usage experiences to software organisations, specifications constructors (e.g., special interest groups and HL7), and management.

Conformance-Testing Environment

In the OpenTE project we are developing a conformance-testing environment for several web-based testing services, for example, CDA R2, lightweight context management, and common service interfaces. We have studied conformance-testing actions in present state in healthcare software companies, and got good ideas for the development of the conformance-testing environment. We have made requirement specification and technical specification of the environment, and functional specifications are now being constructed. Healthcare and software organisations have commented on our specifications, and we have gotten positive feedback. Furthermore, we have made a prototype of the testing environment, and it has been presented in workshops.

The idea of the common testing environment is quite new and progressive, thus comments and ideas have been quite conservative, and we have had difficulties in finding mutual understanding in distribution of work and responsibility questions. The responsibility questions and detailed development of the testing environment will become clear in near future.

Testing environment consists of different service-specific and shared testing services (see Figure 2). At the moment, service-specific testing services cover regional information systems, common services, and lightweight context management. Services can be extended in the future. Shared testing service handles, for example, user authentication, code sets, reports, invoicing, and test log. In the environment, test cases can be derived from different kinds of specifications. Furthermore, test cases can be in different formats,

Figure 2. OpenTE testing environment for conformance testing

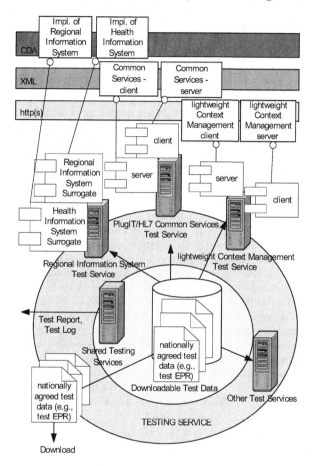

for example, CDA R2, XML, and http. Testing service acts as a needed counterpart in conformance testing. For example, if an implementation of a regional information system attends the testing service, the testing service acts as a surrogate of the health-information system. If a lightweight context-management client attends the service, the testing service acts as a lightweight context-management server. Furthermore, test data can be downloaded through the service — for example, test electronic patient records.

During the project the focus has been changed from CDA R1 to CDA R2, and requirements for test-case derivation have been increased. Thus, we examined different specifications and considered how test cases can be derived from them. Next we give a summary of the test case derivation methods in a healthcare context.

Summary of the Test-Case Derivation Methods in Healthcare Context

Test cases can be derived from formal, semiformal, and natural-language specifications in many different ways. In this section, we study test-case derivation from different kinds of specifications in a healthcare context. The most formal methods are discussed first.

Test cases can be derived automatically from formal languages. However, formal languages are considered to be too complex to use in practice, and they are not very suitable for the healthcare domain. In order to exploit specifications, healthcare clients have to understand them properly but formal languages are difficult to interpret. We think that semiformal languages are more suitable for the healthcare domain, because their notation is more understandable, and easier to use and interpret than formal languages. One disadvantage of semiformal languages is that test cases cannot be derived automatically from the specifications.

We studied how test cases can be derived from an activity diagram, use-case diagram, and state diagram (Jäntti & Toroi, 2004). Activity diagrams show different action flows that a tester must go through in testing. Action flows help testers to develop extensive test cases, although the abstraction level may be too high for testing purposes. UML use cases provide a way to divide the system under test into smaller functional units, and test cases can be organized by use cases. Use-case scenarios include descriptions of exceptional and alternative flows that are often sources of defects. We have noticed that the state diagram is an applicable tool for describing domain-specific concepts (e.g., patient, referral) with relevant states and state transformations, which need to be defined in specifications. Test cases are easy to identify from the UML state diagram and the state transition table. We have also defined test cases based on inputs of different granularities, that is, action flow of users, operation flow of interfaces, and method flow inside software (Toroi, Jäntti, Mykkänen, & Eerola, 2004). Our method is applicable if user actions are described with action diagrams and software is described with use-case and scenario diagrams.

XML-based specifications can be viewed as semiformal specifications. We defined XML-based specifications for common services in the PlugIT project (Mykkänen et al., 2004). Test cases were defined from the specification by hand using reference implementations. Yet, we think that the test cases could have been derived semi-automatically, too. In addition, we have used XML in the OpenTE project when test data was transformed from a legacy system to CDA R2 format, which is needed, for example, to test the electronic patient record. The transformation was quite troublesome.

Governmental laws, recommendations, and specifications created in special interest groups have been written in natural language. In the PlugIT project, we used HL7 Finland specifications, which are national recommendations, and reference implementations in test case generation. Natural language specifications were easy to read and understand but they contained inconsistencies and inaccuracies, further, test case generation by hand was a big disadvantage. It would have been nice to get test cases automatically from the specifications but it was not possible. Furthermore, diversity and adequacy of test cases were not very good. Efficient conformance testing requires that specifications be transformed in semiformal language. The problem here is that it is difficult to find consensus between different organisations. The following questions arise: Who is responsible for transformation? Who is skilful and competent enough to accomplish transformation? Who shall pay the costs? Which organization gets rights to work as conformance tester authorized to issue brands? However, collaboration is necessary to decrease costs and increase quality, efficiency, interoperability, and reliability of software.

Future Trends

We have to study further test-case derivation from the specifications and from the test data. The more automatically derivation is performed, the better. Furthermore, test-case selection in the regression-testing phase is an interesting question. We have to study which test cases have to be retested if implementation has undergone changes, so that not all the test cases have to be selected but conformance can be assured. Different specifications can be used in different situations. We have to study further, which specification style is the best in certain situations and how feasible and efficient methods are in practice in the healthcare domain.

Conclusion

In this chapter, we presented new requirements for the interface specifications from the testability point of view. We found that the form of the specification and exactness were important features. In addition, we noticed that domain-related specifications should be distinguished from technical specifications. Thus, it is good to divide the specification into levels — for example, functional, conceptual, and technical level specifications — where each of the levels contains only certain issues. We described different kinds of specifications, evaluated how useable they are in the healthcare domain, and compared their automatic test-case generation. Formal specifications are exact and test cases can be derived automatically from them. However, they are often too complex to use in practice, and in particular they are not very suitable for the healthcare domain. Natural language specifications are easy to form and understand but they are too ambiguous. Thus, they are more suitable for informal conformance reviews than for conformance testing. We propose that semiformal languages are the most suitable for the healthcare domain, because their notation is more understandable. They are easier to use and interpret than formal languages, and they are more precise than natural languages. Furthermore, we presented a conformance-testing environment developed in the OpenTE project, in which test cases can be derived from different kinds of specifications. Testing service in a testing environment acts as a needed counterpart in conformance testing.

Acknowledgments

This chapter is based on research in the OpenTE project, funded by the National Technology Agency TEKES, software companies, and hospital districts in Finland. The authors thank all the involved participants in this project.

References

Alexander, I. (2003). Misuse cases: Use cases with hostile intent. *IEEE Software, 20*(1), 58-66.

Barden, R., Stepney, S., & Cooper, D. (1994). *Z in practice*. Prentice-Hall.

Bhatti, R., Bertino, E., Ghafoor, A., & Joshi, J. (2004). XML-based specification for Web services document security. *IEEE Computer Society, 37*(4), 41-49.

Binder, R. (1994). Design for testability in object-oriented systems. *Communication of the ACM, 37*(9), 87-101.

Binder, R. (1999). *Testing object-oriented systems: models, patterns and tools*. Addison Wesley.

Carnahan, L., Rosenthal, L., & Skall, M. (1998). Conformance testing and certification model for software specification. In *Proceedings of the ISACC '98 Conference*.

El-Fakih, K., Yevtushenko, N., & Bochmann, G. (2004). FMS-based incremental conformance testing methods. *IEEE Transactions on Software Engineering, 30*(7), 425-436.

Garstecki, L. (2003). Generation of conformance test suites for parallel and distributed languages and APIs. In *Proceedings of the Eleventh Euromicro Conference on Parallel, Distributed and Network-based Processing*, Italy (pp. 308-315).

Gnesi, S., Latella, D., & Massink, M. (2004). Formal test-case generation for UML statecharts. In *Proceedings of the IEEE International Conference on Engineering Complex Computer Systems Navigating Complexity in the e-Engineering Age*, Italy (pp. 75-84).

Herzum, P., & Sims, O. (2000). *Business component factory*. Wiley Computer Publishing.

HIMSS, & RSNA (2002). *Integrating the healthcare enterprise — IHE technical framework volume I — integration profiles*, Revision 5.3. HIMSS/RSNA.

ISO/IEC Guide 2. (1996). 1996 *Standardization and Related Activities: General Vocabulary*.

ITU-T Recommendation X.290. (1996). *OSI conformance testing methodology and framework for protocol recommendations for ITU-T applications — general concepts*.

Jäntti, M., & Toroi, T. (2004). UML-based testing — A case study. *Proceedings of 2nd Nordic Workshop on the Unified Modeling Language*, Finland (pp. 33-44).

Kindrick, J., Sauter, J., & Matthews, R. (1996). Improving conformance and interoperability testing. *StandardView, 4*(1), 1996.

Kirner, D., Porter, R., Punniamoorthy, P., Schuh, M., Shoup, D., Tindall, S., et al. (1999). Extending use cases throughout the software lifecycle. *Software Engineering Notes, 24*(3), 66-68.

Kosanke, K. (2005). ISO standards for interoperability: A comparison. In *Pre-Proceedings of the First International Conference on Interoperability of Enterprise Software and Applications,* Switzerland (pp. 59-67).

Moseley, S., Randall S., & Wiles, A. (2004). In pursuit of interoperability. *International Journal of IT Standards and Standardization Research, 2*(2), 34-48.

Mykkänen, J., Porrasmaa, J., Korpela, M., Häkkinen, H., Toivanen, M., Tuomainen, M., et al. (2004). Integration models in health information systems: Experiences from the PlugIT project. In *Proceedings of the 11th World Congress on Medical Informatics.* San Francisco (pp. 1219-1222).

Rada, R. (1996). Who will test conformance? *Communications of the ACM, 39*(1), 19-22.

Rosenthal, L., & Skall, M. (Eds.). (2002). *Conformance Requirements for Specifications v1.0.* Retrieved December 10, 2004, from http://www.oasis-open.org/committees/download.php/305/conformance_requirements-v1.pdf

Rosenthal, L., Skall, M., Brady, M., Kass, M., & Montanez-Rivera, C. (1997). Web-based conformance testing for VRML. *StandardView, 5*(3), 110-114.

TNT Global Systems (2002). *National electronic healthcare claims standard, conformance and compliance issues* (white paper). Author.

Toroi, T., Jäntti, M., Mykkänen, J., & Eerola, A. (2004). Testing component-based systems—The integrator viewpoint. In *Proceedings of the 27th Information Systems Research Seminar,* Scandinavia, Sweden.

Toroi, T., Mykkänen, J., & Eerola, A. (2005). Conformance testing of open interfaces in healthcare applications—Case context management. In *Pre-Proceedings of the First International Conference on Interoperability of Enterprise Software and Applications,* Switzerland (pp. 535-546).

Tuomainen, M., Mykkänen, J., Rannanheimo, J., Komulainen, A., & Korpela, M. (2004). User-driven clinical context management with low implementation threshold (abstract). In M. Fieschi, E. Coiera, & Y. C. Li, (Eds.), *MEDINFO 2004: Building high performance health care organizations,* San Francisco.

W3C (2005, April 28). *QA framework: Specification guidelines* (working draft). Retrieved May 12, 2005, from http://www.w3.org/TR/qaframe-spec/

Chapter VII

Test-Case
Mutation

Macario Polo, University of Castilla - La Mancha, Spain

Mario Piattini, University of Castilla - La Mancha, Spain

Abstract

*This chapter presents a new testing technique called "test-case mutation." The idea
is to apply a set of specific mutation operators to test cases for object-oriented software,
which produces different versions of the original test cases. Then, the results of the
original test case and of its corresponding mutants are compared; if they are very
similar, the technique highlights the possible presence of a fault in the class under test.
The technique seems useful for testing the correctness of strongly constrained classes.
The authors have implemented a supporting tool that is also described in the chapter.*

Introduction

Source-code mutation is a testing technique whose main goal is to check the quality of
test cases used to test programs. Basically, a program mutant is a copy of the program
under test, but with a small change in its source code, such as the substitution of "+"
by "-."Thus, this small change simulates a fault in the program, the program mutant
therefore being a faulty version of the program under test. If a test case is executed both

on the program being tested and on a mutant and their outputs are different, then it is said that the mutant is "killed." This means that the test case has found the fault introduced in the original program and, therefore, the test case is "good."

Changes in the source code are seeded by mutation operators that, in many cases, are language-dependent (i.e., there are mutation operators specifically designed for Java, C++, etc.).

Although powerful, source-code mutation is computationally a very expensive testing technique (Baudry, Fleurey, Jézéquel, & Traon, in press; Choi, Mathur, & Pattison, 1989; Duncan, 1993; Mresa & Bottaci, 1999; Weiss & Fleyshgakker, 1993). In fact, source-code mutation has several very costly steps:

- **Mutant generation:** Offut, Rothermel, Untch, and Zapf (1996) reported on an experiment that, from a suite of 10 Fortran-77 programs ranging from 10 to 48 executable statements, between 183 and 3010 mutants were obtained. Mresa and Bottaci (1999) showed a set of 11 programs with a mean of 43.7 lines of code that produced 3211 mutants. The Mujava tool (Ma et al., 2004), when applied to a Java version of the triangle-type program with 37 lines of code, produces 469 mutants.

- **Mutant execution:** According to Ma, Offutt, and Kwon (2004), research in this line proposes the use of nonstandard computer architectures (i.e., Krauser, Mathur, & Rego, 1991) and weak mutation. In weak mutation, the state of the mutant is examined immediately after the execution of the modified statement, considering that the mutant is killed even though the incorrect state is not propagated until the end of the program. Weak mutation was initially introduced by Howden. Offut and Lee (1994) concluded that weak mutation is a cost-effective alternative to strong mutation for unit testing of noncritical applications.

- **Result analysis:** Besides the study of mutants, both killed and alive, this step also involves the discovery of functionally equivalent mutants that, for Mresa & Bottaci (1999), "is the activity that consumes the most time."

In order to reduce the number of mutants generated, Mathur (1991) proposed "selective mutation." This line has also been worked by other authors: Mresa and Bottaci (1999), Offut et al. (1996), and Wong and Mathur (1995) conducted experiments to find a set of sufficient mutant operators that decreases the number of mutants generated without information loss. In Mresa and Bottaci (1999) and Wong and Mathur (1995), the respective authors also investigate the power of randomly selected mutants and compare it to selective mutation. In Hirayama, Yamamoto, Okayasu, Mizuno, and Kikuno (2002), the authors proposed a new testing process starting with a prioritization of program functions from several viewpoints; according to these authors, this ordination reduces the number of test cases generated without decreasing the results.

In this very same line, Kim, Clark, and McDermid (2001) analyze the effectiveness of several strategies for test-case generation with the goal of finding out which one gets kills more mutants.

Offut and Pan (1997) demonstrated that it is possible to automatically detect functionally equivalent mutants. A mutant is equivalent to the original program if it is impossible to find any test data to kill the mutant. The authors use constraints for this task. In their experiments, they can detect almost 50% of equivalent mutants.

When testing object-oriented software, it is common to consider a test case for a class K as a sequence of invocations to methods of K. In testing environments such as JUnit, Nunit, and tools of this family, each test case consists of the construction of an instance of the class being tested, and then in the execution of some of the services offered by the class. The obtained object is then compared with the expected object. With other testing tools, such as MuJava (Ma et al., 2004), a test case is also composed of a sequence of calls to some of the class services.

The manual generation of test cases for a class is a hard and costly task. A proposal to facilitate this task was made by Kirani and Tsai (1994), who proposed the use of a technique called "method-sequence specification" to represent the causal relationship between methods of a class. This specification documents the correct order in which the methods of a class can be invoked by client classes, and can be specified using state machines or regular expressions. As it is also interesting to test a class when its methods are invoked in an order different from "the correct" one, the specification (regular expression or state machine) can be also used to generate other sequences.

Once the tester has a set of sequences (correct or not), he or she must combine them with test values to obtain a set of test cases.

From one point of view, a test case composed of a sequence of methods with actual values passed, as parameters can be understood as a way of using the class being tested. Any variation in the test-case results in a different way of using the class. In many cases, the state of the instance after being executed in one or another way should be different. One only needs to think of a bank account, one of the simplest examples. The final state of a new instance is different if we deposit and then withdraw, or if we withdraw and then deposit; the state of the instance will also be different if we deposit 100 euros rather than 200.

As a matter of fact, unit tests are based on the fact that an instance must always be in a correct state; if an instance cannot reach a correct state, it must report throwing an exception. A class is defined by a set of fields and operations; moreover, it may have some class invariants, and some pre- and postconditions annotating its operations.

Class operations are divided into *queries* (which do not change the instance state) and *commands* (which change the instance state). To apply a command to an instance, the instance must:

1. Be in a correct state (*state precondition*). For example, a banking account cannot be locked against withdrawals.

2. Receive correct arguments (*argument precondition*). For example, the amount to be withdrawn must be greater than zero.

The evaluation of the state precondition may require taking into account the argument precondition, since arguments can be invalid by themselves or due to a conflict with the current state of the instance (e.g., if a banking account has a balance of 100, it must be impossible to withdraw 200).

The result of applying a command will be:

1.   An instance in a correct state (*state postcondition*).
2.   Possibly, a return value according to the class semantic (*result postcondition*).

Given a test case composed of a sequence of commands (operations that change the instance state) executed on the same instance, it is possible to obtain many versions by introducing some changes, such as removing a method invocation or repeating one, changing the order of invocation of methods, interchanging the values of two parameters of compatible types, setting to zero the value of a numeric parameter, setting to null a complex parameter, reducing the size of a parameter array, etc. The state of the instance will probably be different depending on which version of the test case has been executed. Each version of the test case may be obtained by applying a test-case mutation operator. If source code mutants simulate faults in the program under test, test case mutants simulate faults in the way of using the class being tested: in strongly-constrained class, we hope that different ways of use put the respective instances in different states. Thus, the test-case mutation technique we present in this chapter is especially useful to test strongly constrained classes.

Initially, the chapter describes the proposed technique, giving some concepts and definitions. Then it presents the results of its application to a set of programs. The tool we have implemented for supporting the technique is later explained. Finally, we draw our conclusions and future lines of work.

Definitions and Preliminaries

Given K a class, a "test template" for K is a sequence composed of (1) an operation of K that builds an instance of K (a constructor or a *factory* method) and (2) a set of public methods of K. More formally:

$$T = \left(c(\overline{p_c}), s'(\overline{p_{s'}}), s''(\overline{p_{s''}}), ..., s'''(\overline{p_{s'''}}) \right),$$

where c is an operation in K that builds an instance of K; s', s'', and so on, are public methods of K, and the different p elements represent the types of the parameters of the corresponding operation (any p can be empty, which means that the operation has no parameters).

Test templates for K proceed from a "method sequence specification" (Kirani & Tsai, 1994) for such class, described as a regular expression of the public operations of K.

A test template is used to generate test cases; a test case proceeds from a \ that has been combined with some test values that are used as parameters. Obviously, if all the methods in the test template do not contain parameters, then the test template will only produce

Table 1. A test template and two test cases

Test template	Test values	Test cases
Account o=new Account() o.deposit(double) o.withdraw(double)	double:{-100.0, 0.0, +100.0}	Account o=new Account() o.deposit(-100.0) o.withdraw(-100.0)
		Account o=new Account() o.deposit(-100.0) o.withdraw(0.0)

a single test case composed by calls to the methods (with no arguments) in the test template, and in the same order as in the test template. So, a test case is:

$$tc = \left(c(\overline{v_c}), s'(\overline{v_{s'}}), s''(\overline{v_{s''}}), ..., s'''(\overline{v_{s'''}}) \right),$$

where *c, s', s''* have the same meaning as previously, and each *v* element represents the set of actual values of the corresponding method in this test case.

The first column of the next table shows a test template for an *Account* and a set of test values for the *double* data type; the second column shows two of the nine possible test cases that could be achieved by a simple combination of the template with the three values that also appear in Table 1.

Test-Case Mutants

Given a test case for a class *K,* a mutation operator for a test case is a function that produces a new valid test case for *K*, probably with some alteration to its code. The word "probably" is important, because sometimes the mutant is exactly equal to the original test case. When this happens following the terminology of source-code mutation, we say that the test case is "functionally equivalent" to the original test case. From now on, with the words "mutant" and "mutation operator" we are referring to "test-case mutant" and "test-case mutation operator," respectively.

Let us suppose we have a mutation operator that substitutes the value of a numeric parameter by zero: This operator applied to the bottom example of Table 1 produces the two mutants on the right side of Table 2; one of them is functionally equivalent to the original test case.

Sometimes a mutant is different from the original test case, but equal to another test case (i.e., a mutation operator can produce repeated test cases). For example, it is possible to have a mutation operator that removes one method of the test case. This operator, applied as shown in Table 3, produces a mutant exactly equal to the original test case in Table 2.

Table 2. Two mutants, one of them functionally equivalent to the original test case (Applying the Zero operator)

Original test case	Mutants
Account o=new Account() o.deposit(-100.0) o.withdraw(0.0)	Account o=new Account() o.deposit(0.0) ← o.withdraw(-100.0)
	Account o=new Account() o.deposit(-100.0) o.withdraw(0.0) ←

Table 3. A mutant different from the original test case, but equal to the original test case shown in Table 2 (Applied operator: Comment line)

Original test case	Mutant
Account o=new Account() o.deposit(-100.0) o.withdraw(0.0) o.deposit(100.0)	Account o=new Account() o.deposit(-100.0) o.withdraw(0.0) /* o.deposit(100.0) */

Situations like those explained in the previous paragraph and table are not worrisome. The important issue is to keep under control the original test cases and their respective mutants, as well as the states of the instances proceeding from the execution of the original test case and from its respective mutants. This "control" is what makes it possible to make comparisons and to know with exactitude what mutants are "killed."

Mutation Operators

Mutation operators introduce some types of change in the sequence of operations composing test cases. shows the mutation operators we have defined. All of them produce ways of using the class under test different than the original one that is provided by the original test case.

Killed, Alive, and Injured Mutants

Many software testing researchers and tools recommend or impose the implementation (or redefinition, if it is inherited and has a default implementation) of an *equals* method in the class under test (Chen, Tse, & Chen, 2001; Doong & Frankl, 1994; JUnit, 2003). *equals* is particularly useful in testing because it allows the comparison of the state of the instance obtained by a test case with the state of the expected instance.

Table 4. Mutation operators for test cases

Operator	Description
CL (Comment Line)	Comments on a method from the test case
IN (Interchange of calls)	Interchanges the order of two calls to methods
PI (Parameter interchange)	Interchanges two parameters of compatible types
RC (Repeat call)	Repeats a call to a method
ZE (Zero)	Substitutes a numeric parameter by zero, or changes a complex parameter by *null*
MAX (Maximum)	Changes a numeric parameter by the maximum value of its corresponding data type
MIN (Minimum)	Changes a numeric parameter by the minimum value of its corresponding data type
NEG (Negativize)	Multiplies by –1 a numeric parameter
ADD (Addition)	Adds 1 to a numeric parameter
SUB (Subtraction)	Subtracts 1 from a numeric parameter

Table 5. A test case and an injured mutant (Applying the IN operator)

Original test case	Mutant
Account o=new Account(); o.deposit(100); o.withdraw(100); *The balance is zero.*	Account o=new Account(); o.withdraw(100); o.deposit(100); *The balance is zero, but an exception has been thrown after withdrawing.*

Being t a test case, the expression $f(t)$ denotes the state of the instance after executing the test case t. Being m a mutant proceeding from t, we say that m is "killed" if and only if $f(t) \neq f(m)$; m is "injured" when $f(t) = f(m)$, but methods in t have thrown different exceptions than operations in m; m is "alive" when $f(t) = f(m)$ and t and m have thrown the same exceptions. The comparison of $f(t)$ and $f(m)$ by means of the "=" sign is made with the *equals* operation which, in most cases, must be specifically redefined for the class under test.

Let us suppose that a banking account throws an exception when one attempts to withdraw and the balance is less than or equal to zero. After executing the constructor in Table 5, the account balance is zero; after executing the original test case, the account balance is zero and no exception has been produced. However, the account balance is also zero after executing the mutant, but an exception has been thrown after the call to withdraw, which has caused the interruption of the execution, thus producing an *injured* mutant.

Table 6. A test case and one of its mutants (Applying the IN operator)

Original test case	Mutant
Account a=new Account(); *a.deposit(100.0);* *a.deposit(50.0);*	*Account a=new Account();* *a.deposit(50.0);* *a.deposit(100.0);*

As we said in the introduction, the test-case mutation technique is especially useful for testing strongly constrained classes, which a banking account should be. If we pass valid values to the parameters of the methods that compose the test cases of a correctly implemented strongly constrained class, we expect the class to kill and injure many mutants. If only a few mutants are killed and injured, then we should suspect that the class being tested has some kind of fault in its implementation.

With invalid values, the correct implementation of a strongly constrained class should leave many mutants alive, because the execution of the test case will be interrupted early due to the exceptions thrown by operations in the test case.

In general, the percentage of injured mutants depends on the position in the test case of the operation that throws the exception.

Functionally Equivalent Mutants

A test case is a way of using the class being tested. We expect that the state of the instances will be different depending on the way of using the class. This affirmation is risky, since its truth will depend on the method's implementation and on the class usage protocol (which can be described by the method sequence specification). In the simple example of the *Account* class, the following test case and mutant put both instances in the same state.

However, most of these situations are due to the functional equivalence of the test case and the mutant, as with the example shown in the previous table.

Therefore, for each test case generated, we will count the number of its mutants killed and injured.

Experiments

This section presents some experiments we have made to validate our technique. First, we present them applied to the TriTyp program, commonly used as a benchmark for validating testing techniques. Second, a discussion of the results with other programs is presented.

Figure 1. Two versions of the TriTyp program

TriTyp1 (from paper)
i : int
j : int
k : int
trityp : int
+ TriTyp1()
+ setI(arg0 : int) : void
+ setJ(arg0 : int) : void
+ setK(arg0 : int) : void
+ type() : int
+ equals(arg) : Object) : boolean

TriTyp2 (from paper)
i : int
j : int
k : int
trityp : int
+ TriTyp2()
+ setIJK(arg0 : int, arg1 : int, arg2 : int) : void
+ type() : int
+ equals(arg) : Object) : boolean
+ toString() : String

Application of the Technique to the TriTyp Program

The TriTyp program is commonly used as a benchmark for validating testing techniques. It receives as inputs three integers representing the lengths of the sides of a triangle, and must answer whether the triangle is equilateral, isosceles, scalene or whether it is not a triangle.

We have written two versions of the program, schematically shown in Figure 1. Both versions have three integer fields corresponding to the lengths of the three sides, plus one additional field representing the triangle type, which is computed inside the *type* method. In both cases, we have redefined the *equals* method to return *true* if the two triangles have the same values in the four fields (the three lengths and the type field). In *TriTyp1*, the side lengths are assigned using the methods *setI, setJ, setK*, which receive an integer parameter. If the received value is less than or equal to zero, they throw an exception, which interrupts the execution of the test case; otherwise, the received argument is assigned to the corresponding field. In *TriTyp2,* the three values are assigned using the *setIJK* method, which receives three integer values, throwing an exception if any of the three values is not valid.

For both programs, original test cases consist of a call to the corresponding constructor, calls to the setter methods (to *setI, setJ, setK* in TriTyp1, and to *setIJK* in TriTyp2), and a call to the *type* method. In the first case, the order of the sequence has a relative importance, since the triangle type does not depend on the order of calls to *setI, setJ,* and *setK.*

We generated test cases for both programs using a set of positive values and a set of zero and negative values. Zero and negative values are invalid arguments. Positive values are valid arguments (i.e., fulfill the argument precondition), but they may produce an invalid triangle (for example, if the sum of two sides is equal to the third one).

Table 7. Results for TriTyp1 with valid and invalid values

Oper.	TriTyp1 (valid values)						TriTyp1 (invalid values)					
	Mutants	Inju-red	%	Killed	%	% total	Mutants	Inju-red	%	Killed	%	% total
CL	256	0	0	256	100	100	256	64	25	0	0	25
IN	384	0	0	180	46	46	384	128	33	64	16	50
PI	Non applicable						Non applicable					
ZE	192	0	0	192	100	100	192	0	0	0	0	0
MAX	192	0	0	192	100	100	192	0	0	64	33	33
MIN	192	0	0	192	100	100	192	0	0	0	0	0
NEG	192	0	0	192	100	100	192	0	0	64	33	33
ADD	192	0	0	192	100	100	192	0	0	0	0	0
SUB	192	0	0	192	100	100	192	0	0	0	0	0
RC	256	0	0	34	13	13	256	0	0	0	0	0

Table 8. Results for TriTyp2 with valid and invalid values

Oper.	TriTyp2 (valid values)						TriTyp2 (invalid values)					
	Mutants	Inju-red	%	Killed	%	% total	Mutants	Inju-red	%	Killed	%	% total
CL	128	0	0	128	100	100	128	0	0	64	50	50
IN	64	0	0	46	71	71	64	0	0	64	100	100
PI	Non applicable						Non applicable					
ZE	192	0	0	192	100	100	192	0	0	0	0	0
MAX	192	0	0	192	100	100	192	0	0	0	0	0
MIN	192	0	0	192	100	100	192	0	0	0	0	0
NEG	192	0	0	192	100	100	192	0	0	0	0	0
ADD	192	0	0	192	100	100	192	0	0	0	0	0
SUB	192	0	0	192	100	100	192	0	0	0	0	0
RC	128	0	0	52	40	40	128	0	0	0	0	0

Tables 7 and 8 show the results of applying the test-case mutation technique using valid and invalid values to TriTyp1 and TriTyp2. As previously noted, we expected to kill and to injure many mutants with valid values, and just a few mutants with invalid values.

Obtaining very different results should make us suspect that the class implementation has some type of fault; this is the case with a strongly constrained class that does not kill or injure many mutants in the presence of valid values. We manually introduced a fault into the TriTyp2 class and re-executed its test cases, obtaining the results in Table 9. As seen, the percentage of injured and killed mutants decreased in the presence of valid values.

Table 9. Results for a faulty implementation of TriTyp2, with valid and invalid values

	Faulty implementation of TriTyp2											
	TriTyp2 (valid values)						TriTyp2 (invalid values)					
Oper.	Mutants	Inju-red	%	Killed	%	% total	Mutants	Inju-red	%	Killed	%	% total
CL	256	0	0	64	25	25	256	64	25	64	25	50
IN	384	0	0	192	50	50	384	64	16	256	66	83
PI	Non applicable						Non applicable					
ZE	192	0	0	64	33	33	192	0	0	144	75	75
MAX	192	0	0	0	0	0	192	0	0	168	87	87
MIN	192	0	0	64	33	33	192	0	0	144	75	75
NEG	192	0	0	64	33	33	192	0	0	128	66	66
ADD	192	0	0	0	0	0	192	0	0	64	33	33
SUB	192	0	0	16	8	8	192	0	0	64	33	33
RC	256	0	0	0	0	0	256	0	0	0	0	0

Other Experiments

Container classes have also been widely used to validate testing techniques (Ball, Hoffman, Ruskey, Webber, & White, 2000; Barnett & Schulte, 2002; Henkel & Diwan, 2003; Hoffman, Strooper, & Wilkin, 2005), probably because its operations can be easily annotated with constraints. With the same goal, we applied the test-case mutation technique to both several standard Java container classes and to versions of these same classes, in which we have manually introduced a fault.

Table 10. Results for a correct and a faulty version of the java.util.Stack class

	Stack											
	Regular expression: Stack().(pop()|push())*; Max length: 5; Number of test cases: 341											
	Right version						Faulty version					
Oper.	Mutants	Inju-red	%	Killed	%	% total	Mutants	Inju-red	%	Killed	%	% total
CL	1252	0	0	918	73	73	1252	0	0	0	0	0
IN	1744	0	0	876	50	50	1744	0	0	0	0	0
ZE	939	0	0	606	64	64	939	0	0	0	0	0
RC	1252	0	0	852	68	68	1252	0	0	0	0	0

The *Stack* Class

The first sample corresponds to the *java.util.Stack* class, whose summary is shown in Table 10 (data corresponding to the nonapplicable operators have been removed). We have generated test cases (and their corresponding mutants) using the regular expression *Stack().(pop()|push())**. Results of this sample are especially notable, since no mutants died in the manipulated version, thus revealing the presence of a fault.

The *LinkedList* Class

The second experiment was carried out with the *java.util.LinkedList* class. In this case, we generated several families of test cases using the four short regular expressions listed in Table 11.

One of the operations referenced by each regular expression contains, in the modified version of the class, one single fault. The goal in this case was to check whether the testing technique helps us to detect the presence of this fault.

Table 12 shows the results of testing this class. Note that the second column references the corresponding regular expression in the previous table and that results of nonapplicable operators (those that produce no mutants) have been removed.

The presence of the fault is clear for regular expressions (a) and (d), whereas the test engineer may have more doubts with cases (b) and (c), since the total percentages of killed and injured (although more correct than in the faulty version), are very similar. However, in these two cases, the number of killed mutants is zero and all the differences between the original and muted test cases are in the injured ones. Thus, the hypothesis that a low number of killed mutants is a good predictor of the existence of faults seems plausible.

The *Vector* Class

The hypothesis mentioned in the last paragraph is also confirmed with another small experiment made with the *java.util.Vector*. In fact, as seen in Table 13, the faulty version of the *java.util.Vector* class does not kill any mutants; the entire contribution to the total percentage comes from the injured mutants.

Table 11. Regular expressions used to test the java.util.LinkedList class

Regular expression	Max length	Number of test cases
LinkedList().add(Object)*	4	40
LinkedList ().add(int, Object)*	3	820
LinkedList ().add(Object)*.remove(int)*	3	26
LinkedList ().add(Object)*.remove(Object)*	4	39

Table 12. Results for the correct and faulty versions of java.util.LinkedList

		LinkedList										
		Correct version						Faulty version				
Operator	Reg. expr.	Mutants	Injured	%	Killed	%	% total	Mutants	Injured	%	Killed	%	% total
CL	(a)	102	0	0	102	100	100	102	0	0	0	0	0
	(b)	2358	519	22	651	27	49	2358	1041	44	0	0	44
	(c)	68	20	29	48	70	100	68	26	38	0	0	38
	(d)	102	102	102	102	102	102	102	102	102	102	102	102
IN	(a)	90	0	0	60	66	66	90	0	0	0	0	0
	(b)	2268	396	17	924	40	58	2268	1188	52	0	0	52
	(c)	60	12	20	33	55	75	60	42	70	0	0	70
	(d)	90	90	90	90	90	90	90	90	90	90	90	90
ZE	(a)	102	0	0	102	100	100	102	0	0	0	0	0
	(b)	4716	0	0	1194	25	25	4716	753	15	0	0	15
	(c)	68	1	1	30	44	45	68	13	19	0	0	19
	(d)	102	102	102	102	102	102	102	102	102	102	102	102
MAX	(b)	2358	753	31	417	17	49	2358	1170	49	0	0	49
	(c)	26	5	19	21	80	100	26	26	100	0	0	100
MIN	(b)	2358	753	31	417	17	49	2358	1170	49	0	0	49
	(c)	26	5	19	21	80	100	26	26	100	0	0	100
NEG	(b)	2358	636	26	144	6	33	2358	780	33	0	0	33
	(c)	26	4	15	9	34	50	26	13	50	0	0	50
ADD	(b)	2358	363	15	768	32	47	2358	1053	44	0	0	44
	(c)	26	5	19	18	69	88	26	26	100	0	0	100
SUB	(b)	2358	663	28	498	21	49	2358	1143	48	0	0	48
	(c)	26	2	7	21	80	88	26	26	100	0	0	100
RC	(a)	102	0	0	102	100	100	102	0	0	0	0	0
	(b)	2358	0	0	417	17	17	2358	234	9	0	0	9
	(c)	68	15	22	48	70	92	68	0	0	0	0	0
	(d)	102	102	102	102	102	102	102	102	102	102	102	102

Implementation of the Tool

The tool uses the standard *Reflection* API of Java to extract the set of public methods in the class and the *java.util.regex.Pattern* class to analyze the regular expression to generate test templates. These ones are generated calculating the spanning tree of the regular expression.

Figure 2 shows the main screen of the tool. The tool user can write the regular expression that will be used to generate the test cases, referencing the first operation with "A," the second with "B," and so on. If there are more than "Z" operations, then the successive

Table 13. Results for the java.util.Vector class

	Vector											
	Regular expression: ().add(Object)*.remove(int)*; Max. length: 4; Number of test cases: 547											
	Correct version						**Faulty version**					
Oper.	Mutants	Inju-red	%	Killed	%	% total	Mutants	Inju-red	%	Killed	%	% total
CL	2004	408	20	1110	55	75	384	102	26	0	0	26
IN	2781	471	16	1365	49	66	351	177	50	0	0	50
ZE	2004	104	5	1032	51	56	384	68	17	0	0	17
MAX	1002	333	33	183	18	51	192	102	53	0	0	53
MIN	1002	333	33	183	18	51	192	102	53	0	0	53
NEG	1002	218	21	126	12	34	192	68	35	0	0	35
ADD	1002	213	21	267	26	47	192	102	53	0	0	53
SUB	1002	276	27	213	21	48	192	102	53	0	0	53
RC	2004	162	8	1023	51	59	384	0	0	0	0	0

Figure 2. Main screen of the tool

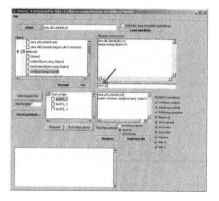

ones are mapped to combinations of letters starting with "(AA)," "(AB)," and so on. The regular expression in the example (*AF{1,3}*) will generate test cases starting with the *java.util.LinkedList()* constructor, followed by from 1 to 3 calls to *add(Object)*.

Test templates must be combined with actual values and additional code to produce the testing methods in the generated testing class. Test values must be manually assigned to parameters by the user, for which he or she can apply his or her best knowledge about

Figure 3. Values assignment

the system, as well as limit the values of assertions, which has been suggested in many studies (Boyapati, Khurshid, & Marinov, 2002; Korel & Al-Yami, 1996; Offut, Liu, Abdurazik, & Amman, 2003; Tracey, Clark, Mander, & McDermid, 2000; Tse & Xu, 1996).

Testing values for arguments of primitive data types are given by hand, using the window shown in Figure 3. Moreover, it is also possible to add pre- and postcode to the test cases, in order to provide the user with the possibility of having a greater control over test cases. Values of nonprimitive data types must be previously serialized. Later, they will be read from the corresponding files and passed as parameters to the operations in the test cases.

The mix of test templates and test values is a file containing testing methods, both original and mutant. When compiled and executed, this program builds a wide set of objects, which are serialized and saved on the disk Then, a result analyzer compares them, writing the results in a XML file and showing a summary table (Figure 4).

Conclusion

This chapter has presented a new testing technique called test-case mutation, whose main goal is to help the test engineer find faults in software. The initial idea is to consider a test case as a way of using the class being tested, and then to assume that to use the class in a different way will produce different results. Obviously, maintaining control of the "original" and the "other" ways of use is central. Each different way of use comes from the original one when a test-case-mutation operator is applied, which introduces a small change in the original test case.

The technique has been shown to be valid for some common problems in software literature. However, still more work and experimental results are required to validate it. Besides this, we are also working on the definition of new mutation operators.

Figure 4. Result file (top) and result analyzer (bottom)

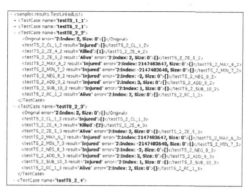

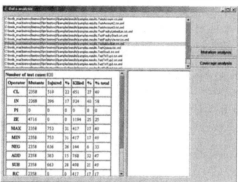

Test-case mutation does not require knowledge of the source code, making it a valid technique for testing components or Web services, when the component user knows only the set of services offered through its interface.

Test-case mutation and source-code mutation are very different: besides working with different artifacts (test cases versus source code), the goal of this one is to check the quality of test cases (the percentage of killed mutants is considered a coverage criteria of the original program), whereas the goal of test-case mutation is to detect the presence of faults in the program. Test-case mutation is an inexpensive testing technique, when an automatic generator is used. Moreover, applying the concepts presented earlier in this chapter, such as regular expressions, reflection and serialization, whose inclusion is now standardized in the most used programming languages, it is not too difficult to write a generator as an standalone or a plugin for an IDE.

References

Ball, T., Hoffman, D., Ruskey, F., Webber, R., & White, L. (2000). State generation and automated class testing. *Software Testing, Verification and Reliability, 10*, 149-170.

Barnett, M., & Schulte, W. (2002). *Contracts, components and their runtime verification on the .NET platform* (Tech. Rep. No. MSR-TR-2002-38). Microsoft Research.

Baudry, B., Fleurey, F., Jézéquel, J. M., & Traon, Y. L. (in press). From genetic to bacteriological algorithms for mutation-based testing. In *Software testing, verification and reliability*.

Boyapati, C., Khurshid, S., & Marinov, D. (2002). *Korat: Automated testing based on Java predicates*. Paper presented at the ACM International Symposium on Software Testing and Analysis (ISSTA).

Chen, H. Y., Tse, T. H., & Chen, T. Y. (2001). TACCLE: A methodology for object-oriented software testing at the class and cluster levels. *ACM Transactions on Software Engineering and Methodology, 10*(4), 56-109.

Choi, B., Mathur, A., & Pattison, B. (1989). *PMothra: Scheduling mutants for execution on a hypercube*. Paper presented at the Proceedings of the ACM SIGSOFT '89 Third Symposium on Software Testing, Analysis, and Verification, Key West, FL.

Doong, R. K., & Frankl, P. G. (1994). The ASTOOT approach to testing object-oriented programs. *ACM Transactions on Software Engineering and Methodology, 3*(2), 101-130.

Duncan, I. M. (1993). *Strong mutation testing strategies*. University of Durham, UK.

Henkel, J., & Diwan, A. (2003). *Discovering algebraic specifications from Java classes*. Paper presented at the 17th European Conference on Object-Oriented Programming (ECOOP).

Hirayama, M., Yamamoto, T., Okayasu, J., Mizuno, O., & Kikuno, T. (2002, October 3-4). *Elimination of crucial faults by a new selective testing method*. Paper presented at the International Symposium on Empirical Software Engineering (ISESE2002), Nara, Japan.

Hoffman, D., Strooper, P., & Wilkin, S. (2005). Tool support for executable documentation of Java class hierarchies. *Software Testing, Verification and Reliability*, in press *(available from Wiley Digital Library)*.

Howden, W. E. (1982). Weak mutation testing and completeness of test sets. *IEEE Transactions on Software Engineering, 8*(4), 371-379.

JUnit (2003). *JUnit, Testing Resources for Extreme Programming*. Retrieved January 5, 2003, from http://www.junit.org

Kim, S. W., Clark, J. A., & McDermid, J. A. (2001). Investigating the effectiveness of object-oriented testing strategies using the mutation method. *Software Testing, Verification and Reliability, 11*, 207-225.

Kirani, S., & Tsai, W. T. (1994). Method sequence specification and verification of classes. *Journal of Object-Oriented Programming, 7*(6), 28-38.

Korel, B., & Al-Yami, A. (1996). *Assertion-oriented automated test data generation.* Paper presented at the International Symposium on Software Testing and Analysis (ISSTA1998), Clearwater Beach, FL.

Krauser, E. W., Mathur, A. P., & Rego, V. J. (1991). High performance software testing on SIMD machine. *IEEE Transactions on Software Engineering, 17*(5), 403-423.

Ma, Y. S., Offutt, J., & Kwon, Y. R. (2004). MuJava: An automated class mutation system. In *Software Testing, Verification and Reliability,* in press *(available from Wiley Digital Library).*

Mathur, A. P. (1991, September). *Performance, effectiveness, and reliability issues in software testing.* Paper presented at the Proceedings of the 15th Annual International Computer Software and Applications Conference, Tokyo, Japan.

Mresa, E. S., & Bottaci, L. (1999). Efficiency of mutation operators and selective mutation strategies: An empirical study. *Software Testing, Verification and Reliability, 9*, 205-232.

Offutt, J., & Lee, S. D. (1994). An empirical evaluation of weak mutation. *IEEE Transactions on Software Engineering, 20*(5), 337-344.

Offut, J., Liu, S., Abdurazik, A., & Amman, P. (2003). Generating test data from state-based specifications. *Software Testing, Verification and Reliability*, (13), 25-53.

Offut, J., & Pan, J. (1997). Automatically detecting equivalent mutants and infeasible paths. *Software Testing, Verification and Reliability, 7*, 165-192.

Offut, J., Rothermel, G., Untch, R. H., & Zapf, C. (1996). An experimental determination of sufficient mutant operators. *ACM Transactions on Software Engineering and Methodology, 5*(2), 99-118.

Tracey, N., Clark, J., Mander, K., & McDermid, J. (2000). Automated test data generation for exception conditions. *Software: Practice and Experience, 30*(1), 61-79.

Tse, T., & Xu, Z. (1996). *Test case generation for class-level object-oriented testing.* Paper presented at the 9th International Software Quality Week, San Francisco.

Weiss, S. N., & Fleyshgakker, V. N. (1993, June). *Improved serial algorithms for mutation analysis.* Paper presented at the International Symposium on Software Testing and Analysis (ISSTA), Cambridge, MA.

Wong, W. E., & Mathur, A. P. (1995). Reducing the cost of mutation testing: An empirical study. *Journal of Systems and Software, 31*(3), 185-196.

Chapter VIII

Discrete Event Simulation Process Validation, Verification, and Testing

Evon M. O. Abu-Taieh, The Arab Academy
for Banking and Financial Sciences, Jordan

Asim Abdel Rahman El Sheikh, The Arab Academy
for Banking and Financial Sciences, Jordan

Abstract

This chapter introduces validation, verification, and testing tools and techniques pertaining to discrete event simulation. The chapter distinguishes between validation and verification within the context of discrete event simulation. Then, we will show the importance of such topic by revealing the amount research done in simulation validation and verification. The chapter subsequently discusses the reasons why simulation projects fail and the sources of simulation inaccuracies. Next, the chapter gives different taxonomies for validation, verification, and testing techniques (VV&T) for both types of simulation systems: object-oriented-based and algorithmic-based. Therefore, the chapter will present a translation of thirteen software-engineering practices suggested for simulation projects. Notwithstanding the significance of providing an objective assessment platform, as such, the chapter will shed light on the independence of VV&T pertaining to simulation systems.

Introduction

Simulation software systems have certain characteristics that make them different from other software systems, consequently, and due to the special nature of simulation-software systems; VV&T techniques of simulation systems must be looked at closely. First, the chapter makes the distinction between validation and verification pertaining to simulation systems. Then, the chapter shows the motivation for VV&T in simulation through two ways:First is the different nature of the VV&T in simulation-software systems. The second is showing the amount of research done in VV&T of simulation-software systems, which only emphasizes the importance of such topic. The chapter subsequently discusses the why simulation projects fail and the sources of simulation inaccuracies. Thus, the chapter gives different taxonomies for VV&T for both types of simulation systems: object-oriented-based and algorithmic-based. Therefore, the chapter will present a translation of thirteen software-engineering practices suggested for simulation projects. Notwithstanding the significance of providing an objective assessment platform, as such, the chapter will shed light on the aspect of the independence of VV&T pertaining to simulation. Finally, the chapter highlights some future trends in the automation of VV&T.

V&V Definition and Distinction

In order to be able to discuss V&V, they must first be based on their original definition, which fully comprehends the true denotation of V&V as related to simulation systems. Sommerville (2001) defines validation by raising the question "are we building the right product?"(p. 420), while defining verification by raising another question "are we building the product right?" (p. 420). This comes from a pure software-engineering point of view, noting that the simulation perspective on the definitions of V&V are similar yet not the same. On another note, Pidd (1998) defines validation as "a process whereby we asses the degree to which the lumped model input: output relation map onto those real systems" (p. 157).

Likewise, Pidd (1998) distinguishes validation from verification by referring to verification as "a process by which we try to assure ourselves that the lumped model is properly released in the computer program. The Lumped model is defined as an explicit and simplified version of the base model and is the one which will be used in management science" (p. 157). While Smith (1998) paraphrases validation as answering the question "Are we building the right product?" (p. 806) and verification as answering the question, "Are we building the product right?" (p. 806), Balci, (1995, 2003), Banks (1999), and Kleignen, Bettonvil, and Gmenendahl (1996) define *model validation* as follows:

Model validation *is substantiating that the model, within its domain of applicability, behaves with satisfactory accuracy consistent with the study objectives. Model validation deals with building the right model. It is conducted by running the model under the "same" input conditions that drive the system and by comparing model behavior with the system behavior.* (Balci, 1995, p. 147)

Balci (1995) defined validation as true simulation science when stressing the words *domain* and *satisfactory*. Also Balci (1995) defines *model verification* as in the following quote:

Model verification *is substantiating that the model is transformed from one form into another, as intended, with sufficient accuracy. Model verification deals with building the model right. The accuracy of transforming a problem formulation into a model specification or the accuracy of converting a model representation in micro flowchart into an executable computer program is evaluated in model verification.* (p. 147)

Again Balci's (1995) definition is stressing here *sufficient accuracy*. Then Balci defines *model testing* as follows:

Model testing *is demonstrating that inaccuracies exist or revealing the existence of errors in the model. In model testing, we subject the model to test data or test cases to see if it functions properly. "Test failed" implies the failure of the model, not the test, Testing is conducted to perform validation and verification.* (p. 147)

As such, the mere distinction between verification and validation is minute yet substantive, acknowledging that validation ensures that the product caters to the needs, whereas, verification ensures the correctness and aptness of the product. Within this context the word *testing* would be the tool to examine these two aspects.

Motivation for V&V in Simulation

Defining simulation in its broadest aspect as embodying a certain model to represent the behavior of a system, whether that may be an economic or an engineering one, with which conducting experiments is attainable. Such a technique enables the management, when studying models currently used, to take appropriate measures and make fitting decisions that would further complement today's growth sustainability efforts, apart from cost decrease, as well as service delivery assurance. As such, the computer-simulation technique contributed in cost decline; depicting the "cause & effect", pinpointing task-oriented needs or service-delivery assurance, exploring possible alternatives, identifying problems, as well as, proposing streamlined measurable and deliverable solutions, providing the platform for change strategy introduction, introducing potential prudent investment opportunities, and finally providing safety net when conducting training courses. Yet, the simulation-development process is hindered due to many reasons. Like a rose, computer-simulation technique, does not exist without thorns; of which the length, as well as, the communication during the development life cycle. Simulation reflects real-life problems; hence, it addresses numerous scenarios with a handful of variables. Not only is it costly, as well as, liable for human judgment, but also, the results are complicated and can be misinterpreted.

Table 1. Published research of V&V in WSC

Year	V & V Papers	Total Published Papers	%
1997	15	280	5%
1998	22	236	9%
1999	26	244	11%
2000	19	280	7%
2001	15	224	7%
2002	1	119	1%
2003	12	263	5%
2004	6	280	2%
Total	**116**	**1,926**	**6%**

Within this context, there are four characteristics that distinguish simulation from any other software-intensive work, which also make VV&T for simulation distinct from VV&T for other software, following are the four characteristics, as discussed by Page and Nance (1997):

- **Time as index variable:** In simulation there is an indexing variable called *TIME*. In discrete event simulation (DES), this indexing variable "establishes an ordering of behavioral events" (Page & Nance, 1997, p. 91).

- *Correctness* **of simulation software:** In software engineering, correctness is one of the objectives like reliability, maintainability, testability, and so on. Yet the Objective of correctness is very special to simulation software for the simple reason How useful is a simulation program "if questions remain concerning its validity" (Page & Nance, 1997, p. 91).

- **Computational intensiveness:** In their paper Page and Nance (1997) clearly state that:

The importance of execution efficiency persists as a third distinctive characteristic. While model development costs are considerable, as is the human effort throughout the period of operation and use, the necessity for repetitive sample generation for statistical analysis and the testing of numerous alternatives forces concerns for execution efficiency that are seen in few software-intensive projects. (p. 91)

- **Uses of simulation:** Ihe uses of simulation are not typical, in fact there is "No typical use for simulation can be described" (Page & Nance, 1997, p. 91).

Within this context, the chapter attempts to shed the light on validation and verification methods and techniques that relate to simulation, which were discussed through 116 research papers in the Winter Simulation Conference (WSC) over the years 1997 through 2004 as seen in and Figure 1, such numbers indicate clearly the importance, inimitable, and unique case of validation and verification of simulation software.

Figure 1. V&V research papers in WSC

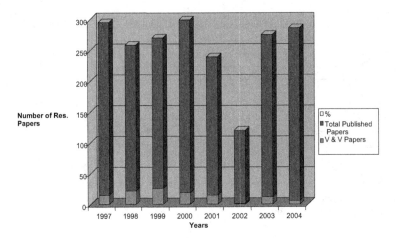

It is worth noting that VV&T — as well as experimentations, execution, and design are so important that Shannon (1998) suggested allowing 40% of the project time for these steps.

Why Simulation Projects Fail

The arising issue of simulation projects falling short to be labeled as successful can be attributed to many reasons, an answer by Robinson (1999) had been put forth, as he listed three main reasons; the first being "poor salesmanship when introducing the idea to an organization" (p. 1702) which includes too much hope in too little time, while identifying the second reason as "lack of knowledge and skills particularly in statistics, experimental design, the system being modeled and the ability to think logically" (p. 1702), and pinpointing the third reason as "lack of time to perform a study properly" (p. 1702). Nevertheless, simulation inaccuracy has become a recurrent condition that instigated a thorough query in its sources.

Sources of Simulation Inaccuracy

There are three sources of inaccuracy in the simulation project might be developing during the three major steps that are in the simulation life cycle, namely: modeling, data extraction, and experimentation (see Figure 2).

Figure 2. The simulation modeling process (simple outline) (Robinson, 1999, p. 1702)

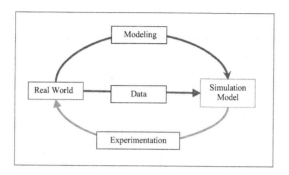

In this regard, the modeling process includes a subordinate set of steps, namely; the modeler understanding the problem, developing a mental/conceptual model, and finally the coding. Noting that from these steps some problems might mitigate themselves, such as: (1) the model could misunderstand the problem, (2) the mental/conceptual model could be erroneous, and (3) the conversion from mental/conceptual model to coding could be off beam.

Furthermore, during the modeling process, the data collection/analysis is a key process element, particularly since the data collected is really the input of the simulation program, and if the data is collected inaccurately then the principle of "garbage in garbage out" is clearly implemented, likewise, the data analysis while using the wrong input model/distribution (Leemis, 2003) is also a problem.

Last but not least, the third source of inaccuracies is experimentation, which uses the collected data from the simulation system and compares the end result to the real world, given that experimentation inaccuracies can result from ignoring the initial transient period, insufficient run-length or replications, insufficient searching of the solution space, not testing the sensitivity of the results.

Within this context, ignoring the initial transient period, labeled as the first inaccuracy source during experimentation process, has been identified by Robinson (1999), who states that "Many simulation models pass through an initial transient period before reaching steady-state" (p. 1705). The modeler, suggests Robinson, can either take into account such period or set the simulation system so that the system has no transient period. Therefore, Robinson suggests two remedies: (1) run the simulation system long enough, or (2) do many reruns (replications). In addition, insufficient searching of the solution space is the third and last source, which in turn would incite the modeler to "only gain a partial understanding of the model's behavior" (Robinson, 1999, p. 1702). Such inaccuracy, obviously leads to erroneous conclusion.

Figure 3. Balci's principles for VV&T (Balci, 1995, pp. 149-151)

Principle 1:	The VV&T must be conducted throughout the entire life cycle of a simulation study.
Principle 2:	The outcome of simulation model VV&T should not be considered as a binary variable where the model is absolutely correct or absolutely incorrect.
Principle 3:	A simulation model is built with respect to the study objectives and its credibility is judged with respect to those objectives.
Principle 4:	Simulation-model VV&T requires independence to prevent developer's bias.
Principle 5:	Simulation-model VV&T is difficult and requires creativity and insight.
Principle 6:	Simulation-model credibility can be claimed only for the prescribed conditions for which the model is tested.
Principle 7:	Complete simulation model testing is not possible.
Principle 8:	Simulation model VV&T must be planned and documented.
Principle 9:	Type I, II, and III errors must be prevented.
Principle 10:	Errors should be detected as early as possible in the life cycle of a simulation study.
Principle 11:	Multiple-response problems must be recognized and resolved properly.
Principle 12:	Successfully testing each submodel does not imply overall model credibility.
Principle 13:	Double-validation problems must be recognized and resolved properly.
Principle 14:	Simulation-model validity does not guarantee the credibility and acceptability of simulation results.
Principle 15:	Formulated-problem accuracy greatly affects the acceptability and credibility of simulation results.

If one acknowledges that errors in the simulation world clearly do not originate only from one source, VV&T are not only considered a necessity but also imperative and crucial. Osman Balci, the well known simulation scientist, declared 15 principles, stated in Figure 3, demonstrating the fundamentality and inevitability of conducting VV&T in the simulation world.

VV&T Techniques

As seen in Balci's fifth principle, VV&T for simulation models is "difficult and requires creativity and insight" (Balci, 1995, p.149), yet the fact remains that "there are no step-by-step procedures available to guide the modeler in performing these important tasks" (Sadowski, 1991, p. 95). It is worth mentioning, however, that many have suggested VV&T techniques and automated tools (Yilmaz, 2001) drawn mainly from software-engineering VV&T techniques like Balci (1994, 1997), Hoffer, George, and Valacich (2005), Pressman (2005), and many more. This is particularly true of Balci (1994), where in his research, he has suggested a taxonomy of 45 V&V techniques, moreover, in another paper, Balci (1997) defined 77 V&V techniques and 38 V&V techniques for object-oriented simulation.

Highlighting the fact that the interest of this chapter is V&V techniques pertaining to simulation, in this regard, the Balci taxonomy should be further reviewed. Balci (1994) categorized 45 VV&T techniques into: informal, static, dynamic, symbolic, constraint, and formal. Later he categorized 115 VV&T techniques to three families: conventional, adaptive, and specific VV&T (Balci, 1997), of which 77 VV&T techniques for conventional simulation were again categorized into informal, static, dynamic, and formal. The remaining 38 VV&T techniques, categorized into the adaptive and specific families, were to be used in object-oriented simulation. Nevertheless, others like Hoffer et al. (2005) and Pressman (2005) categorized the VV&T techniques based on the life-cycle phase. Next, both of Balci's categorizations will be discussed thoroughly.

The first taxonomy (Figure 4) of Balci had come before the object-oriented simulation idea, in which the 45 VV&T techniques were categorized: informal, static, dynamic, and

Figure 4. Taxonomy of VV&T techniques (Balci, 1995, p. 152)

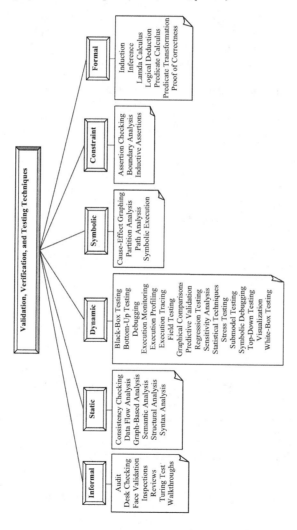

symbolic. Within this context, the *informal VV&T technique* includes tools and approaches that "relay heavily on human reasoning" (Balci, 1994, p. 217) rather than "mathematical formalism" (Balci, 1994, p. 217), this category includes: audit, desk checking, inspection, reviews, turing test, walkthroughs, given the fact that the word *informal* should not reflect lack of structure or formal guidelines as Balci (1994) says.

In the same token, *static VV&T techniques* concentrate on the source code of the model and need not the execution of the code (Hoffer, et al., 2005). More importantly, Balci (1994) has stated that automated tools and language compilers rely on this type of VV&T, since the *static VV&T techniques* category is comprised of: consistency checking, data-flow Analysis, graph-based analysis, semantic analysis, structural analysis, and syntax analysis.

Whereas, the *dynamic VV&T technique's* distinguishing characteristic is for the model execution to evaluate the model as Balci (1994) states, as this category comprises of the following VV&T techniques: black-boxing, bottom-up testing, debugging, execution monitoring, execution profiling, execution tracing, field testing, graphical comparisons, predictive validation, regression testing, sensitivity analysis, statistical techniques, stress testing, submodel testing, symbolic debugging, top-down testing, visualization, and white-box testing. Nonetheless, the *symbolic VV&T techniques* category has been used to asses the model using VV&T techniques like cause-effect graphing, partition analysis, path analysis, and symbolic execution, noting that later in Balci (1997), this category was incorporated with static category and dynamic category, while cause-effect graphing, and symbolic execution were incorporated in the static category, partition analysis and path analysis were incorporated in the dynamic category. On another note, Balci (1994) has stated that "*Constraint VV&T techniques* are employed to assess model correctness using assertion checking, boundary analysis, and inductive assertions" (p. 218). Later, however, such a category also disappeared and was incorporated with others.

Balci (1994), among others, admits that *formal VV&T techniques* are based on mathematical proof, stating that "Current state-of-the-art formal proof of correctness techniques are simply not capable of being applied to even a reasonably complex simulation model" (p. 218).

Given the aforementioned, an elaborated overview will be subsequently given about a group of VV&T techniques, taking into consideration the simulation standpoint.

Conventional Simulation VV&T Techniques

Audit

Zammit (2005), along with many, has considered audits as external type review, while others have classified it as informal VV&T like Balci (1994), either way, the purpose of audit is to substantiate that the system performance meets the requirements, in order to examine the actual code and supporting materials. As such, there are two types of audits: functional configuration audit and physical configuration audit (Zammit, 2005).

Inspections

Balci (1994, 1997) has repeatedly classified inspections as informal type of VV&T, yet, Zammit (2005) has classified tem as review type, nonetheless, the main goal of inspections is to "manually examine code for occurrences of well-known errors," noting that code inspection can detect 60% to 90% of "all software defects as well as provide programmers with feedback that enables them to avoid making the same type of errors in the future work" (Hoffer et al., 2005, p. 576).

Face Validity

Balci (1994, 1997) has recurrently classified *face validity* additionally as informal type of VV&T, although Sargent (2003) has stated that the goal in *face validity* is to ask "individuals knowledgeable about the system whether the model and/or its behavior is reasonable" (p. 41), yet Sargent (2003) has suggested questions, such as: "is the logic in the conceptual model correct?" (p. 41). And "is the model's input-output relationships reasonable?"(p. 41), moreover, Banks, Carson, Nelson, and Nicol (2001) has suggested that sensitivity analysis can be used to check the model validity.

Structured Walkthrough

Balci (1994, 1997) has repeatedly classified structured walkthrough as an informal type of VV&T, yet Zammit (2005) has classified it as review type, however, Hoffer et al. (2005) has stated that *structured walkthrough* can be used to review many system-development deliverables, including logical and physical as well as code, additionally Hoffer et al. explains that since walkthroughs tend to be informal, which in turn makes the programmer less apprehensive about walkthroughs and increase their frequency. Furthermore, it is recommended that walkthroughs to be done on smaller pieces of code, particularly since the longer the code the more defensive the programmer becomes, yet it is worth mentioning that the intention of walkthrough is not fixing the errors, but pointing them out. In this regard, Hoffer et al. gives a guideline for conducting *walkthrough* in Figure 5.

Desk Checking

Balci (1994, 1997) has also classified desk checking as informal type of VV&T. Balci notes that *desk checking* is an informal process, as confirmed additionally by Hoffer et al.

Figure 5. Steps in a typical walkthrough (Hoffer et al., 2005, p. 577)

GUIDELINES FOR CONDUCTING A CODE WALKTHROUGH:

1. Have the review meeting chaired by the project manager or chief programmer who is also responsible for scheduling the meeting, reserving a room, setting the agenda, inviting participants, and so on.
2. The programmer presents his or her work to the reviewers. Discussion should be general during the presentation.
3. Following the general discussion, the programmer walks through the code in detail, focusing on the logic of the code rather than on specific test cases.
4. Reviewers ask to walk through specific test cases.
5. The chair resolves disagreements if the review team cannot reach agreement among themselves and assign duties, usually to the programmer, for making specific changes.
6. A second walkthrough is then scheduled if needed.

(2005), in which the programmer or someone else who understands the logic of the program works through the code with paper and pencil. The programmer executes each instruction, using test cases that may or may not be written down. In a sense, the reviewer acts as the computer, mentally checking each step and its results for the entire set of computer instructions.

Syntax Analysis

Balci (1994, 1997) has classified *syntax analysis* as a static VV&T technique that takes place during the programming phase in the software-development lifecycle (Balci, 1994, 1997). Moreover, the task of syntax analysis is distinctively differentiated, as stated in Sebesta's (2003) book *Concepts of Programming Languages*.

Most compilers separate the task of analyzing syntax into two distinct parts: lexical analysis and syntax analysis. The *lexical analyzer* deals with small-scale language constructs, such as name and numeric literals. It is an essential pattern matcher. The *syntax analyzer* deals with the large-scale constructs, such as expressions, statements, and program units

Hoffer et al.'s (2005) statement that "*Syntax checking* is typically done by compiler. Errors in syntax are uncovered but the code is not executed" (p. 578), explains that syntax checking is an automated and static technique, where, "static testing means that the code being tested is not executed" (p. 578).

Reviews

Much like walkthrough, the main goal of *reviews* is to substantiate, to both management as well as sponsors, that the project is conducted in accordance with the study's objectives, ensuring attainment of appropriate quality level. Highlighting the fact that reviews are more interested in specifications and design deficiency, the review team usually includes managers. Within this context, Freedman and Weinberg (2000) *have* discussed reviews in depth in their book "Handbook Of Walkthroughs, Inspections and Technical Reviews" and made *walkthrough*, *inspection*, and *audit* as types of *reviews*. Additionally, the authors estimate a 10x reduction in errors in products and a 50-80% cost reduction (Freedman & Weinberg). There are different types of reviews, such as management review and technical review. The management review provides an evaluation of project progress and compliance to requirements, whereas, the technical reviews focus mainly on specification and design-meeting product specifications (Zammit, 2005).

Turing Tests

Balci has additionally classified *turing tests* as informal VV&T (Balci, 1994, 1997). However, it is worth mentioning that Sargent (1998, 1999) has addressed the issue that, in turing tests, people who are well-informed and familiar with the operations of a system should be "asked if they can discriminate between system and model outputs" (p. 124), while others had suggested having statistical tests for use with Turing tests.

Correctness Proofs

On another note, Balci (1994, 1997) has classified *correctness proofs* as one of the formal VV&T. Balci (1994), among others, has admitted that "Current state-of-the-art formal proof of correctness techniques are simply not capable of being applied to even a reasonably complex simulation model" (p. 218), while Zammit (2005) signified that "*Correctness proofs* are mathematical proofs of the equivalence between the specification and the program," putting forth two steps to carry out correctness proofs:

1.   Showing that the computation is correct on an ideal computer
2.   Showing that the ideal computation is approximated on an actual computer

Data Analysis

Balci (1994, 1997) has classified data analysis as static VV&T, suggesting that there are types of techniques for *data analysis: data-dependency analysis* and *data-flow analysis*. In this regard, *data dependency analysis* involves the determination of what variables depend on what other variables, particularly used in parallel and distributed applications, this knowledge is critical for assessing the accuracy of process synchro-nization, as in this technique variables are broken down to DEFinition set (DEF) and USE set (USE), where the DEF set is the set of variables modified by a statement, and the USE set is all the variables used in a statement, given that there are two types of dependencies: *flow dependence* and *output dependency*; in the *flow dependency* the intersection of DEF set and USE set is not empty, whereas, in the *output dependency* the intersection of DEF sets is EMPTY (Pressman, 2005). On another note, however, the *data-flow analysis* uses a data-flow graph, in order to detect undefined or unreferenced variables, track maximum and minimum values, track data dependencies and data transformations (Balci, et al. 1996), while the *data-flow graph* depicts the logical control flow using notations in, as seen in Figure 6. Each circle is called *flow-graph node*, representing one or more procedural statements, and the arrows on the flow graph, called *edges* or *links*, representing flow of control (Pressman, 2005). As such, a *data-flow graph* works as follows (Balci et al.):

1.   The program is broken down into blocks (areas of sequential linear code that contain no decisions or loops).

2.   All code within a block is either totally executed or not.

3.   Each of these blocks represents nodes in the graph.

4.   The edges represent the control flow.

Basis-Path Testing

The *basis-path testing* is a white-box testing technique that was first proposed by Tom McCabe. It enables the test-case designer to drive a logical complexity measure of a procedural design and use this measure as a guide for defining a basis set of execution paths. Test cases derived to exercise the basis set are guaranteed to execute every statement in the program at least one time during testing (Pressman, 2005).

Graph-Based Testing Methods

Pressman (2005) has envisaged that *graph-based testing methods* begin by creating a graph of important objects and their relationships, then devising a series of tests that will cover the graph so that each object and relationship is exercised and errors are uncovered, noting that the symbolic representation of graph is composed of nodes, links, and link weights (specific value or state behavior); where:

1.   Nodes are represented as circles.

2.   Links can of different forms: arrows, bidirectional links (symmetrical links), undi-rected, or parallel links.

3.   Arrows indicate relationship moves in only one direction.

Moreover, it is worth noting that bidirectional links imply that the relationship applies in both directions, while parallel links are used when a number of different relationships are established between graph nodes.

Execution Testing

Balci (1994, 1997) has classified *execution testing* as static VV&T. As testing the software or the simulation by executing the software is called *execution testing*, moreover, it has been stated by Balci et al. (1996) that "Its purpose is to reveal the model representational errors (simulation) and to reveal functional and performance errors." Noting that both Balci (1997) and Balci et al. have agreed on the types of execution testing as *execution monitoring, execution tracing, execution profiling*. As the name suggests, this type of test is generally done by collecting and analyzing executable behavior data. In this regard, *execution monitoring*, being the first type, has been described by Balci, et al. as an "Activity/event oriented data about the model's dynamic behavior should be collected and analyzed," providing the following as an example: "in simulation game (fight game) how is the simulations software responding to a user who fights really fast. What is the minimum response time of the system?" Furthermore, *execution tracing*, the second type, has been also described by Balci et al. to "reveal errors by "watching" the line by line execution of a software/simulation," stating that such method produces a huge amount of data which is too complex to analyze. On a last note, *execution profiling*, the third type, has been described by Balci et al. as it "shows the summary of the statistics collected — in most cases the *Trace* results act as inputs to profilers."

Regression Testing

Balci (1997) has classified *regression testing* as dynamic VV&T technique. Moreover, Pressman (2005) has elaborated on integrating the test strategy as follows; "In the context of an integration test strategy *Regression Testing* is the re-execution of some subset of tests that have been already been conducted to ensure that changes have not propagated unintended side affects" (p. 401) and (Kleignen et al., 1996), yet *regression testing* has been known as *regression fault* (Orso, Shi, & Harrold, 2004, p. 241). Regression can be done either manually or automatically, although manual regression has draw backs of inefficiency (e.g., slow, needs labor, etc.), however, a comparison based on the following ten quantitative and qualitative criteria is provided by Baradhi and Mansour (1997) and Mansour and Brardhi (2001).

Equivalence Partitioning

Pressman (2005) has described *equivalence partitioning*, as the program's input is divided into subsets (equivalence class) with one or more elements selected from each subdomain; stating that "Typically, an input condition is either a specific numeric value, a range of values, a set of related values, or Boolean condition" (p. 437). Furthermore, Pressman has defined the *equivalence* as a class according to the following guidelines listed in (p. 437):

1.   If input condition requires a range, one valid and two invalid equivalence classes are defined.

2.   If input condition requires a specific value, one valid and two invalid equivalence classes are defined.

3.   If input condition specifies a member of a set, one valid and two invalid equivalence classes are defined.

4.   If input condition is Boolean, one valid and two invalid equivalence classes are defined.

By applying these guidelines test cases for each input-domain-data object can be developed and executed.

Boundary Value Analysis (BVA)

Boundary value analysis (BVA) leads to selection of test cases that exercise bounding values (boundaries of the input domain), as BVA complement partitioning testing by selecting the edge values and focuses on input and output condition, noting that Pressman (2005) has additionally devised some guidelines that are very much like guidelines of partition testing, which are listed as follows (p. 438):

1.   If input condition specifies a range bounded by values a and b, test cases should be designed with values a and b as well as just above and just below a and b.

2.   If input condition specifies a number of values, test cases should be developed that exercise the minimum and maximum numbers values just above and below minimum and maximum are also tested.

3.   Apply guidelines 1 and 2 to output conditions. For example, assume that a temperature vs. pressure table is required as output from an engineering-analysis program. Test cases should be designed to create an output report that produces the maximum (and minimum) allowable number of table entries.

4.   If internal program-data structures have prescribed boundaries (e.g., an array has a defined limit of 100 entries), be certain to design a test case to exercise the data structure as its boundary.

Assertion Checking

Assertion checking is a dynamic VV&T technique used to compare an execution profile against the expectations of the modeler, and hence, guards model execution against potential errors (Balci, Nance, Arthur, & Ormsby, 2002). Within this technique, assertions are placed in various parts of the software code to monitor its execution, as Balci et al. (p. 656) has stated that "An assertion is a statement that should hold true as a simulation model executes."

Furthermore, assertion checking clearly serves two important needs: "it verifies that the model is functioning within its acceptable domain. Also, assertion statement documents the intentions of the modeler."

However, assertion checking "degrades model performance, forcing the modeler to choose between execution efficiency and accuracy" (Balci et al., 1996).

Bottom-Up Testing

Bottom-up testing is an approach where the lowest level module in the hierarchy is tested first, followed by each successively high level. Balci et al. (1996) quotes Sommerville on how bottom-up-testing is used:

Bottom-up testing is used with bottom-up model development. Many well-structured models consist of a hierarchy of sub models. In bottom-up development, model construction starts with the simulation's routines at the base level, i.e., the ones that cannot be decomposed further, and culminates with the sub models at the highest level. As each routine is completed, it is tested thoroughly. When routines with the same parent, or sub model, have been developed and tested, the routines are integrated and their integration is tested. This process is repeated until all sub models and the model as a whole have been integrated and tested. The integration of completed sub models need not wait for all sub models at the same level to be completed. Sub model integration and testing can be, and often is, performed incrementally.

Some of the advantages of bottom-up testing include, as Balci et al. (1996) states, the fact that it encourages extensive testing and that it is attractive for testing-distributed models and simulation.

Top-Down Testing

Balci (1994, 1997) has repeatedly classified *top-down testing* as a dynamic testing technique, bearing in mind that top-down testing begins with a test of the global model at its highest level. When testing a given level, calls to submodels at lower levels are simulated using *stubs*, which is a dummy submodel that has no function other than to let its caller complete the call (Balci et al., 1996).

Visualization and Animation

Visualization and animation of a simulation greatly assist in model V&V (Sargent, 1998). Displaying graphical images of internal (e.g., how customers are served by a cashier) as well as external (e.g., utilization of the cashier) dynamic behavior of a model during execution exhibits errors. Although witnessing the model in action is very useful in uncovering errors; it nonetheless does not guarantee model correctness (Paul & Balmer, 1998). Therefore, visualization should be used with caution (Balci et al., 1996).

Field Testing

Balci (1994, 1997) has classified *field testing* as a dynamic testing technique, particularly since it operates the model, collecting validation-related information. More importantly, Balci et al. (1996) has stated that "it is usually difficult, expensive, and sometimes impossible to devise meaningful field tests for complex systems, their use wherever possible helps both the project team and decision makers develop confidence in the model" This source has also highlighted major disadvantages pertaining to conducting such a technique, one of which is lacking the adequate test tools and resources necessary to achieve statistically significant results (Balci et al.).

Functional (Black-Box) Testing

Balci (1994, 1997) has repeatedly classified *functional testing*, which is also called black-box testing, as a dynamic VV&T technique. Within this context, Balci et al. (1996) states that since "It is virtually impossible to test all input-output transformation paths for a reasonably large and complex simulation because the paths could number in the millions" (Balci et al.), the technique is used by inputting test data to the model and then assessing the accuracy of consequent output. This is done with the aim of building assurance in the model, not to claim absolute correctness (Balci et al.).

Stress Testing

Stress testing belongs to dynamic VV&T as well. Based on Balci (1994, 1997), it exposes the model to an extreme workload condition, in order to test its validityStress testing and load testing should be distinguished from one another. Stress testing aims to push the model to the threshold, in order to "find bugs that will make that break potentially harmful" (Manta, 2005), whereas, load testing seeks to expose the model to a statistically representative (usually) load (Manta).

Sensitivity Analysis

Balci (1994, 1997) has repeatedly classified *sensitivity analysis* in the dynamic category. Furthermore, Balci et al. (1996) has highlighted its performance, stating that "*Sensitivity analysis* is performed by systematically changing the values of model input variables and parameters over some range of interest and observing the effect upon model behavior" (Balci et al.).

Structural (White-Box) Testing

Balci (1994, 1997) has repeatedly classified *structural testing* in the dynamic category. Alternatively called *white-box testing*, *structural testing* evaluates the model based on its internal structure (how it is built), where as functional (black-box) testing assesses the input-output transformation accuracy of the model (Pidd, 1998), particularly since it employs data-flow and control-flow diagrams to assess the accuracy of internal model structure by examining model elements such as statements, branches, conditions, loops, internal logic, internal data representations, submodel interfaces, and model execution paths. Balci (1997) has stated that *structural (white-box) testing* consists of six testing techniques:

1. **Branch testing:** "runs the model or simulation under test data to execute as many branch alternatives as possible, as many times as possible, and to substantiate their accurate operation" (Balci et al., 1996).

2. **Condition testing:** "runs the model or simulation under test data to execute as many logical conditions as possible, as many times as possible, and to substantiate their accurate operation" (Balci et al., 1996).

3. **Data-flow testing:** "uses the control flowgraph to explore sequences of events related to the status of data structures and to examine data-flow anomalies" (Balci et al., 1996).

4. **Loop testing:** "Runs the model or simulation under test data to execute as many loop structures as possible, as many times as possible, and to substantiate their accurate operation" (Balci et al., 1996).

5. **Path testing:** "runs the model or simulation under test data to execute as many control flow paths as possible, as many times as possible, and to substantiate their accurate operation" (Balci et al., 1996).

6. **Statement testing:** "runs the model or simulation under test data to execute as many statements as possible, as many times as possible and to substantiate their accurate operation" (Balci et al., 1996).

Submodel Testing

Balci (1997) has classified *submodel testing* as conventional dynamic VV&T technique. Given the fact that such testing techniques need to be decomposed (top-down) into submodels, moreover, both the system and the executable model are instrumental in collecting similar data, as such, Balci et al. (1996) consequently states that "Then, the behavior of each submodel is compared with the corresponding subsystem's behavior to judge the sub model's validity." Needless to say, however, that the *validity* of all submodels does not indicate validating for the whole model.

Symbolic Debugging

Balci (1997) has classified *symbolic debugging* as conventional dynamic VV&T technique. Moreover, Balci et al. (1996) has stated that this technique utilizes "a debugging tool that allows the modeler to manipulate model execution while viewing the model at the source code level."

Cause-Effect Graphing

Balci (1997) has classified *cause-effect graphing* as a conventional static VV&T technique. Furthermore, Balci et al. (1996) has stated that this technique "addresses the question of what causes what in the model representation. Causes and effects are first identified in the system being modeled and then their representations are examined in the model specification."

Interface Analysis Techniques

Balci (1997) has classified *interface analysis techniques* as conventional static VV&T techniques, noting that Balci et al. (1996) has appreciatively stated that interface analysis techniques "are especially useful for verification and validation of interactive and distributed simulations." In this regard, however, Balci has suggested two basic techniques, namely; model-interface analysis and user-interface analysis. Where the first "examines submodel-to-submodel interfaces within a model, or federate-to-federate interfaces within a federation, and determines if the interface structure and behavior are sufficiently accurate." (Balci et al.), whereas the latter "examines the user-model interface and determines if it is human engineered to prevent errors during the user's interactions with the model. It also assesses how accurately this interface is integrated into the overall model or simulation" (Balci et al.).

Fault/Failure Analysis

Fault/failure are dynamic VV&T testing techniques (Balci, 1994, 1997), where fault indicates an incorrect model component, whereas Failure indicates incorrect behavior of the model, as such, fault/failure technique examines the input-output transformation, in an attempt to identify how the model could fail (Balci et al., 1996).

Traceability Assessment

Traceability assessment are static VV&T testing techniques (Balci, 1994, 1997), of which the object is to match elements of the model in one phase of the development life cycle with an element in another level. For example, matching elements in the requirement specifications to the design specifications, noting that the matching must be one-to-one (Balci et al., 1996), most importantly, highlighting the fact that unmatched elements indicate unfulfilled requirements, or unintended design.

Graphical Comparison

Balci (1994, 1997) has classified Traceability Assessment as a dynamic VV&T testing technique, within this context, Balci et al. (1996) has superbly described the idea of graph comparison as follows:

The graphs of values of model variables over time are compared with the graphs of values of system variables to investigate characteristics such as similarities in periodicity, skew, number, and location of inflection points; logarithmic rise and linearity; phase shift; trend lines; and exponential growth constants.

The Lambda Calculus

Balci (1994, 1997) has repetitively classified lambda calculus as a formal VV&T testing technique. Moreover, Wikipedia (2005) has given a metaphorical general idea about lambda calculus as follows:

The lambda calculus *can be called the smallest universal programming language. The lambda calculus consists of a single transformation rule (variable substitution) and a single function definition scheme. The lambda calculus is universal in the sense that any computable function can be expressed and evaluated using this formalism. It is thus equivalent to Turing machines. However, the lambda calculus emphasizes the use of transformation rules, and does not care about the actual machine implementing them. It is an approach more related to software than to hardware.*

Acceptance Test

Hoffer et al. (2005) has identified "Acceptance test is testing the system in the environment where eventually be used" (p. 582). Furthermore, Hoffer has explained that in such a case, the users are ready to sign off on the system and accept it once they are satisfied with it, within this context, it should be noted that part of the acceptance tests are Alpha testing and Beta testing.

Alpha Testing

Balci (1994, 1997) has classified alpha testing as a dynamic VV&T testing technique in which the entire system is implemented in a test environment to discover whether the system is overtly destructive to itself or to the rest of environment.

V&V Techniques for Object-Oriented Simulation Models

Joines and Roberts (1998) have stated that "An object-oriented simulation (OOS) consists of a set of objects that interact with each other over time" (p. 141). Indeed assessing the accuracy of a procedural paradigm is a difficult task, it is even harder under the object-oriented paradigm (OOP), particularly since OOP induces various challenges and complexities as stated by Balci (1997), which are "The dynamic and diverse patterns of interactions among groups of objects, nonsequential representation, the partition of the model structure in inheritance and aggregation relationships, and the incremental and iterative nature of model development" (p. 138).

As such, many methodologies have been suggested to test object-oriented software, which can be utilized to test object-oriented simulation systems, one such strategy has been suggested by Pezz and Young (2004) that "Include three main phases: intra-class, inter-class, and system and acceptance testing." Within this context, *intraclass* testing deals with classes in isolation and includes testing of abstract classes, selection of test cases from the ancestors' test suite, and testing state-dependent behavior of the class under test, while, *interclass* testing applies to clusters of classes to be tested incrementally, considering class interactions, polymorphic calls, and exception handling. *System-and-acceptance* testing considers the software as a whole independently from its internal structure and relies on traditional system and acceptance-testing techniques.

Along those lines, Balci (1997) has developed taxonomy of VV&T techniques (see Figure 7) that classified the VV&T techniques into three categories: conventional, specific, and adaptive. Moreover, the taxonomy defined 77 V&V techniques and 38 V&V techniques for object-oriented simulation, noting that most of the techniques are derived from the software-engineering world and modified to the needs of object-oriented simulation systems.

Figure 7. A taxonomy of verification and validation techniques for object-oriented simulation models (Balci, 1997, p. 140)

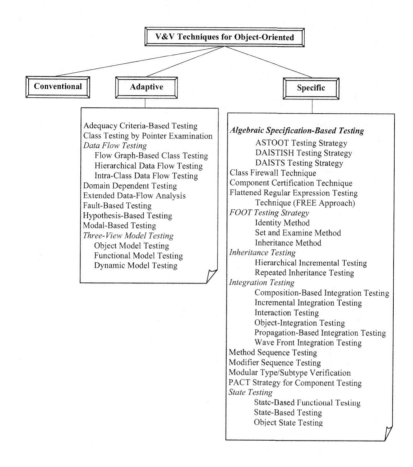

Within this context, *conventional techniques* refer mainly to VV&T techniques used in the object-oriented simulation without any adaptation to OOP, which is further classified as: informal, static, dynamic, and formal categories, highlighting the fact that such categories were previously discussed in the chapter. Likewise, *adaptive techniques*, the second category in the taxonomy, which refers to techniques that were adapted to object-oriented theory including: adequacy criteria-based testing, class testing by pointer examination, *data flow testing which includes* (flow-graph-based class testing, hierarchical data-flow testing, intraclass data-flow testing), domain-dependent testing, extended data-flow analysis, fault-based testing, hypothesis-based testing, model-based testing, and *three-view model testing, which includes* object-model testing, functional-model testing, and dynamic-model testing.

Finally, *specific techniques*, the third category in the taxonomy, are newly created based on object-oriented formalism and used for object-oriented software. It should be taken into consideration that those techniques are algebraic specification-based testing, ASTOOT testing strategy, DAISTISH testing strategy, DAISTS testing strategy, class firewall technique, component certification technique, flattened regular expression testing, technique (FREE approach), FOOT testing strategy, identity method, set and examine method, inheritance method, inheritance testing, hierarchical incremental testing, repeated inheritance testing, integration testing, composition-based integration testing, incremental integration testing, interaction testing, object-integration testing, propagation-based integration testing, wave front integration testing, method sequence testing, modifier sequence testing, modular type/subtype verification, PACT strategy for component testing, state testing, state-based functional testing, state-based testing, object state testing, and graph-based class testing.

Within this context, Balci (1997) has classified *DAISTS* as a specific technique from the *algebraic specification-based testing*. Furthermore, Gannon McMullin, and Hamlet (1981) has stated that *data-abstraction implementation, specification, and testing system (DAISTS)* "permits a program implementing an abstract data type to be augmented with specification axioms and test cases to explore the consistency of axioms and implementation" (p. 212).

In the same token, Balci (1997) has classified *ASTOOT* as a specific technique from the *algebraic specification-based testing*. Furthermore, Doong and Frankl (1994) has stated that *a set of tools for object-oriented testing (ASTOOT)* "includes an interactive specification-based test-case-generation tool and a tool that automatically generates test drivers. For any class C, ASTOOT can automatically generate a test driver, which in turn automatically executes test cases and checks their results. Additionally, when an algebraic specification for C is available, ASTOOT can partially automate test generation. Thus the system allows for substantial automation of the entire testing process" (p. 102).

Likewise, Balci (1997) has classified *Daistish* as a specific technique from the *algebraic specification-based testing*. Hughes and Stotts (1996) have distinguishably described *Daistish* as follows:

Daistish is a tool that performs systematic algebraic testing similar to Gannon's DAISTS tool. However, Daistish *creates effective test drivers for programs in languages that use side effects to implement ADTs; this includes C++ and most other object-oriented languages. The functional approach of DAISTS does not apply directly in these cases.* (p. 1)

It is worth mentioning, however, that Hughes and Stotts (1996) have compared *Daistish* to *ASTOOT* as follows:

Daistish differs from ASTOOT by using Guttag-style algebraic specs (functional notation), by allowing aliasing of type names to tailor the application of parameters in test cases, and by retaining the abilities of DAISTS to compose new test points from existing ones. Daistish *is a Perl script, and is compact and practical to apply.* (p. 1)

Additionally, the *class firewall*, denoted *CFW(X)* for a class X, is the set of classes grouped within *specific techniques* that could be affected by changes to class X and thus, that should be retested when class X is changed (Labiche, Thévenod, Fosse, Waeselynck, & Durand 2000)

Furthermore, *model-based testing* relies on execution traces of behavior models, most importantly since they are used as test cases for an implementation: input and expected output. This complements the ideas of model-driven testing (Pretschner, 2005).

In addition, Balci (1997) has categorized *hierarchical incremental class testing* as a specific inheritance test, Harrold, McGregor, and Fitzpatrich (1992) has explained the process of a *hierarchical incremental class test* as follows:

1. First, a base class is tested by testing each member function individually and then testing the interactions among the member functions.

2. The test suite, execution information, and association between the member functions and test cases is saved in a testing history.

3. Then, when a subclass is defined, the testing history of its parent, the definition of the modifier and the inheritance mapping of the implementation language are used to derive the testing history for the subclass.

4. The subclass's testing history indicates which attributes to (re)test in the subclass and which of the parent's test cases can be reused.

Moreover, *specification fault-based testing* is one of the adaptive VV&T techniques, as Richardson, O'Malley, and Tittle (1989) have stated "The goal of *spec/fault-based testing* is to detect faults in the specification by revealing specification failures or to detect coding faults that are due to misunderstanding the specification by revealing implementation failures" (p. 89). Based on Richardson's description, formal specification language is needed to use such technique.

Binder (1995) has identified that *FREE (flattened regular expression)* is a state-based testing technique, as Balci (1997) has classified FREE as a *specific* VV&T technique, furthermore, Binder has stated FREE "technique can detect four kinds of bugs: missing transition, incorrect transition, incorrect output actions, and incorrect states." (Xu, Xu, & Nygard, 2005). As Xu et al. explain, FREE uses the generation of a transition tree from a state model, then, transition test sequences are transcribed from the tree, thus, FREE shows that the specifications are satisfied.

Furthermore, Unified Modeling Language (UML) has been used in building simulation systems by many, such as: Carr and Balci (2000), Lendermann, Gan, and McGinnis (2001), Ramakrishnan, Lee, and Wysk (2002), and even IBM (2005) advertises such an idea.

Moreover, Linzhang et al. (2004) has stated that: "As a semi-formal modeling language, UML is widely used to describe analysis and design specifications by both academia and industry, thus UML models become the sources of test generation naturally", highlighting the fact that UML's advantage in this case "is that they provide a convenient basis for selecting tests" (Offutt & Abdurazik, 1999).

Mapping Software-Engineering Best Practices to the Discrete Event Simulation Process

Withers (2000) has described 13 software-engineering practices to be applied to simulation project, next an elaborate overview of the suggested best practices, noting that two of which have been compiled from Withers:

1. **Formal risk management:** utilized for modeling risks, which includes access to historical data, documenting existing and planned processes, and the ability to comprehend the lack of management understanding of the modeling process and required sophisticated statistical analyses (Balci & Sargent, 1981; Withers, 2000).

2. **Estimate cost and schedule empirically:** takes place during the project planning, as some "measure of project complexity should be used as a basis" (Withers, 2000, p. 435).

3. **Metric-based scheduling and management and tracking earned** value: reflected in short activities rather than long ones.

4. **Defect tracking:** reflected in tracking defects during the project.

5. **Treating human resources as the most important asset:** such a recommendation is applicable to any project.

6. **Configuration management:** reflected in keeping a log of versions and dates of the simulation system.

7. **Manage and trace requirements:** explaining how the project manager would be capable of keeping check on the project progress.

8. **System-based software design:** indicates the involvement of programmers and software engineers in the design.

9. **Design twice and code once:** which really reflects the need to refrain from coding and give an adequate time to design.

10. **Formal inspections:** Withers (2000) states that this "should be conducted on least the requirements, the project plan, the conceptual model, the model, and the test plans" (p. 437).

11. **Manage testing as a continuous process:** testing like in Balci (1994, 1997) must be managed for the duration of the project.

12. **Compile and smoke test frequently:** Withers (2000) suggests that "Whenever an additional capability is added to the model, a regression test of the prior capabilities should be done first (p. 437).

Independence of VV&T

Many advocate the independence of VV&T pertaining to simulation, particularly since independence provides an objective assessment platform, adds a new analytical perspective, brings its own set of tools and techniques, introduces intermediate users, and significantly enhances testing as well as discovers design flaws and coding errors (Arthur & Nance, 2000). VV&T clearly crystallizes this need when the system is real-time critical software, the program has a high cost of failure, or the cost of error detection, maintenance, or modification exceeds the cost of VV&T. This highlights the fact that with independence we mean: technical, managerial, and financial independence (Arthur & Nance).

Future Trends

Indeed testing is a tedious, mind-numbing, lackluster, repetitive, and long process. Just like compilers started years ago to locate syntax errors, VV&T tools are becoming well known. In fact, as seen in Table 2, there are many tools that test software. Whether the

Table 2. VV&T software tools

Product	Web site	Use For Programming Language	Latest Release Date
vectorCAST	www.vectorcast.com	for c/c++, Delphi, java, Visual Basic, visual c++	—
testcomplete 3	www.automatedqa.com	for win32, java, .NET	—
The Grinder	http://sourceforge.net/projects/grinder	Java load-testing	5/25/ 2005
Mantis	http://www.mantisbt.org/	Php, MySQL, Web-based bug tracking	5/25/ 2005
OpenSTA	http://opensta.org/download.html	Scripted HTTP and HHTPS load test	5/16/ 2005
TestMaker	http://www.pushtotest.com/	solves bugs in the HTTP protocol handler	5/11/ 2005
ProofPower	http://www.lemma-one.com/ProofPower/index/	supporting specification and proof in higher order logic (HOL) and in the Z notation	—

VV&T technique is static or dynamic, formal or informal, many tools have been developed to do the grubby work for the developer. Some tools, like *ProofPower*, go as far as offering supporting proof in higher order logic (HOL) and in the Z notation. As such, those mentioned hereinafter will be part of our life in validation, verification, accreditation, and surly independence.

Conclusion

In conclusion, this chapter gave a full-fledged overview regarding the simulation of VV&T techniques, whether they may be procedural or object-oriented simulations, putting forth various taxonomies for both types of VV&T techniques. Furthermore, the chapter highlighted the fact that the use of UML in simulation can be tuned to serve the purpose of simplifying the VV&T process.

In addition, mapping best practices of software engineering to simulation process, thirteen best practices recommended to be integrated within the simulation system development.

Finally, the chapter pinpointed the significance of the independence of VV&T, identifying the reasons behind advocating for it, the most important of which would be capability to provide an objective assessment platform.

References

Arthur, J., & Nance, R. (2000, December 10-13). Verification and validation without independence: A recipe for failure. In J. A. Joines, R. R. Barton, K. Kang, & P. A. Fishwick (Eds.), *Proceedings of the Winter Simulation Conference* (pp. 859-856). San Diego, CA: Society for Computer Simulation International.

Balci, O. (1994). Validation, verification, and testing techniques throughout the life cycle of a simulation study. *Annals of Operations Research, 53*, 215-220.

Balci, O. (1995). Principles and techniques of simulation validation, verification, and testing. In C. Alexopoulos, K. Kang, W. R. Lilegdon, & D. Goldsman (Eds.), *Proceedings of the 1995 Winter Simulation Conference* (pp. 147-154). New York: ACM Press.

Balci, O. (1997, December 7-10). Verification, validation and accreditation of simulation models. In S. Andradóttir, K. J. Healy, D. H. Withers, & B. L. Nelson (Eds.), *Proceedings of the Winter Simulation Conference*, Atlanta, GA (pp. 135-141). Retrieved April 2003, from http://www.informs-sim.org/wscpapers.html

Balci, O. (2003). Verification, validation, and certification of modeling and simulation applications. *ACM Transactions on Modeling and Computer Simulation, 11*(4), 352-377.

Balci, O., Glasow, P. A., Muessig, P., Page, E. H., Sikora, J., Solick, S., & Youngblood, S. (1996, November). *Department of defense verification, validation and accreditation (VV&A) recommended practices guide*. Alexandria, VA: Defense Modeling and Simulation Office. Retrieved May 25, 2005, from http://vva.dmso.mil/Mini_Elabs/VVtech-dynamic.htm

Balci, O., Nance, R., Arthur, J., & Ormsby, W. (2002, December 8-11). Expanding our horizons in verification, validation, and accreditation research and practice. In E. Yücesan, C. H. Chen, J. L. Snowdon, & J. M. Charnes (Eds.), *Proceedings of the 2002 Winter Simulation Conference* (pp. 653-663). Piscataway, NJ: IEEE.

Balci, O., & Sargent, R. G. (1981, April). A methodology for cost-risk analysis in the statistical validation of simulation models. *Communications of the ACM, 24*(11), 190-197.

Banks, J. (1999, December 5-8). Introduction to simulation. In P. A. Farrington, H. B. Nembhard, D. T. Sturrock, & G. W. Evans (Eds.), *Proceedings of the 1999 Winter Simulation Conference* (pp. 7-13). New York: ACM Press.

Banks, J., Carson, J., Nelson, B., & Nicol, D. (2001). *Discrete-event system simulation* (3rd ed.). Upper Saddle River, NJ: Prentice Hall International Series.

Baradhi, G., & Mansour, N. (1997, September 29-October 2). A comparative study of five regression testing algorithms. In *Proceedings of the Software Engineering Conference*, Australia (pp. 174-182).

Binder, R. V. (1995). State-based testing. *Object Magazine, 5*, 75-78.

Carr, J., & Balci, O. (2000, December 10-13). Verification and validation of object-oriented artifacts throughout the simulation model development life cycle. In A. Joines, R. R. Barton, K. Kang, & P. A. Fishwick (Eds.), *Proceedings of the Winter Simulation Conference* (pp. 866-871). Piscataway, NJ: IEEE.

Doong, R., & Frankl, P. (1994). The ASTOOT approach to testing object-oriented programs. *ACM Trans. on Software Engineering and Methodology, 3*(2), 101-130.

Freedman, D. P., & Weinberg, G. M. (2000). *Handbook of walkthroughs, inspections, and technical reviews: Evaluating programs, projects, and products* (3rd ed.). New York: Dorset House Publishing Co.

Gannon J., McMullin, P., & Hamlet, R. (1981, July). Data-abstraction implementation, specification, and testing. *ACM Transactions on Programming Languages and Systems, 3*(3), 211-223.

Harrold, M., McGregor, J., & Fitzpatrich, K. (1992). Incremental testing of object-oriented class structures. In *Proceedings of the 14th International Conference on Software Engineering*, Melbourne, Australia (pp. 68-80). Retrieved April 2004, from http://citeseer.ist.psu.edu/harrold92incremental.html

Hoffer, J. A., George, J. F., & Valacich, J. S. (2005). *Modern systems analysis and design* (4th ed). Upper Saddle River, NJ: Prentice Hall.

Hughes, M., & Stotts, D. (1996). Daistish: Systematic algebraic testing for OO programs in the presence of side-effects. In *Proceedings of the ACM SIGSOFT Int. Symp. On Software Testing and Analysis* (pp. 53-61). Retrieved June 12, 2005, from http://rockfish.cs.unc.edu/pubs/issta96.pdf

IBM. (n.d.). Retrieved June 12, 2005, from http://www-106.ibm.com/developerworks/rational/library/2797.html

Joines, J., & Roberts, S. (1998, December 13-16). Fundamentals of object-oriented simulation. In D. J. Medeiros, E. F. Watson, J. S. Carson, & M. S. Manivannan (Eds.), *Proceedings of the 1998 Winter Simulation Conference* (pp. 141-149). Los Alamitos, CA: IEEE Computer Society Press.

Kleignen, J., Bettonvil, B., & Gmenendahl, W. (1996). Validation of trace-driven simulation models: Regression analysis revisited. In J. M. Ckrnes, D. J. Morrice, D. T. Brunner, & J. J. Swain (Eds.), *Proceedings of the Winter Simulation Conference* (pp. 352-359). New York: ACM Press.

Labiche, Y., Thévenod, P., Fosse, H., Waeselynck, M., & Durand, H. (2000). Testing levels for object-oriented software. *Proceedings of the 22nd International Conference on Software Engineering*, Limerick, Ireland (pp. 136-145). New York: ACM Press.

Leemis, L. (2003 December 7-10). Input modeling. In S. Chick, P. J. Sánchez, D. Ferrin, & D. J. Morrice (Eds.), *Proceedings of the 2003 Winter Simulation Conference,* New Orleans, LA (pp. 14-24). Retrieved April 2003, from http://www.informs-sim.org/wscpapers.html

Lendermann, P., Gan, B., & McGinnis, L. (2001, December 9-12). Distributed simulation with incorporated aps procedures for high-fidelity supply chain optimization. In B. A. Peters, J. S. Smith, D. J. Medeiros, & M. W. Rohrer (Eds.), *Proceedings of the Winter Simulation Conference,* Arlington, VA (pp. 805-812). Retrieved April 2003, from http://www.informs-sim.org/wscpapers.html

Linzhang, W., Jiesong, Y., Xiaofeng, Y., Jun, H., Xuandong, L., & Guoliang, Z. (2004). Generating test cases from UML activity diagram based on gray-box method. *Apsec*, 284-291.

Mansour, N., & Brardhi, B. R. (2001). Empirical comparison of regression test selection algorithm. *The Journal of System and Software, 57,* 79-90.

Manta. (n.d.). Retrieved June 12, 2005, from http://manta.cs.vt.edu/cs6204

Offutt, J., & Abdurazik, A. (1999, October). Generating tests from UML specifications. In *Second International Conference on the Unified Modeling Language (UML99)*, Fort Collins, CO.

Orso, A., Shi, N., & Harrold, M. J. (2004, October 31-November 6). Scaling regression testing to large software systems. *SIGSOFT'04/FSE-12,* Newport Beach, CA (pp. 241-251).

Page, H., & Nance, R. (1997, July). Parallel discrete event simulation: A modeling methodological perspective. *ACM Transactions on Modeling and Computer Simulation, 7*(3), 88-93.

Paul, R. J., & Balmer D.W. (1998). *Simulation modelling.* Lund, Sweden: Chartwell-Bratt Student Text Series.

Pezz, M., & Young, M. (2004). Testing object oriented software. In *Proceedings of the 26th International Conference on Software Engineering (ICSE'04).*

Pidd, M. (1998). *Computer simulation in management science* (4th ed.). Chichester, UK: John Wiley & Sons.

Pressman, R. (2005). *Software engineering: A practitioner's approach* (6th ed.). New York: McGraw Hill.

Pretschner, A. (2005, May 15-21). Model based testing. In *Proceedings of ICSE'05* (pp.722-723). St. Louis, MO: ACM.

Ramakrishnan, S., Lee, S., & Wysk, R. (2002, December 8-11). Implementation of a simulation-based control architecture for supply chain interactions. In E. Yücesan, C. H. Chen, J. L. Snowdon, & J. M. Charnes (Eds.), *Proceedings of the Winter Simulation Conference*, San Diego, CA. Retrieved April 2003, from http://www.informs-sim.org/wscpapers.html

Richardson, D. J., O'Malley, O., & Tittle, C. (1989, December). Approaches to specification-based testing. In *Proceedings of ACM SIGSOFT Symposium on Software Testing, Analysis and Verification* (pp. 86-96). New York: ACM Press.

Robinson S. (1999, December 10-13). Three sources of simulation inaccuracy (and how to overcome them). In P. A. Farrington, H. B. Nembhard, D. T. Sturrock, & G. W. Evans (Eds.), *Proceedings of the 1999 Winter Simulation Conference*, Orlando, FL (pp. 1701-1708).

Sadowsk, R. P. (1991). Avoiding the problems and pitfalls in simulation. *Winter Simulation Conference Proceedings of the 23rd Conference on Winter simulation* (pp. 48-55), Phoenix, AZ. Washington, DC: IEEE Computer Society.

Sargent, R. (1998, December 13-16). Verification and validation of simulation models. In D. J. Medeiros, E. F. Watson, J. S. Carson, & M. S. Manivannan (Eds.), *Proceedings of the Winter Simulation Conference*, Washington, DC (pp. 121-130). Retrieved April 2003, from http://www.informs-sim.org/wscpapers.html

Sargent, R. (1999, December 10-13). Validation and verification of simulation models. In P. A. Farrington, H. B. Nembhard, D. T. Sturrock, & G. W. Evans (Eds.), *Proceedings of the Winter Simulation Conference*, Orlando, FL (pp. 39-48).

Sargent, R. (2003, December 7-10). Verification and validation of simulation models. In S. Chick, P. J. Sánchez, D. Ferrin, & D. J. Morrice (Eds). *Proceedings of the Winter Simulation Conference*, New Orleans, LA (pp. 39-48). Retrieved April 2003, from http://www.informs-sim.org/wscpapers.html

Sebesta, R. W. (2003). *Concepts of programming languages* (6th ed.). Addison-Wesley.

Shannon, R. (1998, December 13-16). Introduction to the art and science of simulation. In D. J. Medeiros, E. F. Watson, J. S. Carson, & M. S. Manivannan. *Proceedings of the Winter Simulation Conference*, Washington, DC (pp. 7-14). Retrieved April 2003, from http://www.informs-sim.org/wscpapers.html

Smith, R. (1998, December 13-16). Essential techniques for military modeling & simulation. In D. J. Medeiros, E. F. Watson, J. S. Carson, & M. S. Manivannan. *Proceedings of the Winter Simulation Conference*, Washington, DC (pp. 805-812). Retrieved April 2003, from http://www.informs-sim.org/wscpapers.html

Sommerville, I. (n.d.). *Software engineering* (6th ed.). Upper Saddle River, NJ: Addison-Wesley, Pearson Education.

Wikipedia. (n.d.). Retrieved June 12, 2005, from http://en.wikipedia.org/wiki/Lambda_calculus

Withers, D. (2000, December 10-13). Software engineering best practices applied to the modeling process. In J. A. Joines, R. R. Barton, K. Kang, & P. A. Fishwick (Eds.), *Proceedings of the Winter Simulation Conference,* Orlando, FL (pp. 432-439). Retrieved April 2003, from http://www.informs-sim.org/wscpapers.html

Xu, D., Xu, W., & Nygard K. (2005, July 14-16). A state-based approach to testing aspect-oriented programs. In *Proceedings of the 17th International Conference on Software Engineering and Knowledge Engineering (SEKE'05),* Taiwan. Retrieved April 2004, from http://cs.ndsu.edu/~dxu/publications/SEKE05-xu.pdf

Yilmaz, L. (2001). Automated object-flow testing of dynamic process interaction models. In B. A. Peters, J. S. Smith, D. J. Medeiros, & M. W. Rohrer (Eds.), *Proceedings of the Winter Simulation Conference* (pp. 586-594). Retrieved April 2003, from http://www.informs-sim.org/wscpapers.html

Zammit, J. (2005). *Correct cystem, Web site for information systems engineering.* University of Malta. Retrieved June, 18, 2005, from http://www.cis.um.edu.mt/~jzam/vv.html

Chapter IX

The STECC Framework:
An Architecture for Self-Testable Components

Sami Beydeda, Federal Finance Office, Germany

Abstract

Development of a software system from existing components can surely have various benefits, but can also entail a series of problems. One type of problem is caused by a limited exchange of information between the developer and user of a component. A limited exchange and thereby a lack of information can have various consequences, among them the requirement to test a component prior to its integration into a software system. A lack of information cannot only make testing prior to integration necessary; it can also complicate this task. However, difficulties in testing can be avoided if certain provisions to increase testability are taken beforehand. This article briey describes a new form of improving testability of, particularly commercial, components, the self-testing COTS components (STECC) strategy and explains in detail the STECC framework, which implements the necessary technical architecture to augment Java components with self-testability.

Introduction

A major trend in software engineering is that of component-based development. The underlying idea of component-based development is to use existing components for the construction of a software system and to construct it by integrating them instead of programming the software system from scratch. This idea is neither new in the construction of complex systems in general nor in software engineering in particular. In other, more mature engineering disciplines, such as the construction of electronic devices, it is a usual procedure to use existing components. In software engineering, the use of components in software development was suggested more than 30 years ago (McIlroy, 1968).

The expected benefits of using components in software development and the motivations for component-based development are manifold. Among others, components are expected to improve the success factors of software-development projects, such as quality of the system developed and adherence to time and budget restrictions, similar to development projects in other disciplines. However, software components strongly differ from components such as those used in the construction of electronic devices. Software components generally have much more inherent complexity. Appropriate methods to cope with this complexity still do not exist, which gives an indication of the maturity of this paradigm and of software engineering as a whole. Even if some success is achieved with the use of components, component-based development still has to show its full potential.

As one of the success factors, the use of components was assumed to have positively affected the quality of the software system developed. Components were assumed to have reached a high level of quality in a short period of time, for instance, due to market pressure. Also, software systems consisting of such components were expected to inherit this high level of quality. Unfortunately, experience showed that this assumption does not necessarily hold in practice. One reason is a lack of information (Beydeda & Gruhn, 2003b; Beydeda & Gruhn, 2003c), particularly in the case of commercial components. The provider of a component might not be able to anticipate all possible application contexts in which the component might be used. The same also applies to technical environments in which the component might be embedded. Assumptions in the development of a component concerning, for instance, the application environment might be inaccurate or even wrong and quality assurance conducted by the component provider might not be effective. The component might exhibit failures.

A lack of information can also concern the user of a component. The user might also suffer from such a lack insofar that the component might not be sufficiently documented due to inaccurate or incorrect information from the provider with regards to the required documentation. This obviously can have various adverse effects on development and maintenance of a system using the component. Context-dependent tests by the component provider and insufficient documentation often obligate the component user to test a component prior to its use in the development of a software system. A problem, again due to a lack of information, might be encountered when failures are revealed in such tests. The component user usually has to rely on the component provider to remove the faults causing the failures, which is one of the forms in which the component user's development of a system might depend on the component provider's maintenance of the component. A lack of information might also cause other forms of dependence, introducing risks in the development of a component-based system. Moreover, testing itself might also be affected by a lack of information. For instance, source code is seldom available to the user of a component due to various reasons. The user therefore cannot, for instance, conduct program-based testing, even if required in certain cases. A lack of information thus not only necessitates quality assurance to be conducted by the component user but also complicates it.

This article briey introduces the self-testing COTS components (STECC) method and explains in detail the STECC framework. The STECC method aims to meet the requirements of both the provider and user of a component. On the one hand, the provider of a component usually does not wish to disclose certain information. On the other hand, the user needs to test the component that may require this information. The STECC method does not only benefit the user of a component in that the user can test a component as required; it can also benefit its provider, as self-testability provided by an appropriately augmented component can be an advantage in competition.

The underlying idea of this method is to augment a component with the capabilities of testing tools to support testing tasks carried out by the component user. The STECC method obviates access to certain information by the user, since tasks for which the user might require this information are conducted by a STECC self-testable component itself. This information is not disclosed to the user at all; it is processed by the component in an encapsulated form. Specifically, a STECC self-testable component is capable of generating test cases for program-based testing. Source code as the main input for this kind of testing thereby does not need to be disclosed to the tester.

A component might be used in development of various types of systems with distinct quality requirements. A STECC seft-testable component takes this into account insofar that it does not assume a specific adequacy criterion for its testing, but allows its users to specify arbitrary control ow criteria. This exibility is achieved by the binary search-based test case generation (BINTEST) algorithm (Beydeda and Gruhn, 2003a; Beydeda and Gruhn, 2003d), which, together with certain analysis algorithms, constitutes the core of the STECC method. This exibility requires certain provisions, among them the need to augment the component accordingly by integrating it with the STECC framework. The STECC framework mainly implements the BINTEST algorithm as well as the analysis algorithms required by it.

Basic Terms

Components

In recent years, components and component-based development received much attention, certainly due to the explicit support for software reuse and the abstraction principle, two methods of software development. A large number of scientific articles are published on the subjects of components and component-based development and companies have released several component models, allowing the development of component-based systems. The subjects of components and component-based development, however, are still not mature, as definitions of basic terms, such as that of a component, did not converge. The various definitions are not discussed here. According to Szyperski (1998), one can assume that:

- **Definition 1:** A software component is a unit of composition with contractually specified interfaces and explicit context dependences only. A software component can be deployed independently and is subject to composition by third parties.

A similarity between component-based and object-oriented development is the distinction between components and classes, respectively, and their instances. A component is a static description of its instances, while a class is a static description of corresponding objects. The output and behavior of an instance generally depend on two factors, namely its input and its state. Instances, however, are sometimes assumed to be stateless, such as in Szyperski (1998), who shows various consequences. One of the important consequences is that instances of a component do not differ with respect to their output and behavior, which solely depend on the input. A component-based system thus needs to maintain a single instance of a component. However, this does not mean that it cannot be multithreaded. In practice, however, instances are often implemented statefully, and the instances of a component are distinguished from each other with regard to their state. In some applications, it might be necessary to make an instance persistent, for example, by storing its state in a database. Such an instance exists beyond the termination of the creation process and can be identified by its state.

Figure 1. Metamodel of basic terms

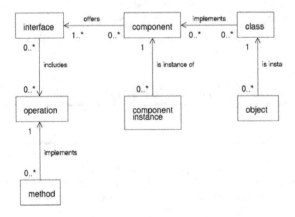

The type of a component is often defined in terms of the interface implemented by it. The component type names all operations of the corresponding interface, the number and types of parameters, and the types of values returned by each operation (Szyperski, 1998). Just as a component can implement several interfaces, it can also be of several types. The operations of a component are accessed through its interfaces and are implemented by its methods. Figure 1 shows a metamodel of the basic terms (Gruhn & Thiel, 2000). Note that the metamodel in Figure 1 also indicates that a component can be implemented according to the object-oriented paradigm. This is, however, not an obligation (Szyperski).

Enterprise JavaBeans

One of the component models widely used in practice is the one following the Enterprise JavaBeans specification released by Sun Microsystems. The Enterprise JavaBeans specification defines the Enterprise JavaBeans architecture for the development of distributed, component-based client-server systems. The initial specification of Enterprise JavaBeans was released in 1998. Since then, the specification was developed further, and several extensions were added to the initial release. In the following, the Enterprise JavaBeans component model and framework are explained with respect to release 2.1 of the specification, which can be found in DeMichiel (2002). Other examples of component models are the CORBA component model proposed by the Object Management Group (2002) and the component object model and related technologies proposed by the Microsoft Corporation (1995).

One of the component types defined by the Enterprise JavaBeans specification is the session bean. The primary purpose of a session bean is to encapsulate business logic. A session bean is usually nonpersistent, that is, its data is not stored in a database and is lost after the session is terminated. Furthermore, multiple clients cannot access a session bean simultaneously. A session bean provides its services through specific interfaces, depending on the type of client and service. Clients that can access a session bean can either be local or remote, and the provided services can be classified as either being related to the lifecycle of a particular session bean or the business logic implemented. In this context, the main distinction between a local and a remote client is that local clients execute in the same Java virtual machine, and that the location of the session bean is not transparent for local clients, whereas a remote client can execute in a different Java virtual machine and thus on a different host, so the location of the session bean is transparent.

Figure 2 shows two session beans embedded in the component framework as specified by the Enterprise JavaBeans specification, which defines a component framework consisting of servers and containers to support the component model. A server is generally responsible for providing technical services such as persistence, transactions, and security, whereas a container provides services related to management of the component lifecycle. An enterprise bean is encapsulated in a container, which is in turn embedded in a server. The Enterprise JavaBeans specification, however, does not clearly separate containers from servers and both terms are often used interchangeably. The component framework consisting of a server and a container is transparent to the user

Figure 2. Client view of session beans deployed in a container

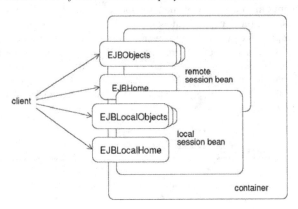

of an enterprise bean, though. Initially, a client intending to access the business logic implemented by a certain session bean needs to create a reference to it. The appropriate methods can be invoked through the home interface of the session bean, which in Figure 2 is called EJBLocalHome and EJBHome for the local session bean and remote session bean, respectively. Note that technically a session bean can implement both types of interfaces; however, this is rarely the case. Having obtained a reference to the session bean, methods implementing the business logic can be invoked through the local interface and remote interface. In Figure 2, these interfaces are called EJBLocalObjects and EJBObjects.

The second component type defined by the Enterprise JavaBeans specification is the entity bean. An entity bean represents a business object. In contrast to session beans, an entity bean can be persistent, that is, data encapsulated in an entity bean can be stored in a database and can thus exist beyond the termination of the component-based system and component framework. Database entries are mapped to entity beans through primary keys, which are unique identifiers of entity beans. Another distinction from a session bean is that several clients can access an entity bean. As several clients might intend to modify data simultaneously, transaction techniques might be required to ensure the consistency of the data. Such techniques, however, are implemented by the server hosting the container of the corresponding entity bean and do not need to be implemented by the entity bean itself. An entity bean provides similar interfaces to those of a session bean, thus Figure 2 is also valid with a minor adaptation for entity beans.

One of the new features in release 2.0 of the Enterprise JavaBeans specification is a third component type called a message-driven bean. However, for an explanation of this third type of component the reader is invited to study the corresponding specification.

Commercial-Off-the-Shelf (COTS) Components

In comparison to other reusable software entities, one of the distinguishing features of components, particularly those referred to as commercial-off-the-shelf (COTS) components, are their market-related aspects. According to Basili and Boehm (2001), a COTS component has the following characteristics:

- The buyer has no access to the source code.
- The vendor controls its development.
- It has a nontrivial installed base.

The term COTS component is, however, not uniquely defined, as a discussion of the various definitions in Morisio and Torchiano (2002) shows, and the above characteristics do not exist to the same degree for each commercially available component. Among other factors, the existence of the above characteristics depends on the organizational relation between the vendor of the component and its buyer. The organizational relations between the component provider and component user can be manifold, and a component can be associated with one of following categories (Carney & Long, 2000):

- **Independent commercial item:** A component can be an independent commercial item that can be purchased from a possibly anonymous component market. This category of components is referred to as COTS components in the following.
- **Special version of commercial item:** A component can also be a special version of a commercial component. The component user might contract with the component provider to produce a customized version of a commercially available component.
- **Component produced by contract:** Depending on the organizational relation, a component can also be produced by contract. The component user can ask the component provider to develop a component for an agreed upon fee.
- **Existing component from external sources:** A component can originate from an external source without being commercial. The component provider and component user might reside in different organizations, but the component could be one developed under a joint contract.
- **Component produced in-house:** Finally, a component can also be developed for a specific project. The component provider and component user might be involved in the same project or the same person can even play the roles of the component provider and component user.

This chapter focuses on COTS components. If not otherwise noted, components are assumed to have the above characteristics of COTS components, and the two terms component and COTS component are used interchangeably. Regarding the organizational relation between the provider and user of a component, components are assumed to be independent commercial items.

Overall Strategy of the STECC Method

Misperceptions in Quality Assurance of Components

It is often argued that the quality of components will improve under certain conditions and less quality assurance actions will be required in the development of a component-based system to satisfy given quality requirements. The conditions under which the quality of components will improve according to this argumentation include (Szyperski, 1998):

- **Frequent reuse:** Reuse is generally supposed to have a positive effect on the quality of the software entity reused. A frequently reused component is expected to improve in quality, since frequent reuse is expected to reveal failures and other adverse behaviors that possibly would not be revealed when, instead of being reused, the component would be redeveloped and tested from scratch.

- **Competitive markets:** Competitive markets are also supposed to contribute to improvements of component quality, since quality is expected to become a success factor in such markets.

One of the implications of this argumentation described in the literature is that quality assurance actions are considered less important in component-based development than in software development in general. Components are supposed to possess a certain degree of quality, which makes further quality assurance actions obsolete, and component-based systems are expected to inherit the quality of its single constituents. However, these arguments do not take into account the following:

Firstly, the quality of an entity, in this context a component, is usually defined with regard to stated or implied needs. In this context, stated and implied needs refer to those of a particular component user. The needs of one component user might contradict those of another user and might also change after some time. Thus, even if the quality of a component might be sufficient according to the needs of a particular component user, additional quality assurance action might nevertheless be necessary prior to use by the same component user due to a change in requirements and by another component user due to a difference the needs.

Secondly, competitive markets also do not necessarily disburden the component user from conducting quality assurance actions. The needs of the component users might not be entirely known to the component provider so that the step taken by the component provider in order to increase quality might not be successful. Such problems are particularly caused by a limited exchange of information between the component provider and component user.

Limited exchange of information between the roles of the component provider and component user does not only limit the positive effect of competitive markets on component quality. It also concerns several other issues in developing components and component-based systems and can even be considered as the main factor in distinguishing testing components from testing software in general.

Organization Relation as an Obstacle for Information Exchange

Various factors impact the exchange of information between the component provider and component user. The information requested by one role and delivered by the other can differ in various aspects, if it is delivered at all. It can differ syntactically insofar that it is, for instance, delivered in the wrong representation, and it can also differ semantically in that it is, for instance, not on the required abstraction level. The differences might be due to various factors, one of them being the organizational relation between the two roles. With respect to the organizational relation, a component can be associated with one of the categories: independent commercial item, special version of commercial item, component produced by contract, existing component from external sources, and component produced in-house. Information exchange between the component provider and component user depends, as one factor, on the category into which the component falls regarding the organizational relation between the two roles.

At one end of the spectrum, the component can be a commercial item. In this case, the quality of information exchange between component provider and component user is often the worst in comparison to the other cases. There are various reasons for this, such as the fact that the component provider might not know the component user due to an anonymous market. In such a case, the component provider can base development of the component on assumptions and deliver only information to the component user that is supposedly needed. Furthermore, several component users might use the component, and the component provider might decide to only consider the needs of the majority of them. The specific needs of a single component user might then be ignored. Finally, the component provider might not disclose detailed technical information even if needed by the component user to avoid another component provider receiving this information. The component provider might decide to only make information available that respects intellectual property and retains competitive advantage.

At the other end of the spectrum, the component can be produced in-house. The quality of information exchange between component provider and component user then is often the best in comparison to the other cases. One of the reasons for this can be the fact that the component is developed in the same project in which it is assembled. The exchange of information in both directions, from the component provider to the component user and in the reverse direction, can take place without any incompatibility in the requested and delivered information. Furthermore, the component provider and component user are roles, so the same person can even play them if the component is used in the same project in which it is developed. Information would not even need to be exchanged in that case.

STECC Approach to Tackle a Lack of Information

A lack of information might require the testing of a component by its user prior to its integration into a system, and might significantly complicate this task at the same time. The component user might not possess the required information for this task. Theoretically, the component user can test a component by making certain assumptions and approximating the information required. Such assumptions, however, are often too imprecise to be useful. For instance, control-dependence information can be approximated in safety-critical application contexts by conservatively assuming that every component raises an exception, which is obviously too imprecise and entails a higher testing effort than necessary (Harrold, 2000; Harrold, Liang, & Sinha, 1999).

Even though source code is often claimed to be required for testing purposes, it is not actually required by itself for testing purposes. Rather, it often acts as the source of other information, for example, with regards to control-dependence. Instead of making source code available to allow the generation of such information, the required information can also be delivered directly to the component user, obviating source code access. This type of information is often referred to as metainformation (Orso, Harrold, & Rosenblum, 2000). Even though the required information might already be available from testing activities, the component provider might still not deliver this information to the component user. One reason may be that detailed and sensitive information, including parts of the source code, may be deduced from it, depending on the granularity of the metainformation. Therefore, there is a natural boundary limiting the level of detail of the information that can be delivered to the user. For some application contexts, however, the level of detail might be insufficient and the component user might not be able to test the component according to certain quality requirements.

The underlying strategy of the STECC method differs from those discussed so far. Instead of providing the component user with information required for testing, component user tests are explicitly supported by the component. The underlying strategy of the method is to augment a component with functionality specific to testing tools. A component possessing such functionality is capable of testing its own methods by conducting some or all activities of the component user's testing processes; it is thus self-testing. Self-testability does not obviate the generation of detailed technical information. In fact, this information is generated by the component itself at runtime and is internally used in an encapsulated manner. The generated information is transparent to the component user and can thus be more detailed than in the above case. Consequently, tests carried out by the component user through the self-testing capability can be more thorough than when using metainformation. Self-testability allows the component user to conduct tests and does not require the component provider to disclose source code or other detailed technical information. It thereby meets the demands of both parties. The overall objective of the STECC method is to provide the component provider and component user the necessary means to enhance a component with this capability and to use it for program-based testing.

Table 1. Typical activities in testing processes and their support by the STECC method

	STECC method supported	Component user's responsibility
Test-plan definition	+	+
Test-case generation	+	-
Test-driver and stub generation	+/-	+
Test execution	+	-
Test evaluation	-	+

Support of Typical Testing Activities

The STECC method supports most of the typical testing activities conducted by the component user, as shown by Table 1. In particular, typical testing activities are impacted as follows:

- **Test-plan definition:** Some decisions usually made during the definition of a test plan are addressed by STECC method conventions. Such decisions concern the target component model and framework. The STECC method technically requires that the component under consideration is a Java component. Furthermore, the decisions taken beforehand also encompass the type of adequacy criteria that measure testing progress. Test cases are generated and testing progress is measured with respect to a control-flow criterion, which can be chosen freely. The component user can specify the control-flow criterion according to the quality requirements of the application context.

- **Test-case generation:** The STECC method includes a test-case generation algorithm. Generation of test cases, particularly according to program-based adequacy criteria, is an integral constituent of self-testability as assumed by the STECC method. Test-case generation is one of the important tasks affected by a lack of information, since a lack of source code strongly hinders generation of test cases by the component user. The task of test-case generation is conducted in the context of the STECC method by the binary search-based test-case generation (BINTEST) algorithm and its auxiliary analysis algorithms.

- **Test-driver and stub generation:** The component user does not need to generate test drivers for testing methods of a component. The STECC framework, which technically supports the STECC method, provides the required test drivers. Stubs, however, might be necessary if the method to be tested needs to invoke methods of absent components. A component can often be embedded in a wide variety of application contexts, so the specific application context can often not be anticipated. The component user either needs to provide the specific stubs or embed the component in the target application context.

- **Test execution:** The execution of methods under consideration with generated test cases is also conducted by the STECC method. The BINTEST algorithm is a dynamic test-case generation algorithm. It approaches appropriate test cases by iteratively identifying a potential test case and executing the method under test to determine its suitability. A useful consequence of this is that the component user does not need to execute tests, since they are already executed during the identification of the respective test cases.

- **Test evaluation:** The evaluation of tests is not conducted by the STECC method due to the oracle problem. Even if it might be possible to use certain heuristics for test evaluation purposes, the STECC method does not cover this activity and expected outputs and behaviors are not identified in test-case generation. Thus, the component user needs to act as test oracle by determining expected output and behavior and comparing them with the observations.

The two activities entirely supported by the STECC method are those of test-case generation and test execution. Both activities are supported by the BINTEST algorithm, which is therefore also referred to as the core of the STECC method.

Example: The CartJB Component

The STECC framework is explained in the following using a simple scenario taken from Sun Microsystems (2001). The scenario shows how a component, the CartEJB component, can be augmented with STECC self-testability and how self-testability can be used for testing this component during development of a component-based system. The CartEJB component is treated as a commercial component in this scenario. The component is developed and augmented accordingly by a company and is delivered to a customer without source code and detailed technical information. Rather, the company delivers a jar-file containing interfaces and classes in compiled form, that is, their class-files.

Even though additional information concerning the implementation of the component can be obtained in this scenario, these possible information sources are not explored, as they are specific to the Java programming language and to the Enterprise JavaBeans component model. Such possible information sources are, for instance:

- **Source decompiler:** A class-file can often be decompiled using a Java decompiler and its source code be obtained (Nolan, 1998).
- **Source-deployment descriptor:** The jar-file generated by the component provider usually also includes a XML deployment descriptor that can also provide relevant information.
- **Source reflection:** An EJB component can also provide information by reflection through its remote interface.

In terms of the various roles defined in Enterprise JavaBeans Specification (DeMichiel, 2002), the company acts as "Enterprise bean provider" and the customer as "application assembler." The company performs the Enterprise bean provider role, as the main task of the company is the development of the CartEJB component. The customer conducts the integration of that component with other software, thus the customer plays the role of the application assembler. Both parties can also assume other roles, but these possibilities are not considered, as they are not relevant for this scenario. The impact of the STECC framework is restricted to the development of a component and its integration with other software; both are typical tasks of the Enterprise bean provider and application assembler, respectively. We assume in the following that the company, that is, the component provider, finished the development of the CartEJB component and that it proceeds with augmenting the component with self-testability according to the STECC method.

Figure 3. Bean class of the CartEJB component

```
        [...]
        public class CartBean implements SessionBean {
          String customerName;
          String customerId;
          Vector contents;
        [...]
        public void ejbCreate(String person, String id) throws CreateException {
B1        if (person == null) {
B2          throw new CreateException("Null person not allowed.");
          }
          else {
B3          customerName = person;
          }
          Id = id.trim(); // inserted for demonstration purposes
B4        IdVerifier idChecker = new IdVerifier();
          If (idChecker.validate(id)) {
B5          customerId = id;
          }
          else {
B6          throw new CreateException("Invalid id: " + id);
          }
B7        contents = new Vector();
        }
        public void addBook(String title) {
          contents.addElement(title);
        }
        public void removeBook(String title) throws BookException {
          boolean result = contents.removeElement(title);
          If (result == false) {
            throw new BookException(title + " not in cart.");
          }
        }
        [...]
        }
```

Figure 4. Remote home interface of the CartEJB component

```
[...]
public interface CartHome extends EJBHome {
[...]
  Cart create(String person, String id) throws RemoteException,
    CreateException;
}
```

The CartEJB component represents a virtual shopping cart in an online bookstore. A cart, such as the one in this scenario, is associated with a certain customer and contains the books the customer intends to purchase. Specifically, the virtual cart only exists during the period in which the customer is in the online bookstore and does not exist beyond that. The CartEJB component is therefore implemented as a remote stateful-session bean, with the state corresponding to the contents of the modeled cart. A session bean generally consists of the session-bean class, various interfaces, and possibly helper classes. The explanations below do not cover these classes and interfaces entirely; they rather focus on parts which are referenced later. A more thorough explanation of technical details can be found in Sun Microsystems (2001).

- **Session-bean class:** Figure 3 shows an extract from the original session-bean class of the CartEJB component. The bean class of the CartEJB component implements the functionality required to model a cart. It encapsulates three attributes, namely customerName, customerId, and contents. The first and second attribute identify the customer by name and a numeric ID, respectively. The numeric ID is not, as one would expect, stored as a primitive numeric type, such as int, but is stored as a string for accuracy reasons. The third attribute represents the books put in the cart. Additionally, the bean class of the CartEJB component also provides methods to initialize the cart and to access its contents. The CartEJB component implements two ejbCreate methods of which one is depicted in Figure 3. This ejbCreate method sets the initial values to the attributes after performing certain checks. Such a check, for instance, aims at ensuring that the ID passed by the user as a string represents a numeric value. The bean class also implements methods allowing access to the cart's contents, particularly a method to add a book to the cart (addBook) and to remove a book from the cart (removeBook).

- **Remote home interface:** The remote home interface of the CartEJB component can be found in Figure 4. The remote home interface of a bean mainly declares methods related to the management of its lifecycle. In the case of the CartEJB component, its remote home interface particularly includes a create method to set up a CartEJB component with a particular customer name and ID.

- **Remote interface:** Figure 5 shows the remote interface of the CartEJB component. The remote interface of an EJB component usually declares the business methods,

Figure 5. Remote interface of the CartEJB component

```
[...]
public interface Cart extends EJBObject {
  public void addBook(String title) throws
    RemoteException;
  public void removeBook(String title) throws
    BookException, RemoteException;
[...]
}
```

Figure 6. A helper class of the CartEJB component

```
[...]
public class IdVerifier {
[...]
  public boolean validate(String id) {
    boolean result = true;
    for (int i = 0; i < id.length(); i++) {
     if (Character.isDigit(id.charAt(i)) == false)
       result = false;
    }
   return result;
  }
}
```

which in the case of the CartEJB component are mainly methods permitting access to the cart's contents. In our context, we solely consider the method to add a book to the cart (addBook) and the counterpart (removeBook), the method to remove a book.

- **Helper classes:** The CartEJB component also encompasses two helper classes with one of these helper classes depicted in Figure 6. The IdVerifier class is required, as its name suggests, for performing checks to ensure that an ID passed by the user represents a valid numerical value.

Even though the STECC approach is elucidated in the following using the EJB component CartEJB, neither its conceptual foundation nor its implementation, that is, the STECC framework, is tailored to the Enterprise JavaBeans component model. The STECC method conceptually assumes a component as defined in Definition 1 and does not conceptually require properties specific to EJB components. The conceptual foundation of the STECC method abstracts as far as possible from the concrete component model and framework. However, the concrete component model and framework cannot be ignored at a technical level. The STECC framework technically supporting the STECC method assumes that the component conforms to the Enterprise JavaBeans specification.

Figure 7. A component after passing the STECC preprocessing phase

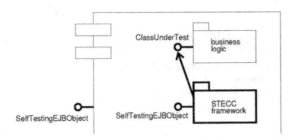

STECC Framework

Architecture

The BINTEST algorithm as well as the analysis algorithms are implemented as part of a framework, called the STECC framework. Figure 7 shows a component after its integration with the STECC framework, after generating a self-testing version of it. The necessary fimodifications in order to generate the self-testing version are drawn bold. This fifigure shows that the component's implementation of business logic and the STECC framework implementing self-testing capability are functionally separated as two distinct sub-systems within the component. The interaction between the two subsystems mainly takes place through interfaces, which are also required for a component user's access to the self-testability features.

The STECC method does not prescribe the phase of the development process in which the STECC preprocessing phase has to be conducted and the STECC framework has to be integrated with the component. These tasks can be carried out prior to delivery to the component user, or alternatively during the development process depending on budget and time constraints. Carrying them out during the development process allows the use of component self-testability also by the component provider. The component provider can use this capability for his or her own testing tasks and therefore does not need to incorporate other analysis and testing tools. The STECC method avoids the above outlined drawbacks by considering self-testability as a capability of a certain component class rather than a functionality of a particular component and giving the component provider the freedom of choice as to when to augment the component with this capability.

Figure 8 shows the UML class diagram of the STECC framework as integrated with the CartEJB component. This class diagram was modeled with the tool Together ControlCenter (Borland Software Corporation, 2003). The explanations in the following solely cover those parts of class diagram relevant for comprehension of the STECC method and its application. Attributes and private methods are hidden for the sake of clarity.

The STECC framework is implemented in the programming language Java and is intended for use with the Enterprise JavaBeans component model. Let C be the self-testing EJB component, M be a method of C testable by C itself, and f be a method invoked during the execution of M. The implementation of the STECC framework consists of the following interfaces and classes:

- **Interface Self-testing EJBObject:** This interface provides access to the self-testing capability and is, having a black-box view to the component such as the component user, the only difference between self-testing and non-self-testing components. It extends the EJBObject interface and needs to be extended itself by the remote interface of C. It declares a single method, called selfTest, which can be invoked by the component user to test M with respect to an arbitrary adequacy criterion.

- **Interface ClassUnderTest:** This interface links C's bean class and the STECC framework with each other in a loose manner. Once implemented by the bean class of C, classes of the STECC framework can reference the bean class through this interface, which avoids close coupling and contributes to a clear separation of C and the STECC framework. The methods declared by this interface are methodUnderTest, toBigDecimal, fromBigDecimal and monotonyBehaviours. The first method is mainly a wrapper; it is invoked by the selfTest method to invoke M by casting its input to the class required, if necessary. The second and third methods are required to map an object to and from a BigDecimal object, that is, a real number. The BINTEST algorithm, based on the corresponding real numbers, carries out operations on objects, such as comparing two objects or computing their midpoint. Finally, monotonyBehaviours gives for method f invoked by M the subsets in its domain on which it is monotone, which are required for the binary search-based test-case generation.

- **Class MonotonyBehaviour:** This abstract class gives the form in which the monotony behavior of a method f has to be specified in order to be usable for the binary search conducted by the BINTEST algorithm. The monotony behavior of f can be specified in two steps: first, extending this class, which includes overwriting method numberOfArgs; second, defining the subsets in f's domain on which it is monotone. Method numberOfArgs gives, as its name suggests, the number of f's arguments, required for tracing purposes. Subsets in f's domain need to be defined by extending abstract class MonotoneSubset. The corresponding objects, that is, the subsets in f's domain, can be retrieved using method getConditions.

- **Class MonotoneSubset:** This abstract class is used to represent a subset in f's domain on which it is monotone. The concrete class representing a particular subset needs to extend this class by inheriting a method called correctMonotonyAss and implementing the method consistentMove. Method consistentMove mainly validates that f's input lies between the least and greatest element of the subset and thereby ensures the monotony of the traversal condition which is composed of f. Class MonotoneSubset furthermore provides correctMonotonyAss validating the monotony assumption.

Figure 8. Class diagram modeling the STECC framework and the CartEJB component

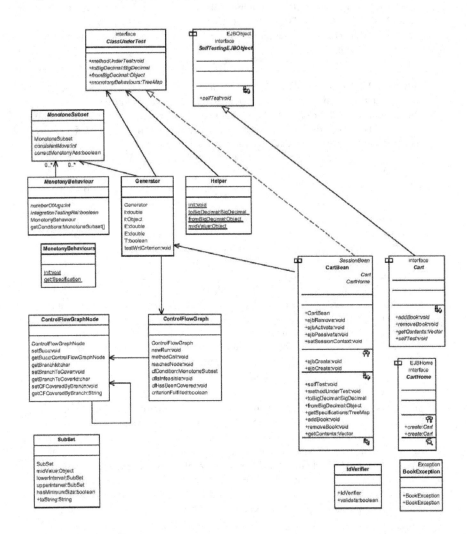

- **Class MonotonyBehaviours:** This class is mainly a container including the monotony behaviors of standard methods. It provides a method called "get," allowing access to the monotony fispecification of a particular method.

- **Class Helper:** This class is similar to class MonotonyBehaviours in that it contains methods that can be applied to standard classes. These methods, toBigDecimal, fromBigDecimal, and midValue, are required by the implementation of the BINTEST algorithm. The first two methods correspond to those explained in the context of interface ClassUnderTest. Here, they are intended for the use in the case of standard classes, whereas in the context of interface ClassUnderTest they are intended for use in the case of specific classes implemented by C. Method midValue gives, as its name suggests, the object between two others.

- **Class Subset:** This class models a subset in M's domain in which an input is searched traversing a particular path. It provides the methods required by the implementation of the BINTEST algorithm: methods midValue, lowerSubset, upperSubset, and hasMinimumSize. The fifirst method determines the element in the middle of the subset modeled. The second and third method bisects the subset and returns the lower and upper half, respectively. The last method hasMinimumSize checks if the subset reached its minimum size, that is, if it is empty.

- **Class ControlFlowGraph:** This class represents the control flow graph of M, which is required, for instance, for the identification of paths to be traversed according to the criteria specified by the tester. This class provides two groups of methods, namely methods to link the execution of M with its control flow graph and methods to select the paths to be traversed according to the control flow criteria passed by the component user. The first group of methods includes method newRun, mainly required for initialization purposes. This group further includes method reachedNode, invoked after entering a basic block to identify the position in the control flow graph, if the corresponding node exists. The second group encompasses method cfCondition identifying a path in the control flow graph whose traversal covers certain segments and defining the necessary conditions for its traversal. Methods cfIsInfeasible and cfHasBeenCovered are two other methods belonging to the second group. They are invoked after detecting that the path considered cannot be covered and after covering it, respectively. Finally, the second group of methods includes criterionFulfilled, indicating whether the control flow criteria specified by the component user are satisfied by the paths traversed.

- **Class ControlFlowGraphNode:** This class models a node in M's control flow graph. It implements mainly methods to set and get attributes, namely setSucc, getSucc, getBranchId, setBranchToCover and getBranchToCoverId. The first two methods are primarily required for creation purposes. Method getBranchId returns the ID of the branches originating from the node modeled, which is, for instance, necessary to compute the control flow segments covered based on the regular expression specification of the criterion. setBranchToCover and getBranchToCoverId are used to mark the branch to be covered and to obtains its ID after its coverage, respectively.

- **Class Generator:** This class can be considered as the main class of the STECC framework, as it implements the BINTEST algorithm. Besides the implementation of the BINTEST algorithm, it also includes methods for tracking the execution of M. Method testWrtCriteria implements the BINTEST algorithm and conducts the test-case generation. Methods I, E, and T are required for tracking M's execution and need to be inserted in the source code of M. Method E is invoked right after the invocation of a method. Method I observes the input of the method invoked. Finally, method T represents the counterpart of method E invoked right after the evaluation of the expression within a condition statement.

STECC Preprocessing Phase

Integration of a component with the STECC framework and thus enhancing it with self-testability is conducted in the context of the STECC method in a preprocessing phase. Two tasks have to be performed during the STECC preprocessing phase (see the following paragraphs).

Firstly, the STECC framework requires that the component under consideration needs to conform to a certain component type. From a technical point-of-view, the component needs to implement a certain interface. The remote interface and the bean class of the EJB component need to implement the interfaces Seft-testingEJBObject and ClassUnderTest, respectively.

Secondly, the methods that the user might wish to test need to be instrumented with tracing statements. These methods can only be those visible to the user and thus appearing in either the remote interface or home interface of the JavaBean. Other methods, particularly those having private access, do not need to be instrumented.

An important factor affecting acceptance of the component provider is the effort required to conduct the above two tasks. Even though a component exhibiting a self-testing capability might be more preferable to the component user than a component not possessing such a feature, the component provider is usually only willing to invest a certain effort to gain such an advantage of other suppliers. The STECC preprocessing phase therefore needs to be automated as much as possible to keep the effort required by the component provider at a minimum.

However, the two tasks cannot be fully automated. The first task in particular requires component-specific information to implement the methods declared by the interfaces, which cannot be automatically deduced from the source code of the component. The methods to be implemented by the bean class of the EJB component consist of selfTest, methodUnderTest, toBigDecimal, fromBigDecimal, and monotonyBehaviours. Method selfTest, as the first method in this list, requires information indicating the methods to be made testable. Furthermore, the initial search subset in the domain of each of these methods needs also to be known. The second method, methodUnderTest, is invoked by selfTest and invokes in turn the method to be tested. The information necessary to implement methodUnderTest concerns the input of the method to be tested, since methodUnderTest might receive the input with which the method to be tested is to be invoked not in the form required and might thus need to transform it appropriately.

Methods toBigDecimal and fromBigDecimal also necessitate component-specific information, which primarily concerns the objects processed during the execution of the method to be tested. The objects processed, or more clearly their classes, need to be known to implement injective functions and their inverses. Finally, monotonyBehaviours also requires component-specific information. This information concerns the methods invoked during the execution of that which is to be tested. The monotony behavior of each of these methods needs to be known to implement monotonyBehaviours, which obviously can only be hardly determined from the source code of the component.

Even though some parts of the information necessary might be obtained on the basis of the component source code, the information necessary cannot be obtained entirely on the basis of this source. The STECC framework, however, provides prototypes of these methods that have to be completed by the component provider. It should also be noted that the component provider solely needs to implement these methods for classes and their methods developed in the context of the component. The corresponding methods for most standard Java classes are already available in classes Helper and MonotonyBehaviours of the STECC framework.

Contrary to the first task, the second task that has to be performed during the STECC preprocessing phase can be automated, even if not entirely. This task consists of inserting tracing code for obtaining information for following purposes:

- Firstly, the tracing code has the objective of delivering the information required for the dynamic generation of the control flow graph of the method to be tested. The information required consists of the basic blocks within the method's source code and an adjacence matrix giving for each basic block those that can be entered next after its traversal. Assuming that the basic blocks are distinguished by unique IDs, successively executing the method and observing the basic blocks traversed can incrementally assemble this information.

- Secondly, another objective of the tracing code is to deliver the information necessary to validate that the inputs of the methods invoked during the execution of the method under test lie in the corresponding subsets of the methods' domains. The information required consists of an ID identifying the method invoked, an ID identifying the invocation and the input passed.

- Thirdly, the objective of the tracing code is also to collect the necessary information to determine the path traversed during the execution of the method under test. The path traversed can be uniquely determined by observing the edges selected by the conditional statements. The edge selected by a conditional statement generally depends on a Boolean expression, and the edge selected can identified by observing the values of these expressions.

The STECC framework, or more clearly the Generator class, offers for this purpose the three aforementioned methods I, E, and T. These methods have to be inserted at the appropriate positions in the source code of the method under test.

- **Method I:** This method has the purpose of observing the value of an arbitrary expression without interfering with its execution. Such an expression might be an argument in a method call or the expression within a conditional statement according to which alternative executed is next chosen. For instance, in the case of f(x) being a method invocation, the tracing statement has to be inserted in this method invocation so that the value of x is observed. It can be achieved by f(I(x)).

- **Method E:** This method has the purpose of identifying the ID of the method invoked, again without interfering with the invocation. This can be achieved by inserting an invocation of E right after the invocation of a method without explicitly giving its ID. In the case of the above example, this can be accomplished by the STECC framework as E("f", f(I(x))).

- **Method T:** This method can be considered to be the counterpart of E for use in the context of conditional statements. Similar to method E, which indicates that a method is invoked, method T indicates that a conditional statement is reached. For instance, an if-statement such as if (x == 2) ... this is accomplished by if (T(1,(x == 2))) ... with 1 being the ID of this conditional statement.

The information necessary to conduct the second task of the STECC preprocessing phase can often be obtained by syntactic analysis of the source code of the method under test as also apparent by the above brief explanation of the three methods. Tools capable of parsing the Java programming language can, for instance, compute this information. Such a tool was generated in the context of the STECC method using the parser generator ANTLR (Parr, 2003). The tool generated parses the bean class of the EJB component and inserts the tracing statements at the appropriate positions. The parser generator, as well as the grammar definition used, is not explained in the following, since they do not necessarily contribute to comprehension of the STECC method. The reader is, however, invited to examine http://www.antlr.org/fieldguide/whitespace, which gives an introduction to translating source code. The first example in Figure 9 shows the remote interface of CartEJB after insertion of selfTest's declaration. The instrumented source code of CartEJB's bean class is given in Figures 10 and 11.

Figure 9. The remote interface of CartEJB after inserting selfTest

```
[...]
public interface Cart extends Seft-testingEJBObject {
  public void addBook(String title) throws RemoteException;
  public void removeBook(String title) throws BookException,
    RemoteException;

[...]
  public void selfTest(String methodUnderTestId, String
    adequacyCriterion) throws RemoteException;

}
```

Figure 10. Instrumented bean class of the CartEJB component (1/2)

```java
public class CartBean implements SessionBean, ClassUnderTest {

    String customerName;
    String customerId;
    Vector contents;

    String state;

    int methodUnderTestId;
    Generator G;

    public void selfTest(int methodUnderTestId, String
      intramethodCriterion, String intermethodCriterion) {
      this.methodUnderTestId = methodUnderTestId;

      G = new Generator(this, intramethodCriterion,
                  intermethodCriterion, 10);
      Interval initialInterval[];
      if (methodUnderTestId == 0) {
         initialInterval = new Interval[2];
         initialInterval[0] = new Interval("a", "u");
         initialInterval[1] = new Interval("", "z");
         G.testWrtCriterion(initialInterval);
      }
    }

    public void methodUnderTest(Object input[]) {
      try {

         if (methodUnderTestId == 0) {
         state = (String) input[1];
           ejbCreate((String) input[0]);

         }
      }
      catch (Exception e) {

    System.out.println(e);
    }
}

public BigDecimal toBigDecimal(Object o) {
  return null;

}

public Object fromBigDecimal(Object o, BigDecimal d) {
  return null;

}
```

Figure 11. Instrumented bean class of the CartEJB component (2/2)

```
public TreeMap getSpecifications() {
  return new TreeMap();
  }

public void ejbCreate(String person, String id) throws CreateException {
  if (G.T(0,G.I(G.E("==",G.I(person)==G.I(null))))) {
    throw new CreateException("Null person not allowed.");
  }
  else {
    customerName = person;
  }

  G.I(id);
  id = G.E("trim", id.trim());
  IdVerifier idChecker = new IdVerifier();
  if (G.T(1,G.I(G.E("validate",idChecker.validate(G.I(id)))))) {
    customerId = id;
  }
  else {
    throw new CreateException("Invalid id: " + id);
  }

  contents = new Vector();

}

[...]

}
```

Note that the STECC framework does not assume a specific component model, even though in Figures 9, 10, and 11, the component under consideration is an EJB type component. The assumption made by the STECC framework is that the component is implemented using the Java programming language. The integration of a component with the STECC framework does not require, for instance, interfaces specific to certain component models. Thus, a regular Java class can also be considered in this context as a component.

Access to the Self-Testing Capability

According to the STECC method, a self-testing component conforms to a certain type, which technically means that it implements a certain interface. The self-testing capability of a component can be accessed through a single method, called selfTest, which implements parts of the required functionality and invokes methods of the STECC

Figure 12. Client for the access of the self-testing feature

```
[...]
public class CartClient {
  public static void main(String[] args) {
    try {
    Context initial = new InitialContext();
    Object objref = initial.lookup("java:comp/env/ejb/SimpleCart");
    CartHome home = (CartHome) PortableRemoteObject.narrow(objref,
      CartHome.class);
    Cart shoppingCart = home.create("Duke DeEarl","123");
    shoppingCart.selfTest(0, "..");
    shoppingCart.remove();
    System.exit(0);
  } catch (Exception ex) {
    System.err.println("Caught an unexpected exception!");
    ex.printStackTrace();
    System.exit(1);
  }
 }
}
```

Figure 13. Output produced by selfTest method

```
[STECC] Input: (k, =)
[STECC] Covered: bc (bc, )
[STECC] Input: (a, =)
[STECC] Covered: bd (bd, )
[STECC] Input: (k, k)
[STECC] Covered: ac (ac, ) [...]
[STECC] Input: (a, a)
[STECC] Covered: ad (ad, )
[STECC] #Test cases: 4, #Iterations: 1862
```

framework transparently to the component user. This method is invoked with the following two arguments:

- **Argument methodUnderTestId:** The first argument specifies the method to be tested by its ID, which needs to be known by both parties.
- **Argument adequacyCriterion:** The second argument specifies the adequacy criterion according to which the method under consideration is to be tested.

A task that the component user has to conduct is the implementation of a client invoking method selfTest. The client, which might also be that implemented by the component user to access business logic, only needs to invoke this method and can thus have a single

Table 2. Comparison between the STECC method and testable beans approach

	STECC approach	Testable beans approach
Test-case generation	+	-
Test observation	-	+

line of self-testability specific code. Thus, access to the self-testing feature of a component does not require any further provisions, except the knowledge of which methods provided by a component are self-testing. Once one has the IDs of these methods, they can be tested through method selfTest.

Assume the component user wishes to test the ejbCreate method of CartEJB so that all segments having a length of two edges are traversed. The specification of this criterion in form of a regular expression can be formulated as '..'. The information required for this is the ID of that method, which needs to be defined by the component provider. Let 0 designate the ID of this method. Furthermore, the component user either needs to insert a line of code into the client used to access the business logic implemented or to implement a specific client for executing the self-testing functionality. Assume that the component user decides to implement a specific client, which is shown in Figure 12. After having implemented the client, the component user can invoke method selfTest with the appropriate arguments to test ejbCreate according to the criteria selected. The output produced by the selfTest method is given in Figure 13.

The BINTEST algorithm conducted 1862 iterations to satisfy the criterion specified. The output produced includes the test cases generated together with the segments traversed. Note, that the output has solely an informative purpose insofar that the component user does not need to execute four tests with the test cases generated. The tests were already executed as iterations during test-case generation. Once test cases have been obtained, a comparison of the corresponding results with those expected needs to be conducted by the tester in order to detect potential failures. In the case of a failure, the tester also needs to conduct a debugging phase.

Table 3. Comparison between the STECC method and built-in testing approaches

	STECC approach	Built-in testing approaches, predefined set of test cases	Built-in testing approaches, test-case generation on-demand
Adequacy criterion specification	+	-	-
Storage consumption	+	-	+
Computation time consumption	-	+	-

Related Work

Testable Beans Approach

A lack of information can complicate testing of components in various aspects, and several approaches are proposed to tackle such difficulties. One of these approaches is proposed in Gao Gupta, Gupta, and Shim (2002). It addresses potential difficulties by improving component testability. Component testability depends, besides other factors, on the ability of a component to support test execution and test observation, and can thus be increased by augmenting a component with capabilities that support these tasks. A component augmented with such capabilities is called a testable bean in this context, which indicates, at least technically, the target component model and framework of the approach, namely the Enterprise JavaBeans component model and framework.

One of the difficulties in testing a component is that the component user generally has very limited possibilities of observing the execution of tests. A component usually does not possess the necessary capabilities to allow the component user observation of test execution, and such capabilities cannot be added to the component by the component user, since these capabilities generally require the source code and other detailed information. The necessary provisions thus need to be implemented by the component provider.

A component, in this context an EJB component, needs to satisfy certain requirements and possess certain features in order to become a testable bean:

Firstly, a testable bean is deployable and executable. A testable bean can be used in exactly the same way as a regular component and does not require specific provisions for its operation.

Secondly, a testable bean is traceable. A testable bean possesses certain capabilities that permit the component user to observe its behavior during a test, which would be encapsulated without such capabilities.

Thirdly, a testable bean implements the test interface. A testable bean implements a consistent and well-defined interface which allows access to the capabilities supporting its testing.

Fourthly, a testable bean includes the necessary provisions to interact with external testing tools. The approach suggests functionally separate business logic from the testing-specific logic at an architectural level.

From a technical point of view, the test interface is probably the most obvious difference between a testable bean and a regular component that is visible to the component user. The test interface declares three methods. One of them initializes a test, giving the class and method to be tested, as well as the test case; another method executes the test as initialized; and the last method finally evaluates the test. The methods declared by the test interface and implemented by a testable bean can be used in two possible ways:

Firstly, other tools can use the test interface. For instance, tools in the environment that the testable bean is embedded in can use it. In Gao et al. (2002) and Gao, Zhu, and Shim

(2000), an environment containing two tools, called test agent and tracking agent, is described. The first one triggers the tests, while the second one's main purpose is monitoring.

Secondly, the testable bean itself can also use the test interface. A testable bean can contain built-in test scripts that access the methods declared in the test interface, as necessary. These test scripts, possibly comprising test cases, can initialize tests, execute them, and evaluate the results autonomously.

Built-In Test Approaches

A lack of information cannot only complicate the observation of test execution, but also complicate the generation of test cases. The testable beans approach tackles the difficulties in observing test execution and can also provide support for test-case generation in the form of built-in test scripts. Other authors also suggest built-in testing to support the component user's tests. A component can contain the test cases or possess facilities capable of generating test cases that the component can use to test itself and its own methods. The component user thus does not need to generate test cases, and difficulties that the component user would otherwise face cannot complicate the component user's tests.

A built-in test approach can be found in Wang, King, and Wickburg (1999). According to this approach, a component can operate in two modes, namely in normal mode and maintenance mode. In normal mode, the built-in test capabilities are transparent to the component user, and the component does not differ from other, non-built-in testing-enabled components. In maintenance mode, however, the component user can test the component with the help of its built-in testing features. The component user can invoke the respective methods of the component, which execute the test, evaluate results autonomously, and print out a test summary. The authors describe a generic technical framework for enhancing a component with built-in tests. One of the few assumptions is that the component is implemented as a class. Under this assumption, it is suggested to implement built-in testing by additional methods that either contain the test cases to be used in hardwired form or are capable of generating them. The integral benefit of such an implementation is that the methods for built-in testing can be passed to subclasses by inheritance.

A built-in testing approach is also proposed in Baudry, Hanh, Jezequel, and Traon (2000), Baudry, Hanh, Jezequel, and Traon (2001), Deveaux, Frison, and Jezequel (2001), Jezequel, Deveaux, and Traon (2001), and Traon, Deveaux, and Jezequel (1999). Even though its authors call this approach a self-testing approach, it is referred to as a built-in testing approach for the sake of consistency. The features characterized by those authors as self-testing significantly differ from those characterized as self-testing in the context of the STECC method, and resemble those of the above approach. This approach and that previously explained share several properties. Besides various modes of operation, a component is assumed to be implemented using object-oriented languages, particularly Java. Built-in testing is implemented by additional methods. Each component method that is testable with built-in testing capabilities possesses a testing method as a counterpart that invokes it with predefined arguments. An oracle is implemented by means of a component invariant — method pre- and postconditions. Invariants, pre- and postconditions are determined based on the specification of the component and embedded in the source code of the component by the component provider. The necessary functionality to validate them and other functionality, for example, for tracing and reporting purposes, is implemented by a framework, which technically requires that the component, or more precisely the main class of the component, implements a certain interface. Similarly to the above approach, the built-in testing capability can be passed to subclasses by inheritance. The authors propose to measure test completion by means of fault injection, which is, however, not feasible in this context, since it requires source code access, which the component user does not have. The component user therefore has to assume that the built-in tests are sufficient.

Another built-in test approach, the component+ approach, can be found in Atkinson and Groß (2002) and Hörnstein and Edler (1994). A shortcoming of the previous built-in testing approach is that test cases or a description of their generation need to be stored within the component. This can increase the resource consumption of the component, which, particularly taking into account that the built-in testing capabilities of a component are often required only once for deployment, can be an obstacle for its use. To avoid this shortcoming, the authors define an architecture consisting of three types of components, namely BIT components, testers and handlers. The BIT components are the built-in testing-enabled components. These components implement certain mandatory interfaces. Testers are components which access to the built-in testing capabilities of BIT components through the corresponding interfaces and which contain the test cases in a certain form. In the other approaches, a built-in testing-enabled component also encompasses the functionality of the testers. Here, however, they are separated with the benefit that they can be developed and maintained independently, and that they do not increase the resource requirements of BIT components in the operational environment. Finally, handlers are components in this architecture that do not contribute to testing, but can be required, for instance, to ensure recovery mechanisms in the case of failures.

The presented built-in testing approaches do not restrict the tests that can be conducted insofar that they are not constrained to specification-based testing. Built-in testing approaches which are constrained to specification-based testing, such as those in Edwards (2000, 2001a, 2001b), and Martins, Toyota, and Yanagawa (2001), are not discussed here, since specification-based testing does not necessarily require provisions by the component provider. Assuming a specification is given, the component user can obtain the appropriate test cases and test the component in principle without the component provider's support. Specification-based built-in testing capabilities undoubtedly have the potential of simplifying component user's tests by improving component testability, but the corresponding tasks can usually also be accomplished by the component user.

Note that approaches supporting and facilitating information exchange between the component provider and component user, such as the component metadata, retro-components, reective wrapper, and component test-bench approaches, can also form a basis for built-in testing. Depending on the type of information, it is in principle possible to automatically generate test cases using such information and conduct tests. A respective application of the reective wrapper approach is given in Edwards (2000), Edwards (2001a), and Edwards (2001b).

Relation to the STECC Method

Testable Beans Approach

Both the testable beans approach and the STECC approach can be assigned to the second category of approaches. They both aim at tackling the difficulties that the component user can encounter while testing a component. However, they address different difficulties in testing components and differ in various aspects. The testable-beans approach and the STECC approach differ in the following points:

Firstly, the testable-beans approach supports the testing of component with an emphasis on monitoring test execution. The STECC approach in contrast does not focus on monitoring test execution, even though the STECC framework provides basic capabilities.

Secondly, the testable-beans approach does not cover the generation of test cases. Test cases can be statically incorporated as part of built-in test scripts, but cannot be dynamically changed by the component user. The STECC approach allows generation of test cases according to the needs of the component user.

Objectively, it is not possible to identify one approach as being better or dominating the other. Both approaches have their benefits and one approach can be more appropriate in certain circumstances than the other. Both, however, require specific provisions by the component provider. The component user cannot add them to a component, but, since their existence can be a selection criterion in component evaluation, the component provider needs to carefully choose the approach with which to augment a component.

Built-In Testing Approaches

Similar to the STECC approach, the built-in testing approaches in Atkinson and Groß (2002), Baudry et al. (2000), Baudry et al. (2001), Deveaux et al. (2001), Hörnstein and Edler (1994), Jezequel et al. (2001), Traon et al. (1999), and Wang et al. (1999) can be assigned to the second category of component-testing approaches, taking into account a lack of development-relevant information. Both aim at tackling difficulties in testing components caused by such a lack and the resulting difficulties in test-case generation in particular. The STECC approach has the same objective, so the three approaches can be directly compared to it. A comparison highlights several differences, including the following:

Firstly, the built-in testing approaches explained here are static in that the component user cannot influence the test cases employed in testing. A component which is built-in testing enabled according to one of the explained approaches either contains a predetermined set of test cases or the generation, even if conducted on-demand during runtime, solely depends on parameters which the component user cannot influence. Specifically, the component user cannot specify the adequacy criterion to be used for test-case generation. However, the component user might wish to test all components to be assembled with respect to an unique adequacy criterion. Built-in testing approaches, at least those described, do not allow this. The STECC approach does not have such a restriction. Adequacy criteria, even though constrained to control flow criteria, can be freely specified. Note that this restriction of built-in testing approaches depends on the size of the test-case set used. A large set of test cases generally satisfies more adequacy criteria than a small set, but at the same time increases resource requirements.

Secondly, built-in testing approaches using a predefined test-case set generally require more storage than the STECC approach. Specifically, large components with high inherent complexity might require a large set of test cases for their testing. A large set of test cases obviously requires a substantial amount of storage, which, however, can be difficult to provide taking into account the additional storage required for execution of large components. This is also the case if test cases are stored separately from the component, such as proposed by the component+ approach. In contrast, the STECC method does not require predetermined test cases and does not store the generated test cases.

Thirdly, built-in testing approaches using a predefined test-case set generally require less computation time at the component user's site. In such a case, the computations for test-case generation were already conducted by the component provider and obviously do not have to be repeated by the component user, who thus can save resources, particularly computation time, during testing. Savings in computation time are even increased if the component user needs to conduct tests frequently, for instance due to volatility of the technical environment of the component. Storage and computation time consumption of a built-in testing-enabled component obviously depends on the implementation of the corresponding capabilities, and the component provider needs to decide carefully between the two forms of implementation — predefined test case set or generation on-demand — in order to ensure a reasonable trade-off.

The STECC approach has several benefits that make it more preferable than one of the built-in testing approaches. Except for computation time consumption, the STECC approach dominates the three explained built-in testing approaches and should be the first choice if a component is to be enhanced to facilitate a component user's testing. However, in some circumstances, computation time might be crucial so that built-in testing approaches, particularly those that do not generate test cases on-demand but contain a fixed set of test cases, are more preferable. Such a circumstance might be, as mentioned, one in which the technical environment of the component is volatile.

Conclusion and Future Research

In this chapter, the STECC approach to testing components has been briefly introduced with a detailed explanation of the STECC framework. The STECC framework provides a technical platform for augmenting components developed using the Java programming language such those according to the EJB component model with self-testability.

So far, the STECC method can be used for intracomponent testing, that is, the testing of components in isolation. However, an issue also relevant for the component user is the integration of components. The component user needs usually to carry out integration testing in order to gain confidence that the components used for building a system interact as intended.

Our research in the future will particularly focus on integration testing of STECC self-testable components. We do believe that integration testing can also be conducted as part of the self-testability feature of components. For this purpose, a protocol can be defined among STECC self-testable components so that information required for integration testing can be exchanged in an encapsulated manner, for example, encrypted. So, this would still satisfy the requirements of both the component user and the component provider. The component user can integration test without requiring detailed technical information, which the component provider might not be willing to disclose.

An important issue in the future will concern case studies. From an academic point of view, the STECC approach seems to be very promising for testing COTS components. However, the STECC framework needs to be used and validated in industrial size project in order to assess aspects such as acceptance by practitioners, costs, and benefits.

References

Atkinson, C., & Groß, H. G. (2002). Built-in contract testing in model-driven, component-based development. In *ICSR Workshop on Component-based Development Processes* (LNCS 2319, pp. 1-15). Berlin: Springer Verlag.

Basili, V. R., & Boehm, B. (2001). COTS-based systems top 10 list. *IEEE Computer, 34*(5), 91-93.

Baudry, B., Hanh, V. L., Jezequel, J. M., & Traon, Y. L. (2000). Trustable components: Yet another mutation-based approach. In *Proceedings of the Symposium on Mutation Testing (Mutation)* (pp. 69-76). Retrieved from http://www.irisa.fr/triskell/perso_pro/bbaudry/mutation2000.pdf

Baudry, B., Hanh, V. L., Jezequel, J. M., & Traon, Y. L. (2001). Trustable components: Yet another mutation-based approach. In W. E. Wong (Ed.), *Mutation testing for the new century* (pp. 47-54). Dordrecht: Kluwer Academic Publishers.

Beydeda, S., & Gruhn, V. (2003a). BINTEST — Binary search-based test case generation. In *Proceedings of the Computer Software and Applications Conference (COMPSAC)* (pp. 28-33). Los Alamitos, CA: IEEE Computer Society Press.

Beydeda, S., & Gruhn, V. (2003b). Merging components and testing tools: The self-testing COTS components (STECC) strategy. In *Proceedings of the EUROMICRO Conference Component-based Software Engineering Track (EUROMICRO)* (pp. 107-114). Los Alamitos, CA: IEEE Computer Society Press.

Beydeda, S., & Gruhn, V. (2003c). The self-testing COTS components (STECC) strategy — a new form of improving component testability. In M. H. Hamza (Ed.), *Software Engineering and Applications Conference (SEA)* (pp. 222-227). Anaheim: ACTA Press.

Beydeda, S., & Gruhn, V. (2003d). Test case generation according to the binary search strategy. In *Proceedings of the International Symposium on Computer and Information Sciences (ISCIS)* (LNCS 2869, pp. 1000-1007). Berlin: Springer Verlag.

Borland Software Corporation (2003). *Together ControlCenter*. Retrieved June 2003, from http://www.togethersoft. com

Carney, D. & Long, F. (2000). What do you mean by COTS? Finally, a useful answer. *IEEE Software, 17*(2), 83-86.

DeMichiel, L. G. (2002). *Enterprise javabeans specification, version 2.1* (Technical report). Sun Microsystems. Retrieved from http://java.sun.com/products/ejb/docs.html

Deveaux, D., Frison, P., & Jezequel, J. M. (2001). Increase software trustability with self-testable classes in java. In *Australian Software Engineering Conference (ASWEC)* (pp. 3-11). Los Alamitos, CA: IEEE Computer Society Press.

Edwards, S. (2000). A framework for practical, automated black-box testing of component-based software. In *Proceedings of the International ICSE Workshop on Automated Program Analysis, Testing and Verification* (pp. 106-114). New York: ACM Press.

Edwards, S. H. (2001a). A framework for practical, automated black-box testing of component-based software. *Software Testing, Verification and Reliability, 11*(2), 97-111.

Edwards, S. H. (2001b). Toward reective metadata wrappers for formally specified software components. In *Proceedings of the OOPSLA Workshop Specification and Verification of Component-based Systems (SAVCBS)* (pp. 14-21). New York: ACM Press.

Gao, J., Gupta, K., Gupta, S., & Shim, S. (2002). On building testable software components. In *Proceedings of the COTS-Based Software Systems (ICCBCC)* (LNCS 2255, pp. 108-121). Berlin: Springer Verlag.

Gao, J., Zhu, E. Y., & Shim, S. (2000). Monitoring software components and component-based software. In *Proceedings of the Computer Software and Applications Conference (COMPSAC)* (pp. 403-412). Los Alamitos, CA: IEEE Computer Society Press.

Gruhn, V., & Thiel, A. (2000). *Komponentenmodelle: DCOM, JavaBeans, Enterprise JavaBeans, CORBA*. München: Addison-Wesley.

Harrold, M. J. (2000). Testing: A roadmap. In *The Future of Software Engineering, Special Volume of the Proceedings of the International Conference on Software Engineering (ICSE)* (pp. 63-72). New York: ACM Press.

Harrold, M. J., Liang, D., & Sinha, S. (1999). An approach to analyzing and testing component-based systems. In *Proceedings of the International ICSE Workshop Testing Distributed Component-based Systems*. Retrieved from http://www-static.cc.gatech.edu/aristolte/Publications/Papers/icse99-workshop.pdf

Hörnstein, J., & Edler, H. (1994). Test reuse in cbse using built-in tests. In *Proceedings of the Workshop on Component-based Software Engineering, Composing systems from components, 2002*. Retrieved from http://www.idt.mdh.se/~icc/cbse-ecbs2002/Jonas-Hornstein.pdf

Jezequel, J. M., Deveaux, D., & Traon, Y. L. (2001). Reliable objects: Lightweight testing for oo languages. *IEEE Software, 18*(4), 76-83.

Martins, E., Toyota, C. M., & Yanagawa, R. L. (2001). Constructing self-testable software components. In *Proceedings of the International Conference on Dependable Systems and Networks (DSN)* (pp. 151-160). Los Alamitos, CA: IEEE Computer Society Press.

McIlroy, M. D. (1968, October 7-11). Mass produced software components. In P. Naur & B. Randell (Eds.), *Software Engineering: Report of a Conference Sponsored by the NATO Science Committee, Garmisch, Germany*, NATO, Scientific Affairs Division, Brussels.

Microsoft Corporation. (1995). *The component object model specification*. Retrieved July 2003, from http://www.microsoft.com/COM/resources/COM1598D.ZIP

Morisio, M., & Torchiano, M. (2002). Definition and classification of COTS: A proposal. In *Proceedings of the COTS-Based Software Systems (ICCBSS)* (LNCS 2255, pp. 165-175). Berlin: Springer Verlag.

Nolan, G. (1998). *Decompiling Java*. McGraw-Hill.

Object Management Group (2002). *Corba components*. Retrieved June 2003, from http://www.omg.org/cgi-bin/doc? formal/02-06-65.pdf

Orso, A., Harrold, M. J., & Rosenblum, D. (2000). Component metadata for software engineering tasks. In *International Workshop on Engineering Distributed Objects (EDO)* (LNCS 1999, pp. 129-144). Berlin: Springer Verlag.

Parr, T. (2003). *ANTLR website*. Retrieved May 2003, from http://www.antlr.org

Sun Microsystems (2001). *The J2EE tutorial*. Retrieved April 2003, from http://java.sun.com/j2ee/tutorial

Szyperski, C. (1998). *Component software beyond object oriented programming*. New York: Addison-Wesley.

Traon, Y. L., Deveaux, D., & Jezequel, J. M. (1999). Self-testable components: From pragmatic tests to design-to-testability methodology. In *Proceedings of the Technology of Object-oriented Languages and Systems (TOOLS)* (pp. 96-107). Los Alamitos, CA: IEEE Computer Society Press.

Wang, Y., King, G., & Wickburg, H. (1999). A method for built-in tests in component-based software maintenance. In *Proceedings of the European Conference on Software Maintenance and Reengineering (CSMR)* (pp.186-189). Los Alamitos, CA: IEEE Computer Society Press.

Chapter X

Certifying Properties of Programs Using Theorem Provers

J. Santiago Jorge, University of A Coruña, Spain

Víctor M. Gulías, University of A Coruña, Spain

David Cabrero, University of A Coruña, Spain

Abstract

Proving the correctness of a program, even the simplest one, is a complex and expensive task; but, at the same time, it is one of the most important activities for a software engineer. In this chapter, we explore the use of theorem provers to certify properties of software; in particular, two different proof-assistants are used to illustrate the method: Coq and PVS. Starting with a simple pedagogic example, a sort algorithm, we finally reproduce the same approach in a more realistic scenario, a model of a block-allocation algorithm for a video-on-demand server.

Introduction

The difficulty of certifying the correctness of a program makes the process very expensive in the cycle of software development. The most frequent validation method consists of running the target program on a set of selected inputs. Unfortunately, although *testing* can detect some bugs, it does not guarantee the correctness of our software because the input set is generally incomplete (Ghezzi, Jazayeri, & Mandrioli, 1991). Formal methods, on the other hand, are proposed to complement traditional debugging techniques, assuring that some relevant property holds in any execution of the program (Clarke et al., 1996; Gunter & Mitchell, 1996). Through formal methods we understand tools, techniques, or languages that help us to develop certified software. Those methods state that a program is correct with respect to a particular *specification*. Two main techniques are taken into account:

- **Model checking:** Proves that every possible state of the program satisfies a specification
- **Theorem proving:** Derives a proof establishing that the program satisfies a specification

It must be mentioned that formal methods are not intended to provide absolute reliability. The strength of formal methods resides in increasing the reliability (Clarke et al., 1996; Peled, 2001). They assist us in producing quality software by improving our confidence in programs. However, they are not the panacea for detecting software errors. Software verification methods do not guarantee the correctness of actual code, but rather allow the verification of some abstract model of it. In addition, this verification is done with respect to a given specification, which is written manually, and it is sometimes incomplete or may not express accurately the expected program behaviour. Besides, large systems are difficult to study as a whole and therefore, they must be separated into small pieces in order to study each one.

The literature about model checking (Bérard et al., 2001; Clarke, Grumberg, & Peled, 1999; Nielson, Nielson, & Hankin, 1999; Roscoe, 1994) is more prolific than that of theorem proving; however, in the present chapter we explore the use of theorem provers to check particular properties of software. These formal proofs should help us understand programs better. Two approaches are considered:

- **Manual proofs:** We reason directly over the source code, applying techniques like equational reasoning and structural induction. The proof methods are rigorous, though error-prone.
- **Theorem provers:** Besides assisting us in the development of the proofs, they guarantee their correctness, preventing bugs that may be introduced in a hand-made proof.

Theorem provers are usually based on a logic, like first-order logic, higher-order logic, or a version of set theory which provides a framework for the formalization of mathematics. Interactive proof assistants require a human user to give hints to the system. Depending on the degree of automation, significant proof tasks can be performed automatically. Available implementations of generic theorem provers are ACL2 (Kaufmann, Mannolios, & Moore, 2000a, 2000b), *Coq* (Bertot & Casteran, 2004; The Coq Development Team, 2004), HOL (Gordon & Melham, 1993), Isabelle (Paulson,

1990, 1994), LCF (Gordon, Milner, & Wadsworth 1979), *PVS* (Owre, Rushby, & Shankar, 1992; Owre, Shankar, & Rushby, 1995), and so on.

In our study, *Coq* and *PVS* are going to be used as theorem provers. By comparing two theorem provers to each other (and also with handmade proofs), conclusions about their suitability can be stated. *Coq* is a proof tool developed at INRIA-Rocquencourt and ENS-Lyon. It provides a very rich and expressive typed language, a higher-order constructive logic, and the possibility of extracting automatically functional programs from the algorithmic content of the proofs. On the other hand, *PVS* is a verification system built on nearly 20 years experience at SRI. It integrates an expressive specification language and powerful theorem-proving capabilities. *PVS* has been applied successfully to large applications in both academic and industrial settings. However, the proofs presented in this chapter can also be constructed easily with other similar tools.

For the implementation of our algorithms and models, we propose the use of *functional programming* (Bird & Wadler 1988; Hudak, 1989; Paulson, 1996). Functional languages treat computation as the evaluation of mathematical functions rather than the execution of commands, as done in imperative languages. A functional program consists of a set of (possibly recursive) definitions and the system evaluates (reduces) an expression to compute a result value. The choice of using functional languages is due to a powerful mathematical property of this paradigm: *referential transparency*, that assures that equational reasoning — that is, $f x$ *is always* $f x$ — makes sense. As a matter of fact, the mathematical way of proving theorems can be applied to functional programs.

In this chapter, a list-sorting algorithm is firstly used as a running example for proving the correctness of a piece of software. Even though this is a simple pedagogic example, some interesting problems arise when proving properties of an actual implementation. As concrete programming language, we choose the functional language *Objective Caml* (Leroy et al., 2004; Weis & Leory, 1999) due to its wide coverage in the research and academic environments. Then, we reproduce the same approach in a more realistic scenario, a model of a block allocation algorithm for a video-on-demand server (Gulías, Barreiro, & Freire, 2005), developed using the concurrent functional language *Erlang* (Armstrong, Virding, Wikström, & Williams, 1996)

Theorem Proofs

Before proving the correctness of a piece of software, we have to specify its algorithms and the properties that define that correctness. Afterwards, a formal proof will be developed to verify whether those properties hold or not.

As said before, a classic sorting algorithm is chosen as our running example. The implementation in the functional language *Objective Caml* is done using an auxiliary function ins. Given a relation le, an element x of a generic type 'a and a list of elements with appropriate type, ordered with respect to the relation le, the function ins returns a new list where the new element x has been placed in the right place, according to the relation le.

```
(* ins : ('a -> 'a -> bool) -> 'a -> 'a list -> 'a list *)
let rec ins le x = function [] -> [x]                      (* ins_0 *)
                  | y::ys -> if (le x y)  then x::y::ys     (* ins_1 *)
                                          else y::ins le x ys   (* ins_2 *)
```

The definition explores two different cases depending on the structure of the input list. If the input list is empty, the result is trivially a singleton list with the new input element. If the list is not empty, and the new element is less than or equal to the first element of the list, the new element must be at the head of the result; otherwise, the head of the result is the head of the input list and we proceed recursively with the tail of the list.

The sort algorithm is now defined by inserting the elements of the input list into an empty list.

```
(* sort : ('a -> 'a -> bool) -> 'a list -> 'a list *)
let rec sort le = function [] -> []                        (* sort_0 *)
                  | x::xs -> ins le x (sort le xs)          (* sort_1 *)
```

The sorting criterion is defined by a reflexive, antisymmetric, transitive, total-relation, named le. Proving the correctness of sort involves proving two different properties: (a) the result must be an ordered list, and (b) the result is a permutation of the input list. The correctness of the specification is as important as the proof itself. For example, without the second property, the following dummy definition would be erroneously certified as a correct sorting algorithm.

```
let dummy mylist = []
```

As the final step, we should prove whether the properties hold or not, using mathematical tools such as equational reasoning and structural induction (Paulson, 1996). In our example, we start proving the first property: Given a total order le, and a finite list l, it holds that the result of sort le l is an ordered list. To state the property, we use the predicate ord, which expresses that the elements of a list are ordered under the relation le.

```
(* ord : ('a -> 'a -> bool) -> 'a list -> bool *)
let rec ord le = function [] -> true                       (* ord_0 *)
                  | [x] -> true                             (* ord_1 *)
                  | x::y::ys -> (le x y) && ord le (y::ys)  (* ord_2 *)
```

Hence, the property to certify is stated as:

*   **Lemma 1:** *For every finite list* l, *every relation* le *and every element* x *of appropriate type:*

    ord le l $\Rightarrow$ ord le (ins le x l)

    Proof: By structural induction on l.

    Base case: l = [].

    ord le (ins le x [])
    = ord le [x]   { (1) by definition of ins_0 (left to right) }
    = true   { (2) by definition of ord_1 (left to right) }

The equality has been proved starting with one expression and replacing "equals by equals" until the other has been achieved. Each step has been justified unfolding a definition; in other cases, we may apply a previously proved property, the induction hypothesis, and so on.

Induction step: l = y::ys. The induction hypothesis is ord le (ins le x ys). There are two alternatives:

1. le x y.

    ord le (ins le x (y::ys))
    = ord le (x::y::ys)   {(1) by definition of ins_1 (left to right)}
    = le x y $\wedge$ ord le (y::ys)   {(2) by definition of ord_2 (left to right)}
    = ord le (y::ys)   {(3) by case analysis le x y}
    = true   {(4) by hypothesis}

2. not (le x y) $\Rightarrow$ le y x. We take into account three different sub-cases:

    a.   ys = [].

        ord le (ins le x (y::[]))
        = ord le (y::ins le x [])   {(1) by definition of ins_2 (left to right)}

= ord le (y::[x])   {(2) by definition of ins_0 (left to right)}

= le y x ∧ ord le [x]   {(3) by definition of ord_2 (left to right)}

= ord le [x]   {(4) by case analysis le y x}

= true   {(5) by definition of ord_1 (left to right)}

b.   ys = z::zs ∧ le x z.

ord le (ins le x (y::z::zs))

= ord le (y::ins le x (z::zs))   {(1) by definition of ins_2 (left to right)}

= ord le (y::x::z::zs)   {(2) by definition of ins_1 (left to right)}

= le y x ∧ ord le (x::z::zs)   {(3) by definition of ord_2 (left to right)}

= ord le (x::z::zs)   {(4) by case analysis le y x}

= ord le (ins le x (z::zs))   {(5) by definition of ins_1 (right to left)}

= true   {(6) by induction hypothesis}

c.   ys = z::zs ∧ not (le x z).

ord le (ins le x (y::z::zs))

= ord le (y::ins le x (z::zs))   {(1) def. of ins_2 (left to right)}

= ord le (y::z::ins le x zs)   {(2) def. of ins_2 (left to right)}

= le y z ∧ ord le (z::ins le x zs)   {(3) def. of ord_2 (left to right)}

= ord le (z::ins le x zs)   {(4) hypoth. ord le (y::z::zs)}

= ord le (ins le x (z::zs))   {(5) def. of ins_2 (right to left)}

= true   {(6) by induction hypothesis}

The proof of the law ends here.   *Q.E.D.*

This lemma can be used now to demonstrate new properties, as shown in the following theorem.

- **Theorem 1:** *For every finite list l,*

  ord le (sort le l)

Proof: By structural induction on l.

Base Case: l = [].

ord le (sort le [])

= ord le [] $\{(1)$ by definition of sort_0 (left to right)$\}$

= true $\{(2)$ by definition of ord.0 (left to right)$\}$

Induction step: l = x::xs. The induction hypothesis is sort le xs.

ord le (sort le (x::xs))

= ord le (ins le x (sort le xs)) $\{(1)$ by definition of sort_1 (left to right)$\}$

= true $\{(2)$ by lemma 1 and by induction hypothesis$\}$

So, it has been stated that the program sort returns an ordered list.   *Q.E.D.*

To complete the certification, we should demonstrate the second property: sort returns a permutation of the input list. We could provide the definition of *permutation* of a list and show that the output of sort is a permutation of the input list. However, we can also show that the input and output of sort are the same *multiset* (see chapter 6 of Paulson, 1996). In this case, we define count as that which returns the number of occurrences of an element w in a list l.

```
(* val count : 'a -> 'a list -> int *)
let rec count w = function [] -> 0                    (* count_0 *)
                  | x::xs -> if w = x then 1 + count w xs    (* count_1 *)
                            else count w xs              (* count_2 *)
```

It is necessary to prove that for every list l and for all element w of appropriate type, it holds that count w l = count w (sort l). This can be proved using the following auxiliary laws.

- **Lemma 2:** *For all finite lists l1 and l2 and all elements w and n of appropriate type:*

count w l1 = count w l2 $\Rightarrow$ count w (cons n l1) = count w (cons n l2)

Proof: By equational reasoning. There are two sub-cases:

○   w = n

      count w (n::l1)

      = 1 + count w l1   {(1) by definition of count_1 (left to right)}

      = 1 + count w l2   {(2) by hypothesis}

      = count w (n::l2)   {(3) by definition of count_1 (right to left)}

○ $w \neq n$. The proof is similar to the previous case.   *Q.E.D.*

- **Lemma 3:** *For every finite list l and all elements w, n and m of appropriate type:*

count w (n::m::l) = count w (m::n::l)

Proof: Equational reasoning using the definition of count easily solves this lemma. There are four sub-cases.   *Q.E.D.*

Now, we prove that ins le n l has the same number of occurrences of every element in n::l.

- **Lemma 4:** *For every finite list l, every relation le and all elements w, n of appropriate type:*

count w (ins le n l) = count w (n::l)

Proof: By structural induction on l:

Base case: l = [].

count w (ins le n [])

= count w [n]   {(1) by definition of ins_0 (left to right)}

Induction step: l = x::xs. There are two sub-cases:

○   le n x

    count w (ins le n (x::xs))

    = count w (n::x::xs)   {(1) by definition of ins_1 (left to right)}

○   not (le n x)

    count w (ins le n (x::xs))

= count w (x::ins le n xs)	{(1) by definition of ins_2 (left to right)}
= count w (x::n::xs)	{(2) by lemma 2 and by induction hypothesis}
= count w (n::x::xs)	{(3) by lemma 3}

This finishes the proof.   Q.E.D.

Finally, we state and prove the main theorem based on previous results.

- **Theorem 2:** *For every finite list l, every relation le and every element w of appropriate type:*

count w (sort le l) = count w l

Proof: By structural induction on l:

Base case: l = [].

count w (sort le [])
= count w []   {(1) by definition of sort_0 (left to right)}

Induction step: l = x::xs.

count w (sort le (x::xs))
= count w (ins le x (sort le xs))   {(1) by definition of sort_1 (left to right)}
= count w (x::sort le xs)   {(2) by lemma 4}
= count w (x::xs)   {(3) by lemma 2 and induction hypothesis}

This ends the certification of sort.   Q.E.D.

Theorem Provers

Manual proving is tedious, costly, and error-prone. By using theorem provers, some of these problems are alleviated. Even though the proof process developed using a proof assistant is similar to the one done with manual proofs, there are two main differences: The proof itself is more or less automatic, and we must include a preamble declaring those functions, types, and so on that we intend to use in the description of the algorithm and its properties.

Using the running example in the previous section, we describe the proof process using both *Coq* and *PVS* as theorem provers. From now on, the code of the examples as well as the user's input will be typed in Arial font whilst the system answer will be in italics.

The Preamble

The first task to be carried out is to declare all the resources required for the proof: types of data, structures, hypotheses, axioms, and so on. Let us see this preamble with the proof assistant *Coq*. For an introduction to *Coq*, refer to Giménez (1998), Huet, Kahn, G., and Paulin-Mohring (2002).

First, we axiomatize a generic type to contain the elements of the lists in our sorting algorithm. In addition, *Coq* demands that the decidability of the equality should be explicitly stated for the new type.

```
Variable A: Set.
Hypothesis eq_dec: forall a b: A, {a=b}+{~a=b}.
```

A total relation order over A, leA, is introduced together with some hypotheses about its properties.

```
Variable leA: A -> A -> Prop.
Hypothesis leA_refl: forall a: A, (leA a a).
Hypothesis leA_trans: forall a b c: A, (leA a b)->(leA b c)->(leA a c).
Hypothesis leA_antisym: forall a b: A, (leA a b)->(leA b a)->a=b.
Hypothesis leA_tot: forall a b: A, (leA a b) \/ (leA b a).
```

We also state that relation leA is decidable from a computational point of view.

```
Hypothesis leA_dec: forall a b: A, {leA a b}+{~(leA a b)}.
```

Finally, we use the predefined definition of lists of the system *Coq*.

```
Inductive list (A : Set):Set := nil : list A | cons : A -> list A -> list A
```

The lists are parametric inductive definitions with two constructors: nil and cons. The former represents the empty list, and the latter takes an element of a generic type A and a list of elements of type A to construct another list of type list A. The lists follow this induction principle:

list_ind : forall (A : Set) (P : list A -> Prop), P nil ->

(forall (a : A) (l : list A), P l -> P (a :: l)) -> forall l : list A, P l

Let us take a look to the same preamble using a different proof assistant, *PVS*. For a tutorial relating to *PVS*, refer to Crow, Owre, Rushby, Shankar, and Srivas (1995). As we previously did with *Coq*, a type A for the elements of a list is introduced.

A: TYPE

There is an equality predicate on each type specified in *PVS*, that is it is possible to decide whether two elements of type A are the same or not. A relation leA over A is introduced. The relation is described as a function that takes two elements of A and it returns a value of built-in type bool.

leA: [A, A -> bool]

It is axiomatized that the relation order leA is total.

leA_refl: AXIOM FORALL (a: A): leA(a, a)

leA_trans: AXIOM FORALL (a, b, c: A): leA(a, b) => leA(b, c) => leA(a, c)

leA_antisym: AXIOM FORALL (a, b: A): leA(a, b) => leA(b, a) => a = b

leA_tot: AXIOM FORALL (a, b: A): leA(a, b) OR leA(b, a)

The predefined definition of lists is used to state the insertion sort algorithm in *PVS*. The list datatype takes a single-type parameter and it has constructors null and cons.

As seen, *PVS* is less demanding than *Coq* regarding the decidability of types and relations defined by the user.

The Algorithm

Following the workflow of the proof, once the preamble is completed the algorithm and the properties that are to be proved should be defined.

The algorithm is first defined in *Coq*. We define the function ins. Definitions by structural induction can be programmed directly through the Fixpoint construct (Giménez, 1998). From the point of view of function definition, this construct is similar to the let rec statement of *Objective Caml*. The body of the function has three alternatives; case analysis is applied on leA_dec a x that returns (left p) if a proof (p: le a x) exists or (right q) if it exists (q: ~(le a x)).

```
Fixpoint ins (a: A) (l: (list A)) {struct l}: (list A) :=
 match l with nil => (cons a l)
          | (cons x xs) => match (leA_dec a x) with (left p) => (cons a l)
                                                    | (right q) => (cons x (ins a xs))
                       end
 end.
```

The function is defined by structural induction on the second argument, list l. This is denoted by {struct l}. In order to be accepted, this argument has to decrease structurally in the recursive calls. It is also possible to define functions in *Coq* by general recursion specifying a well-founded relation that guarantees termination (Giménez, 1998; Bertot & Casteran, 2004).

Now, using ins, the function sort can be defined.

```
Fixpoint sort (l: (list A)) {struct l}: (list A) :=
 match l with nil => nil
          | (cons x xs) => (ins x (sort xs))
 end.
```

On the other hand, in *PVS* the function ins is a recursive declaration that takes an element of type A and a list, and it returns a new list.

```
ins(a: A, l: list[A]): RECURSIVE list[A] =
 CASES l OF null: cons(a, null),
   cons(x, xs): IF leA(a, x) THEN cons(a, l) ELSE cons(x, ins(a, xs)) ENDIF
 ENDCASES
MEASURE length(l)
```

There is a MEASURE function specified in order to guarantee that the definition is total. *PVS* uses the MEASURE to generate a *proof obligation* to ensure that the function is total. This proof obligation is generated as a *type-correctness condition* (TCC). In this case, this clause is used to show that ins terminates by indicating the argument that decreases through recursive calls. The proof of this TCC is postponed until the algorithm and its properties have been specified.

The insertion sort function is defined by using the definition of ins.

```
sort(l: list[A]): RECURSIVE list[A] =
 CASES l OF null: null, cons(x, xs): ins(x, sort(xs)) ENDCASES
 MEASURE length(l)
```

As shown, *Coq* and *PVS* have different approaches to the definition of primitive recursive functions. *Coq* is more restrictive in the sense that it demands to use structural induction on one argument of the function. Although this restriction improves mathematical soundness, it is less flexible than the approach chosen by *PVS*, particularly with complex recursive definitions.

The Properties

After defining the algorithm, the properties to be proved have to be stated as done in the first section.

*   **The result must be an *ordered list*:** In *Coq*, the predicate ord expresses this first property: whether a list is ordered with respect to the predicate leA or not. It is defined inductively. These three clauses are mathematical axioms translated into *Coq*.

```
Inductive ord: (list A) -> Prop :=
 | ord_1 : (ord nil)
 | ord_2 : forall a: A, (ord (cons a nil))
 | ord_3 : forall a b: A, forall l: (list A),
       (ord (cons b l)) -> (leA a b) -> (ord (cons a (cons b l))).
```

In *PVS*, the predicate ord specifies whether a list is ordered or not with respect to a relation order. It is a recursive declaration with a MEASURE clause.

```
ord(l: list[A]): RECURSIVE bool =
   CASES l OF
       null: TRUE,
        cons(x, xs):
            CASES xs OF null: TRUE, cons(y,ys): leA(x,y) AND ord(xs) ENDCASES
       ENDCASES
   MEASURE length(l)
```

*   **The result is a *permutation* of the input list:** As in the manual proof (first section), the second property is specified by means of an auxiliary function count that counts the number of occurrences of an element in a list. Therefore, it is necessary to prove that for every list l and for any element w of appropriate type, it holds that count w l = count w (sort l). In *Coq*, count can be defined using Fixpoint.

```
Fixpoint count (w:A) (l: (list A)) {struct l}: nat :=
match l with nil => O
               | (cons x xs) => match (eq_dec w x) with
                                      | (left p) => (S (count w xs))
                                      | (right q) => (count w xs)
                                end
    end.
```

And the lemma that states the desired property is:

```
Lemma count_sort: forall l: (list A), forall w:A,
  (count w l)=(count w (sort l)).
```

In *PVS*, count is defined as a direct translation of the *Caml* program in first section.

```
count(w: A, l: list[A]): RECURSIVE nat =
  CASES l OF null: 0,
       cons(x, xs): IF w = x THEN 1 + count(w, xs) ELSE count(w, xs) ENDIF
     ENDCASES
    MEASURE length(l)
```

To guarantee termination, the MEASURE clause indicates that the list decreases through recursive calls. With count, we state the desired property:

```
count_sort: THEOREM FORALL (l: list[A]), (w: A):
  count(w, l) = count(w, sort(l))
```

As seen, there are no remarkable differences between *Coq* and *PVS* in the example.

The Proof

As the final step, the properties defined in the previous section have to be proved. A theorem prover assists by applying logical rules during the proof and, in some cases, proving the theorems automatically. Frequently, the theorem prover cannot perform the proof automatically and the problem needs to be decomposed by introducing intermediate lemmas and properties to guide the system, and, even, manually pointing out the logical rules to be applied.

In *Coq*, each property constitutes a goal to be proven. The proof of a property is carried out applying successive tactics that solve the goal or that transform the current goal into new subgoals. The proof ends when no subgoal remains unproved. This methodology, initially developed in the LCF system, allows a total control over the proof. In proof mode, the system displays the current goal below a double line and the hypothesis above the line.

In *PVS*, on the other hand, each proof goal is a *sequent*. A sequent is a formula like:

$$(A_1 \wedge A_2 \wedge \ldots \wedge A_n) \Rightarrow (C_1 \vee C_2 \vee \ldots \vee C_m)$$

where each subformula A_i is an *antecedent*, and each subformula C_i is a *consequent*. It needs to be established that the conjunction of the formulas above the line implies the disjunction of the formulas below the line. A proof starts with no antecedent and a single consequent. This is the initial goal. In *PVS*, a sequent is displayed as:

```
-1   A₁            For example:
 .    .
 .    .
 .    .
-n   Aₙ            ord_ins_aux :
-------            |--------
 1   C₁            [1] FORALL (l: list[A]), (a, b: A):
 .    .                    ord(cons(a,l)) => leA(a,b) => ord(cons(a,ins(b,l)))
 .    .
 .    .
 m   Cₘ
```

PVS waits for a prover command to transform the sequent. A *PVS* proof command can be applied either to a consequent or an antecedent. A command may specify the line number in the current goal where it should be applied.

In both *Coq* and *PVS*, some tactics or commands may split the proof into branches or subgoals. The law is proved when all branches are finished.

The Result of sort must be an Ordered List

Coq The lemma 1, presented in the first section, is split into two simpler ones. The first one, which comprehends the second alternative of that mentioned lemma, is stated as follows:

$$\forall l \in (\textit{listA}), \ \forall a,b \in A, \ \textit{ord}(a :: l) \wedge a <= b \Rightarrow \textit{ord}(a :: \textit{ins } b \ l)$$

The proof engine is entered using Lemma, followed by a name and the conjecture to verify.

```
Lemma ord_ins_aux: forall l: (list A), forall a b: A,
  (ord (cons a l)) -> (leA a b) -> (ord (cons a (ins b l))).
```

```
1 subgoal
 A : Set
 eq_dec : forall a b : A, a = b + a <> b
 leA : A -> A -> Prop
 leA_refl : forall a : A, leA a a
 leA_trans : forall a b c : A, leA a b -> leA b c -> leA a c
 leA_antisym : forall a b : A, leA a b -> leA b a -> a = b
 leA_tot : forall a b : A, leA a b  leA b a
 leA_dec : forall a b : A, {leA a b} + {~ leA a b}
 ============================
   forall (1 : list A) (a b : A), ord (a :: l) -> leA a b -> ord (a :: ins b l)
```

As the function ins is defined by structural recursion on l, it is important to try to prove the property by induction on l. The tactic induction allows the use of the induction scheme associated to lists (list_ind). In general, eliminating a hypothesis with induction applies the corresponding induction scheme. The induction principle generates the cases depending on the definition of the type that the property is applied to. Now, we have two subgoals depending on l being an empty list or not; only the hypotheses of the first subgoal are shown.

```
induction l.
```

```
2 subgoals
    ⋮
  leA_dec : forall a b : A, {leA a b} + {~ leA a b}
 ============================
   forall a b : A, ord (a :: nil) -> leA a b -> ord (a :: ins b nil)
```

```
subgoal 2 is: forall a0 b: A, ord (a0::a::l) -> leA a0 b -> ord (a0::ins b (a::l))
```

intros. 2 subgoals . . . leA_dec : forall a b : A, {leA a b}+{~ leA a b} a : A b : A H : ord (a :: nil) H0 : leA a b ======================== ord (a :: ins b nil) subgoal 2 is: ...	The tactic **intros** transfers universal quantifiers and the premises of the implications, in order, from the current goal to the hypothesis context.
simpl. 2 subgoals . . . ======================== ord (a :: b :: nil) subgoal 2 is: ...	The tactic *simpl* carries out a simplification doing all the possible β-reductions (the β-reduction expresses the idea of function application). Here, the use of this tactic corresponds to the manual step (first section) in which equational reasoning over the definition of ins was realized.
constructor 3. 3 subgoals . . . ======================== ord (b :: nil) subgoal 2 is: leA a b subgoal 3 is: ...	When the current subgoal of the proof is an inductive type, the nth constructor of the type definition is applied by means of the tactic **Constructor** *n*. It is now when the third introduction rule of ord is used. This replaces the actual subgoal with two new ones: ord (b :: nil) and leA a b.

Then, the second introduction rule of ord is applied. This terminates the first subgoal. In order to solve the second subgoal, we just have to notice that the goal is available as hypothesis H0 in the hypothesis context. Such an easy step is solved by an automatic tactic, called auto.

constructor 2. auto.

Figure 1. Derivation tree from the application of case (leA_dec y a) in lemma ord_ins_aux

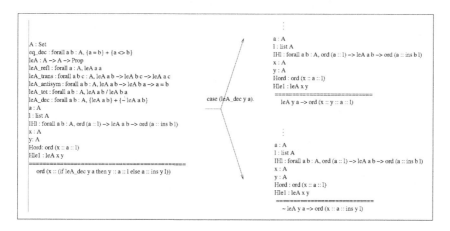

The inductive step follows. First, the universal quantifiers and the premises of the implications are moved into the hypothesis context (the tactic intros allows the identification names as argument). Then, all possible β-reductions are carried out, that is the definition of ins is expanded by using simpl.

intros x y Hord Hle1. simpl.

The resulting subgoal is the root of the proof tree shown in Figure 1. Afterwards, the problem is split into two subcases: leA y a and ~ leA y a. The tactic Case *t* allows the definition of a proof by case analyses on the term t. In Figure 1 the proof subtree generated by the tactic case (leA_dec y a) in this context is displayed.

The first of the two subcases, leA y a, is studied now. The premise of the implication is moved into the hypotheses context and the third introduction rule of ord is applied twice to the current goal.

intros Hle2. constructor 3. constructor 3.

4 subgoals

  ·
  ·
  ·

 IHI : forall a b : A, ord (a :: 1) -> leA a b -> ord (a :: ins b 1)
 x : A
 y : A
 Hord : ord (x :: a :: 1)
 Hle1 : leA x y
 Hle2 : leA y a

```
=============================
```
ord (a :: 1)

subgoal 2 is: leA y a
subgoal 3 is: leA x y
subgoal 4 is: ...

inversion Hord. *4 subgoals* . . *Hord : ord (x :: a :: l)* *Hle1 : leA x y* *Hle2 : leA y a* *H1 : ord (a :: l)* *H3 : leA x a* `============================` *ord (a :: l)* *subgoal 2 is: leA y a* *subgoal 3 is: leA x y* *subgoal 4 is: ...*	One of the premises of the inductive hypothesis ord (x :: a :: l) is the current subgoal. The introduction rules of an inductive type are derived with the tactic inversion. Every possible premise is generated.

Proving the actual subgoal, and the two successive ones, is trivial when using the hypotheses: H1, Hle2 and Hle1.

The second subcase, ~ leA y a, whose proof is similar to the previous alternative, is carried out now. The premise of the implication is moved into the hypotheses context and the third introduction clause of ord is used.

intros Hle2. constructor 3.

2 subgoals

   .

   .

```
=============================
```
ord (a :: ins y l)

subgoal 2 is: leA x a

<table>
<tr><td>

apply IHl.

3 subgoals
.
.
.
=============================
ord (a :: l)

subgoal 2 is: leA a y
subgoal 3 is: leA x a

</td><td>

The current goal may be obtained from the induction hypothesis IHl, provided the truth of ord (a :: l) and leA a b are established. Tactic apply fulfills this piece of reasoning.

</td></tr>
</table>

The first subgoal is solved by the inversion tactic analysing the hypothesis Hord. The second subgoal is achieved with the help of the auxiliary law not_leA_leA which states that $\forall a, b \in A, a \nleq b \Rightarrow b \leq a$ and that is easy to prove. Finally, the last goal is also proved analysing the hypothesis Hord.

inversion Hord; auto.

apply not_leA_leA; auto.

inversion Hord; auto.

Qed.

The demonstration of the law ord_ins_aux ends here. Figure 2 displays the proof tree of this lemma. Now, the same proof built in lemma 1 is developed in *Coq*. It establishes that the insertion of an element in an ordered list returns another ordered list. The previously proved lemma will be used in the proof.

Lemma ord_ins: forall a: A, forall l: (list A), (ord l) -> (ord (ins a l)).

Again, the proof is done by structural induction on l. The base case is solved using the definitions of ins and ord.

induction l. simpl. constructor 2.

1 subgoal

A : Set
eq_dec : forall a b : A, a = b + a <> b
leA : A -> A -> Prop
leA_refl : forall a : A, leA a a

leA_trans : forall a b c : A, leA a b -> leA b c -> leA a c
leA_antisym : forall a b : A, leA a b -> leA b a -> a = b
leA_tot : forall a b : A, leA a b leA b a
leA_dec : forall a b : A, {leA a b} + {~ leA a b}
a : A

Figure 2. Proof tree of the lemma ord_ins_aux developed in Coq

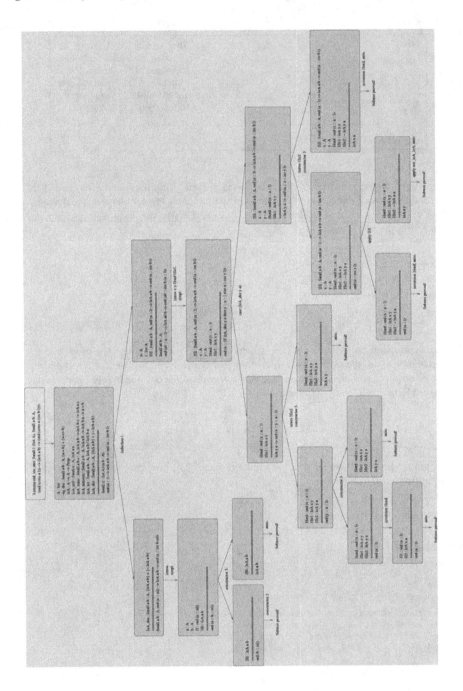

```
a0 : A
l : list A
IHl : ord l -> ord (ins a l)
=============================
  ord (a0 :: l) -> ord (ins a (a0 :: l))
```

In the inductive step, a case analysis is done. The first alternative is demonstrated employing the third clause of ord. The auxiliary law ord_ins_aux and the induction hypothesis are used in the second one. Notice that tactic combination with ";" that is tact1; tact2 consists on the application of tact2 to all the subgoals generated by tact1.

```
intros Hord. simpl. case (leA_dec a a0).
intros Hle. constructor 3; auto.
intros Hle. apply ord_ins_aux; auto. apply not_leA_leA; auto.
Qed.
```

By means of this law and following the same steps used in the manual proof, it is certified that sort returns a sorted list.

```
Theorem ord_sort: forall l: (list A), (ord (sort l)).
induction l.
simpl. constructor 1.
simpl. apply ord_ins. auto.
Qed.
```

So far it has been demonstrated in the proof assistant *Coq* that the result of the insertion sort program is an ordered list: theorem ord_sort.

PVS In *PVS*, the definition of recursive functions must include MEASURE functions in order to guarantee that the definition is total. *PVS* uses MEASURE to generate an obligation to ensure that the function is total. This *proof obligation* is generated as a *type-correctness condition* (TCC). In the case of the previously defined ins function this clause is used to show that ins terminates indicating the argument that decreases through recursive calls.

```
ins_TCC1: OBLIGATION FORALL (x: A, xs: list[A], a: A, l: list[A]):
  l = cons(x, xs) AND NOT leA(a, x) IMPLIES length[A](xs) < length[A](l);
```

This obligation is proved automatically by *PVS*'s standard strategy for proving TCCs. Below is the TCC generated by *PVS* using the MEASURE clause to ensure that the function sort always terminates. This TCC is also proved automatically by *PVS*.

sort_TCC1: OBLIGATION FORALL (x: A, xs: list[A], l: list[A]):
l = cons(x, xs) IMPLIES length[A](xs) < length[A](l);

As happened before, the predicate ord specifies whether a list is ordered or not with respect to a relation order. It is a recursive declaration with a MEASURE clause. The generated TCC is subsumed by sort_TCC1 proof obligation.

Now, we should demonstrate that the insertion of an element in a sorted list returns another sorted list. As has been done before with *Coq*, lemma 1 is split into two simpler ones: ord_ins_aux, and ord_ins.

ord_ins_aux: LEMMA FORALL (l: list[A]), (a, b: A):
  ord(cons(a, l)) => leA(a, b) => ord(cons(a, ins(b, l)))

In this first example, we use mainly basic strategies to keep the proving process as close as possible to the one performed in *Coq*. The initial goal is ord_ins_aux.

ord_ins_aux :
|———
[1] FORALL (l:list[A]),(a,b:A): ord(cons(a,l)) => leA(a,b) => ord(cons(a,ins(b,l)))

(induct "l") *Inducting on l on formula 1,* *this yields 2 subgoals:* *ord_ins_aux.1 :* *|----* *[1] FORALL (a, b: A):* * ord(cons(a, null)) => leA(a, b)* * => ord(cons(a, ins(b, null)))*	First, the command induct is used automatically applying the list induction scheme. The resulting formula is then β-reduced and simplified into the base and induction subcases. *PVS* shows the first of these subgoals.

The command skolem eliminates the external universal quantification in a consequent (or the external existential quantification in an antecedent). The command flatten simplifies the current goal, performing repeatedly one or more of the following simplifications:

• Removing negation by transforming an antecedent formula ¬x into the consequent formula x, or by translating a consequent ¬x into the antecedent x.

- Breaking a conjunction by converting an antecedent formula of the form x ∧ y into two antecedent formulas x and y.

- Breaking a disjunction by replacing a consequent formula x ∨ y by two consequents x and y.

- Transforming a consequent x ⇒ y into an antecedent x and a consequent y.

(skosimp*) *ord_ins_aux.1 :* *[-1] ord(cons(a!1, null))* *[-2] leA(a!1, b!1)* *|----* *[1] ord(cons(a!1, ins(b!1, null)))*	The command **skosimp*** is a short form for repeatedly applying skosimp and then flatten.

(expand "ins") *ord_ins_aux.1 :* *[-1] ord(cons(a!1, null))* *[-2] leA(a!1, b!1)* *|----* *[1] ord(cons(a!1, cons(b!1, null)))*	The next step in the proof consists of applying equational reasoning on the definition of ins. To expand (and simplify) a definition we use the command **expand**.
(expand "ord" +) *ord_ins_aux.1 :* *[-1] ord(cons(a!1, null))* *[-2] leA(a!1, b!1)* *|----* *[1] leA(a!1, b!1) AND ord(cons(b!1, null))*	Now, the definition of **ord** is rewritten only in the consequent.

The command split separates the current subgoal as follows:

- If the current goal has an antecedent of the form x ∨ y, it creates two subgoals, in the first one the antecedent above is replaced by x and in the second one by y.

- If the current goal has a consequent of the form x ∧ y, it creates two subgoals, in the first one the above consequent is replaced by x, and in the second it is replaced by y.

(split)

Splitting conjunctions, this yields 2 subgoals:
ord_ins_aux.1.1 :
[-1] ord(cons(a!1, null))
[-2] leA(a!1, b!1)

```
 |——
[1]  leA(a!1, b!1)
```
which is trivially true. This completes the proof of ord_ins_aux.1.1.

```
ord_ins_aux.1.2 :
[-1]  ord(cons(a!1, null))
[-2]  leA(a!1,  b!1)
  |——
[1]   ord(cons(b!1, null))
```

(expand "ord" +) ord_ins_aux.1.2 : [-1] ord(cons(a!1, null)) [-2] leA(a!1, b!1) |---- [1] TRUE *which is trivially true.* *This completes the proof of ord_ins_aux.1.2.* *This completes the proof of ord_ins_aux.1.*	The first branch generated by the application of split is trivially true. The second one is solved by rewriting the definition of ord.

The base case is then proved. We could have solved the base case just with the sophisticated command grind. The grind command is usually a good way to complete a proof that only requires definition expansion, arithmetic, equality, and quantifier reasoning. It is advisable to use the most powerful commands first and only rely on simpler ones when the former fail.

```
ord_ins_aux.2 :
  |——
[1]    FORALL (cons1_var: A, cons2_var: list[A]):
          (FORALL (a,b: A): ord(cons(a,cons2_var)) =>
                           leA(a,b) => ord(cons(a,ins(b,cons2_var))))
          IMPLIES (FORALL (a,b: A): ord(cons(a,cons(cons1_var,cons2_var))) =>
                           leA(a,b) => ord(cons(a,ins(b,cons(cons1_var,cons2_var)))))
```

(skosimp*)
(expand "ins" +)
 	
ord_ins_aux.2 :
[-1] FORALL (a, b: A):
       ord(cons(a, cons2_var!1)) =>
        leA(a, b) =>
         ord(cons(a, ins(b, cons2_var!1)))
[-2] ord(cons(a!1, cons(cons1_var!1, cons2_var!1)))
[-3] leA(a!1, b!1)
  |----
[1]   ord(cons(a!1,IF leA(b!1,cons1_var!1)
                 THEN cons(b!1,cons(cons1_var!1,cons2_var!1))
                 ELSE cons(cons1_var!1,ins(b!1,cons2_var!1))
                 ENDIF))
	In the induction step, we begin eliminating universal quantifiers from the consequent, transforming the implications, and expanding the definition of ins.

(lift-if)
 	
Lifting IF-conditions to the top level,
this simplifies to:
ord_ins_aux.2 :
  .
  .
  .
  |----
[1]   IF leA(b!1, cons1_var!1)
     THEN ord(cons(a!1, cons(b!1,
                  cons(cons1_var!1, cons2_var!1))))
     ELSE ord(cons(a!1, cons(cons1_var!1,
                   ins(b!1, cons2_var!1))))
     ENDIF
	As the if-then-else structure in the consequent is not at the outermost level, we issue a lift-if command. It is used to bring the case analysis in an expanded definition to the top level of the sequent where it can be propositionally simplified.

(split 1)
 	
Splitting conjunctions,
this yields 2 subgoals:
ord_ins_aux.2.1 :
  .
  .
  .
  |----
[1] leA(b!1, cons1_var!1) IMPLIES
  ord(cons(a!1, cons(b!1,
    cons(cons1_var!1, cons2_var!1))))
	With split, case analyses in the current subgoal are performed. As the consequent is of the form if x then y else z, the goal is splitted into two subgoals: $x \Rightarrow y$ and $\neg x \Rightarrow z$.

(flatten)
(expand "ord" +)
 	
ord_ins_aux.2.1 :
  .
  .
  .
  |----
 	
[1]   leA(a!1, b!1) AND ord(cons(b!1, cons(cons1_var!1, cons2_var!1)))
	In the first subgoal, the implication is broken and the definition of ord expanded.

(split)
(expand "ord" +)
(split)
 	
ord_ins_aux.2.1.2.2 :
 	
   .
   .
   .
 	
[-3] ord(cons(a!1, cons(cons1_var!1,
       cons2_var!1)))
[-4] leA(a!1, b!1)
 |----
[1] ord(cons(cons1_var!1, cons2_var!1))
	We continue the proof combining the commands split and expand.

(expand "ord" -3)
 	
ord_ins_aux.2.1.2.2 :
   .
   .
   .
 	
[-3] leA(a!1, cons1_var!1) AND
   ord(cons(cons1_var!1, cons2_var!1))
[-4] leA(a!1, b!1)
 |----
[1] ord(cons(cons1_var!1, cons2_var!1))
	The current subgoal can be solved expanding the definition of ord in the antecedent -3.

(flatten -3) This completes the proof of ord_ins_aux.2.1.2.2. This completes the proof of ord_ins_aux.2.1.2. This completes the proof of ord_ins_aux.2.1.	Now the application of flatten to the antecedent -3 completes the proof of this branch.

ord_ins_aux.2.2 :
[-1] FORALL (a, b: A):
     ord(cons(a, cons2_var!1)) =>
     leA(a, b) => ord(cons(a, ins(b, cons2_var!1)))
[-2] ord(cons(a!1, cons(cons1_var!1, cons2_var!1)))
[-3] leA(a!1, b!1)
 |——
[1] NOT leA(b!1, cons1_var!1) IMPLIES
       ord(cons(a!1, cons(cons1_var!1, ins(b!1, cons2_var!1))))

At this point, the second alternative of the case analysis is reached. As in the first one, the implication is broken and the definition of ord expanded. It should be noted that flatten transforms an antecedent ¬x into the consequent x, and it transforms a consequent ¬x into the antecedent x.

```
(flatten)
(expand "ord" 2)
```
    .

    .

    |——
[1] leA(b!1, cons1_var!1)
[2] leA(a!1, cons1_var!1) AND ord(cons(cons1_var!1, ins(b!1, cons2_var!1)))

(split 2)
(expand "ord" -2)
(flatten -2)
 	
[-1] FORALL (a, b: A):
    ord(cons(a, cons2_var!1)) => leA(a, b) =>
        ord(cons(a, ins(b, cons2_var!1)))
[-2] ord(cons(a!1, cons(cons1_var!1, cons2_var!1)))
[-3] leA(a!1, b!1)
  |----
[1] ord(cons(cons1_var!1, ins(b!1, cons2_var!1)))
[2] leA(b!1, cons1_var!1)
	We split the second consequent yielding two subgoals. The first one, leA(a!1, cons1_var!1), is proved by replacing ord in the antecedent -2 with its definition.

(rewrite -1 1)
 	
Rewriting using -1, matching in 1,
this yields 2 subgoals:
ord_ins_aux.2.2.2.1 :
 	
    .
    .
    .
  |----
[1] leA(cons1_var!1,b!1)
[2] ord(cons(cons1_var!1,
      ins(b!1,cons2_var!1)))
[3] leA(b!1,cons1_var!1)
	The current goal can be obtained from the inductive hypothesis (the antecedent -1). The command rewrite tries to automatically determine the required substitutions by matching a sequent against expressions in a formula, for example, rewrite -1 1 finds and rewrites an instance of the antecedent -1 throughout the consequent 1. With rewrite, it is also possible to rewrite instances of previously checked proofs.

```
(lemma "leA_tot")

ord_ins_aux.2.2.2.1 :
[-1] FORALL (a, b: A): leA(a, b) OR leA(b, a)
[-2] FORALL (a, b: A):
        ord(cons(a, cons2_var!1)) => leA(a, b) =>
            ord(cons(a, ins(b, cons2_var!1)))
[-3] ord(cons(a!1, cons(cons1_var!1, cons2_var!1)))
[-4] leA(a!1, b!1)
  |----
[1]  leA(cons1_var!1, b!1)
[2]  ord(cons(cons1_var!1, ins(b!1, cons2_var!1)))
[3]  leA(b!1, cons1_var!1)
```

This branch of the proof is true because the order relation leA is total. The command lemma introduces an instance of a lemma.

```
(inst? -1)
(split -1)

ord_ins_aux.2.2.2.2 :

[-1] FORALL (a,b:A): ord(cons(a,cons2_var!1))=>
            leA(a,b)=>ord(cons(a,ins(b,cons2_var!1)))
[-2] ord(cons(a!1,cons(cons1_var!1,cons2_var!1)))
[-3] leA(a!1,b!1)
  |----
[1]  ord(cons(cons1_var!1,cons2_var!1))
[2]  ord(cons(cons1_var!1,ins(b!1,cons2_var!1)))
[3]  leA(b!1,cons1_var!1)
```

Finding substitutions in the antecedent -1 and splitting it completes this branch of the proof because the subgoals are trivially true. The command inst? tries to instantiate quantified variables in a formula by pattern-matching against the subexpressions in the consequent formulas. The above command lemma "leA_tot" and inst can be combined into a simpler one: use "leA_tot".

```
(expand "ord" -2)

Q.E.D.
```

The last branch is solved by replacing ord with its definition in the antecedent -2.

So we finished the proof of the lemma ord_ins_aux. Now we are going to present and prove the law which states that inserting an element in an ordered list returns another ordered list in *PVS*. The proof is done by induction on the list.

ord_ins: LEMMA FORALL (a: A), (l: list[A]): ord(l) => ord(ins(a, l))

With the help of this lemma and carrying out the same proof steps as in the manual proof and in the *Coq* proof, it is demonstrated that sort returns a sorted list.

ord_sort: THEOREM FORALL (l: list[A]): ord(sort(l))

Figure 3. Proof trees in PVS for the laws ord_ins and ord_sort

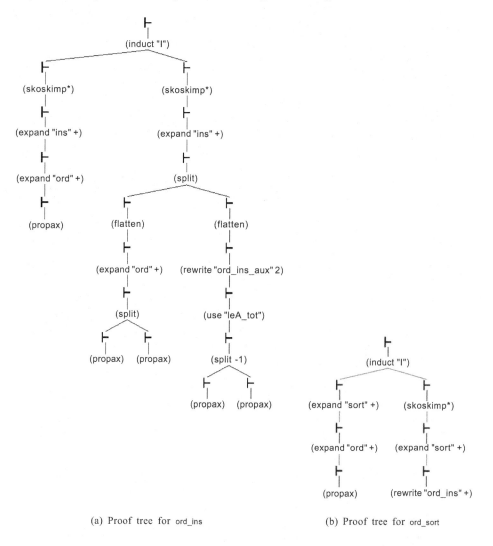

(a) Proof tree for ord_ins   (b) Proof tree for ord_sort

Figures 3(a) and 3(b) show the proof trees for ord_ins and ord_sort, respectively.

The Result of sort is a Permutation of Elements

Coq As a first step we prove auxiliary laws count_cons and count_cons_cons. In order to do this, it is only necessary to apply β-reductions and to perform case analyses. The system solves automatically each alternative.

Lemma count_cons: forall l1 l2: (list A), forall w n: A,
  (count w l1)=(count w l2) -> (count w (cons n l1))=(count w (cons n l2)).
intros. simpl. case (eq_dec w n); auto.
Qed.

Lemma count_cons_cons: forall l: (list A), forall n m w: A,
  (count w (cons n (cons m l)))=(count w (cons m (cons n l))).
intros. simpl. case (eq_dec w m); case (eq_dec w n); auto.
Qed.

Now, we prove lemma 4 which states that each element appears the same number of times in ins n l as in n::l. The proof is carried out by induction in l. The base case is automatically solved by means of β-reductions.

Lemma count_ins: forall l: (list A), forall n w: A,
  (count w (ins n l))=(count w (cons n l)).
induction l.
intros. simpl. auto.

```
1 subgoal
 A : Set
 eq_dec : forall a b : A, a = b + a <> b
 leA : A -> A -> Prop
 leA_refl : forall a : A, leA a a
 leA_trans : forall a b c : A, leA a b -> leA b c -> leA a c
 leA_antisym : forall a b : A, leA a b -> leA b a -> a = b
 leA_tot : forall a b : A, leA a b leA b a
 leA_dec : forall a b : A, {leA a b} + {~ leA a b}
 a : A
 l : list A
 IHl : forall n w : A, count w (ins n l) = count w (n :: l)
 ============================
  forall n w : A, count w (ins n (a :: l)) = count w (n :: a :: l)
```

In the inductive step, universal quantifiers are moved into the hypothesis environment and the definition of ins is expanded.

intros. simpl ins.

```
1 subgoal

 .

 .

 .
 ============================
 count w (if leA_dec n a then n :: a :: l else a :: ins n l) =
   count w (n :: a :: l)
```

A case analysis is carried out. The first subcase becomes trivial. The second one is solved using previous auxiliary laws and the induction hypothesis.

```
case (leA_dec n a); intros Hle. auto.
rewrite count_cons_cons.
apply count_cons.
apply IHl.
Qed.
```

Finally, by means of this result, it is proved that the number of occurrences of any element is the same in the sort argument as in its return value.

```
Lemma count_sort: forall l: (list A),
                forall w: A, (count w l)=(count w (sort l)).
induction l.
simpl; auto.
intros. simpl sort.
rewrite count_ins.
apply count_cons. apply IHl.
Qed.
```

Thus, this is the end of the formalization in *Coq*, which states that the insertion sort algorithm interchanges the order of the elements in the argument list.

PVS Regarding the previously defined function count, the MEASURE clause indicates that the list decreases through recursive calls. The type-correctness condition generated by *PVS* is proved automatically by the system. In the *PVS theory*, we demonstrate exactly the same laws as we have done in the *Coq* system. Next, the declarations can be seen.

```
count_cons: LEMMA FORALL (l1, l2: list[A]), (w, n: A):
  count(w, l1) = count(w, l2) =>
    count(w, cons(n, l1)) = count(w, cons(n, l2))

count_cons_cons: LEMMA FORALL (l: list[A]), (n, m, w: A):
  count(w, cons(n, cons(m, l))) = count(w, cons(m, cons(n, l)))
```

These two auxiliary laws are directly solved with the powerful command grind that tries skolemization, instantiation, and if-lifting repeatedly. Figure 4 shows the proof trees of the remaining two laws.

Figure 4. Proof trees of the lemma count_ins and the theorem count_sort in PVS

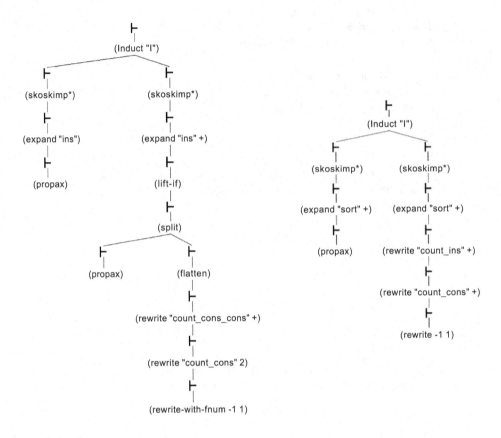

(a) Proof tree for count_ins   (b) Proof tree for count_sort

count_ins: LEMMA
    FORALL (l: list[A]), (n, w: A): count(w, ins(n, l)) = count(w, cons(n, l))

count_sort: THEOREM
    FORALL (l: list[A]), (w: A): count(w, l) = count(w, sort(l))

A Case Study

In this section, we present the verification of part of a real-world application, the implementation of a distributed video-on-demand server (Gulías, Barreiro, & Freire, 2005) that has been developed in the concurrent functional language *Erlang* (Armstrong et al., 1996). As the application of a formal method to a large system is extremely difficult or even impossible, we apply the techniques presented in Jorge (2004) to verify relevant properties of a part of this system separately, so that when, later, we combine other partial results, conclusions on the whole system could be drawn.

An Overview of the VoDKA Server

A *video-on-demand* server is a system that provides video services to several clients simultaneously. A user can request a particular video at any time, with no pre-established temporal constraints. A video-on-demand server is a quite complex distributed system that must satisfy some critical requirements, including large storage capacity, many concurrent users, high bandwidth, reliability, scalability, adaptability to the underlying topology, and low cost.

VoDKA (video-on-demand kernel architecture, http://vodka.lfcia.org) is a project devoted to providing broadband-quality video-on-demand services to cable clients. Clusters built from cheap off-the-shelf components are proposed as an affordable solution for the huge demand of resources of the system. However, the main problem is how to design and implement the distributed application to control the cluster, achieving the demanding requirements of a video-on-demand system (e.g., scalability, adaptability, availability, flexibility). As a first approach, cluster resources were organized as a hierarchical storage system, identifying three different layers: (a) *repository level*, to store all the available media; (b) *cache level*, in charge of storing videos read from the repository level, before being streamed; and (c) *streaming level*, a frontend in charge of protocol adaption and media streaming to the final client.

The Problem: Cache Block Allocation

The cache layer provides a large aggregate throughput that alleviates usual deficiencies (in terms of bandwidth and concurrency) of the repository level. It is composed by a set of physical nodes each running agents and modules implementing different algorithms and policies — some quite tricky and error prone. The piece of software to be verified in this example is (a simplification of) part of the cache subsystem: the block allocation algorithm. Other formal techniques have been also applied to other subsystems (Arts & Sánchez, 2002; Gulías, Valderruten, & Abalde, 2003).

The local disk of each node of the cache level acts as a *local cache*, divided into fixed-size blocks (e.g., 8 MB), which store fragments of a media object. In order to attend a request, media object is firstly looked up in local caches, avoiding the access to the repository layer if possible.

If a media object must be fetched to cache (because of a cache miss), enough space must be booked to load the object from the storage. In order to release some blocks, we have to assure that these blocks are not in use by other pending tasks, either readings from cache to the streaming level or fetchings from repository to cache. As locality in cache is important for performance, blocks of the same media object are in close proximity and we can speak of *block intervals*.

Representing Block Intervals

A block interval is modeled as a triple (a,b,x): the interval between blocks a and b (inclusive) has x pending tasks. To store the whole sequence of block intervals, a list is used as shown:

$$[(a_1,b_1,x_1), (a_2,b_2,x_2), ..., (a_n,b_n,x_n)]$$

For the sake of efficiency, intervals are kept sorted $\forall i, a_i \leq b_i \wedge b_i < a_{i+1}$. Moreover, space is saved if the sequence is kept compact, that is, $\forall i, x_i \neq 0$, and $(x_i \neq x_{i+1}) \vee ((x_i = x_{i+1}) \wedge (b_i + 1 < a_{i+1}))$

Several definitions are needed before translating algorithms on blocks, intervals, and sequences into a model. We show both *Coq* and *PVS* approaches to highlight differences between provers.

Coq A *block interval* is defined as a triple of natural numbers including the initial and final block and the number of pending requests requiring the interval. Interval is an inductive definition with one constructor, tuple.

Inductive interval: Set:= tuple: nat -> nat -> nat -> interval.

A *sequence* is then represented as a list of blocks using an inductive type. Constructor Nil represents an empty sequence while Cons represents a sequence constructed from an interval and a sequence.

Inductive seq: Set:= Nil: seq | Cons: interval -> seq -> seq.

Intervals are kept sorted in ascending order, that is, for every sequence $[(a_1,b_1,x_1), (a_2,b_2,x_2), ..., (a_n,b_n,x_n)]$, the predicate $\forall i, a_i \leq b_i \wedge b_i < a_{i+1}$ holds.

PVS Definitions are analogous to the ones used in the *Coq* model: An interval is a tuple of three elements, and a sequence is a list of intervals.

```
interval: TYPE = [nat, nat, nat]
sequence: TYPE = list[interval]
tuple(a, b, x: nat): interval = (a, b, x)
```

Some additional definitions ease the sequence manipulation:

```
empty: sequence = null
ins(i: interval, l: sequence): sequence = cons(i, l)
```

The Algorithm: Block Allocation

The core of the algorithm is the *Erlang* function add which sums up a new block request over an interval sequence, computing the new interval sequence in addition to all the new blocks allocated. Testing showed up several bugs but, unfortunately, this does not guarantee the correctness of the software.

To improve the confidence on our program, a model is written from the actual *Erlang* code. The disadvantage of this approach is that it does not guarantee the correctness of the code, but some abstract model of it; however this helps increasing the reliability on the system (Peled, 2001).

In Box A, (a part of) the *Coq* model is presented in the first column and the same translation into *PVS* in the second one. The function is defined using structural recursion over the second argument: the interval sequence. As the final sequence must be kept sorted, there are seven alternatives. Observe that some cases produce the splitting of an interval into two or three fragments.

Proving a Property of add in Coq

First of all, an auxiliary function nth is defined to return the number of pending requests on the nth block. This function, certified in Jorge (2004), is going to be used to state the specification.

```
Fixpoint nth [n:nat; l:seq]: nat->nat:= [default]
  Cases l of
  | Nil => default
  | (Cons (tuple a b x) l') => Cases (le_lt_dec a n) of
                                | (left _) => Cases (le_lt_dec n b) of
                                              | (left _) => x
```

Box A.

```
Fixpoint add [n:nat; l: seq]: seq :=          add(n: nat, l: seq): RECURSIVE seq =
Cases l of                                    CASES l
| Nil => (Cons (tuple n n (S O)) Nil)          OF null: make(tuple(n,n,1), null),
| (Cons (tuple a b x) l') =>                    cons(i, l1):
  Cases (le_lt_dec a n) of                       IF i`1 <= n THEN
  | (left _) =>                                    IF n <= i`2 THEN
    Cases (le_lt_dec n b) of                         IF i`1 = n THEN
    | (left _) =>                                       IF n = i`2 THEN
      Cases (eq_nat_dec a n) of                            make(tuple(i`1,i`2,i`3+1), l1)
      | (left _) =>                                       ELSE
        Cases (eq_nat_dec n b) of                           make(tuple(i`1,i`1,i`3+1),
        | (left _) =>                                          make(tuple(i`1+1,i`2,i`3), l1))
          (Cons (tuple a b (S x)) l')                      ENDIF
        | (right _) =>                                    ELSE
          (Cons (tuple a a (S x))                           IF n = i`2 THEN
            (Cons (tuple (S a) b x) l'))                       make(tuple(i`1,i`2-1,i`3),
        end                                                     make(tuple(i`2,i`2,i`3+1), l1))
      | (right _) =>                                       ELSE
        Cases (eq_nat_dec n b) of                           make(tuple(i`1,n-1,i`3),
        | (left _) =>                                          make(tuple(n,n,i`3+1),
          (Cons (tuple a (pred b) x)                             make(tuple(n+1,i`2,i`3), l1)))
            (Cons (tuple b b (S x)) l'))                    ENDIF
        | (right _) =>                                    ENDIF
          (Cons (tuple a (pred n) x)                     ELSE make(i, add(n, l1))
            (Cons (tuple n n (S x))                      ENDIF
              (Cons (tuple (S n) b x) l')))            ELSE make(tuple(n,n,1), l)
        end                                            ENDIF
      end                                            ENDCASES
    | (right _) =>                                   MEASURE length(l)
      (Cons (tuple a b x) (add n l'))
    end
  | (right _) => (Cons (tuple n n (S O)) l)
  end
end.
```

```
                              | (right _) => (nth n l' default)
                              end
                    | (right _) => default
                    end
  end.
```

Function add must satisfy that, in the resulting interval sequence, the number of requests over the requested block is incremented by one, while all the other blocks remain unchanged.

$$\text{nth } n \text{ (add } i \text{ 1) 0} = \begin{cases} \text{nth } n \text{ 1 0} & \text{if } i \neq n \\ \text{nth } n \text{ 1 0} + 1 & \text{if } i = n \end{cases}$$

This property is split into two theorems provided that i equals n or not.

Theorem nth_add_1:

  (l: seq; n,i: nat) i=n -> (nth n (add i l) O)=(S (nth n l O)).

Both the definition of add and nth are carried out by structural recursion on the sequence of block intervals. Thus, we proceed by induction on l.

Induction l.

Intros; Rewrite H; Simpl.

2 subgoals

  ⋮

 H : i=n

 =============================

  (Cases (le_lt_dec n n) of

    (left _) => Cases (le_lt_dec n n) of

           (left _) => (1)

        | (right _) => (0)

       end

  | (right _) => (0)

  end)=(1)

subgoal 2 is: ...

The case analysis applied to le_lt_dec n n returns either (left _) with a proof of le n n, or (right _) with a proof of lt n n. As every natural number equals itself, the second alternative leads to an erroneous hypothesis n < n and this is easily proved. In fact, this common proof pattern suggested us the creation of a new ad-hoc tactic, DecLeLt, that may be used in the future.

DecLeLt n n.

1 subgoal

l : seq

=============================

 (i:interval; s:seq)

 ((n,i:nat)i=n->(nth n (add i s) (0))=(S (nth n s (0))))

 ->(n,i0:nat)i0=n->(nth n (add i0 (Cons i s)) (0))

  =(S (nth n (Cons i s) (0)))

The inductive step starts by introducing the universal quantifiers, the induction hypothesis, and the theorem hypothesis in the hypotheses environment. The theorem hypothesis is rewritten in the conclusion and all the β-reductions are carried out.

Clear l;IntroInt a b x;Intros l indH n j Heq.

Rewritec Heq; Simpl.

1 subgoal

⋮

indH : (n,i:nat)i=n->(nth n (add i l) (0))=(S (nth n l (0)))
n : nat
j : nat
============================
```
(nth n
   Cases (le_lt_dec a n) of
      (left _) =>
         Cases (le_lt_dec n b) of
            (left _) =>
               Cases (eq_nat_dec a n) of
                  (left _) => Cases (eq_nat_dec n b) of
                               (left _) => (Cons (tuple a b (S x)) l)

                               | (right _) =>
                                  (Cons (tuple a a (S x)) (Cons (tuple (S a) b x) l))
                             end
                  | (right _) =>
                     Cases (eq_nat_dec n b) of
                        (left _) => (Cons (tuple a (pred b) x) (Cons (tuple b b (S x)) l))
                        | (right _) =>
                           (Cons (tuple a (pred n) x)
                              (Cons (tuple n n (S x)) (Cons (tuple (S n) b x) l)))
                     end
               end
            | (right _) => (Cons (tuple a b x) (add n l))
            end
      | (right _) => (Cons (tuple n n (1)) (Cons (tuple a b x) l))
      end (0))
   = (S Cases (le_lt_dec a n) of
            (left _) => Cases (le_lt_dec n b) of
                           (left _) => x
                           | (right _) => (nth n l (0))
                        end
            | (right _) => (0)
      end)
```

Using the structure of function add, we perform several case analyses:

```
CaseEq '(le_lt_dec a n) Hle1 le1.
CaseEq '(le_lt_dec n b) Hle2 le2.
Case (eq_nat_dec a n); Intro Heq1.
Rewritec Heq1.
Case (eq_nat_dec n b); Intro Heq2.
```

5 subgoals

·
·
·

indH : (n,i:nat)i=n->(nth n (add i l) (0))=(S (nth n l (0)))
n : nat
j : nat

```
Hle1 : (le a n)
le1 : (le_lt_dec a n)=(left (le a n) (lt n a) Hle1)
Hle2 : (le n b)
le2 : (le_lt_dec n b)=(left (le n b) (lt b n) Hle2)
Heq2 : n=b
=============================
(nth n (Cons (tuple n b (S x)) l) (0))=(S x)
```

subgoal 2 is: ...

The first alternative is easily proved replacing b with n, doing all β-reductions and then applying the defined tactic DecLeLt.

RewritecL Heq2. Simpl. DecLeLt n n.

4 subgoals

```
        .
        .
        .

indH : (n,i:nat)i=n->(nth n (add i l) (0))=(S (nth n l (0)))
n : nat
j : nat
Hle1 : (le a n)
le1 : (le_lt_dec a n)=(left (le a n) (lt n a) Hle1)
Hle2 : (le n b)
le2 : (le_lt_dec n b)=(left (le n b) (lt b n) Hle2)
Heq2 : ~n=b
=============================
(nth n (Cons (tuple n n (S x)) (Cons (tuple (S n) b x) l)) (0))=(S x)
```

subgoal 2 is: ...

The rest of alternatives but one are solved similarly. The remaining one requires the induction hypothesis.

Simpl. DecLeLt n n.
Case (eq_nat_dec n b); Intro Heq2.
RewritecL Heq2. Simpl. Rewrite le1.
DecLeLt n '(pred n). DecLeLt n n.
Simpl. Rewrite le1.
DecLeLt n n. DecLeLt n '(pred n).
Simpl. Rewrite le1. Rewrite le2.
Apply indH; Auto.
Simpl. DecLeLt n n.
Qed.

The second theorem to be proved is quite similar (though larger):

Theorem nth_add_2: (l:seq; n, i:nat) ~i=n->(nth n (add i l) O)=(nth n l O).

Proving a Property of add in PVS

As done in *Coq*, we define an auxiliary function nth to state the specification:

```
nth(n: nat, l: sequence, default: nat): RECURSIVE nat =
  CASES l OF null: default,
              cons(i, l1): IF i'1 <= n THEN
                             IF n <= i'2 THEN i'3 ELSE nth(n, l1, default) ENDIF
                           ELSE default
                           ENDIF
  ENDCASES
  MEASURE length(l)
```

The resulting theorems are stated as:

```
nth_add_1: THEOREM FORALL (m, n: nat), (l: sequence):
  m = n => nth(n, add(m, l), 0) = 1 + nth(n, l, 0)
```

```
nth_add_2: THEOREM FORALL (m, n: nat), (l: sequence):
  NOT (m = n) => nth(n, add(m, l), 0) = nth(n, l, 0)
```

In this case, *PVS* proofs are carried out by the system *automagically* using the advanced command induct-and-simplify. A great deal of work is carried out by *PVS* if compared with *Coq* version.

Assuring the Canonical Form of Interval Sequences

The representation of interval sequences should be canonical (in the sense that two different representations always correspond to two different objects) to achieve better space and time behaviour. Theorem provers can help us to assure that sequences are always delivered in canonical form. We should demonstrate that the application of add to an interval sequence in canonical form always delivers a new canonical sequence. First, we present the property that states that intervals in a sequence are in ascending order. The predicate ascend asserts whether a sequence $[(a_1,b_1,x_1), ..., (a_n,b_n,x_n)]$ is sorted in ascending order, that is, it shows whether $\forall i, a_i \leq b_i \wedge b_i < a_{i+1}$ is true or not. In the rest of the presentation, *Coq* code is shown in the left column and *PVS* approach in the right one.

```
Inductive ascend: seq -> Prop:=          ascend(l: sequence): RECURSIVE bool =
| Ascend1: (ascend Nil)                    CASES l
| Ascend2: (a, b, x: nat)                   OF null: TRUE,
   (le a b) ->                              cons(i, l1):
   (ascend (Cons (tuple a b x) Nil))          CASES l1
| Ascend3: (a, b, x, c, d, y: nat; l:seq)      OF null: i`1 <= i`2,
   (ascend (Cons (tuple c d y) l)) ->          cons(j, l2):
   (le a b) -> (lt b c) ->                         ascend(l1) AND i`1 <= i`2
   (ascend (Cons (tuple a b x)                     AND i`2 < j`1
        (Cons (tuple c d y) l))).          ENDCASES
                                          ENDCASES
                                          MEASURE length(l)
```

This predicate is not enough to define the canonical representation because the same sequence could be represented in different ways, e.g. the sequence [(2,2,3),(3,6,3),(8,9,2)] could also be represented by [(2,6,3),(8,9,2)] which is more compact. The representation must also be *packed*, that is, it must hold that $\forall i, a_i \leq b_i \wedge ((x_i \neq x_{i+1} \wedge b_i < a_{i+1}) \vee (x_i = x_{i+1} \wedge b_i + 1 < a_{i+1}))$.

```
Inductive packed: seq -> Prop:=          packed(l: sequence): RECURSIVE bool =
| Packed1: (packed Nil)                    CASES l
| Packed2: (a, b, x: nat)                   OF null: TRUE,
   (le a b) ->                              cons(i, l1):
   (packed (Cons (tuple a b x) Nil))          CASES l1
| Packed3: (a, b, x, c, d, y: nat; l: seq)     OF null: i`1 <= i`2,
   (packed (Cons (tuple c d y) l)) ->          cons(j, l2):
   (le a b) -> ~x=y -> (lt b c) ->                packed(l1) AND
   (packed (Cons (tuple a b x)                   i`1 <= i`2 AND
        (Cons (tuple c d y) l)))                 ((NOT (i`3 = j`3)
| Packed4: (a, b, x, c, d, y: nat; l: seq)        AND i`2 < j`1)
   (packed (Cons (tuple c d y) l)) ->           OR (i`2 + 1) < j`1)
   (le a b) -> (lt (S b) c) ->              ENDCASES
   (packed (Cons (tuple a b x)            ENDCASES
        (Cons (tuple c d y) l))).         MEASURE length(l)
```

The output of add holds the predicate ascend but it does not hold packed. In order to satisfy the specification, a new function pack is defined to convert the result of add.

```
Fixpoint packAux [i:interval;l:seq]:seq        packAux(i: interval, l: sequence):
:=Cases i of                                                RECURSIVE sequence =
| (tuple a b x) =>                             CASES l
  Cases l of                                    OF null: ins(i, empty),
  | Nil => (Cons (tuple a b x) Nil)              cons(i1, l1):
  | (Cons (tuple c d y) l') =>                     IF i`3 = i1`3 THEN
    Cases (eq_nat_dec x y) of                        IF i`2 + 1 = i1`2 THEN
    | (left _) =>                                      packAux(tuple(i`1,i1`2,i`3),l1)
      Cases (eq_nat_dec (S b) c) of                  ELSE ins(i, packAux(i1, l1))
      | (left _) =>                                  ENDIF
        (packAux (tuple a d x) l')               ELSE ins(i, packAux(i1, l1))
      | (right _) =>                               ENDIF
        (Cons (tuple a b x)                    ENDCASES
         (packAux (tuple c d y) l'))           MEASURE length(l)
      end
    | (right _) =>                             pack(l: sequence): sequence =
      (Cons (tuple a b x)                      CASES l OF
       (packAux (tuple c d y) l'))             null: empty,
    end                                        cons(i, l1): packAux(i, l1)
  end                                          ENDCASES
end.

Definition pack [l: seq]: seq:=
Cases l of
  Nil => Nil
| (Cons i l') => (packAux i l')
end.
```

To complete the canonical representation, we need a predicate that guarantees that every block in the sequence has at least one request.

```
Inductive strictPosit: seq -> Prop:=           strictPosit(l: sequence): RECURSIVE bool =
| StrictPosit1: (strictPosit Nil)              CASES l OF
| StrictPosit2: (l:seq; a, b, x: nat)           null: TRUE,
  (strictPosit l) -> ~x=O ->                     cons(x, xs): strictPosit(xs) AND x`3>0
  (strictPosit (Cons (tuple a b x) l)).         ENDCASES
                                               MEASURE length(l)
Inductive canonical: seq -> Prop:=
  Canonical: (l: seq) (packed l) ->            canonical(l: sequence): bool =
  (strictPosit l) -> (canonical l).            packed(l) AND strictPosit(l)
```

We should show that pack returns an interval sequence equivalent to the one it gets as argument as long as it is sorted in ascending order.

```
Lemma nth_pack: (l:sequence;n:nat)            nth_pack: LEMMA
  (ascend l) ->                                FORALL (n: nat), (l: sequence):
  (nth n l O) = (nth n (pack l) O).            ascend(l) =>
                                                 nth(n, l, 0) = nth(n, pack(l), 0)
```

Now, it is proved that the result of add is a sequence sorted in ascending order and that the result of the application of pack on an ascending sequence delivers a packed one.

```
Lemma ascend_add: (l:seq)(i:nat)        ascend_add: LEMMA
  (ascend l) -> (ascend (add i l)).        FORALL (l: sequence) (n: nat):
                                             ascend(l) => ascend(add(n,l))
Lemma packed_pack: (l: seq)             packed_pack: LEMMA
  (ascend l) -> (packed (pack l)).         FORALL (l: sequence):
                                             ascend(l) => packed(pack(l))
```

It is also proved that add and pack does not leave any block without requests.

```
Lemma strictPosit_add: (l:seq; i:nat)        strictPosit_add: LEMMA
  (strictPosit l) -> strictPosit (add i l)).   FORALL (l: sequence)(n: nat):
Lemma strictPosit_pack: (l:seq)                strictPosit(l)=>strictPosit(add(n,l))
  (strictPosit l) ->(strictPosit (pack l)).  strictPosit_pack: LEMMA
                                               FORALL (l: sequence):
                                                 strictPosit(l)=>strictPosit(pack(l))
```

Finally, we conclude that the composition of pack and add delivers a canonical sequence.

```
Theorem canonical_pack_add: (l:seq;n:nat)   canonical_pack_add: THEOREM
  (canonical l) ->                             FORALL (l: sequence)(n: nat):
  (canonical (pack (add n l))).                canonical(l) =>
Intros l n Hpack.                                canonical(pack(add(n, l)))
Inversion_clear Hpack.                       (skosimp*)
Constructor.                                 (expand "canonical")
                                             (flatten)
2 subgoals                                   (split)
  l : seq
  n : nat                                    canonical_pack_add.1 :
  H : (packed l)                             [-1] packed(l!1)
  H0 : (strictPosit l)                       [-2] strictPositive(l!1)
  ============================                 |----
    (packed (pack (add n l)))                [1]  packed(pack(add(n!1, l!1)))

subgoal 2 is:(strictPosit(pack(add n l)))   (use "packed_pack")(split -1)
                                             (use "ascend_add")(split -1)
Apply packed_pack. Apply ascend_add.         (use "packed_ascend")(split -1)
Apply packed_ascend. Auto.                   (use "strictPosit_pack")(split -1)
Apply strictPosit_pack.                      (use "strictPosit_add")(split -1)
Apply strictPosit_add. Auto.
Qed.
```

Table 1. Quantitative information of the development

Theory	Lines	Defs.	Laws	Prop
SeqDefs	49	4	0	12
SeqLaws	144	9	5	10
SeqCan	601	8	21	20
totals	794	21	26	16

(a) *COQ* theories

Theory	Lines	Defs.	Laws	Prop
SeqDefs	47	7	0	6
SeqLaws	14	0	2	7
SeqCan	323	6	22	11
totals	384	13	24	10

(b) *PVS* theories

Table 1(a) presents quantitative information on each *Coq* theory for this example, showing the number of lines of code, the number of definitions (including new tactics) and the number of laws and the relation between the number of lines and the number of laws and definitions which can be used as a complexity measure for the theory. Table 1(b) shows the same information on *PVS* theories, where each provided command for the development of proofs has been counted as one line of code.

Summary

We present how formal methods, and in particular theorem provers, help to perform software verification, assuring that some relevant properties hold in a program. We suggest developing programs using side-effect free languages, such as functional languages, where tools like equational reasoning make sense and can ease the analysis of programs.

In the chapter, proofs of properties have been carried out both in an informal and exhaustive style (on functional programs), and with the help of *Coq* and *PVS* proof assistants. In general, the elaboration of proofs is based on the syntactic structure of the program. As usual, complexity is managed by dividing the problem in smaller problems using auxiliary lemmas and laws. The explored provers have different philosophies: *Coq* formalizes higher-order logic with inductive types, which gives a rigorous notion of proof and the possibility of extracting automatically functional programs from the algorithmic content of the proof. On the other hand, *PVS* does not have such a rigorous notion of proof but it incorporates powerful automatic theorem-proving capabilities that reduce the amount of work for the developer.

As a first example, we present the pedagogic case study of an insertion sort algorithm over lists of elements. The sorting criteria is defined by some reflexive, antisymmetric, transitive, and total relation. The proving procedure is kept as general as possible. Though the example is simple, the procedure to be accomplished for more complex pieces of software follows the same pattern.

As an example of a real-world application, we applied the method to a distributed video-on-demand server developed using a functional language. So far, we have expounded separately the formal verification of part of the functionality of the server. Other partial results would be necessary to reach conclusions on the whole system. The verification is not done on the real system but on some abstract model of it.

Formal methods are not intended to provide *absolute* reliability, but to *increase* software reliability. Specification and verification yield a better understanding of the program. A correctness proof is a detailed explanation of how the program works. Formal methods can be used to improve the design of systems, its efficiency, and to certify its correctness. It is often difficult to apply formal methods to a whole system, so we should look for compositional techniques. We think that the future of program verification heads for a general proposal: to obtain certified software libraries.

Acknowledgment

This work is partially supported by projects MEC TIN2005-08986 and XUGA PGIT05TIC10503PR.

References

Armstrong, J., Virding, R., Wikström, C., & Williams, M. (1996). *Concurrent programming in Erlang*. Hertfordshire, UK: Prentice Hall.

Arts, T., & Sánchez, J. J. (2002). Global scheduler properties derived from local restrictions. In *ACM SIGPLAN Workshop on Erlang* (pp. 49-57). Pittsburgh, PA: ACM Press.

Bérard, B., Bidoit, A. F. M., Laroussine, F., Petit, A., Petrucci, L., Schoenebelen, P., et al. (2001). *Systems and software verification. Model-checking techniques and tools*. Springer-Verlag.

Bertot, Y., & Casteran, P. (2004). *Interactive theorem proving and program development, Coq'Art: The calculus of inductive constructions*. Springer-Verlag.

Bird, R., & Wadler, P. (1988). *Introduction to functional programming*. Hertfordshire, UK: Prentice Hall.

Clarke, E. M., Grumberg, O., & Peled, D. A. (1999). *Model checking*. Cambridge, MA: MIT Press.

Clarke, E. M., Wing, J. M., Alur, R., Cleaveland, R., Dill, D., Emerson, A., et al. (1996). Formal methods: State of the art and future directions. *ACM Computing Surveys, 28*(4), 626-643.

Coq Development Team, The. (2004). *The Coq proof assistant reference manual, version 8.0*. Rocquencourt, France.

Crow, J., Owre, S., Rushby, J., Shankar, N., & Srivas, M. (1995). A tutorial introduction to PVS. In *Wift '95 Workshop on Industrial-Strength Formal Specication Techniques*. Boca Raton, FL: Computer Science Laboratory, SRI International.

Ghezzi, C., Jazayeri, M., & Mandrioli, D. (1991). *Fundamentals of software engineering*. Englewood Cliffs, NJ: Prentice Hall.

Giménez, E. (1998). *A tutorial on recursive types in Coq* (Tech. Rep. No. 0221). Rocquencourt, France: INRIA. (for Coq V6.2)

Gordon, M. J., Milner, A. J., & Wadsworth, C. P. (1979). *Edinburgh LCF: A mechanised logic of computation: Vol. 78*. Springer-Verlag.

Gordon, M. J. C., & Melham, T. F. (1993). *Introduction to HOL: A theorem proving environment for higher order logic*. New York: Cambridge University Press.

Gulías, V. M., Barreiro, M., & Freire, J. L. (2005). VODKA: Developing a video-on-demand server using distributed functional programming. *Journal of Functional Programming, 15*(4).

Gulías, V. M., Valderruten, A., & Abalde, C. (2003). Building functional patterns for implementing distributed applications. In *IFIP/ACM Latin America Networking Conference: Towards a Latin American Agenda for Network Research (LANC '03)* (pp. 89-98). New York: ACM Press.

Gunter, C., & Mitchell, J. (1996). Strategic directions in software engineering and programming languages. *ACM Computing Surveys, 28*(4), 727-737.

Hudak, P. (1989). Conception, evolution, and application of functional programming languages. *ACM Computing Surveys, 21*(3), 359-411.

Huet, G., Kahn, G., & Paulin-Mohring, C. (2002). *The Coq proof assistant: A tutorial, version 7.3* (Technical report). INRIA.

Jorge, J. S. (2004). *Estudio de la verificación de propiedades de programas funcionales: De las pruebas manuales al uso de asistentes de pruebas*. Unpublished doctoral dissertation, University of A Coruña, Spain.

Kaufmann, M., Mannolios, P., & Moore, J. S. (2000a). *Computer-aided reasoning: ACL2 case studies*. Boston: Kluwer Academic Publishers.

Kaufmann, M., Mannolios, P., & Moore, J. S. (2000b). *Computer-aided reasoning: An approach*. Norwell, MA: Kluwer Academic Publishers.

Leroy, X., et al. (2004). *The Objective Caml system: Documentation and user's manual, release 3.08*.

Nielson, F., Nielson, H. R., & Hankin, C. (1999). *Principles of program analysis*. Springer-Verlag.

Owre, S., Rushby, J. M., & Shankar, N. (1992). PVS: A prototype verication system. In *The 11th International Conference on Automated Deduction* (Vol. 607, pp. 748-752). New York: Springer-Verlag.

Owre, S., Shankar, N., & Rushby, J. M. (1995). *The PVS specification language*. Menlo Park, CA: Computer Science Laboratory, SRI International.

Paulson, L. C. (1990). Isabelle: The next 700 theorem provers. In P. Odifreddi (Ed.), *Logic and computer science* (pp. 361-386). London: Academic Press.

Paulson, L. C. (1994). *Isabelle: A generic theorem prover*. New York: Springer-Verlag.

Paulson, L. C. (1996). *ML for the working programmer* (2nd ed.). New York: Cambridge University Press.

Peled, D. A. (2001). *Software reliability methods*. Berlin; Heidelberg; New York: Springer-Verlag.

Roscoe, A. W. (1994). Model-checking CSP. In A. W. Roscoe (Ed.), *A classical mind: Essays in honour of C. A. R. Hoare* (pp. 353-378). Hertfordshire, UK: Prentice-Hall.

Weis, P., & Leroy, X. (1999). *Le langage Caml* (2nd ed.). Paris: Dunod.

Chapter XI

Static Type Systems:
From Specification
to Implementation

Pablo E. Martínez López,
LIFIA, Facultad de Informática, UNLP, Argentina

Abstract

*Static type systems are fundamental tools used to determine properties of programs
before execution. There exist several techniques for validation and verification of
programs based on typing. Thus, type systems are important to know for the practicioner.
When designing and implementing a technique based on typing systems, there is usually
a gap between the formal tools used to specify it, and the actual implementations. This
gap can be an obstacle for language designers and programmers. A better understanding
of the features of a type system and how they are implemented can help enourmously
to the good design and implementation of new and powerful verification methods based
on type systems. This chapter addresses the problem of specifing and implementing a
static type system for a simple language, but containing many of the subtleties found
in bigger, mainstream languages. This contributes to the understanding of the techniques,
thus bridging the gap between theory and practice. Additionally, the chapter contains
a small survey of some of the existing developments in the static typing area and the
static analysis based on typing.*

Introduction

When someone speaks about verification and validation of programs, it is not very common that a static type system comes to one's mind. However, static typing techniques have been a foundation for many of the developments in the theory and practice of this area of computing science.

A static type system (Cardelli, 1997; Cardelli & Wegner, 1985; Curry & Feys, 1958; Hindley, 1969; Hindley, 1995; Milner, 1978; Pierce, 2002) is a fundamental tool used to determine properties of programs before execution — for example, the absence of some execution errors — and to provide rudimentary documentation when coding solutions in a programming language. The main motivation for the use of these systems is that every program with a type calculated statically — that is, based only on the text of the program and not on its computation — is free from some kinds of errors during execution. The classic motto coined by Robin Milner is "well-typed programs cannot go wrong" (1978). This guarantees a certain correctness of the code and also helps omit specific checks in the executable code to avoid these kinds of problems, thus obtaining a more efficient program.

When designing static type systems, a trade-off between expressiveness and decidability has to be made. The computation prescribed by a static type system is limited — it may happen that given a type system, a decidable inference algorithm does not exist; it is usually said that the system is not decidable. So, the choices are: Design a decidable system discarding some number of correct programs, or design a precise system but with a noncomputable notion of typing. Both alternatives have been thoroughly studied.

When choosing the first alternative, the goal is to maximize the expressiveness of the system — that is, the number of correct accepted programs be as large as possible, while minimizing the number of incorrect accepted ones — without losing decidability. In this line of research appear polymorphic type systems (Damas & Milner, 1982; Jim, 1996; Milner, 1978; Reynolds, 1983) as the one of ML (Clément, Despeyroux, Despeyroux, & Kahn, 1986; Rèmy & Pottier, 2004) or Haskell (Peyton Jones & Hughes, 1999), and systems with subtypes (Henglein & Rehof, 1997; Mitchell, 1991; Palsberg, Wand, & O'Keefe, 1997), overloading (Jones, 1994a; Jones, 1996; Thatte, 1992), recursive types (Tiuryn & Wand, 1993), records (Gaster & Jones, 1996; Rèmy, 1989), and so on.

In the second case, the idea is to design semiautomatic tools to help in the construction of programs, maximizing the ability to perform automatic type inference. In this line of research appear Girard's System F (Girard, 1989; Reynolds, 1974), and dependent type systems as the Type Theory of Martin-Löf (Nordström, Petersson, & Smith, 1990) — on which a tool like Alf (Thorsten, Altenkirch, Gaspes, Nordström, & von Sydow, 1994) is based — and the calculus of constructions (Coquand & Huet, 1988) — on which the Coq proof assistant (Bertot & Castéran, 2004; The Coq proof assistant, 2004) is based.

This chapter concentrates on the first of these two choices.

Static type systems are an integral part of the definition of a language, similar to the grammar defining the syntax of programs. Furthermore, just as there is a tool implementing the grammar — the parser — there is a tool implementing the type system. It can be either a type checker, or a type inferencer (the difference between typechecking and type inference will be discussed in subsequent sections). Usually, there is a gap between the formal tools used to specify a type system, and the actual implementations. Once a type system has been designed, finding an algorithm for typechecking or type inference may be from really easy to extremely hard, or even impossible. There are usually two hindrances when implementing type inference: inherent subtleties of the system and techniques used to improve performance. This gap can be an obstacle for language designers and programmers. A better understanding of the features of a type system, and how they are implemented can help enourmously to the good design and implementation of new and powerful verification methods based on type systems.

Type systems are intrinsically related to the semantics of the language. The main property of a type system is *soundness*, which states that any typeable program is free of the errors addressed by the system. However, a purely syntactic treatment of types is enough for the purpose of this chapter — that is, no formal semantics will be given to the language, and no proof of soundness for the type system. These issues have been addressed in the literature — Reynolds (1998), for example.

What this chapter addresses is the problem of specifying and implementing a static type system for a simple language, but which contains many of the subtleties found in bigger, mainstream languages. The chapter begins explaining in detail the basic techniques for specification of the type systems and then discusses a straightforward way to implement it, showing the relationship between the two. This contributes to the understanding of the techniques, thus bridging the gap between theory and practice; this contribution may help in the design of other techniques for verification and validation of programs. Continuing with the chapter, a small survey of some of the existing developments in the static typing area and the static analysis based on typing are given, such as the addition of records and variant types, recursive and overloaded types, register allocation, sized types, type specialization, and so on, is given. Finally, some conclusions are drawn.

The Basic Language and Its Typing

The development of a formal system — a system used to capture essential features of the real world by means of a formal language and deductive mechanisms — always starts by defining the syntax of the languages involved. The language used in this chapter is a very simple one, but has enough constructs to present the more subtle problems of typing: It has numbers, Booleans, higher-order functions, tuples, and recursion. A functional language (Bird, 1998) has been chosen because of its simplicity, allowing for easy illustration of the features of the type system.

Functional programming is a programming paradigm that concentrates on the *description of values* rather than on the sequencing of commands. For that reason, its semantics is easy, assigning a value to each valid expression. The interesting feature about functional programming is the existence of a special kind of values, called *functions*, that are used to describe the relation between two sets of values and that can also be interpreted as the prescription of information transformation — that is, a *program*. In functional languages, functions are treated just like any other value, and thus can be passed as parameters, returned as values, and used in data structures, and so the expressive power is very high.

- **Definition 2.1:** *Let x denote a term variable from a countably infinite set of variables, n, a number, and b, a Boolean (that is, either* **True** *or* **False***). A term, denoted by e, is an element of the language defined by the following grammar:*

$$
\begin{array}{llll}
e & ::= & x & | & n & | & e + e \\
& | & b & | & e == e & | & \text{if } e \text{ then } e \text{ else } e \\
& | & (e, \ldots , e) & | & \pi_{n,n}\, e \\
& | & \lambda x.e & | & e\, e & | & \textbf{fix } e \\
& | & \textbf{let } x = e \textbf{ in } e
\end{array}
$$

where + is chosen as a representative numeric operation, and == as a representative relational operation.

The expression $(e_1, \ldots, e_n)$ in the last definition represents a tuple of arity n for every positive number n (this is an ordered pair when $n = 2$), and $\pi_{i,n}\, e$ is the i-th projection of the n-tuple e. The expression $\lambda x.e$ is an anonymous function that returns e when given an argument x, and $e_1\, e_2$ is the application of the value of e_1 — expected to be a function — to argument e_2. The expression **let** is used to provide (self-contained, i.e., in a single expression) local definitions, and the expression **fix** e provides recursion vía fixpoint operators (Mitchell, 1996). A *fixpoint* of a given function f is a value of its domain that is returned without changes by f. When writing expressions, some conventions are taken: Addition, multiplication, and other operators have the usual precedence; functional application has higher precedence than any other operator, and associates to the left; and finally, parentheses are used whenever needed to eliminate ambiguity (even when no parenthesis are explicitly given in the grammar). This is an example of abstract syntax as seen in McCarthy (1962) and Reynolds (1998).

A program is any closed term of this language — that is, those with no free variables. To define the concept of free variable, the notion of *binder* (i.e., the *definition point* of a variable) is needed, together with its *scope* (i.e., where the definition is valid); those occurrences of the variable defined by the binder that appear in the scope are called bound occurrences, and the variable is said to be a bound variable; those variables that are not bound are said to be *free*. For the language used here, the binders are the λ and **let** expressions, and the scopes are the body of the λ-expression, and the expression following the **in** in the **let** expression, respectively.

Very simple examples are arithmetic expressions, like $1 + 1$, and $(4 - 1)*3$, relational expressions, like $x == 0$, $2 + 2 > 4$, etc., and example of tuples and projections, like $(2, \textbf{True})$, $\pi_{2,2}(\pi_{2,2}(1,(\textbf{True},3)))$, etc. Still simple, but less common, are anonymous functions, such as $(\lambda x.x)$, $(\lambda p.\pi_{1,2}\, p)$, etc.

Growing in complexity, there are examples using local definitions and conditionals:

let $fst = \lambda p.\ \pi_{1,2}\, p$
in $fst\,(2,5)$

and

let $max = \lambda x.\ \lambda y.$ **if** $x > y$ **then** x **else** y
 in $max\ 2\ 5$

Finally, recursion is the most involved feature; the factorial is an example of a recursive function:

let $fact = $ **fix** $(\lambda f.\ \lambda v.$ **if** $v == 0$
                        then 1
                        else $v * f\ (v-1))$
in $(fact\ 2, fact\ 5)$

Observe how recursion is expressed using the **fix** operator. An equivalent way to provide this is to use a construct similar to **let**, but allowing recursive definitions (typically called **letrec**, and assumed implicitly in many languages); it can be defined as syntactic sugar, by using **fix** in the following way:

letrec $f = e$ **in** e' $\equiv$ **let** $f = $ **fix** $(\lambda f.e)$ **in** e'

In this way, the previous example can be rewritten as:

letrec $fact = \lambda v.$ **if** $v == 0$
                       then 1
                       else $v * fact\ (v-1)$
in $(fact\ 2, fact\ 5)$

which is a more common way of finding recursion. Had this construct been added instead of **fix**, the set of binder expressions would have to be extended with it, and the scope of the new binder defined as both expressions appearing in the **letrec**.

A naive approach for ruling out typing errors is using syntactic categories to discriminate expressions of different types — for example, instead of having a single syntactic category e of programs, a naive designer would have defined one category e_i for integer expressions, one category e_b for Boolean expressions, and so on. The main problem is that the set of typed terms is not context free. This is shown in two ways: First of all, there are expressions in the language that can take different types — for example, conditionals, or local definitions — and so they have to be replicated on each syntactic category; but second, and much more important, there is usually an infinite number of sets of values to discriminate, but there cannot be an infinite number of syntactic categories — context-free grammars are finite tools.

The specification of the type system is given in two steps: First, all the nonfunctional parts (that is, numbers, Booleans, and tuples) are presented, and then, functions are added to the system. The reason is that functions introduce many of the subtleties that make the system complex (and interesting).

Typing Nonfunctional Elements

The type system is specified as a relation between an expression and a *type*, denoted by τ, which is a term of a new language used to classify programs according to the kind of value they may produce when executed (if they terminate). In a naive interpretation, a type can be identified with a set of values.

- **Definition 2.2:** *A type, denoted by τ, is an element of the language defined by the following grammar:*

  $$\tau ::= \textbf{Int} \mid \textbf{Bool} \mid (\tau, \dots, \tau) \mid \tau \to \tau$$

Naive interpretations for types are the set of numbers for type **Int**, the set of truth values for type **Bool**, the cartesian product of types for tuples, and the function space for the function type ($\to$).

A key property that any static analysis must have is that it has to be *compositional* — that is, the analysis of a given program has to be constructed based on the result of the analysis of its subprograms. Type systems are no exception. However, the restriction that programs are closed terms complicates achieving this property, because subprograms do not fulfil it; they may contain free variables. This is a very common problem when defining a static analysis — that is, subexpressions may have different restrictions than full programs — and several ways to address it exist. Here, *environments* are used; they are similar to the symbol table of a compiler.

- **Definition 2.3:** *A typing environment, denoted by Γ, is a (finite) list of pairs composed by a variable and a type, written $x : \tau$, where all variables appear at most once.*

The idea of a typing environment is to provide information about the type of free variables. However, in order to allow flexibility (needed in the formal development to prove the desired properties), larger environments — that is, with more than just those variables free in the term — can also be used when typing a term. An operation used for environments is the elimination of a pair containing a given variable x, denoted by Γ_x; this is needed before extending the environment with a new pair for x.

The typing relation takes three elements: a typing environment, a term, and a type. It is denoted by the statement $\Gamma \vdash e : \tau$ (written $\vdash e : \tau$ when Γ is empty); this statement is called a *typing judgement*. There are two ways to read a typing judgement: The first says that Γ, e, and τ are in the typing relation, and the other says that if *the typing environment Γ associates the free variables of e with some types, then e has type τ*. The former brings out the relational nature of the typing, while the latter emphasizes the algorithmic nature; the usual reading is the latter. When the elements appearing in the judgement are in the typing relation, the judgement is called *valid* (and the term, *well typed*) and if that is not the case, it is called *invalid* (and the term, *ill typed*). Thus, the typing relation is completely specified by the set of all valid judgements. For example, $\vdash 1 + 1 : \mathbf{Int}$ is a valid judgement, while $\vdash 2 + (\text{True}, 5) : \mathbf{Bool}$ is invalid. It is important to understand that well typed terms are free of certain execution errors, but ill typed terms may either contain those errors, or simply cannot be assured that they are free of errors. In the example above, the term contains an error: The representation in memory for numbers and pair are surely different (e.g., two bytes for the number and three for the pair), but addition will expect to receive a two-bytes operand; thus if the addition is executed, it will either need to check that each memory location corresponds to the numbers, or wrongly access the memory portion of the pair as if it corresponds to a number! For an ill-typed term that does not contain errors, see the last example in Section "Designing an Algorithm for Type Inference."

There are several ways to determine when a typing judgement is valid. The most common is to use a system of rules, called the *typing system* or *type system*. This system is a particular case of a formal proof system (collection of rules used to carry out stepwise deductions). Each rule has some judgements as premises and a judgement as conclusion, allowing in this way the desired compositional nature of the specification; when the number of premises of a rule is zero, it is called an axiom. Rules are written with premises above a horizontal line, and the conclusion below it; if some condition is needed for the application of the rule, it is written by its side. A rule states that when all premises are valid (and the conditions satisfied), so is the conclusion; thus, axioms are direct assertions that a judgement is valid.

Using the rules, a tree, called a *derivation tree* or also a *typing derivation*, or *derivation* for short, can be constructed; it has judgements as labels, and instances of rules as nodes; leaves are instances of axioms. One important property of derivation trees is that the judgement labelling the root of these trees is always a valid judgement. The common method to determine the validity of a given judgement is to build a derivation tree with it as the root; if no such tree exists, the judgement is invalid.

The typing rules for the nonfunctional part of the language are given in Figure 1. The rules are named for easy reference. Rule (VAR) establishes that Γ, x, and t are in the typing relation for every Γ containing the pair $x : \tau -$ or, using the algorithmic reading, if the typing environment G associates x with type τ, then x has type t. Rule (INT) states that numbers have type **Int** in any environment, and similarly, rule (BOOL) states that Boolean

Figure 1. Typing system (non-functional part)

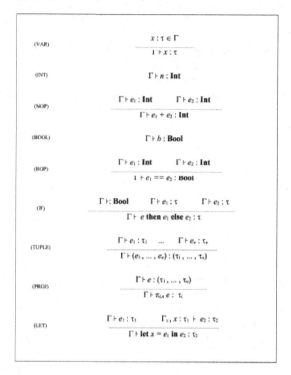

constants have type **Bool**. Rules (NOP) and (ROP) provide the typing of arithmetic and relational operations, respectively. Rule (IF) gives the typing for conditional construction-s: If the guard is a Boolean and the two branches have the same type t, then the conditional have type t as well. The typing for tuples and projections is given by rules (TUPLE) and (PROJ), with straightforward meaning. Finally, the typing for local definitions provided by **let** expressions is given by rule (LET): The free ocurrences of x in the body of the **let** are assumed to have the type of the definition of x, and then the whole expression have the type of the body.

Once the system has been given, derivation trees can be constructed to prove that a given judgement is valid. For example, in order to prove that $\Gamma \vdash 1 + 1 : $ **Int** is valid, the following derivation can be constructed for any Γ:

$$\frac{\Gamma \vdash 1 : \textbf{Int} \qquad \Gamma \vdash 1 : \textbf{Int}}{\Gamma \vdash 1 + 1 : \textbf{Int}}$$

On the other hand, there are no derivations for the judgement $\vdash 2 + (\textbf{True}, 5) : \textbf{Bool}$, because the only possibility to construct one is to use rule (NOP), but the second premise is not of the right form; it is expected that the operand must be an **Int**, and here it is a pair.

A more complex derivation is given for a term using a **let** and a conditional. The example has x and y as free variables, and for that reason, the pairs $x : \textbf{Int}$ and $y : \textbf{Int}$ must appear in the environment used in the judgements — in the derivation given, the environment $\Gamma^{xy} = x : \textbf{Int}, y : \textbf{Int}$ is used, which is the minimal useful one. (After introducing functions, the variable *max* shall be transformed into a function.)

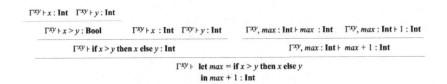

Observe, in particular, how the axiom stating that 1 has type **Int** in the right subtree of the derivation uses a larger environment than the minimal one needed for that judgement in isolation.

There are two main ways to use a type system: It can be used to check if a triple Γ, e, τ belongs to the relation, or, given Γ and e, a type τ can be constructed such that they are related (if it exists). The former is called *typechecking*, while the latter is called *type inference*.

One important property of this fragment of the type system is that it is *functional* — that is, given Γ and e, there exists at most one single type τ related to them. This facilitates the implementation of type inference, and reduces typechecking to infer the type and compare it with the given one. In order to compute the type of an expression, the implementation of type inference will recursively compute the type of each subexpression and then compare them to those needed to build a derivation. For example in (NOP), after the types of the operands have been obtained, they can be directly compared with **Int**, and if they are different, an error can be returned immediately, and similarly in other rules, as (IF). The functionality of the system comes from the fact that all the decisions have only one choice, and thus they can be taken locally. However, it is not always the case that static analyses are functional. Several decisions have multiple choices, and the information to decide about the right one can appear in some other part of the derivation. (See the example of the identity function in the next section.) So, more complex techniques are needed for implementation.

Typing Functions

The real expressive power of this language comes with the use of functions. The expression ($\lambda x.e$) denotes an anonymous function: When this function is given an argument in place of x, the body e of the function is returned. Thus, the type of this expression is a function space: If under the assumption that x has type τ_2, e has type τ_1, then the function has type ($\tau_2 \rightarrow \tau_1$). Corresponding with this notion, the application ($f\,e$) is the operation that provides the argument e to a function f: if f is the function ($\lambda x.e\,'$), the meaning of ($f\,e$) is the value of the body $e\,'$, where x is substituted by e. For example, when f is ($\lambda x.x+x$), the meaning of ($f\,2$) is $2 + 2$, that is, 4.

A common notational convention is that function types associate to the right, in accordance with the convention that function application associates to the left; thus, when considering the function *plus*, defined as ($\lambda x.\lambda y.x + y$), the application is written ($plus\,2\,3$) — for (($plus\,2$) 3) — while its type is written ($\mathbf{Int} \rightarrow \mathbf{Int} \rightarrow \mathbf{Int}$) — for ($\mathbf{Int} \rightarrow (\mathbf{Int} \rightarrow \mathbf{Int})$); the meaning is that *plus* is a function taking an integer x and returning a function of y into the result. By means of this convention it is simpler to understand *plus* as a function "with two arguments," even when formally it has only one. This is called *currification*; see later.

The typing rules for the functional fragment of the language, originally due to Hindley (1969), are given in Figure 2. Rule (LAM) establishes the typing of functions as explained above. Rule (APP) establishes the typing of applications: When e_1 is a function and e_2 has the type of its argument, then the application ($e_1\,e_2$) has the type of the result. Finally, rule (FIX) establishes the typing for recursive expressions: As (**fix** e) is a fixpoint of e, its type is that of the arguments, or identically, the results, of the function.

Figure 2. Typing system (functional part)

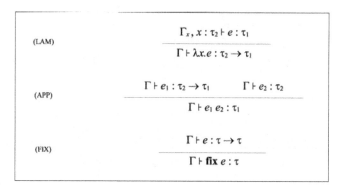

Copyright © 2007, Idea Group Inc. Copying or distributing in print or electronic forms without written permission of Idea Group Inc. is prohibited.

The simplest example is that of the function mapping a number to its successor:

$$\cfrac{\cfrac{x :_, \mathbf{Int} \vdash x : \mathbf{Int} \qquad x : \mathbf{Int} \vdash 1 : \mathbf{Int}}{x : \mathbf{Int} \vdash x + 1 : \mathbf{Int}}}{\vdash \lambda x. x + 1 : \mathbf{Int} \to \mathbf{Int}}$$

The operation of addition forces both the argument x and the result to have type **Int**. A slightly more complex example is that of a function projecting an element from a tuple:

$$\cfrac{\cfrac{p : (\mathbf{Int, Int}) \vdash p : (\mathbf{Int, Int})}{p : (\mathbf{Int, Int}) \vdash \pi_{1,2}\, p : \mathbf{Int}}}{\vdash \lambda p.\ \pi_{1,2}\, p : (\mathbf{Int, Int}) \to \mathbf{Int}} \qquad \cfrac{\cfrac{\Gamma^{fst} \vdash fst : (\mathbf{Int, Int}) \to \mathbf{Int}}{\Gamma^{fst} = fst : (\mathbf{Int, Int}) \to \mathbf{Int} \vdash fst\ (2,5) : \mathbf{Int}}}{\vdash \mathbf{let}\ fst = \lambda p.\ \pi_{1,2}\, p\ \mathbf{in}\ fst\ (2,5)\ : \mathbf{Int}}$$

$$\cfrac{\Gamma^{fst} \vdash 2 : \mathbf{Int} \qquad \Gamma^{fst} \vdash 5 : \mathbf{Int}}{\Gamma^{fst} \vdash (2,5) : (\mathbf{Int, Int})}$$

Observe that the built-in construct $\pi_{1,2}$ that cannot be used alone as a full expression, can be transformed into a function *fst* by means of anonymous functions. The typing of *fst* is chosen as to match the typing of the argument (2,5); this issue is discussed below. As before, the assigning of names to contexts is used to simplify the reading of the derivation.

Another interesting example is a function "with two arguments:" As mentioned before, that is represented by a higher-order function taking one argument and returning another function that completes the work. (This is called *currification*, and the function is said to be *curried*.) Here, the function calculating the maximum of two numbers has been chosen (a similar derivation can be constructed for function *plus* above):

$$\cfrac{\cfrac{\cfrac{(as\ before)}{\Gamma^{xy} = x : \mathbf{Int}, y : \mathbf{Int} \vdash \mathbf{if}\ x > y\ \mathbf{then}\ x\ \mathbf{else}\ y : \mathbf{Int}}}{x : \mathbf{Int} \vdash \lambda y.\ \mathbf{if}\ x > y\ \mathbf{then}\ x\ \mathbf{else}\ y : \mathbf{Int} \to \mathbf{Int}}}{\vdash \lambda x.\ \lambda y.\ \mathbf{if}\ x > y\ \mathbf{then}\ x\ \mathbf{else}\ y : \mathbf{Int} \to \mathbf{Int} \to \mathbf{Int}}$$

$$\cfrac{\cfrac{\Gamma^{max} \vdash max : \mathbf{Int} \to \mathbf{Int} \to \mathbf{Int} \qquad \Gamma^{max} \vdash 2 : \mathbf{Int}}{\Gamma^{max} \vdash max\ 2 : \mathbf{Int} \to \mathbf{Int} \qquad \Gamma^{max} \vdash 5 : \mathbf{Int}}}{\Gamma^{max} = max : \mathbf{Int} \to \mathbf{Int} \to \mathbf{Int} \vdash max\ 2\ 5 : \mathbf{Int}}$$

$$\vdash \quad \mathbf{let}\ max = \lambda x.\ \lambda y.\ \mathbf{if}\ x > y\ \mathbf{then}\ x\ \mathbf{else}\ y \\ \mathbf{in}\ max\ 2\ 5 \qquad\qquad : \mathbf{Int}$$

The derivation of the conditional in the body of the function has already been given in Section "Typing Nonfunctional Elements." It can be noted that the typing of $(\lambda x.\lambda y. \ldots)$ gives $(\mathbf{Int} \rightarrow (\mathbf{Int} \rightarrow \mathbf{Int}))$, but the notational convention is used. Observe that it is the comparison between x and y which forces their type to be **Int**.

An important example is that of a recursive function; first the function itself is typed:

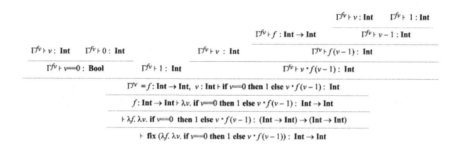

and having the derivation for the function, a complete expression using it can be typed:

Oddly enough, after the addition of functions the type system is no longer functional — that is, there are expressions that admit more than one typing. The simplest example of one of these expressions is the identity function; it can be typed as the identity on numbers:

$$\frac{x : \mathbf{Int} \vdash x : \mathbf{Int}}{\vdash \lambda x.x : \mathbf{Int} \rightarrow \mathbf{Int}}$$

and it can also be typed as the identity on Booleans:

$$\frac{x : \textbf{Bool} \vdash x : \textbf{Bool}}{\vdash \lambda x.x : \textbf{Bool} \to \textbf{Bool}}$$

In fact, it can be typed as the identity on any fixed type τ:

$$\frac{x : \tau \vdash x : \tau}{\vdash \lambda x.x : \tau \to \tau}$$

At first sight, the loosing of the functionality is not a very important issue. However, it has a high impact in the implementation of the type inference algorithm. For example, in the following typing derivation, the subderivation for the identity function must produce a function from numbers to numbers:

$$\frac{x : \textbf{Int} \vdash x : \textbf{Int}}{\vdash \lambda x.x : \textbf{Int} \to \textbf{Int}} \qquad \frac{\Gamma^{idI} \vdash id : \textbf{Int} \to \textbf{Int} \qquad \Gamma^{idI} \vdash 3 : \textbf{Int}}{\Gamma^{idI} = id : \textbf{Int} \to \textbf{Int} \vdash id\, 3 : \textbf{Int}}$$
$$\vdash \textbf{let } id = \lambda x.x \textbf{ in } id\, 3 : \textbf{Int}$$

But suppose that the number 3 is changed by the Boolean **True**. Will that mean that the expression has no longer a type? The answer is no. The following derivation can be constructed:

$$\frac{x : \textbf{Bool} \vdash x : \textbf{Bool}}{\vdash \lambda x.x : \textbf{Bool} \to \textbf{Bool}} \qquad \frac{\Gamma^{idB} \vdash id : \textbf{Bool} \to \textbf{Bool} \qquad \Gamma^{idB} \vdash \textbf{True} : \textbf{Bool}}{\Gamma^{idB} = id : \textbf{Bool} \to \textbf{Bool} \vdash id\, \textbf{True} : \textbf{Bool}}$$
$$\vdash \textbf{let } id = \lambda x.x \textbf{ in } id\, \textbf{True} : \textbf{Bool}$$

The typing of the identity function is different in the two examples. However, in a type inference algorithm, when making the recursive call to produce a type for the identity function, there is no information about which type must be chosen. The problem is that the decision about which type to assign to the function's argument x is needed inside the derivation of the defining expression, but cannot be taken until the body is processed; however, the type of the defining expression is needed to process the body.

The problem just mentioned is common to many static analysis techniques: The analysis of certain subexpressions may depend on information coming from the context where they are used. In the type system, the information coming from the context is the type of the argument in the rule (LAM). The solution to this problem is to use a mechanism to defer decisions and another one to take those deferred decisions and communicate them to the rest of the algorithm. Such a solution is presented in the next section.

The Implementation of Type Inference

In the previous section, the specification of a type system has been studied, and the problem regarding the implementation of type inference was stated. In this section, an algorithm is completely designed and implemented. The correctness and completeness of the given algorithm is stated, and although the proof is not given, similar proofs can be found in the literature — for example, Jones (1994a).

This section is divided into two parts. Firstly, the design of the algorithm is presented in the style of proof systems; however, the rules presented here are completely functional, and so they can be read directly as the design of a program. This design, originally introduced by Rèmy (1989), uses two formal mechanisms: variables and substitutions. Additionally, the correctness and completeness of the algorithm are stated as two theorems. Second, an almost direct coding in the language Java is presented, discussing its relation with the given design. More efficient ways to code the algorithm can be given, but the one presented here illustrates better the important features to be taken into account, without the clutter of subtle implementation tricks.

Designing an Algorithm for Type Inference

For the design of the algorithm for type inference, two mechanisms are needed. The first one is the addition of type variables in order to be able to express decisions that are deferred: When a decision has to be made but there is not enough information available, a new type variable is introduced; later, when the information becomes available, the variable can be replaced by the correct information. These new type variables are not part of the language presented to the programmer, but only a tool used inside the implementation (this will change when adding polymorphism). So, for the algorithm, the actual type language used is the following one:

$$\tau ::= t \mid \mathbf{Int} \mid \mathbf{Bool} \mid (\tau, \dots , \tau) \mid \tau{\rightarrow}\tau$$

The new syntactic category t stands for a countably infinite set of type variables (disjoint from the set of term variables). Observe that type variables can appear in any place where a type is needed; however, only ground types (i.e., with no variables) are accepted as result of the algorithm.

The second mechanism needed to design the type inference algorithm is one allowing the recording of decisions taken, in order to propagate them to the rest of the derivation tree. Substitutions are perfect for this task.

- **Definition 3.1:** *A substitution, denoted by S, is a function from type variables to types (formally, $S : t \rightarrow \tau$), where only a finite number of variables are mapped to something other than themselves.*

The denotation for the application of a substitution S to a variable t is written $(S\,t)$. The substitution mapping every variable to itself — the identity substitution — is denoted **Id**. The substitution mapping variable t to type τ, and all the rest to themselves is denoted $[t := \tau]$, so $[t := \tau]\,t = \tau$, and $[t := \tau]\,t' = t'$ for $t' \neq t$. Similarly, a substitution mapping t_i to type τ_i for $i = 1..n$ is denoted $[t_1 := \tau_1, \ldots, t_n := \tau_n]$.

Substitutions are extended to operate on types in a homomorphic way—that is, every variable t appearing in the type being substituted is replaced by $(S\,t)$. Formally this is denoted as S^*, and defined as:

$$\begin{cases} S^*t = St \\ S^*\text{Int} = \text{Int} \\ S^*\text{Bool} = \text{Bool} \\ S^*(\tau_1,...,\tau_n) = (S^*\tau_1,...,S^*\tau_n) \\ S^*(\tau_1 \rightarrow \tau_n) = (S^*\tau_1) \rightarrow (S^*\tau_n) \end{cases}$$

By abuse of notation, the form $(S\,\tau)$ is also used for types.

The composition of substitutions is defined using the extension to types; the composition of substitution S with substitution T is denoted $(S\,T)$, and defined as $(S\,T)\,t = S^*\,(T\,t)$. However, by using the abuse of notation, this definition can also be written as $(S\,T)\,t = S\,(T\,t)$, thus resembling the standard notion of function composition.

The final notion regarding substitutions is its extension to operate on typing environments. The idea is that applying a substitution to an environment amounts to applying the substitution to every type appearing in the environment. Thus, if $\Gamma = x_1 : \tau_1, ..., x_n : \tau_n$, then $S^*\,\Gamma = x_1 : S^*\,\tau_1, ..., x_n : S^*\,\tau_n$. Once again, the notation can be abused, thus defining $S\,\Gamma = x_1 : S\,\tau_1, ..., x_n : S\,\tau_n$ instead.

Variables are used to defer decisions, and substitutions are used to record a decision that has been taken. But, where are decisions actually taken? In order to formalize that idea, the notion of *unifier* has to be introduced. A unifier for types τ and τ' is a substitution S such that $S\,\tau = S\,\tau'$. If given two types, there exists a unifier for them, the types are said to be *unifiable*.

Unifiers are not unique, but they can be ordered by a more general order: A unifier S for τ and τ' is more general than a unifier T for the same types, denoted $S > T$, if there exist a substitution R such that $T = R\,S$. The composition of substitutions is used in the definition. The idea is that a unifier is more general than another one if it takes less decisions to unify the two types; the substitution R is encoding the remaining decisions taken by T. Given two unifiable types, there always exists a most general unifier, that is, a unifier that is more general than any other for those types; most general unifiers are not unique, however they differ only in the name of variables. This can be observed in the above-mentioned substitution R: It only maps variables to variables (and it is called a *renaming* for that reason).

For example, taking $\tau = \mathbf{Int} \to t_1 \to t_2$ and t' = $\tau_3 \to \mathbf{Bool} \to t_4$, two possible unifiers for τ and τ' are $S_1 = [t_1 := \mathbf{Bool}, t_2 := t_4, t_3 := \mathbf{Int}]$ and $S_2 = [t_1 := \mathbf{Bool}, t_2 := t_5 \to t_5, t_3 := \mathbf{Int}, t_4 := t_5 \to t_5]$; in this case, $S_1 > S_2$, being $R = [t_4 := t_5 \to t_5]$; it is the case also that S_1 is a most general unifier. Another most general unifier for the two types is $S_3 = [t_1 := \mathbf{Bool}, t_2 := t_6, t_3 := \mathbf{Int}, t_4 := t_6]$; observe that $S_1 > S_3$, by virtue of $R_1 = [t_4 := t_6]$ and also that $S_3 > S_1$, by virtue of $R_2 = [t_6 := t_4]$ — observe that both R_1 and R_2 are renamings.

It may be the case that given two types, there exist no unifier for them. There are two sources for this situation in the language presented here. The first one is common to any language with constants and type constructors: Two expressions constructed with different constructors cannot be unified. For example, there is no unifier for types **Int** and **Bool**, or for types **Bool** and **Int** → **Int**, and so on. The second one is subtler: It is related with the unification of a variable t with a type containing an occurrence of such a variable. For example, there are no unifiers for t_1 and $(t_1 \to \mathbf{Int})$, because the only choice is to substitute t_1 for an infinite type $((\ldots \to \mathbf{Int}) \to \mathbf{Int}) \to \mathbf{Int})$; however this language contains no infinite types. There are languages of types where there is a solution for the unification of these two types. (See the extension of the typing system with recursive types in Section *Recursive Types*.)

The first part of the implementation is to design an algorithm calculating the most general unifier of two given types. This algorithm, called *unification*, is written using judgements of the form $\tau \sim^S \tau'$, meaning that S is a most general unifier for τ and τ'. The rules defining the unification system are given in Figure 3.

Figure 3. Unification algorithm

$$\mathbf{Int} \sim^{Id} \mathbf{Int}$$

$$\mathbf{Bool} \sim^{Id} \mathbf{Bool}$$

$$t \sim^{[t:=\tau]} \tau \qquad (t \text{ does not occur in } \tau)$$

$$\tau \sim^{[t:=\tau]} t \qquad (t \text{ does not occur in } \tau)$$

$$\frac{\tau_1 \sim^{S_1} \tau'_1 \qquad S_1 \tau_2 \sim^{S_2} S_1 \tau'_2}{\tau_1 \to \tau_2 \sim^{S_2 S_1} \tau'_1 \to \tau'_2}$$

$$\frac{\tau_1 \sim^{S_1} \tau'_1 \qquad S_1 \tau_2 \sim^{S_2} S_1 \tau'_2 \qquad \ldots \qquad S_{(n-1)} \ldots S_1 \tau_n \sim^{S_n} S_{(n-1)} \ldots S_1 \tau'_n}{(\tau_1, \ldots, \tau_n) \sim^{S_n \ldots S_1} (\tau'_1, \ldots, \tau'_n)}$$

These rules can be read as function calls: the types are passed to the unification function, and the substitution is returned as the result. Observe, in particular, how in the second premise of the rule for functions, the substitution S_1 produced by the first recursive call is applied to types τ_2 and τ'_2 before making the second recursive call; the reason for this is to propagate decisions that may have been taken in the first call. Correctness is given by the following proposition.

Figure 4. Type inference algorithm

- **Proposition 3.2:** *Types τ and τ' are unifiable iff $\tau \sim^S \tau'$ for some substitution S satisfying that $S\tau = S\tau'$ and for all T such that $T\tau = T\tau'$, $S > T$. That is, the types τ and τ' are unifiable iff the unification algorithm returns a substitution S that is a most general unifier for τ and τ'.*

A coding of the unification algorithm must take into account the possibility of failure, encoding it in an appropriate form — for example, by returning a boolean establishing the success of the operation, and the substitution in case that the boolean is **True**.

The algorithm for type inference is also specified by using a formal system whose rules that can be understood as function calls. The judgments used for this system have the form $S\ \Gamma \vdash_W e : \tau$, where the environment Γ and the expression e are inputs, and the substitution S and the type τ are outputs (the W in the judgement is there for historical purposes. Such was the name used by Milner for his inference algorithm). The rules for this system are given in Figure 4.

The rules look much more complicated than they really are, because of the need to propagate substitutions obtained in each recursive call to subsequent calls. In particular, the notation $S_2 (S_1\ \Gamma)$ is used to indicate that the environment $(S_1\ \Gamma)$ is used as input, and substitution S_2 is obtained as output. In contrast with $(S_2\ S_1)\ \Gamma$, used to indicate that Γ is the input and the composition $(S_2\ S_1)$, the output (see rules (W-NOP), (W-ROP), (W-IF), (W-TUPLE), (W-LET), and (W-APP)). Another important thing to observe is that no assumption is made about the type returned by a recursive call. Instead, unification is used to make decisions forcing it to have the desired form afterwards (see rules (W-NOP), (W-ROP), (W-IF), (W-PROJ), (W-APP), and (W-FIX)). A final observation is concerned with the side conditions of the form (t new variable). The idea is that t is a variable not used in any other part of the derivation tree. This is a global condition, and any implementation has to take care of it.

As an example, the use of the algorithm to type the identity function is presented:

$$\frac{\mathbf{Id}\ (x : t_x) \vdash_W x : t_x}{\mathbf{Id}\ \varnothing \vdash_W \lambda x.x : t_x \to t_x} \qquad (t_x \text{ new variable})$$

Observe how a type containing variables is returned (together with the identity substitution).

Considering again the two uses of the identity function on numbers and booleans, but using the algorithm to obtain the derivations, it can be seen that the recursive call for typing the identity is always the same, and that it is the unification in rule (W-APP) which gives the variable its right value.

$$\frac{\mathbf{Id}\ (x : t_x) \vdash_W x : t_x \quad \mathbf{Id}\ \Gamma^{id} \vdash_W id : t_x \to t_x \quad \mathbf{Id}\ \Gamma^{id} \vdash_W 3 : \mathbf{Int}\ \ t_x \to t_x \sim^{[t_x:=\mathbf{Int},\ t:=\mathbf{Int}]} \mathbf{Int} \to t}{\frac{\mathbf{Id}\ \varnothing \vdash_W \lambda x.x : t_x \to t_x \quad [t_x:=\mathbf{Int},\ t:=\mathbf{Int}]\ (\Gamma^{id} = id : t_x \to t_x) \vdash_W id\ 3 : \mathbf{Int} = [t_x:=\mathbf{Int},\ t:=\mathbf{Int}]\ t}{[t_x:=\mathbf{Int},\ t:=\mathbf{Int}]\ \varnothing \vdash_W \mathbf{let}\ id = \lambda x.x\ \mathbf{in}\ id\ 3 : \mathbf{Int}}}$$

The relation of this new system with the old one — stated in Theorems 3.3 and 3.4 — is simple because the original system has a very important property: There is at most one rule for every construct in the language. This property is expressed by saying that the system is *syntax-directed*. Syntax-directed systems are relatively easy to implement because they provide only one rule for every construct. When specifying the extension to polymorphism, this property will be lost, giving much more work to implement that system. (See Section "Adding Parametric Polymorphism.")

The correctness and completeness of the algorithm are stated in the following theorems.

- **Theorem 3.3:** *If $S \Gamma \vdash_w e : \tau$, then $(S \Gamma) \vdash e : \tau$. That is, the type returned by the algorithm is a type for e.*

- **Theorem 3.4:** *If $(S \Gamma) \vdash e : \tau$ for some S, then $T \Gamma \vdash_w e : \tau'$ for some T and τ', and such that there exists R satisfying that $S = R\ T$, and $\tau = R\ \tau'$. In other words, any type for e can be obtained by a suitable substitution from a type given by the algorithm.*

These two properties, together with the fact that the system $\vdash_w$ is functional (up to the renaming of new variables), state that in order to type a term it is enough to run the algorithm once and later calculate the right substitution on every use.

However, as presented, this system only allows the calculation of the substitution once and for all, instead of at every use.

$$\mathbf{Id}\ (x : t_x) \vdash_w x : t_x \quad \mathbf{Id}\ \Gamma^{id} \vdash_w id : t_x{\to}t_x \quad \mathbf{Id}\ \Gamma^{id} \vdash_w \mathbf{True} : \mathbf{Bool} \quad t_x{\to}t_x \sim^{[t_x:=\mathbf{Bool},\, t:=\mathbf{Bool}]} \mathbf{Bool} \to t$$

$$\mathbf{Id}\ \varnothing \vdash_w \lambda x.x : t_x{\to}t_x \quad [t_x:=\mathbf{Bool}, t:=\mathbf{Bool}]\ (\Gamma^{id} = id : t_x{\to}t_x) \vdash_w id\ \mathbf{True} : \mathbf{Bool} = [t_x:=\mathbf{Bool}, t:=\mathbf{Bool}]\ t$$

$$[t_x:=\mathbf{Bool}, t:=\mathbf{Bool}]\ \varnothing \vdash_w \mathbf{let}\ id = \lambda x.x\ \mathbf{in}\ id\ \mathbf{True} : \mathbf{Bool}$$

When typing (id **True**), the variable t_x from the type of id was already substituted by **Int**, and so, the unification with **Bool** fails. For this reason, the term has no type, and is thus rejected by the type system. However, the term has no errors; it is the type system that has not enough expressive power. This kind of problem can be fixed by extending the system with parametric polymorphism. (This system is sketched in Section "Adding Parametric Polymorphism.")

The design of the algorithm is complete. In the following section, a coding of this algorithm using the object-oriented paradigm in the language C++ (Stroustrup, 2000) is presented.

Coding Type Inference with Objects

The presentation of the algorithm given before has been divided into three parts: the representation of terms and types, the unification algorithm, and the type inference algorithm. In a functional language, where the usual concern is how data is created (Nordlander, 1999), this separation would have been clear. Terms and types would have been represented as algebraic types, and unification and type inference would have been functions on those types. However, the object-oriented paradigm concentrates in how data is used — it being a dual view of programming (Nordlander, 1999) — and thus, the separation is not so clear. Recalling that the goal of this chapter is to bridge the gap between specification and implementation, that the gap is broader in the object-oriented paradigm than in the functional one, and that object-oriented languages are much more widespread, the implementation explained here will be done for the object-oriented paradigm. An implementation using a functional language can be found in Martínez López (in press).

The coding in the object-oriented paradigm uses several common patterns, such as the Composite, Singleton, or Template Methods (Gamma, Helm, Johnson, & Vlissides, 1995), so, for an experienced object-oriented programmer with a thorough understanding of the previous sections, it will not present a challenge.

In order to represent terms and types, the pattern Composite has been used. Abstract classes Term and Type represent those elements, and its subclasses indicate the corresponding alternative; each subclass has internal variables for its parts and the corresponding getters and (internal) setters. This idea is depicted in Figure 5 graphically using class diagrams (Object Management Group, 2004).

Type inference is represented by means of a message to terms, and type unification by means of a message to types. Abstract methods are used to allow each subclass to have the right behaviour by providing a hook method. This is an example of the Template Method Pattern. For unification, the abstract method unify() is redefined by each subclass, providing the right behaviour through hook methods. Additionally, unification uses double dispatching: When a type receives the message of unify with some other type, it sends to it the message unifyWithXX(), where XX is its own class. For example, class Function redefines unify'() to the following:

```
void Function:: unify'(Type *t){
                t->unifyWithFunction(this);
        }
```

and unifyWithFunction to:

```
void Function:: unifyWithFunction(Function *t){
                this->getOperator()->unify (t->getOperator());
                this->getOperand()->unify(t->getOperand());
        }
```

where getOperator() and getOperand() are the getters of Function's components.

Regarding type inference, the important coding decision is to represent the substitution being calculated as a global element. This is obtained by the instance variable state of class GlobalState in class Term. Instances of GlobalState contain two components:

- the current substitution, represented as a mapping between TypeVariables and Types, with operations setType() to associate a variable with a type, hasAssociation()

Figure 5. Class diagram for type inference in the object-oriented paradigm

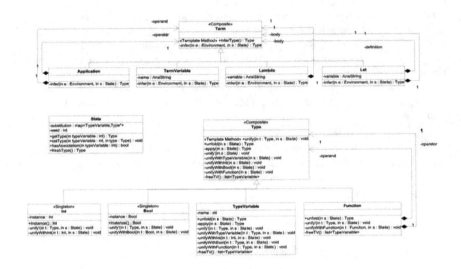

informing if a given variable has an association, and getType() returning the type associated to a variable if it exists, and

- a seed, with an operation freshType() used to calculate a new type variable (one never used before in the derivation; thus its global nature) in those rules that require it.

Instead of performing the application of the substitution to every element immediately, the substitution is recorded in the state, and applied only when the type has to be accessed. The coding of this behaviour is given by the methods apply() and unfold() of class Type: apply() represents the application of a substitution to a type variable (i.e., it stops the application of the substitution as soon as something different from a variable is found), while unfold() represents the application of a substitution to a type (i.e., it applies the substitution to all the parts of the type, recursively). The difference between apply() and unfold() is due to the behaviour of unification. When unification is performed, new associations between type variables and types (corresponding to the decisions taken by the algorithm) are made on every subterm, and those new associations would have not been taken into account by unfold(); instead, apply() is used at every subterm, performing an incremental unfolding that has taken into account the last associations calculated. The code of apply() and unfold() is identical at class TypeVariable, but differs in Function.

```
type* Type:: unfold(State s){
        return this;
}
Type* TypeVariable:: unfold(State s){
        if (!s->hasAssociation(this->getName)) return this;
        else return (s->getType(this->getName())->unfold(s));
}
Type* Function:: unfold(State s){
        this->setOperand(this->getOperand()->unfold(s));
        this->setOperator(this->getOperator()->unfold(s));
        return this;
}
Type* Type:: apply(State s){
        return this;
}
Type* TypeVariable:: apply(State s){
        if (!s->hasAssociation(this->getName)) return this;
        else return (s->getType(this->getName())->apply(s));
}
```

The coding of method inferType in class Term just resets the global state with a new state (with the identity substitution and a base seed), and then it calls the abstract method infer, letting the subclasses provide the actual behaviour through hook methods. Environments used in the internal method infer are represented as mappings from TermVariables to Types.

```
Type* Term:: inferType(){
        State* state = new State;
        state->initialState();
        Environment* g = new Environment;
        Type* t = this->infer(g,state)->unfold(state);
        delete g;
        return t;
}
```

Adding Parametric Polymorphism

In the last example of the section "Designing an Algorithm for Type Inference" a term having no type, but without errors, has been given. That example shows the limitations of the simple type system presented. In this section, the basic type system is extended with parametric polymorphism, making it more powerful, and so, capable of typing terms like the one presented in the example.

Recall that the problem was that the simple type system only allows the calculation of the substitution once and for all, instead of at every use. In order to solve the problem, some mechanism allowing multiple different instances for a given variable is needed. The solution is to quantify universally a type with variables, thus indicating that the quantified variables can take many different values. However, this has to be done with care. If universal quantification is added in the same syntactic level as the rest of the typing constructs, the system obtained becomes undecidable (Wells, 1994, 1998). In order to have polymorphism keeping decidability, Damas and Milner separate the quantification in a different level (Damas & Milner, 1982), thus having (monomorphic) types in one level, and type schemes (polymorphic types) in another one. The type system is designed in such a way that only declarations made in a **let** construct are allowed to be polymorphic. For that reason, it is sometimes called let-bounded polymorphism. Another solution is to add type annotations into terms (Reynolds, 1998), resulting in the language called *second order lambda calculus*, but that alternative is not described here. The term language is the same, but the type language is changed.

- **Definition 4.1:** *Types for a let-bounded polymorphic language are given by two syntactic categories: monomorphic types, called also* monotypes, *denoted by* τ, *and polymorphic types, called* type schemes, *denoted by* σ. *The grammars defining these categories are the following:*

$$\tau ::= t \mid \mathbf{Int} \mid \mathbf{Bool} \mid (\tau, \dots, \tau) \qquad \mid \tau \to \tau$$
$$\sigma ::= \tau \mid t.\sigma$$

Observe how monotypes can be seen as type schemes, but not the other way round. Once a quantification has been introduced, no other type constructions can be used. This forces the elements of tuples and the arguments and results of functions to be monomorphic (they can be made polymorphic in an outer level, but, for example, no polymorphic function can be passed as argument. See the example at the end of this section). The addition of quantification to types implies that the variables of a type expression are now divided into two groups: those that are quantified (*bound* variables) and those that are not (*free* variables). This notion is exactly the same as the one of free variables in the term language, where   is the binder and the s following it, its scope.

The judgements to determine the typing of terms in the polymorphic system are very similar to those of the simply typed system. The only differences are that environments associate variables with type schemes (instead of monotypes as before), and that the resulting type can be a type scheme. That is, the form of judgements is $\Gamma \vdash e : \sigma$, where Γ contains pairs of the form $x : \sigma$. The rules specifying the polymorphic typing are given in Figure 6 (rules (P-INT), (P-NOP), (P-BOOL), and (P-ROP) are omitted because, being monomorphic in nature, they are identical to their counterpart in the simply typed system).

The formulation of this system deserves explanation, because at first glance, it may seem almost identical to the one given in the previous sections. However, the changes make it more powerful. On the one hand, there are two new rules ((P-GEN) and (P-INST)) to allow the quantification of type variables and their removal (by using substitutions). On the other hand, some rules have been changed to incorporate the notion of type scheme ((P-VAR), (P-IF), and, most notably, (P-LET)), while others ((P-TUPLE), (P-PROJ), (P-LAM), (P-APP), and (P-FIX)) remained exactly as before. This fact is represented by the use of τs and σs in the appropriate places. It is very important that these rules remain unchanged; the reason is that, as functions and tuples cannot handle polymorphic components, their typing must remain monomorphic, and thus the rules are identical to their simply typed counterparts (remember that allowing functions to have polymorphic components turns the system undecidable). The other rules are changed to consider type schemes; the most important of these is (P-LET), because it is the one allowing the actual use of polymorphism. See the following example, considering again the typing of the identity function used twice on different types.

$$
\cfrac{
\cfrac{x : t_s \vdash x : t_s}{
\cfrac{\vdash \lambda x.x : t_s \to t_s \quad \text{(P-GEN)}}{\vdash \lambda x.x : \forall t_s.t_s \to t_s}
}
\quad
\cfrac{
\cfrac{\Gamma^{id} \vdash id : \forall t_s.t_s \to t_s \quad \text{(P-INST)}}{\Gamma^{id} \vdash id : \text{Int} \to \text{Int} \quad \Gamma^{id} \vdash 3 : \text{Int}}
}{\Gamma^{id} \vdash id\ 3 : \text{Int}}
\quad
\cfrac{
\cfrac{\Gamma^{id} \vdash id : \forall t_s.t_s \to t_s \quad \text{(P-INST)}}{\Gamma^{id} \vdash id : \text{Bool} \to \text{Bool} \quad \Gamma^{id} \vdash \text{True} : \text{Bool}}
}{\Gamma^{id} \vdash id\ \text{True} : \text{Bool}}
\quad
1^{id} = id : \forall t_s.t_s \to t_s \vdash (id\ 3, id\ \text{True}) : (\text{Int, Bool})
}{\vdash \text{let } id = \lambda x.x \text{ in } (id\ 3, id\ \text{True}) : (\text{Int, Bool})}
$$

Observe how the use of the new rules (marked with their names in the derivation) allows the two subderivations to use different types for the identity. This example, that was not typable under the simply typed system, shows that this extension gives more power.

An important thing to observe is that only let-bounded variables are polymorphic. In order to see this, consider the operationally equivalent term $(\lambda id.\ (id\ 3, id\ \textbf{True}))(\lambda x.x)$. This term is not typable on this system. The problem is the use of an anonymous function to bind the variable id to the identity function $(\lambda x.x)$; it has to be monomorphic. Observe a possible derivation:

$$
\cfrac{
\cfrac{\textbf{Id}\ (x : t_s) \vdash_w x : t_s}{\textbf{Id}\ \varnothing \vdash_w \lambda x.x : t_s \to t_s}
\quad
\cfrac{
\cfrac{\textbf{Id}\ \Gamma^{id} \vdash_w id : t_s \to t_s \quad \textbf{Id}\ \Gamma^{id} \vdash_w 3 : \text{Int}}{t_s \to t_s \sim^{S = [t_s = \text{Int}, t_1 = \text{Int}]} \text{Int} \to t_1}
}{
\cfrac{S\Gamma^{id} \vdash_w id\ 3 : \text{Int} = S\ t_1}{}
}
\quad
\cfrac{
\cfrac{S\Gamma^{id} \vdash_w id : \text{Int} \to \text{Int} \quad S\Gamma^{id} \vdash_w \text{True} : \text{Bool}}{\text{Int} \to \text{Int} \sim \text{Bool} \to t_2\ !!!}
}{
?? (S\ \Gamma^{id}) \vdash_w id\ \text{True} : ??
}
}{
?? (\Gamma^{id} = id : t_s \to t_s) \vdash_w (id\ 3, id\ \text{True}) : ??
}
$$

$$
?? \varnothing \vdash_w \text{let } id = \lambda x.x \text{ in } (id\ 3, id\ \text{True}) : ??
$$

The implementation of this system requires some care. The problem is that the system is not syntax directed — that is, more than one rule can be applied to type a given term. However, it can be noted that this is the result of the addition of rules (P-GEN) and (P-INST), so, if the use of these two rules can be limited to certain parts of a derivation, they can be incorporated to the other rules. Fortunately, this is the case: The only meaningful uses of (P-GEN) are either before the use of (P-LET), or at the end of a derivation; and the only meaningful uses of (P-INST) are just after the use of (P-VAR). All the other uses can be either removed or changed into one of those mentioned.

Figure 6. Typing system for let-bounded polymorphism

$$(\text{P-VAR}) \quad \frac{x : \sigma \in \Gamma}{\Gamma \vdash x : \sigma}$$

$$(\text{P-IF}) \quad \frac{\Gamma \vdash e : \textbf{Bool} \quad \Gamma \vdash e_1 : \sigma \quad \Gamma \vdash e_2 : \sigma}{\Gamma \vdash \textbf{if } e \textbf{ then } e_1 \textbf{ else } e_2 : \sigma}$$

$$(\text{P-TUPLE}) \quad \frac{\Gamma \vdash e_1 : \tau_1 \quad \ldots \quad \Gamma \vdash e_n : \tau_n}{\Gamma \vdash (e_1, \ldots, e_n) : (\tau_1, \ldots, \tau_n)}$$

$$(\text{P-PROJ}) \quad \frac{\Gamma \vdash e : (\tau_1, \ldots, \tau_n)}{\Gamma \vdash \pi_{i,n} \, e : \tau_i}$$

$$(\text{P-LET}) \quad \frac{\Gamma \vdash e_1 : \sigma_1 \quad \Gamma_x, x : \sigma_1 \vdash e_2 : \sigma_2}{\Gamma \vdash \textbf{let } x = e_1 \textbf{ in } e_2 : \sigma_2}$$

$$(\text{P-LAM}) \quad \frac{\Gamma_x, x : \tau_2 \vdash e : \tau_1}{\Gamma \vdash \lambda x.e : \tau_2 \to \tau_1}$$

$$(\text{P-APP}) \quad \frac{\Gamma \vdash e_1 : \tau_2 \to \tau_1 \quad \Gamma \vdash e_2 : \tau_2}{\Gamma \vdash e_1 \, e_2 : \tau}$$

$$(\text{P-FIX}) \quad \frac{\Gamma \vdash e : \tau \to \tau}{\Gamma \vdash \textbf{fix } e : \tau}$$

$$(\text{P-GEN}) \quad \frac{\Gamma \vdash e : \sigma}{\Gamma \vdash e : \forall t.\sigma} \quad \text{(if } t \text{ does not appear free in } \Gamma)$$

$$(\text{P-INST}) \quad \frac{\Gamma \vdash e : \forall t.\sigma}{\Gamma \vdash e : [t := \tau] \, \sigma}$$

There are two mechanisms to incorporate the uses of these rules to a syntax-directed version: one to capture (P-GEN), and the other for (P-INST). The first one is an operation to quantify exactly those variables that are important.

- **Definition 4.2:** *Let* $A = \{t_1, ..., t_n\}$ *be the set of free variables of type* τ, *from which the free variables appearing in* Γ *have been removed. Then* $Gen_\Gamma(\tau) = \forall t_1. ... \forall t_n.\tau$. *That is, the operation Gen quantifies all the free variables of a type except those that appear free in the environment.*

The correspondence of this notion with the use of (P-GEN) is given in the following proposition:

- **Proposition 4.3:** *If* $\Gamma \vdash e : \tau$, *then* $\Gamma \vdash e : Gen_\Gamma(\tau)$, *and both derivations differ only in the use of rule* (P-GEN).

The second mechanism is a relationship between type schemes, according to how general they are. In order to define it, the notion of generic instance of a type scheme has to be defined first.

- **Definition 4.4:** *A type* τ' *is a* generic instance *of a type scheme* $\sigma = \forall t_1. ... \forall t_n.\tau$ *if there are types* $\tau_1, ..., \tau_n$ *such that* $[t_1 := \tau_1, ..., t_n := \tau_n] \tau = \tau'$.

For example, **Int** $\rightarrow$ **Int** is a generic instance of $\forall t.t \rightarrow t$, and $(t, t') \rightarrow$ **Bool** is a generic instance of $\forall t_1. \forall t_2.t_1 \rightarrow t_2$.

- **Definition 4.5:** *A type scheme* σ *is said to be* more general *than a type scheme* σ', *written* $\sigma \geq \sigma'$, *if every generic instance of* σ' *is a generic instance of* σ.

For example, $\forall t_1. \ t_2.t_1 \rightarrow t_2$ is more general than $\forall t.\forall t'.\forall t''.(t, t') \rightarrow$ **Bool**. Observe that there can be any number of quantifiers on the less general type scheme, as long as the variables do not clash with those in the more general one.

This definition of *"more general"* does not provide an easy way to calculate when two types are related. The following proposition provides a characterization giving a syntactic way to do that:

- **Proposition 4.6:** *Let* $\sigma = \forall t_1. ... \forall t_n.\tau$, *and* $\sigma' = \forall t'_1. ... \forall t'_m.\tau'$. *and suppose none of the* t'_i *appears free in* σ. *Then* $\sigma \geq \sigma'$ *if, and only if, there are types* $\tau_1, ..., \tau_n$ *such that* $[t_1 := \tau_1, ..., t_n := \tau_n] \tau = \tau'$.

Figure 7. Syntax directed system for let-bounded polymorphism

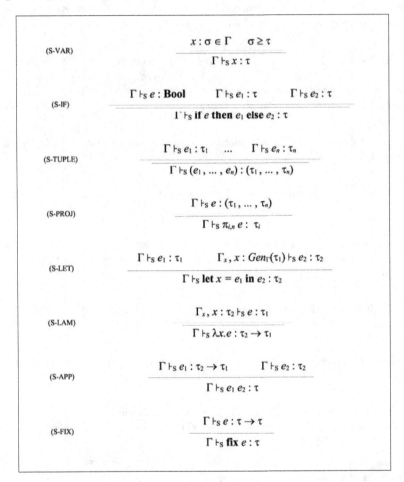

By means of Proposition 4.6, the relationship between two type schemes can be calculated by pattern matching — a restricted form of unification — of τ against τ'.

With all these elements, a syntax-directed version of the polymorphic type system can be introduced. The judgements have the form $\Gamma \vdash_s e : \tau$, where Γ contains pairs of the form $x : \sigma$, but the result is a monotype. The rules are given in Figure 7.

Observe the use of the operation *Gen* in the rule (S-LET), and the use of $\geq$ in the rule (S-VAR). They capture the uses of rules (GEN) and (INST). Correctness and completeness of the syntax-directed version with respect to the specification are given in the following two theorems. Completeness is a bit more complicated because the two systems return elements of different syntactic categories; the specification returns a type scheme, and the syntax directed version, a monotype. However, they can be related by using *"more general."*

- **Theorem 4.7:** *If* $\Gamma \vdash_s e : \tau$, *then* $\Gamma \vdash e : \tau$. *That is, the type returned by the syntax-directed version is a type for e according to the specification.*

- **Theorem 4.8:** *If* $\Gamma \vdash : \sigma$, *then* $\Gamma \vdash_s e : \tau$ *for some* τ, *and* $Gen_\Gamma(\tau) \geq \sigma$. *In other words, any type scheme for e can be obtained by instantiation of the generalization of a type given by the syntax-directed system.*

Consider a derivation of a type of the identity function using the syntax directed system:

$$\frac{x : t_x \vdash_S x : t_x}{\vdash_S \lambda x.x : t_x \to t_x}$$

Its generalization is $\forall t_x.t_x \to t_x$, and any other type scheme obtainable for the identity function (e.g., $\forall t.(t, t) \to (t, t)$, $\forall t'.\forall t''.(t' \to t'') \to (t' \to t'')$, **Int** $\to$ **Int**, etc.) can be obtained from the former by instantiation.

The algorithm to calculate a type scheme for a given term in the polymorphic system is very similar to the one given for the simply typed system. The most interesting rule is that of variables, because it has to implement the instantiation prescribed by the "more general" relation. This is obtained by substituting the quantified variables for new ones on *every use* of the rule, thus having the desired effect. All the remaining rules are easily deducible.

(WP-VAR)
$$\frac{x : \forall t_1. \dots \forall t_n.\tau \in \Gamma}{\text{Id } \Gamma \vdash_{WP} x : [t_1 := t'_1, \dots, t_n := t'_n] \, \tau} \qquad (t'_1, \dots, t'_n \text{ new variables})$$

The coding of this algorithm is an easy extension of the one presented in Section "Coding Type Inference with Objects." The only possible complication is the representation of bound variables because free and bound variables can be mixed, and thus can cause confusion. A good solution is to have two different representations for free and bound variables and code the algorithms for generalization and instantiation accordingly.

Other Extensions
to the Basic Type System

Type systems have been designed for almost all kinds of paradigms in programming, and for almost all features — for example, records, arrays, variant types, not to mention extensions to the language, overloading (Jones, 1994a, 1996; Odersky, Wadler, & Wehr, 1995), recursive types, type systems for imperative features (Hoang, Mitchell, & Viswanathan, 1993; Wright, 1992, 1995), object oriented languages (Abadi & Cardelli, 1996; Nordlander, 1999; Nordlander, 2000; von Oheimb & Nipkow, 1999; Syme, 1999; Wand, 1987), inheritance (Breazu-Tannen, Coquand, Gunter, & Scedrov, 1991; Wand, 1991, 1994), persistency (Atkinson, Bailey, Chisholm, Cockshott, & Morrison, 1983; Atkinson & Morrison, 1988; Dearle, 1988; Morrison, Connor, Cutts, Kirby, & Stemple, 1993), abstract datatypes (Mitchell & Plotkin, 1988), reactive systems (Hughes, Pareto, & Sabry, 1996; Nordlander, 1999), mobile systems (Freund & Mitchell, 1998; Igarashi & Kobayashi, 2001; Knabe, 1995), and others (Pottier, 2000; Shields & Meijer, 2001) in the field of language features.

There are also other ways to present type inference systems, the main alternative being the use of constraints (Aiken, 1999; Sulzmann, Odersky, & Wehr, 1997). In these systems, there are two phases for type inference: the first one, when the term is traversed and constraints on type variables are collected, and a second phase of constraint solving, where a solution for all the constraints gathered is calculated. This form of presentation allows much more flexibility for the use of heuristics during constraint solving, and it is more suitable when typing extensions to the basic system presented here. The theory of qualified types for overloading and the framework of type specialization discussed below use this variation.

In this section, some extensions will be presented. In the first part, basic extensions to the language are considered. In the second part, extensions to the type system to consider advanced features are covered. And in the last one, different type-based analyses are discussed.

Extending the Basic Language

Two important extensions a good language has to consider are the ability to manage records and variant types (or sum types).

Records

Most languages provide records instead of tuples. Records are a variation of tuples with named components. Instead of referencing the elements by their position, there are labels that can be used to retrieve them. The projections $\pi_{i,n} e$ are then replaced by the accessing operation $e.l_i$.

- **Definition 5.1:** *The term language is extended with* records *in the following way:*

$$e ::= ... \mid \{l=e, ... , l=e\} \mid e.l \mid \textbf{with } \{l = x, ... , l = x\} = e \textbf{ in } e$$

where l is an element of a set of identifiers called labels.

Examples of record types are $\{x = 0, y = 0\}$, to represent the origin vector in a two dimension space, $\{name = $ "Juan Pérez", $age = 55, address = $ "C.Pellegrini 2010"$\}$ to represent a person, and $\{subst = idSubst, seed = 0\}$ to represent a global state (with *idSubst* a proper representation of the identity substitution). Different languages have different rules regarding the scope of labels and whether records can be "incomplete" or not (that is, having some labels with an undefined value or not). For example, in Pascal, any record can contain any label and records may be incomplete, while in O'Haskell (Nordlander, 1999), labels are global constants — thus contained by at most one record type. O'Haskell uses subtyping, thus alleviating the problems that this "global policy" may produce (Nordlander, 2000) — and records have to determine uniquely a record type already declared.

In order to type records, the language of types has to be extended. There are two common choices for doing this: to have named records, and using the name as the type, or to have anonymous records, using the structure as the type. Here, the second option is taken, because it is more illustrative and the other version can be easily reconstructed.

- **Definition 5.2:** *The extension of the type language to consider records is the following:*

$$\tau ::= ... \mid \textbf{Struct}\{l : \tau, ... , l : \tau\}$$

Examples of record types are **Struct**$\{x : \textbf{Int}, y : \textbf{Int}\}$, to represent a vector of two integers, **Struct**$\{name : \textbf{String}, age : \textbf{Int}, address : \textbf{String}\}$ to represent the type of a person, and **Struct**$\{subst : \textbf{Int} \rightarrow \textbf{Type}, seed : \textbf{Int}\}$ to represent the type of a global state (for a suitable representation of **Type**s). A common abbreviation used to simplify the writing of record types is to group several labels with the same type by putting them separated by commas before the type, as in **Struct**$\{x, y : \textbf{Int}\}$, but this is just syntactic sugar.

The extension of the simply typed system to type records is given in Figure 8.

In addition to the accessing operation using a label name, some languages provide a **with** construct, to bind all the elements of a record simultaneously. This construct is similar to the **let** used before. In some languages, the binding of variables to label is left implicit — for example, Pascal — with the consequence that scoping depends thus on typechecking, causing a difficulty to find errors due to hidden variable clashes.

The implementation of type inference for this extension is an easy exercise.

Figure 8. Typing system (records)

$$\text{(RECORD)}\quad \frac{\Gamma \vdash e_1 : \tau_1 \quad \ldots \quad \Gamma \vdash e_n : \tau_n}{\Gamma \vdash \{l_1 = e_1, \ldots, l_n = e_n\} : \mathbf{Struct}\{l_1 : \tau_1, \ldots, l_n : \tau_n\}}\quad (l_i \text{ all distinct})$$

$$\text{(LABEL)}\quad \frac{\Gamma \vdash e : \mathbf{Struct}\{l_1 : \tau_1, \ldots, l_n : \tau_n\}}{\Gamma \vdash e.l_i : \tau_i}$$

$$\text{(WITH)}\quad \frac{\Gamma \vdash e_1 : \mathbf{Struct}\{l_1 : \tau_1, \ldots, l_n : \tau_n\} \qquad \Gamma_x, x_1 : \tau_1, \ldots, x_n : \tau_n \vdash e_2 : \tau_2}{\Gamma \vdash \{l_1 = x_1, \ldots, l_n = x_n\} = e_1 \ \mathbf{in}\ e_2 : \tau_2}$$

The combination of records and higher-order functions has been used to provide objects without classes in the language O'Haskell (Nordlander, 1999). This is an example of the power that a good discipline of types providing neat combinations of different elements can achieve.

Sum Types (Unions, Variants, or Tagged Types)

Sum types are important types for expressiveness, although they are less known than the rest of the type constructs. They consist of the union of several types, discriminating from which addend a given value comes from; the usual way to discriminate is by means of *tags*, and for that reason they also receive the name of *tagged types*. Another way in which they appear in programming languages is as variant records, although that is only a weak implementation of the real notion of sums. The main purpose of variant records is to save memory and not to add expressiveness.

There are several ways to present sum types. The most simple one consists of allowing several named tags — called *constructors* — with a single argument each; constructors with more arguments can be expressed using tuples, and a special type called **Unit** or **Void** needed to have constant constructors. Other versions allow for constructors with multiple arguments, to use unnamed tags (using indexes instead of constructors), to have only binary sums (multiple sums are obtained by combination), and so on.

To start the presentation, the **Unit** type is given first. This type contains a single value, usually called **unit**, and it can be identified with a tuple with zero elements (so, following the notation used for tuples, both the type and its single element can be denoted by a pair of parenthesis — **()**). Another common notation for this type is to call it **void**, and its single element also **void** (for example, in C). The purpose of **unit** is to indicate that some uninteresting or unnecessary argument or result is being used.

- **Definition 5.3:** *The term language is extended with* **unit** *in the following way:*

  $e ::= ... \mid ()$

- **Definition 5.4:** *The extension of the type language to consider the* **Unit** *type is the following:*

  $t ::= ... \mid ()$

There is only one typing rule for **unit**, presented in Figure 9, with the rules for sum types. As a simple example of the use of unit, consider its use as filler:

let $fst = \lambda p. \, \pi_{1,2} \, p$
in $(fst\,(2,()), fst\,(\mathbf{True},()))$

Here, the type of the first instance of *fst* used in the body of the local definition is (**Int**, ()) $\rightarrow$ **Int**, and that of the second one is (**Bool**, ()) $\rightarrow$ **Bool**. More involved examples are given in conjunction with sums.

Sum types are built with constructors — a special kind of function — and they are inspected with a construct called **case**; they can be thought of as a generalization of the notion of booleans, with constructors in place of **True** and **False**, and **case** in place of **if-then-else**. The syntax used here for sum types is given as follows:

- **Definition 5.5:** *The term language is extended with* sums *in the following way:*

  $e ::= ... \mid C\,e \mid \mathbf{case}\ e\ \mathbf{of}\ C\,x\,.\,e; ...; C\,x\,.\,e$

  where C is an element of a set of identifiers called constructors.

The simplest example of sum types is an enumerative type. For example, to model colors, constructors with the names of the colors can be used — as in **Red** (), **Blue** (), and so on. Constructors need an argument, but as colors are supposed to be constants, they are given the meaningless unit value.

Sum types used to type expressions using constructors respect the following syntax:

- **Definition 5.6:** *The extension of the type language to consider sum types is the following:*

  $\tau ::= ... \mid \mathbf{Variant}\{C:\tau, ..., C:\tau\}$

This presentation provides anonymous sums, that is, they are represented by the possible constructors used to build elements of the type. Different languages made different decisions regarding this choice. The most used one is to assign a name to a sum type, and then use the name when referring to it. The most important difference between these alternatives is how the equivalence of two given types is calculated: They can be considered equal if they have the same set of constructors, regardless of their order — in one extreme — to being considered equal only if they have the same name — in the other one.

In the case of the modelling of colors, their type can be, for example, **Variant{Red**:(), **Yellow**:(), **Blue**:()}, if only primary colors are modelled, or **Variant{Red**:(), **Yellow**:(), **Blue**:(), **Orange**:(), **Green**:(), **Purple**:()}, if both primary and secondary colors are modelled.

A slightly more complex example is that of basic geometric shapes. They can be represented as the following type: **Variant{Circle** : **Int**, **Rectangle** : (**Int**,**Int**)}, and some of its elements can be given as **Circle** 10, **Rectangle** (3,5), and so on.

The typing rules for expressions involving constructors are given in Figure 9. In the case of rule (CONSTR), there is some freedom in the choice of the constructors not mentioned in the term; some variants regarding the possible accepted constructors there are possible, and the choices are given by the restrictions in the equivalence of types, as described. In the rule (CASE), this presentation forces the construct **case** to have one branch for every constructor appearing in the type; however, other choices are also possible, allowing less constructors to be used. Again, this issue is related with type equivalence between different sums.

By using the case construct, functions over sums can be constructed. For example, the following function calculates the area of a given shape (although in the given definition of the language there are only integers, this example uses operations on floating point numbers, as the decimal number 3.14 as an approximation to number p, and the division by two):

Figure 9. Typing system (unit and sum types)

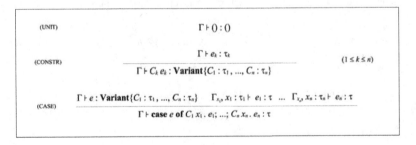

let *area* = λ*s*. **case** *s* **of** **Circle** *x*. 3.14*(x^2);

$$\text{Rectangle } xy. \ (\pi_{1,2} \ xy * \pi_{2,2} \ xy)/2$$

in (*area* (**Circle** 5), *area* (**Rectangle** (2,4)))

The type of function *area* in this example is **Variant{Circle : Int, Rectangle : (Int,Int)}** →**Int**.

Sums can be combined with type variables, to obtain very flexible types. A classic example is that of a variant type used to model the possibility of failure; several names for constructors can be used. Here, they are called **Error** and **Ok**. Thus, the type is **Variant{ Error : String, Ok : τ}**, for some τ. This type can be used to model the result of a function calculating the minimum of a sequence of values, where **Error** "Empty sequence" can be used to model when there are no values, and **Ok** *v* to model that *v* is the minimum.

The real power of sums can be seen when combined with other types, as the case of recursive types, presented in the following section.

Extending the Type System

Some important extensions are better considered extensions to the type system, rather than extensions to the language. Among those, recursive and qualified types are considered here.

Recursive Types

Recursive types are a powerful addition to a type system. Several different ways to introduce recursion with types exist, being the most common one to use recursive definition of types (in combination with named types). However, the formal presentation of recursive types using names and equations is more complex than the anonymous one, thus, as the goal here is to keep simplicity, the latter have been chosen.

The introduction of recursive types usually do not introduce new expressions on the term language, although the presentation is more simple introducing two constructs as follows:

- **Definition 5.7:** *The term language is extended with two new constructs in the following way:*

  e ::= ... | **in** *e* | **out** *e*

These two constructs, **in** and **out**, are usually implicitly assumed in practical languages. Their purpose is to map a recursive type into its expansion, and back.

The syntax of recursive types is obtained with an operator similar to **fix**: it maps a type function into its fixpoint. For historical purposes, this operator is denoted with the greek letter μ. The syntax of types is thus extended as follows:

- **Definition 5.8:** *The extension of the type language to consider recursive types is the following (in addition to type variables, as described in Section "Designing an Algorithm for Type Inference"):*

$$\tau ::= \ldots \mid \mu t.\tau$$

The intended meaning of the type expression $\mu t.\tau$ is the solution of the equation $t = \tau$, where variable t may occur in τ. A simple way to obtain that is to make $\mu t.\tau$ and $[t:=\mu t.\tau]\tau$ isomorphic (i.e., having the same structure); the result of this is that, assuming that $\mu t.\tau$ represents the solution of the equation, replacing on every occurrence of t in τ must give the same result. The term constructs **in** and **out** are functions from $[t:=\mu t.\tau]\tau$ to $\mu t.\tau$, and from $\mu t.\tau$ to $[t:=\mu t.\tau]\tau$, respectively. This is captured by the typing rules given in Figure 10.

Recursive types provide infinite expansion of type constructs. This feature allows, in particular, extending the solutions to unification. When unifying a type variable t with a type containing it, say $t \rightarrow$ **Int**, the type $\mu t.\ t \rightarrow$ **Int** is a solution for it in this system; observe that the expansion of $\mu t.\ t \rightarrow$ **Int** is isomorphic to it, being that the condition needed.

The real power of recursive types comes from the combination with other type constructs, as sums and tuples. A classic example is that of lists of a type t_x; they can be represented as the type $\mu t_l.$**Variant**$\{$ **Nil** : (), **Cons** : $(t_x,t_l)\}$. For example, the elements of this type when t_x is **Int** are (**in** (**Nil** ())), (**in** (**Cons** (1, **in** (**Nil** ())))), (**in** (**Cons** (2, **in** (**Cons** (1, **in** (**Nil** ())))))), etc., as the following derivation shows:

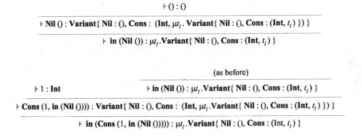

Figure 10. Typing system (recursive types)

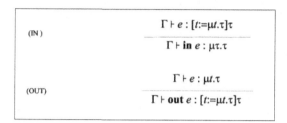

Observe the use of **in** to indicate when an expansion has to be injected into the recursive type.

Another important example is that of functions over recursive types, or returning a recursive type. In the first case, consider the function counting the number of elements in a list:

let *len* = λ*l*. **case** (**out** *l*) **of**   **Nil** *x*.   0;

Cons *p*.   1 + *len* ($\pi_{2,2}$ *p*)

in *len* (**in** (**Cons** (3, **in** (**Cons** (4, **in** (**Nil** ()))))))

The type of *len* in the previous expression is (μt_l. **Variant**{ **Nil** : (), **Cons** : (**Int**, t_l) }) → **Int**. If the abbreviation **List_of** t_x is used for (μt_l. **Variant**{ **Nil** : (), **Cons** : (t_x, t_l) }), then the type of *len* is **List_of Int** → **Int**. For an example of a function returning a recursive type, consider the function generating a list of repeated elements:

let *repeat* = **fix** (λ*rep*. λ*x*. λ*n*. **if** (*n*==0)   **then in** (**Nil** ())

else in (**Cons** (*x*, *rep* *x* (*n*-1))))

in *repeat* **True** 3

The type of the function *repeat* used is **Bool** → **Int** → (μt_l. **Variant**{ **Nil** : (), **Cons** : (**Bool**, t_l) }), which, using the abbreviation **List_of** t_x can be written as **Bool** → **Int** → **List_of Bool**. Observe the use of recursion on integers to generate a finite list of the indicated length.

An important family of recursive types is that of trees. A *tree* is any recursive type where one of the alternatives has two or more uses of the recursively bound variable. Examples of tree types are μt. **Variant**{ **Leaf** : t_x, **Node** : (t_x, t, t) }, μt. **Variant**{ **Null** : (), **Bin** : (t, t_x, t) }, μt. **Variant**{ **Tip** : t_x, **Branch** : (t, t) }, and so on. Going deeper into these examples is beyond the scope of this chapter. However, a lot of literature exists on it (Bird, 1998; Okasaki, 1998).

A final curiosity about the power of recursive types is that in a language with recursive types, the operator **fix** can be constructed. Thus, there is no need to provide it as a primitive. A possible way to construct it is:

let *prefix* = λ*m*. λ*f*. *f* (**out** *m m f*)
in *prefix* (**in** *prefix*)

The type of *prefix* is $(\mu t. t \rightarrow (t_x \rightarrow t_x) \rightarrow t_x) \rightarrow (t_x \rightarrow t_x) \rightarrow t_x$, and thus the type of (**in** *prefix*) is $\mu t. t \rightarrow (t_x \rightarrow t_x) \rightarrow t_x$ obtaining the required type, $(t_x \rightarrow t_x) \rightarrow t_x$, for **fix**. Verifying that this term has the desired behaviour is an easy exercise.

Qualified Types for Overloading

The theory of qualified types (Jones, 1994a) is a framework that allows the development of constrained type systems in an intermediate level between monomorphic and polymorphic type disciplines. Qualified types can be seen in two ways: either as a restricted form of polymorphism, or as an extension of the use of monotypes (commonly described as *overloading*, in which a function may have different interpretations according to the types of its arguments).

Predicates are used to restrict the use of type variables, or, using the second point of view, to express several possible different instances with one single type (but without the full generality of parametric polymorphism). The theory explains how to enrich types with predicates, how to perform type inference using the enriched types, and which are the minimal properties predicates must satisfy in order for the resulting type system to have similar properties as in the Hindley-Milner one. In particular, it has been shown that any well-typed program has a *principal type* that can be calculated by an extended version of Milner's algorithm.

As we have seen, polymorphism is the ability to treat some terms as having many different types, and a polymorphic type can be expressed by means of a *type scheme*, using universal quantification to abstract those parts of a type that may vary. The idea of qualified types is to consider a form of restricted quantification. If *P(t)* is a predicate on types and *f(t)* a type possibly containing variable *t*, the type scheme ∀ *t.P(t)*⇒*f(t)* can be used to represent the set of types:

{ *f*(τ) s.t. τ is a type such that *P(τ)* holds. }

and accurately reflect the desired types for a given term.

Thus, a key feature in the theory is the use of a language of *predicates* to describe sets of types (or, more generally, relations between types). The exact set of predicates may vary from one instance of the framework to another, but the theory effectively captures the minimum required properties by using an entailment relation (⊩) between (finite) sets of predicates satisfying a few simple laws. If Δ is a set of predicates, then $\Delta \Vdash \delta$ indicates that the predicate δ can be inferred from the predicates in Δ.

The language of types is stratified in a similar way as in the Hindley-Milner system, where the most important restriction is that qualified or polymorphic types cannot be an argument of functions. That is, types are defined by a grammar with at least the productions:

$$\tau ::= t \mid \tau \to \tau$$

and, on top of them, are constructed qualified types of the form:

$$\rho ::= \tau \mid \delta \Rightarrow \rho$$

and then type schemes of the form

$$\sigma ::= \rho \quad \mid \quad t.\sigma$$

Type inference uses judgements extended within a context of predicates $\Delta \mid \Gamma \vdash e : \sigma$, representing the fact that when the predicates in Δ are satisfied and the types of the free variables of e are as specified by Γ, then the term e has type σ. Valid typing judgements can be derived using a system of rules that is an extension of the basic one presented here.

As mentioned, one of the uses of the theory of qualified types is to express overloading of functions (Jones, 1996), as it has been done for the language Haskell. Consider the Haskell declaration:

```
member x [] = False
member x (y:ys) = x == y || member x ys
```

The following typing judgement will hold for it:

$$\varnothing \mid \varnothing \vdash \text{member} : \quad a.\mathbf{Eq}(a) \Rightarrow a \to [a] \to \mathbf{Bool}$$

Observe how the use of the overloaded function (==) in the body of the function member is reflected in the predicate qualifying the variable a in the resulting type; this predicate states precisely that a type implements its own version of the overloaded function.

The implementation of a qualified type system follows the line of the presentation given in this chapter, with additions to keep track of predicates, and to simplify the set of predicates obtained for a type (Jones, 1994b).

Type-Based Analysis

The influence of the type discipline on program analysis, however, does not stop there. Typing techniques have been the inspiration for several developments in the fields of program analysis and validation and verification techniques. Typing techniques have been modified to be applied to the calculation of different kinds of effects like type and effects systems (Talpin & Jouvelot, 1992; Jouvelot & Gifford, 1991) — for example, typing references (Wright, 1992), register allocation (Agat, 1997), and so on—control flow analysis (Mossin, 1996; Volpano, Smith, & Irvine, 1996), compilation (Wand, 1997), program transformation (Danvy, 1998; Hannan & Hicks, 1988; Hughes, 1996b; Romanenko, 1990), code splicing (Thiemann, 1999), security (Volpano & Smith, 1997), and other forms of program analysis (O'Callahan, 1998).

In the rest of this section, some of these developments are discussed.

Types and Effects

Types and effects are based on the idea of considering *effects*, which are an abstraction extending types to express the consequence of imperative operations on certain *regions* — the abstraction of possible aliased memory locations. A basic example of effects is that of reading and writing a persistent memory — a possible syntax, where ε denotes effects and ρ regions, is given by:

$$\varepsilon ::= \varnothing \mid \varsigma \qquad \mid \textit{init}(\rho,\tau) \mid \textit{read}(\rho) \mid \textit{write}(\rho) \mid \varepsilon \cup \varepsilon$$

where $\varnothing$ denotes the absence of effects, ς denotes effect variables, the operators *init*, *read*, and *write* approximate effects on regions, and operator $\cup$ gathers different effects together. Types are extended to express effects by adding an effect expression to the function type: $\tau \rightarrow^\varepsilon \tau$, and a special type $\textit{ref}_\rho(\tau)$ to express a reference to an element of type τ in region ρ. Typing judgements are also extended with effects, becoming $\Gamma \vdash e : \tau,\varepsilon$; the rules of the formal system are extended as well. Finally, basic operations on memory locations are given types with effects. For example, the operator $:=$ for assignment receives the type $\forall t.\forall \rho.\forall \varsigma.\forall \varsigma'.\textit{ref}_\rho(t) \rightarrow^\varsigma t \rightarrow^{\varsigma' \cup \textit{write}(\rho)} ()$, expressing that the assignment takes a reference to a location and a value, and returns a command (of type $()$) whose effect is writing in the given region; other operations on locations are treated similarly.

Types for Register Allocation

Register allocation is the process of deciding where, in which register or in the memory, to store each value computed by a program being compiled. In modern architectures, the difference in access time between a register and a memory cell can be as much as 4 to 10 times (or much more, if a cache miss occurs) (Henessy & Patterson, 1990). Moreover, typical RISC arithmetic can handle only register operands, and thus the difference in the number of required operations to add two numbers stored in registers against two stored in memory is of three instructions (two loads and a store of difference). For that reason, an optimal process of register allocation is crucial to obtain efficient programs.

By its very nature, register allocation must be done late in the compilation process, when the order of evaluation of every subterm has been decided. Typical algorithms to perform register allocation operate on assembly-code level, when all structure and type information of the compiler's intermediate language is lost. This means that calls to statically unknown functions must be made with some rigid calling convention, thus having the risk of requiring much more expensive operations due to misuse of registers. That is, if the register behaviour of the callee is known, the code produced to invoke the function can be optimized to use the best register allocation.

Types and effects, as described in the previous section, can be used to provide a type system describing the behaviour of register usage of all objects in a program (Agat, 1997, 1998). Types are enriched with register usage information, and the type system can be extended to perform optimal interprocedural register allocation, even when the function invoked is statically unknown. The main idea, then, is to move the register allocation phase from assembly-code to intermediate code, thus having all the power of types at hand.

Each type τ is annotated where the value of that type is, or is expected to be, stored, thus becoming τ_r. Function types are modified to be of the form $\tau_r \rightarrow^{k;d} \tau_r$, where k, called the *kill-set*, is a description of the registers that might be modified when the function is applied, and d, called the *displacement*, describes which registers contain values that might then be referenced. Examples of such types are:

- $\textbf{Int}_{R3}$: Integer value stored in register 3.
- $\textbf{Int}_{S8}$: Integer value stored in slot 8 of the current stack frame.
- $(\textbf{Int}_{R2} \rightarrow^{\{R6,R4\};\{R3\}} \textbf{Int}_{R4})_{R5}$: Function accepting an integer argument in register 2 and returning an integer result in register 4. While computing the result, registers 6 and 4 might be altered, and the value currently in register 3 might be needed in the computation. The pointer to the function closure is stored in register 5.

There are several benefits to using such a typed system expressing the register assignments made by a register allocator. Since all values have a type, and types describe register behaviour, specialized calling conventions can be used for *all* applications, even those whose functions are not known statically; it is the type of the argument function that tells how to call it. Additionally, a clean and simple setting for reasoning about the correctness of the register-allocation algorithm is gained. Finally, several optimizations can be performed — for example, keeping values required by commonly used functions in registers as much as possible.

Sized Types

In the domain of safety-critical control systems (Levenson, 1986), a correct program is a program not causing any (unintentional) harm — like injury, damage, or death — to its environment. Correctness properties like these require system-level reasoning. A particular way in which one of these systems may cause harm is when some component exceeds its memory limits, thus causing unintentional state changes, or even damage, to the whole system. Errors of this kind are easy to introduce — a small change can do it, without notice — but are completely unacceptable. A formal technique allowing to reason about the memory limits of programs is thus a must.

The theory of sized types (Pareto, 1998) is a framework composed by a language aimed at control systems programming, accompanied by tools asserting program correctness from the memory consumption point of view. The main tool is a variation of a type system accepting only programs whose memory behaviour can be predicted. Some principles of design underlying the theory of sized types guide the development of programs. Basic principles are that types may exclude bottom (a particular theoretical value that represent nonterminating or erroneous computations) — that is, certain types can only be used for type terminating programs — that types may distinguish finite, infinite, and partial values. For example, the availability of data from a given source can be assured by typing it with an infinite type with no partial values, and types may bound their values by size parameters in several dimensions. So, an upper bound in the number of elements of a list, or a lower bound on the number of elements produced by a data source can be determined (and those elements can also be bounded in size).

The particular way to achieve the principles is by using data declarations with additional information. For example, consider the following declarations:

```
data Bool = False | True

idata List (ω) a = Nil | Cons a (List (ω) a)

codata Stream (ω) a = Make a (Stream (ω) a)

data BS k = BS (Stream k Bool)
```

The first declaration establishes the type Bool as a sum type, but excludes explicitly the possibility of undefined or nonterminating expressions of this type. Thus, if a program can be typed with Bool, it can be asserted that it terminates and produces a value either False or True.

The second declaration defines recursive sum types for lists, but adding an extra parameter ω. This new parameter is a bound on the size of the elements of the type, and the keyword **idata** establishes that several new types are introduced, all finite: one for lists of size less than k for each possible natural number k, and the classical type for lists of any (finite) size.

The third declaration uses the keyword **codata** to define that the elements of the declared type are infinite. It also has a bound parameter, but in this case it is used to determine a lower bound on the size of the streams. So, again, several new types are introduced: one for each natural number k of streams of size bigger than k, and one for streams that will always produce new data on demand.

The last declaration has a parameter that fixes the size of the lower bound for the stream of Booleans declared.

A carefully defined syntax for programs, and its corresponding semantics are needed to assure that all the desired principles are valid. A type system assigning sized types to programs is defined, and also an algorithm calculating the assignment. In this way, the type system can be used to assure the property of bounded size on typable programs (Hughes, Pareto, & Sabry, 1996).

Type Specialization

Program specialization is a form of a automatic program generation taking a given program as input to produce one or more particular versions of it as output, each specialized to particular data. The program used as input is called the *source program*, and those produced as output are called the *residual programs*.

Type Specialization is an approach of program specialization introduced by John Hughes in 1996 (Hughes, 1996a, 1996b, 1998) for typed languages. The main idea of type specialization is to specialize *both* the source program and its type to a residual program and residual type. In order to do this, instead of a generalized form of evaluation — as the one used in partial evaluation, the most common form of program specialization — type specialization uses a generalized form of type inference.

The key question behind type specialization is:

How can the static information provided by the type of an expression be improved?

An obvious first step is to have a more powerful typesystem. But, it is also desirable to *remove* the static information expressed by this new type from the code in order to obtain a simpler and (hopefully) more efficient code. So, type specialization works with two typed languages: the source language, in which the programs to be specialized are coded, and the residual language, in which the result of specialization is expressed. The source language, whose elements are denoted by e, is a two-level language where every construct is marked as either static or dynamic. Static information is supposed to be moved to the type, while a dynamic one is supposed to be kept in the residual term; source types, denoted by τ, reflect the static or dynamic nature of expressions, and thus they also contain the marks. The residual language, whose terms and types are denoted by e' and τ' respectively, has constructs and types corresponding to all the dynamic constructs and types in the source language, plus additional ones used to express the result of specializing static constructs.

In order to express the result of the specialization procedure, Hughes introduced a new kind of judgement and a formal system of rules to infer valid judgements. These judgements, similar to typing judgements in the source language, make use of environments to determine the specialization of free variables. The new judgements have the form $\Gamma \vdash e : \tau \leadsto e' : \tau'$ which can be read as "if the free variables in e specialize to the expressions indicated in Γ, then source expression e of source type τ specializes to residual expression e' and residual type τ'". The valid judgements are obtained by using a system of rules specifying how to specialize a given typed term; this system follows the same ideas of typing systems.

A very interesting example of type specialization is to specialize an interpreter for a language to a given term: given an interpreter int for a language and a program p written in it, the specialization of int to p is a program equivalent to p. This is called a Futamura projection (Futamura, 1971), and it compiles by specializing the interpreter. When this way of compiling programs can be done optimally for all the programs in the language, then it can be assured that the specialization method can tackle all the constructs in it. Type specialization was the first approach obtaining optimality for compilation of typed languages by specialization.

The implementation of a type specialization algorithm is rather tricky, and although John Hughes has provided a prototype implementation (Hughes, 1997), it is difficult to understand, and properties about it are difficult to prove. However, Martínez López has given a systematic way to implement type specialization following the lines presented in this chapter (Martínez López & Hughes, 2002; Martínez López, 2005), together with a proof of a very important property of the system: the existence of a principal specialization for every source term. Current research on type specialization involves the addition of sum types to the principal specialization system, and the addition of dynamic recursion.

Conclusion

Type-based analyses are an important way to structure a system for verification or validation of programs. However, the design of a type-based analysis usually does not directly suggest a good way to implement it. This chapter has addressed the problem of going from a specification of a type system to its implementation, showing several of the common subtleties that are a hindrance for designers and implementers. Additionally, the correctness and completeness of the implementation's design were stated as theorems; their proofs are easy examples of induction on derivations, including several lemmas and additional propositions. The case presented here is the most basic one, but it is useful in order to cast light on the techniques needed.

In addition, several extensions to the basic system were discussed, and several type-based analyses were mentioned and referenced. Some of the most important among them are register allocation, sized types, and type specialization; other approaches, such as control-flow analysis and code splicing, that have not been considered are also important.

Acknowledgments

I am very grateful to my colleague Eduardo Bonelli for his careful reading and his many suggestions to improve the material presented here. I am also in debt to Jerónimo Irazábal because he agreed to translate my functional code to C++, even when the task was not as easy as it seemed at first. Two more people deserving my gratitude are Andrés Fortier, who has given his time to help me with the subtleties of the object oriented paradigm, and Alejandro Russo, who reviewed the early drafts. Finally, the anonymous referees, because they have given many suggestions on how to improve the chapter.

References

Abadi, M., & Cardelli, L. (1996). *A theory of objects*. Springer-Verlag.

Aiken, A. (1999). Introduction to set constraint-based program analysis. *Science of Computer Programming, 35*, 79-111.

Agat, J. (1997). Types for register allocation. In *IFL '97* (LNCS 1467).

Agat, J. (1998). *A typed functional language for expressing register usage*. Licenciate Dissertation. Chalmers University of Technology.

Altenkirch, T., Gaspes, V., Nordström, B., & von Sydow, B. (1994). *A user's guide to ALF* (Technical report). Sweden: Chalmers University of Technology.

Atkinson, M. P., Bailey, P. J., Chisholm, K. J., Cockshott, W. P., & Morrison, R. (1983). An approach to persistent programming . *Computer Journal, 26*(4), 360-365.

Atkinson, M. P., & Morrison, R. (1988). Types, bindings and parameters in a persistent environment. In M.P. Atkinson, O. P. Buneman, & R. Morrison (Eds.), *Data types and persistence*. Springer-Verlag.

Bertot, Y., & Castéran, P. (2004). Interactive theorem proving and program development. Coq'Art: The calculus of inductive constructions. In *Texts in theoretical computer science. An EATCS Series*. Springer-Verlag.

Bird, R. (1998). *An introduction to functional programming using Haskell*. Prentice-Hall.

Breazu-Tannen, V., Coquand, T., Gunter, C. A., & Scedrov, A. (1991). Inheritance as implicit coercion. *Information and Computation, 93*, 172-221.

Cardelli, L. (1997). Type systems. In *CRC Handbook of computer science ad engineering* (2nd ed.). CRC Press.

Cardelli, L., & Wegner, P. (1985). On understanding types, data abstraction, and polymorphism. *Computing Surveys, 17*(4), 471-522.

Clément, D., Despeyroux, J., Despeyroux, T., & Kahn, G. (1986). A simple applicative language: Mini-ML. In *Proceedings of the 1986 ACM Conference on LISP and Functional Programming* (pp. 13-27). Cambridge, MA: ACM Press.

The Coq proof assistant (2004). Retrieved from http://coq.inria.fr/ ECurry, H. B., & Feys, R. (1958). *Combinatory logic*. Amsterdam, The Netherlands: North Holland.

Coquand, T., & Huet, G. (1988). The calculus of constructions. *Information and Computation, 76*(2/3), 95-120.

Damas, L., & Milner, R. (1982). Principal type-schemes for functional languages. In *Proceedings of the Ninth Annual ACM Symposium on Principles of Programming Languages,* Albuquerque, NM (pp. 207-212).

Danvy, O. (1998). Type-directed partial evaluation. In J. Hatcliff, T. E. Mogensen, & P. Thiemann (Eds.), *Partial evaluation — Practice and theory* (LNCS 1706, pp. 367-411). Copenhagen, Denmark: Springer-Verlag.

Dearle, A. (1988). *On the construction of persistent programming environments.* PhD thesis, University of St. Andrews.

Freund, S. N., & Mitchell, J. C. (1998). A type system for object initialization in the Java bytecode language. In *Proceedings of the ACM Conference on Object-Oriented Programming: Systems, Languages and Applications (OOPSLA'98)* (pp. 310-328).

Futamra, Y. (1971). Partial evaluation and computation process — an approach to a compiler-compiler. *Computer, Systems, Controls, 2*(5), 45-50.

Gamma, R., Helm, R., Johnson, R., & Vlissides, J. (1995). *Design patterns: Elements of reusable object-oriented software.* Addison Wesley.

Gaster, B. R., & Jones, M. P. (1996). *A polymorphic type system for extensible records and variants* (Tech. Rep. No. NOTTCS-TR-96-3). Department of Computer Science, University of Nottingham.

Girard, J. Y. (1989). *Proofs and types.* Cambridge University Press.

Hannan, J. J., & Hicks, P. (1988). Higher-order arity raising. In *Proceedings of the ACM SIGPLAN International Conference on Functional Programming (ICFP'98)* (pp. 27-38). Baltimore: ACM.

Henglein, F., & Rehof, J. (1997). The complexity of subtype entailment for simple types. In *Proceedings, Twelfth Annual IEEE Symposium on Logic in Computer Science* (pp. 352-361). Warsaw, Poland.

Hennessy, J. L. & Patterson, D. A. (1990). *Computer architecture: a quantitative approach.* Palo Alto: Morgan Kaufmann Publishers.

Hindley, J. R. (1969). The principal type-scheme of an object in combinatory logic. *Transactions of the American Mathematical Society, 146,* 29-60.

Hindley, J. R. (1995). *Basic simplet Type Theory.* Cambridge University Press.

Hoang, M., Mitchell, J. C., & Viswanathan, R. (1993). Standard ML: NJ weak polymorphism and imperative constructs. In *Proceedings of the Eighth Annual IEEE Symposium on Logic in Computer Science (LICS).* Journal version appeared in (Mitchell & Viswanathan, 1996).

Hughes, J. (1996a). An introduction to program specialisation by type inference. In *Functional Programming.* Scotland: Glasgow University. Published electronically.

Hughes, J. (1996b). Type specialisation for the λ-calculus; or, a new paradigm for partial evaluation based on type inference. In Olivier Danvy, Robert Glück, and Peter Thiemann (Eds.), *Selected papers of the International Seminar "Partial Evaluation"* (LNCS 1110, pp. 183-215). Springer-Verlag.

Hughes, J. (1997). *Type specialiser prototype.* Retrieved from http://www.cs.chalmers.se/~rjmh/TypeSpec2/

Hughes, J. (1998). Type specialisation. In *ACM Computing Surveys, 30.* ACM Press. Article 14. Special issue: electronic supplement to the September 1998 issue.

Hughes, J., Pareto, L., & Sabry, A. (1996). Proving the correctness of reactive systems using sized types. In *Proceedings of the 23rd ACM SIGPLAN-SIGACT Symposium on Principles of Programming Languages.* FL: ACM Press.

Igarashi, A., & Kobayashi, N. (2001). A generic type system for the Pi-calculus. *ACM SIGPLAN Notices, 36*(3), 128-141.

Jim, T. (1996). What are principal typings and what are they good for? In *Proceedings of POPL '96: The 23rd ACM SIGPLAN-SIGACT Symposium on Principles of Programming Languages* (pp. 42-53). St. Petersburg Beach, FL: ACM Press.

Jones, M. P. (1994a). Qualified types: Theory and practice. In *Distinguished dissertations in computer science.* Cambridge University Press.

Jones, M. P. (1994b). *Simplifying and improving qualified types* (Tech. Rep. No. YALE/DCS/RR-989). Yale University.

Jones, M. P. (1996). Overloading and higher order polymorphism. In E. Meijer & J. Jeuring (Eds.), *Advanced functional programming* (LNCS 925, pp. 97-136). Springer-Verlag.

Jouvelot, P., & Gifford, D. (1991). Algebraic reconstruction of types and effects. In *Conference Record of the Eighteenth Annual ACM Symposium on Principles of Programming Languages.* Orlando, FL: ACM Press.

Knabe, F. (1995). *Language support for mobile agents.* PhD thesis. Pittsburgh, PA: Carnegie Mellon University.

Leveson, N. G. (1986). Software safety: Why, what, and how. *ACM Computing Surveys, 18*(2), 25-69.

Martínez López, P. E. (2005). *The notion of principality in type specialization.* PhD thesis, Argentina: University of Buenos Aires. Retrieved from http://www-lifia.info.unlp.edu.ar/~fidel/Work/Thesis.tgz

Martínez López, P. E. (in press). Static type systems: A functional implementation (Technical report). LIFIA, Facultad de Informática, Universidad Nacional de La Plata.

Martínez López, P. E., & Hughes, J. (2002). Principal type specialisation. In W. N. Chin (Ed.), *Proceedings of the 2002 ACM SIGPLAN Asian Symposium on Partial Evaluation and Semantics-based Program Manipulation* (pp. 94-105). ACM Press.

McCarthy, J. (1962). Towards a mathematical science of computation. In C. Popplewell (Ed.), *Information processing 1962: Proceedings of IFIP Congress 62.* Amsterdam, The Netherlands: North-Holland.

Milner, R. (1978). A theory of type polymorphism in programming. *Journal of Computer and System Sciences, 17*(3).

Mitchell, J. C. (1991). Type inference with simple subtypes. *Journal of Functional Programming, 1*(3), 245-285.

Mitchell, J. C. (1996). *Foundations for programming languages.* MIT Press.

Mitchell, J. C., & Plotkin, G. D. (1988). Abstract types have existential type. *ACM Transactions on Programming Languages and Systems, 10*(3), 470-502.

Mitchell, J. C., & Viswanathan, R. (1996). Standard ML-NJ weak polymorphism and imperative constructs. Information and Computation, *127*(2), 102-116.

Morrison, R., Connor, R. C. H., Cutts, Q. I., Kirby, G. N. C., & Stemple, D. (1993). Mechanisms for controlling evolution in persistent object systems. *Journal of Microprocessors and Microprogramming, 17*(3), 173-181.

Mossin, C. (1996). *Flow analysis of typed higher-order programs.* PhD thesis. Denmark: DIKU, University of Copenhagen.

Nordlander, J. (1999). *Reactive objects and functional programming.* PhD thesis. Chalmers University of Technology.

Nordlander, J. (2000). Polymorphic subtyping in O'Haskell. In *Proceedings of the APPSEM Workshop on Subtyping and Dependent Types in Programming.*

Nordström, B., Petersson, K., & Smith, J. M. (1990). *Programming in Martin-Löf's Type Theory.* Oxford University Press.

O'Callahan, R. (1998). *Scalable program analysis and understanding based on type inference.* PhD thesis proposal. Pittsburgh, PA: School of Computer Science, Carnegie Mellon University.

Object Management Group (2004). *Unified Modelling Language specification, version 2.0.* Retrieved from http://www.uml.org/#UML2.0

Odersky, M., Wadler, P., & Wehr, M. (1995). A second look at overloading. In *Proceedings of ACM Conference on Functional Programming and Computer Architecture.* ACM Press.

Okasaki, C. (1998). *Purely functional data structures.* Cambridge University Press.

Palsberg, J., Wand, M., & O'Keefe, P. (1997). Type inference with non-structural subtyping. *Formal Aspects of Computer Science, 9,* 49-67.

Pareto, L. (1998). *Sized types.* PhD thesis. Chalmers University of Technology.

Peyton Jones, S., & Hughes, J. (Eds.). (1999). *Haskell 98: A non-strict, purely functional language.* Retrieved from http://haskell.org

Pierce, B. (2002). *Types and Programming Languages.* MIT Press.

Pottier, F. (2000). A 3-part type inference engine. In G. Smolka (Ed.), *Proceedings of the 2000 European Symposium on Programming (ESOP '00)* (LNCS 1782, pp. 320-335). Springer-Verlag.

Rèmy, D. (1989). Typechecking records and variants in a natural extension of ML. In *Proceedings of the Sixteenth Annual ACM Symposium on Principles of Programming Languages* Austin, TX.

Rèmy, D., & Pottier, F. (2004). The essence of ML type inference. In B. Pierce (Ed.), *Advanced topics in types and programming languages*. MIT Press.

Reynolds, J. C. (1974). Towards a theory of type structure. In *Proceedings of the Symposium on Programming* (LNCS 19, pp. 408-423). Springer-Verlag.

Reynolds, J. C. (1983). Types, abstraction, and parametric polymorphism. In R. E. A. Mason (Ed.), *Information Processing '83. Proceedings of the IFIP 9th World Computer Congress* (pp. 513-523). Amsterdam, The Netherlands: North-Holland.

Reynolds, J. C. (1998). *Theories of programming languages*. Cambridge University Press.

Romanenko, S. (1990). Arity raising and its use in program specialisation. In N. D. Jones (Ed.), *Proceedings of 3rd European Symposium on Programming (ESOP '90)* (LNCS 432, pp. 341-360). Copenhagen, Denmark: Springer-Verlag.

Shields, M., & Meijer, E. (2001). Type-indexed rows. In *Proceedings of the 28th ACM SIGPLANSIGACT Symposium on Principles of Programming Languages (POPL '01)*, London (pp. 261-275).

Stroustrup, B. (2000). *The C++ programming language* (special 3rd ed.). Addison-Wesley.

Sulzmann, M., Odersky, M., & Wehr, M. (1997). Type inference with constrained types. In *Fourth International Workshop on Foundations of Object-Oriented Programming (FOOL 4)*. Journal version appeared in (Sulzmann, Odersky, & Wehr, 1999).

Sulzmann, M., Odersky, M., & Wehr, M. (1999). Type inference with constrained types. *Theory and Practice of Object Systems, 5*(1), 33-55.

Syme, D. (1999). Proving Java type soundness. In J. Alves-Foss (Ed.), *Formal syntax and semantics of Java* (LNCS 1523, pp. 119-156). Springer-Verlag.

Talpin, J. P., & Jouvelot, P. (1992). The type and effect discipline. In *Proceedings of the Seventh Annual IEEE Symposium on Logic in Computer Science*. Santa Cruz, CA: IEEE Computer Society Press.

Thatte, S. R. (1992). *Typechecking with ad-hoc polymorphism* (Technical report preliminary manuscript). Potsdan, NY: Clarkson University, Department of Mathematics and Computer Science.

Thiemann, P. (1999). Higher-order code splicing. In S. D. Swierstra (Ed.), *Proceedings of the Eighth European Symposium on Programming* (LNCS 1576, pp. 243-257). Springer-Verlag.

Tiuryn, J., & Wand, M. (1993). Type reconstruction with recursive types and atomic subtyping. In *CAAP '93: 18th Colloquium on Trees in Algebra and Programming*.

von Oheimb, D. & Nipkow, T. (1999). Machine-checking the Java specification: Proving type-safety. In J. Alves-Foss (Ed.), *Formal syntax and semantics of Java* (LNCS 1523, pp. 119-156). Springer-Verlag.

Volpano, D., & Smith, G. (1997). A type-based approach to program security. In *Proceedings of TAPSOFT '97, Colloqium on Formal Approaches in Software Engineering*.

Volpano, D., Smith, G., & Irvine, C. (1996). A sound type system for secure flow analysis. *Journal of Computer Security, 4*(3), 1-21.

Wand, M. (1987). Complete type inference for simple objects. In *Proceedings of the 2nd IEEE Symposium on Logic in Computer Science* (pp. 37-44).

Wand, M. (1991). Type inference for record concatenation and multiple inheritance. *Information and Computation, 93*, 1-15. Preliminary version appeared in *Proc. 4th IEEE Symposium on Logic in Computer Science* (1989), 92-97.

Wand, M. (1994). Type inference for objects with instance variables and inheritance. In C. Gunter & J. C. Mitchell (Eds.), *Theoretical aspects of object-oriented programming* (pp. 97-120). MIT Press. Originally appeared as Northeastern University College of Computer Science (Tech. Rep. No. NU-CCS-89-2), February 1989.

Wand, M. (1997). Types in compilation: Scenes from an invited lecture. In *Workshop on Types in Compilation (invited talk), held in conjunction with ICFP97.*

Wells, J. B. (1994). Typability and typechecking in second-order lambda calculus are equivalent and undecidable. In *Proceedings of the 9th Annual IEEE Symposium Logic in Computer Science.* Superseded by (Wells, 1998).

Wells, J. B. (1998). Typability and typechecking in System F are equivalent and undecidable. *Annals of Pure and Applied Logic, 98*(1-3), 111-156.

Wright, A. K. (1992). Typing references by effect inference. In B. Krieg-Bruckner (Ed.), *Proceedings of ESOP '92, 4th European Symposium on Programming* (LNCS 582, pp. 473-491). Springer-Verlag.

Wright, A. K. (1995). Simple imperative polymorphism. *Lisp and Symbolic Computation, 8*(4), 343-355.

Chapter XII

Generic Model of the Business Model and Its Formalization in Object-Z

Marcela Daniele, Universidad Nacional de Río Cuarto, Argentina

Paola Martellotto, Universidad Nacional de Río Cuarto, Argentina

Gabriel Baum, Universidad Nacional de Río Cuarto, Argentina

Abstract

This chapter shows the generic model of the business model, represented graphically with a UML class diagram, product of the analysis of the artifacts that compose the business model and their relationships, according to rational unified process (RUP) (2000). Moreover, the chapter defines a set of rules that the model must verify. It has been demonstrated that graph modeling is useful to visualize, specify, build, and document the artifacts of a system, offering a common language, easy to understand and apply. However, it lacks a precise semantics, which causes problems of ambiguities that in turn generate incorrect or different interpretations. In order to improve upon this, the generic model is translated into a formal specification language. This translation, carried out in Object-Z, allows the expression of a specific business model in a particular domain without ambiguity, and it facilitates the analysis of the properties of the system, showing possible inconsistencies, ambiguities, or incompleteness.

Introduction

The purpose of the development of a software system is to solve problems through programs that present a variety of characteristics such as efficiency, robustness, data safety, dynamism, and portability among others. The design of such a system is only possible once the problem has been identified, followed by a proposal of possible solutions.

The unified software development process (Jacobson, Booch, & Rumbaugh, 1999; RUP, 2000) is a methodology that defines who is doing *what*, *when*, and *how* to build or improve a software product. This method uses UML (unified modeling language) (Booch, Rumbaugh, & Jacobson, 1999; UML 2.0, 2003) as a way to express the different models that are created in the different stages of development. Business modeling allows one to obtain an abstraction of the organization. This is a set of activities whose goal is to help one visualize and understand business processes. As applied to software systems or other systems, a business model acts as a blueprint that guides the construction of the system. In effect, the model becomes an operational description of the business that can illuminate value/cost tradeoffs, priorities, and risks. This level of understanding is frequently essential to helping system analysts, designers, and developers make informed decisions about the processes they are automating and the technologies most appropriate for implementing them.

There are basic reasons to model a business. The first is to re-engineer a business. This involves analyzing and fundamentally rethinking how the business operates and interacts with the outside world. For this highest-risk form of process and system design, business modeling is essential. Second is to improve a business process, to streamline how the business works, and/or to enhance its competitiveness. Third is toto automate a business process. The goal here is to reduce the resource requirements associated with a process by enabling more of it to happen without human intervention. In this context, a model of the current business allows one to understand the environment in which a software system will function. Whether the plan is to re-engineer the business or to automate an existing process, business modeling is the first step toward defining a software system that will solve the precise business problem and is fundamental to capturing and to structuring the system requirements.

Business-process automation is also the focus of the business-modeling discipline in the rational unified process. The business modeling is proposed by RUP (2000) through the development of a group of artifacts by means of which the business is completely modeled.

Research on business modeling that refers specifically to the unified software development process use the definition of artifacts as presented by their authors. In this context, it is worth mentioning Eriksson and Penker's (2000) definition of an extension of UML to describe business processes. In addition to this, they describe a set of business rules in object constraint language (OCL) as well as how to use business models in use cases. Ortín, García Molina, Moros, and Nicolás (2001) propose a systematic method for obtaining the requirements model from the business model. Salm (2003) uses the extensions to UML for the business modeling proposed by the Object Management

Group (OMG) (2001). Sinogas et al. (2001) propose an extension to UML with the definition of a profile for the business model.

Firstly, this chapter describes the analysis of the artifacts that compose the business model in accordance with the unified software development process and presents a generic model of the business model represented graphically in terms of UML through a class diagram (Figure 1), and sets the basis for specifying a concrete business model. The application of the set of rules defined for each artifact and the relationships among each of them help to build the business model that makes it possible for the designers to acquire the knowledge of the context that is required. Furthermore, the generic model can also be used to verify a previously built concrete business model.

UML is a graphical language for modeling and specifying software systems. It has been demonstrated that graph modeling is very useful for visualizing, specifying, building, and documenting the artifacts of a system, offering a common language that is easy to understand and apply. However, it does not have a precise semantics, and therefore, it allows for ambiguities that cause problems of incorrect or different interpretations. In this sense, we need to translate the generic model of the business model, proposed with a UML class diagram, to a formal specification language such as Object-Z, which allows one to express concrete business models in particular domains without ambiguity. Although the application of formal methods does not guarantee the correction of a system a priori, it facilitates the analysis of the properties of the system considerably, showing possible inconsistencies, ambiguities, or incompleteness.

The formal specifications are expressed in mathematical notation; therefore, they have syntax and semantics that are defined precisely. The formal specification of the systems complements the informal specification techniques.

Object-Z (Smith, 2000a) is a language Z extension (Spivey, 1992) that facilitates the formal specification of object-oriented systems. It is an extension because all Z's syntax and associated semantics are also a part of Object-Z. A Z specification is also an Object-Z specification. Object-Z facilitates the formal specification of object-oriented systems because it does not enforce any particular style of specification but provides constructs to aid the specification of systems in a particular way. The constructs provided enable specifications using classes, objects, inheritance, and polymorphism.

The choice of Object-Z as the formal specification language has been driven by the following considerations. Object-Z provides a uniform-representation formalism and semantics for expressing diagrammatical models (e.g., UML class diagrams). In addition, the language preserves most features of the object-oriented structure of informal UML models, and Object-Z models seem to be more accessible to software engineers than other standard formal specifications. In addition, there are many works in this area.

The following paragraphs summarize some of the works that present formal definitions of the UML semantics through translation to formal languages like Object-Z.

Kim and Carrington (1999, 2000) propose the formal basis for the syntactic and semantic structure of the modeling components of the UML and define a reasoning mechanism about UML models. For the formal description of UML constructors' Object-Z classes are used (Smith, 1995). Any verification of the UML models can be done using corresponding Object-Z specifications using the reasoning techniques that the language provides. In 2001, Kim and Carrington (2001) presented a metamodel based on the transformation between UML and Object-Z, and three years later (Kim & Carrington, 2004), they introduced the definition of consistence restrictions between UML models and the use Object-Z with the aim showoff showing how such a metamodel can be extended to consistence restrictions for UML models.

Similarly, Moura et al. (2000) propose a practical use of the formal methods where fragments of specification Object-Z language are included in the UML classes, also called an integration between UML and formal methods. From the work of Roe, Broda, and Russo (2003), as well as from the work of Becker and Pons (2003), it can be inferred that UML class diagrams complemented with OCL expressions are translated into Object-Z expressions. The purpose for this is to provide a formalization of the graphic models expressed in UML/OCL that allows the application of classical verification techniques and theorem testing on the models. Both authors use similar notation to apply their translation mechanism.

In view of this, the UML class diagrams do not describe the set of specification aspects to be taken into account in a precise way. Therefore, it is necessary to translate the generic model of the business model proposed with a UML class diagram to a formal specification language such as Object-Z, which allows one to express concrete business models in particular domains without ambiguity.

The definition of a formal generic model guarantees that any business model of a particular domain is correctly built according to the generic specification presented for this kind of problem. Although the application of formal methods does not assure the correction of a system a priori, it facilitates the analysis of the properties of the system considerably, showing possible inconsistencies, ambiguities, or incompleteness.

Taking all this into account, this chapter presents the generic model of the business model, represented graphically through the UML class diagram. Then, it develops a formalization of generic model in the specification language Object-Z.

The Unified Process and the Business Model

The unified process (Jacobson et al., 1999) is a developing software methodology that defines who is doing what, when, and how in order to build or improve a software product. It acts as a guide for every participant in the project: clients, users, developers, and directors. It organizes the team, managing the tasks for every developer and team member. It also specifies the artifacts that need to be developed and offers criteria for control and measurement. It also reduces risks and makes everything more predictable.

The unified process uses UML (Booch et al., 1999; UML 2.0, 2003) as a means of expressing the different models that are created during different stages of development. UML is a standard modeling language that allows the visualization, specification, creation, and documentation of the artifacts of a software.

The unified process is use-case driven. Every use case together constitutes the use-case model that describes the functionality of the whole system. Based on the use-case model, the developers create models for the analysis, design, and implementation that will carry out the use cases. The unified process is architecture-centric, due to the architecture of a software system being described through different views of the system of construction. The unified process is iterative and incremental. Therefore, it is sensible to divide the whole project into smaller miniprojects. Each miniproject is an iteration that results in an increment. These iterations refer to the different steps in the workflow, and the increments, refer to growth in the product. To be most effective, the iterations must be controlled, and they must be selected and carried out in a planned way.

The Life of the Unified Process

The unified process is structured along two dimensions. The *time* dimension is the segmentation of the lifecycle in phases and iterations and involves the following phases: *inception, elaboration, construction, and transition.* The *components* dimension of the process is the production of specific models to represent an aspect of the system and includes the following activities: *business modeling, requirement specifications, analysis, design, implementation, and testing.* Each activity of the component dimension of the process is carried out in each phase of the time dimension.

Business Model

Modeling the business is an essential part of any software-development process. It allows the analyst to see the general scheme and procedures that govern the system. This model provides a description of where the software system is going to adjust, taking into account the business habitual process within the organizational structure.

A company organizes its activity through a set of *business processes*. Each one of them is characterized by a collection of data that are produced and managed through a set of *task*s, in which certain agents (e.g., workers or departments) participate in agreement with the specified *workflow*. In addition to this, these processes are subject to a set of business rules governing the company's policies and information structure. Therefore, the aim of the business model is to describe each business process by specifying its data, activities, roles, and business rules. Its purposes can be summarized as: to provide an abstraction of the organization, to understand the structure and dynamics of the organization in which the system is developed, to identify current problems and propose potential improvements, to assure clients, users and developers that they all have the same vision of the organization and to infer the system requirements that are needed to sustain the structure and dynamics of the organization.

Artifacts of the Business Model

According to the creators of the process (Jacobson et al., 1999; RUP, 2000), two main artifacts support the business model: the business use-case model and the business-analysis model. The business use-case model describes the business processes of a company in terms of business use cases and business actors that correspond, respectively, to the business processes and the clients. It presents a system from the perspective of their use, and it shows how it provides value to their users. On the other hand, the business-analysis model is a model internal to a business that describes how each business use case is carried out by a group of workers that use business entities and work units. All the artifacts of the business model capture and present the context of the system and are useful as input and references for the definition of the system requirements.

The artifacts of business modeling can be categorized into *model, model element,* or *document.*

Models

- **Artifact – Business use-case model:** The use-case model represents business functions. It is used as a means to identify the role in the organization for it describes the business processes of a company in terms of the business use case and business actors.

- **Artifact – Business-analysis model:** The businessanalysis model is an internal business model that describes how each business use case is carried out by the business workers that use the set of business entities and work units, usually called business use-case realization. A business entity represents something that workers take, inspect, manipulate, produce, or use in a business use case. These entities are equivalent to the domain classes in a domain model. A work unit represents a group of entities. Each worker, entity, or work unit can participate in one or more business use-case realizations. The domain model is a subset of the business-analysis model that does not include responsibilities. The aim of domain modeling is to understand and describe the most important classes in the system's context.

Model Elements

- **Artifact – Business use case:** A business use case is a sequence of actions the business develops to obtain an observable result for a particular business actor. They are useful to know the value the business offers and the way in which it interacts with its environment. Each business use case must sustain at least one business goal. The business strategies are transferred to business goals which are concrete and measurable, and which can be sustained by processes or business use cases. The definition of relationship in the business goals and business use cases makes it possible for the business processes to align with the business strategies. The existence of such a relationship helps prioritize and factorize the business use cases.

- **Artifact – Business actor:** In order to understand the purpose of a business it is essential to know those "who" interact with it, that is to say, the ones who make demands or the ones who are interested in its outputs. These are represented as the business actors. The term business actor refers to the role that somebody or something has when interacting with the business.

- **Artifact – Business use-case realization:** A business use-case realization describes how business workers, entities, and events collaborate to carry out a particular business use case. The structure of such realizations goes along with the business use cases and responds to the questions of who is doing what in the organization. This artifact is part of the business-analysis model and can be excluded. The business use-case realizations must be modeled if the organizational workflow is important or if the potential changes can affect the way in which the actual business operates. While the business use case is described from an external perspective with the aim to describe what steps will be taken to attach value to a stakeholder, a business use-case realization describes how the steps will be taken inside the organization from an internal perspective.

- **Artifact – Business system:** A business system groups a set of roles, resources, and defined responsibilities that are capable of achieving a specific purpose. The business system is part of the business-analysis model.

- **Artifact – Business entity:** A business entity represents a piece of information that is persistent and meaningful, which is manipulated by business actors and workers. The entities are passive, that is to say, they do not initiate interactions. The business entities are part of the business-analysis model.

- **Artifact – Business worker:** A business worker is an abstraction of the human or software system that stands for a role within the business use-case realizations. This abstraction allows the identification of potential improvements in the business processes. A worker cooperates with others; he or she is notified of business events and manipulates entities to perform his or her responsibilities. A business worker belongs to the business-analysis model.

- **Artifact – Business event:** The business events represent the important things that happen in the business, and as such, they help manage complexity. They are sent and received by actors, workers, and business entities while they interact with the use-case realization.

Documents

- **Artifact – Business glossary:** The business glossary defines the common vocabulary, using the most common terms and expressions concerning the problem domain. Each term contains a textual description that must be used in a consistent way during all the development.

- **Artifact – Business rules:** The business rules are some types of requirements that establish how the business must operate. They define a restriction or invariant that the business must satisfy. This restriction can be of two different kinds: behavioral or structural. They are normally described in natural language, in object constraint language (OCL), through a set of reserved words, or through formal language.

- **Artifact – Business goal:** The aim of business goals is to direct the business strategies into a concrete and measurable form, to make it possible for the business operations to be driven through the correct path and improved if necessary. These measurements are quantitative. An organization has a business vision that is transformed into a business strategy. The business goals that are finally measured in organization's operations should summarize this strategy.

- **Artifact – Target organization assessment:** It describes the current state of the organization. The description is carried out in terms of current processes, tools, competencies, activities, clients, competitors, technical tendencies, problems, and improvement areas.

- **Artifact – Business vision:** The business vision is defined as the set of objectives on which the business model should focus. It highly impacts the business goals and it provides an entrance for the approval process. It communicates the WHATS and HOWS that are fundamental to the project, and is the basis on which future decisions will be validated.

- **Artifact – Supplementary business specification:** The supplementary business specification presents quantifiers or restrictions that are not in the business use-cases model, or the business-analysis model.

Generic Model of the Business Model

The generic model of the business model is a well-formed reconstruction of the original model presented by RUP (2000). It allows the user to visualize and specify in a precise, unambiguous, and complete way the artifacts of the business model and their relationships. Moreover, it is used to represent a business model in some particular context. The original proposal uses natural language to describe the artifacts and their relationships. However, it is known that this brings about risks such as imprecision and ambiguity that can be very dangerous when translated to formal and semiformal notation (for example the typical UML diagrams), due to the fact that the designer has to interpret, add and/or delete information in order to be able to perform the task.

Figure 1 shows the generic model of the business model. This proposed generic model solves the problem of business modeling in a simple manner since it summarizes in only one UML class diagram every artifact that composes the business model as well as the relationships among them. In addition to this, the semantic of the UML class diagram (relationship types, multiplicity, navigability, etc.) allow one to visualize and specify the artifacts that are obligatory and those that are optional as well. The set of rules defined for the generic model of the business model contribute to the creation of the correct

Table 1. Labels for the artifacts of the business model

MODEL			
BUCM	Business Use-case Model		
BAM	Business-analysis Model		

MODEL ELEMENT		DOCUMENT	
BUM	Business Use Case	**BG**	Business Glossary
BA	Business Actor	**TOA**	Target Organization Assessment
BUCR	Business Use-case Realization	**BV**	Business Vision
BS	Business System	**BAD**	Business Architecture Document
BE	Business Entity	**SBS**	Supplementary Business Specification
BW	Business Worker	**BR**	Business Rules
Bev	Business Event	**BGo**	Business Goal

model, which is verified during the construction process of the business model. In addition to this, the rules are useful in verifying a previously built model. This generic model of the business model does not modify what was introduced by RUP (2000), which defines how to build each artifact. This model aims at simplifying business modeling considerably since the developer does not need to analyze the relationships among artifacts, or determine which artifacts to build in a particular order, or to decide which are unnecessary. It is important to highlight the fact that the definitions and rules of the generic model assure that the results obtained will be correct and satisfactory so as to continue with the development process.

In order to build the generic model, each artifact of the business model is defined as a class. Table 1 shows the references to the labels used for each artifact as grouped according to the characteristics defined in the model.

The class diagram in Figure 1 shows the graphic representation of the generic model proposed for the business model. It allows to clearly visualize the artifacts that compose the complete business model highlighting the models with the stereotype <<model>>, the model elements with the stereotype <<element>> and the documents with the stereotype <<document>> which stand for the supplementary definitions for the two fundamental models identified by BUCM and BAM.

The BUCM is the most important of the models to build in the business modeling. If the BUCM and its relationships with the other artifacts are analyzed in detail, the class diagram proposed specifies that for each BUCM there should exist an associated BG, BR, and BGo. Therefore, in order to create the BUCM it will be necessary to have realized the business strategies in BGo, because once these have been defined the BUCM can aim at achieving them. As shown in the class diagram (Figure 1), the relationship between BUCM and BGo is a simple association towards the BGo with multiplicity which equals 1 and 0..1 in BUCM. In addition to this, such relationship also expresses partially the business goals that are required before the description of the business use-case model. The same analysis is applied to the relationship expressed between the BUCM and the

Figure 1. Generic model of the business model

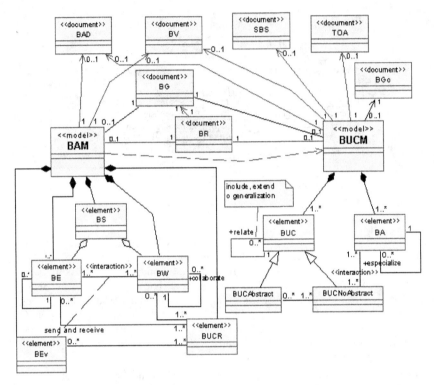

BG and BR artifacts. Moreover, it is known that each one of these artifacts will evolve gradually with the building of the general model.

Since the terms defined in the BG possess a unique textual description that has to be respected by every other element in the business model, this could be indicated in the class diagram with a dependency relationship from each artifact to the BG. This is not done to make clear the visualization of the diagram and this is textually expressed in one of the rules.

The model rules exist in any context that is studied and, therefore, it is visualized and specified that the BR artifact must exist whenever a BUCM is built. This contributes an important definition in the building of a solution where the developer is able to determine which artifacts must be defined in every business model. After this, depending on the context of the problem to be solved and the size of the business to be modeled, there are documents that supplement the BUCM and may be included or excluded from the general model. These are expressed in the class diagram as BAD, SBS, BV, and TOA. The relationship between each document and the BUCM is an *association* with 0..1 multiplicity and navigability to the document. To build these documents is not obligatory; however, if they are built they must be related to the BUCM of the general model.

In addition to this, after observing the relations in the diagram between the BUCM and its BUC and BA components, a developer can infer that to build a BUCM the definition of the BUC and BA must be taken into account. Besides, every BA must be associated to at least one BUCNoAbstract and a BUCNoAbstract must be associated to at least one BA.

According to the definition provided by the RUP (2000), when the project team understands the business analysis, the BAM can be excluded. If this action is taken, it can be observed that by excluding the BAM its associated components are excluded as well. This is due to the definition of the relations of composite aggregation or composition, where there is a strong ownership and coincident lifetime as part of the whole, in this particular case, between the BAM and the model elements BUCR, BE, BW, BEv and BS. In some cases, the BAM can be completely built or it can only be defined with the *Domain Model* that is formed with the business entities, BE. The class model proposed specifies that in order to realize the BAM one or more BE must be defined, that it is based on the BUCM and that the BR document as well as the BG can be used, revised and even updated as the BAM evolves.

The BAM is related to the BUCM given the fact that its purpose is to describe how the BUC are developed and executed. Therefore, a semantic relationship is shown to hold between both models indicating that the BAM uses the BUCM definition. A *dependency* is a using relationship, specifying that a change in the specification of one thing (BUCM) may affect another thing that uses it (BAM), but not necessarily the reverse.

Even though every business document has a purpose and is particularly important, the document that contains the business rules is the BR. It is an essentially important artifact because each rule defines a restriction or invariant that the business must satisfy and maintain during the development of the project. There are behavioral and structural restrictions that affect the sequence of actions that define a BUC such as pre and post conditions that must be satisfied by the BUCR. When the *domain model* is built, it is generally represented with a UML class diagram which reflects the structural rules as relations and/or multiplicity between the BE. In addition to this, the rules of the BR are also associated with the BG because the maintenance of policies and conditions require constant revision of the terms defined in the BG.

Translation of the
UML Class Diagram into Object-Z

Object-Z (Smith, 2000a) is an extension object oriented to Z (Spivey, 1989). It is a formal specification language based on states in which the different states of a system, the initial state and the operations, are modeled by schemes that involve a set of variable declarations associated to a predicate called *class schema*. Smith defines the specification of recursive structures in Object-Z. The type corresponding to a class schema is a set of identifiers that refer to objects of the class. That is, the objects they reference behave according to the definitions in the class schema. The identifiers themselves, however, are independent of these definitions. This independence allows us to relax the notion of "definition before use" of Z. This notion prevents, for example, a schema S including a variable whose value is an instance of S. In Object-Z, however, a class may contain a state variable that is an instance of the type defined by that class. Each class in Object-Z has an implicitly declared constant *self* that for a given object of the class denotes that object's identifier.

A UML class diagram represents the generic model of the business model. UML is a common language, easy to understand and apply, however, it lacks a precise semantics, which causes problems of ambiguities that in turn generate incorrect or different interpretations. Then, the generic model of the business model is translated into the formal specification language Object-Z, which allows the expression of a specific business model in a particular domain without ambiguity, and also facilitates the analysis of the properties of the system, showing possible inconsistencies, ambiguities or incompleteness.

For the translation of the UML class diagram into Object-Z expressions, the definitions exposed in Roe et al. (2003), Becker and Pons (2003), and Kim and Carrington (1999, 2000) are considered and the following translation mechanism is defined:

- Firstly, BM is defined as a package that contains all the classes of the diagram.

- Each class of the diagram is mapped into an Object-Z class, using the same class label to which the BM, package name, is prefixed.

- The associations among classes are expressed as attributes in the Object-Z class created. An attribute, which is named after the opposite class, is added to the class with a navigable association end. In addition to this, the type of the attribute will depend on multiplicity, the relations with 0..1 multiplicity the type of the attribute is that of the opposite class, and when there is more than one, the type will be represented as a set of elements belonging to the opposite class type. However, if both ends are navigable a restriction is added to indicate so.

- For the composition, the symbol © is added to each attribute which is a "part" of the whole in the compound class. In addition to this, a restriction is added to indicate that each "part" is also contained in the whole.

- The association class is represented as a class outline with an attribute for each associated class and a restriction that indicates that there is only one instance of the association class that belongs to an instance of the associated classes.

- In the generalization, the name of the parent class is added at the beginning of the child's class outline.

Figure 2. Class scheme of business glossary (BG)

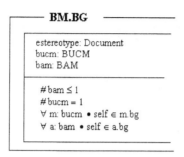

Figure 3. Class scheme of business rules (BR)

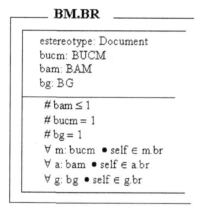

Formalization of the Generic Model of the Business Model

The BM is a "package" that groups every artifact out of which it is composed. In addition to this, three basic types are defined, namely, model, element and document, which allow to indicate the artifact that corresponds to each stereotype.

Using the class diagram and using the translation mechanism described above, Object-Z expressions are built. Each class scheme that translates each artifact has an attribute that indicates the stereotype to which it is associated.

The BG presents an association relationship with navigability in both ends of the BAM and the BUCM, therefore it contains two attributes, a restriction to indicate the multiplicity and a restriction that indicates navigability, both for each attribute. Figure 2 shows the class scheme that represents the translation of the BG with each of its elements.

Figure 4. Class scheme of business use-case model (BUCM)

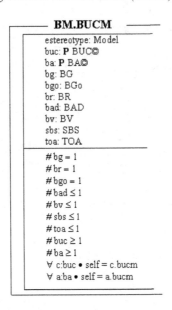

The BR document is associated to the BUCM, BAM, and BG. The latter relationship is only navigable from the BR to the BG and not in the reverse direction; therefore, in addition to the BUCM and BAM attributes, this class has a BG type attribute, three restrictions that define multiplicity and three restrictions that define navigability. Figure 3 shows the class scheme that translates the BR of the original class diagram.

In the BUCM, there is an attribute for each one of the <<document>> classes and there are two attributes to represent the BUC and BA type. These attributes are defined as a set of elements and they have the © to indicate that they are related to the *whole*, the

Figure 5. Class Scheme for Business Use Case (BUC)

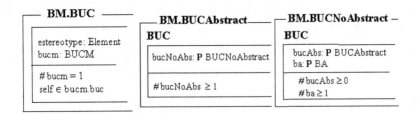

Figure 6. Class scheme for business actor (BA)

```
┌──  BM.BA  ──────────────────────────┐
│                                     │
│  estereotype: Element               │
│  bucm: BUCM                         │
│  bucNoAbs: P BUCNoAbstract          │
│  ba: P BA                           │
│ ─────────────────────────────────── │
│  # bucm = 1                         │
│  # bucNoAbs ≥ 1                     │
│  self ∈ bucm.ba                     │
│  (# ba ≥ 0 ∧  #self = 1) ∨ (#ba = 0 ∧ #self = 0) │
│                                     │
└─────────────────────────────────────┘
```

Figure 7. Class scheme for business entity (BE)

```
┌──  BM.BE  ──────────────────────┐
│                                 │
│  estereotype: Element           │
│  bam: BAM                       │
│  bs: BS                         │
│  bw: P BW                       │
│  bucr: P BUCR                   │
│ ─────────────────────────────── │
│  # bam = 1                      │
│  # bs ≤ 1                       │
│  # bw ≥ 1                       │
│  # bucr ≥ 1                     │
│  self ∈ bam.be                  │
│  (# ba ≥ 0 ∧  #self = 1) ∨ (#ba = 0 ∧ #self = 0) │
│                                 │
└─────────────────────────────────┘
```

BUCM. The multiplicity of each class is translated and two restrictions that indicate the *composition* relationship are added. Figure 4 shows the class scheme for this artifact.

The BUC is part of the BUCM and, similar to the BA, has a restriction that indicates so. In addition to this, BUC is the parent class for BUCAbstract and BUCNoAbstract, therefore the class scheme that represents them indicates such a *generalization* relationship. See Figure 5.

In the Figure 6 shows the class scheme for the artifact BA. More important is a restriction indicating that there can be a relationship among the actors is also defined in BA.

The BE element is part of the BAM model and part of the BS element. In addition, BE is associated to the BUCR and BW. In the class scheme of the Figure 7 the restrictions are defined that indicate these associations and their multiplicity.

Figure 8. Class scheme for business-analysis model (BAM)

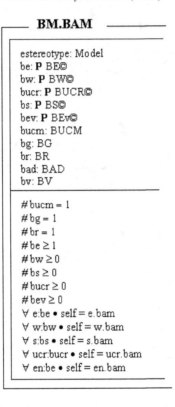

In the BAM model there is an attribute by each one of the <<element>> that composes it. These attributes are defined as a set of elements and they have the © to indicate that they are related or are *parts* to the *whole*, the BAM. There are restrictions for translate the multiplicity and indicate the *composition* relationship. In addition to this, are translated the association relationship that specifiies that the BG, BR, BAD, and BV documents are connected to the BAM model. Figure 8 shows the class scheme that translates the BAM of the original class diagram.

Using the translation mechanism described, the representation of the other classes of the diagram is analogous to the one shown for any of the previous classes.

Definition and Formalization of Rules

In order to complete the definition of the generic model of the business model they define a set of associate rules that cannot be modeled through the UML class diagram.

The class diagram proposed plus the set of rules displayed in this section will help the software engineer to verify that a concrete business model is built correctly from such generic model, or to determine if a previously built business model complies with these rules and therefore it is the right one.

The rules given below impose relations and conditions among the artifacts, however, without taking into account the conditions to be considered for the internal construction of each artifact.

The defined rules are grouped into general rules for the business model, rules that are associated to the business use-case model and, finally, rules that correspond to the business-analysis model. Each group is identified with the labels BM, BUCM, and BAM, followed by a correlative number.

The rules defined in natural language and its formalization into Object-Z expressions are shows in the following tables.

- **Rules defined for the business model (BM):**

Natural Language	Object-Z
(BM.1) BM={**artifact**} A BM is defined as a set of artifacts.	$\forall$ bm: BM $\bullet$ bm: P artifact
(BM.2) Each artifact has only one instance for a particular BM.	$\forall$ a: artifact, bm: BM $\bullet$ a $\in$ bm $\Rightarrow$ # a = 1
(BM.3) Every BM must have a BG, BGo, BR and BUCM.	$\forall$ bm: BM $\bullet$ ($\exists$ bg: BG, bgo: BGo, br: BR, bucm: BUCM $\bullet$ # bg = 1 $\wedge$ # bgo = 1 $\wedge$ # br = 1 $\wedge$ # bucm = 1)
(BM.4) Each BG term must be included in the description of at least one BUC.	BG = {(term,description)} BUC = {(specification,description)} $\forall$ bg:BG, buc:BUC $\bullet$ (t $\in$ dom bg $\Rightarrow$ t $\in$ ran buc)

- **Rules defined for the business use-case model (BUCM) and its elements:**

Natural Language	Object-Z
(BUCM.1) A BUCAbstract is not related to any BA, therefore it will never be instantiated.	$\forall$ buc: BUCAbstract, ba: BA $\bullet$ # buc.ba = 0
(BUCM.2) A BUC can relate to other BUC by means of include, extend, or generalization relations.	TR ::= include | extend | generalization $\forall$ buc1,buc2: BUC, tr:TR $\bullet$ (# buc1.buc2 > 0 $\Rightarrow$ buc1.buc2 = tr) $\wedge$ (# buc2.buc1>0 $\Rightarrow$ buc2.buc1 = tr)
(BUCM.3) A BUC cannot be related to itself.	$\forall$ buc1,buc2:BUC $\bullet$ # buc1.buc2 > 0 $\vee$ # buc2.buc1 > 0 $\Rightarrow$ buc1 $\neq$ buc2
(BUCM.4) An BA cannot be related to itself.	$\forall$ ba1,ba2:BA $\bullet$ # ba1.ba2 >0 $\vee$ # ba2.ba1 > 0 $\Rightarrow$ ba1$\neq$ba2

- **Rules defined for the business-analysis model (BAM) and its elements:**

Natural Language	Object-Z
(BAM.1) An BE can be related to itself or to other BE.	$\forall$ be1,be2: BE • # be1.be2 $\geq$ 0 $\wedge$ # be2.be1 $\geq$ 0
(BAM.2) Each BW, BE and BEv must participate in at least one BUCR.	$\forall$ bw:BW, be:BE, bev:BEv • ($\exists$ bucr:BUCR • # bw.bucr > 0 $\wedge$ #be.bucr > 0 $\wedge$ # bev.bucr > 0)
(BAM.3) Each BE must be documented in the BG.	BG = {(term,description)} $\forall$ e:BE; bg:BG • e $\in$ Dom BG

Application of the Generic Model to a Case Study

An example of application is given to show the capacity of the method proposed. This example shows the relations built among artifacts such as BG, BGo, BR, BUCM, and BAM:BE. It is important to mention that according to the generic model and its rules the BUCM cannot be built in isolation for it needs the following artifacts to be created as well: BG, Bgo, and BR. Besides, in order to create the BAM or a part of it, it is necessary to have created the BUCM. The generic model proposed imposes an order in the creation of some artifacts that need to be constantly revised during the process of construction of the actual model.

Case Study: Credit Card Information Service

A hypothetical credit card company requires a business model for an information service. Since the information service works through the telephone the company has a phone number and a series of lines. The average number of daily calls is 150 and the company provides the information service from 9:00 am. to 5:00 pm, that is to say, 8 hours every day. The highest demand for the service takes place from 10:00 am. to 1:00pm when an average of 60% of calls are produced. In an attempt to satisfy client's demands, the company has arranged that from 9:00 to 10:00 and from 1:00 to 5:00 pm. there will only be one telephone operator, while there will be three during the hours of highest demand. A telephone call proceeds as follows: a client calls, the telephone operator records the following information in a call registration form: client's full name, identity number, card number, security code number — at the back of the card, a description of the call and the code that corresponds to the call. The company has categorized the following reasons why clients call: card loss, Internet purchasing, movement and balance, due dates and payments, promotions and travel assistance. At the beginning of his or her shift, the operator opens the call registration form, and it is closed at the end. After this, the record is filed with all the other call records.

Building the Business Model

In order to create a business model for a credit card information service, a BG has to be defined followed by the BGo and the BR. Based on this, the BUCM is built and the BE are identified and grouped in a *domain model* which corresponds to the BAM.

The different steps are described in detail below:

1. First, the problem to be solved is carefully analyzed and the most important terms for the business are defined. Each term will be described within a text that will be considered all along the project. These terms will be redefined as the other artifacts are built, and they represent an instance of the artifact BG in the generic model.

    Then, the BG instance is:

    - **Artifact: BG:**
        - **Line:** telephone line used by the client to consult the operator.
        - **Call:** action performed by the client to contact and consult an operator. Each call corresponds to a specified reason.
        - **Reason:** what causes the consultation. The reasons are categorized as follows: credit card loss, Internet purchasing, movement and balance, due dates and payments, promotions and travel assistance.
        - **Operator:** person assigned to answer incoming calls.
        - **Client:** person who holds one of this company's credit cards and uses the service to consult the company.
        - **Form:** it is a sheet with five columns to record the following information about the client: Surname and Name, identity number, card number, security code, and the code specified for the call.

2. Second, the business goals are defined and they turn the business strategies into concrete and measurable strategies. In this example, a business goal is defined and documented in BGo.

    - **Artifact: BGo:**
        - **Name of the objective:** *always replying an incoming call.*
        - **Description:** every time a client makes a call, the company must handle it by answering the caller's questions provided it has been previously categorized.

3. Third, the business policies determine the business operation and control. The following is a list of each rule in natural language.

    - **Artifact: BR:**
        a. There must always be at least one phone line and an operator available.
        b. An operator can answer any phone line in any of his or her shifts.
        c. A client can call as many times as she or he wishes to consult an operator.

    d.   Each call is associated to a single reason.

    e.   A call is answered in only one line.

    f.   If the company does not categorize the reason expressed by the client, then the information exchanged must not be recorded.

    g.   If the call corresponds to a reason categorized by the company then it must be recorded in a form.

    h.   A call registration form must be opened and closed by the same operator.

4.   The following step is to identify and describe the business use cases and actors that constitute the business use-case model. In the example, we concentrate on the use case "Consultation" and informally describe pre and post conditions, actors involved, and events flow. Both business actors, operator and client, are defined as terms in the BG. The following UML diagram models business use case defined and the actors proposed.

- **Artifact: BUCM:**

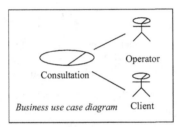

Business use case diagram

- **Textual description of the artifact BUC:** *Consultation*

A client calls the company, the operator answers the call and asks for the following information: client's full name, identity number, card number, security code number, a description of the call and records the reason that corresponds to the call. The operator records the information in a call registration file. If the call does not correpond to one of the categories considered by the company, the information is not recorded. Finally, the operator either satisfies the client's requests or not and ends the call.

Business Use Case: *Consultation*
Business Actors: Operator and Client
Precondition: there is one available line and operator during client assistance hours.
Actions: 1. The client makes a phone call.   2. The operator answers the call and records the following information in a form: full name, identity number, card number, security code, reason, and description for the consultation.   3. The operator provides the information required.   4. The operator ends the call.
Alternative path: 2.1. If the reason for the call does not fit to one of the categories considered by the company, the call is not recorded and communication is ended.
Postcondition: the client's purpose has been satisfactorily achieved or the purpose for the call is not categorized and therefore it is disregarded.

5. The domain model is a BAM's subset that clarifies the business context since it defines the most important entities and their relations. It is usually represented by means of a UML class diagram. The domain model consists of business entities identified in the BE of the generic model.

- **Artifact: BE. Domain Model:** The domain model consists of the following BE: line, operator, client, reason, form, call. The next class diagram graphically represents the domain model.

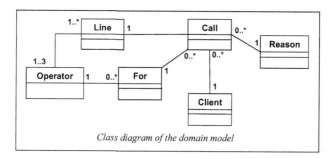

Class diagram of the domain model

In this way, the different artifacts of the one specific business model in a particular domain are realized, that it is based on generic model.

- **Verification of the Proposed Rules:** This section shows the verification of the rules associated to the generic model of the business model for the case study previously presented.

  In the case study of the credit card information service are defined a BG, BGo, BR, and BUCM, which are all artifacts of the BM, with which rules number 1, 2, and 3 of the BM are verified.

  The rule BM.4 establishes that each BG term must be included in the description of at least one BUC. In the example:

  o **Line:** it appears in the precondition of BUC *Consultation.*

  o **Call:** it appears in the description of the actions, the alternative path and the postcondition of BUC *Consultation.*

  o **Reason:** it appears in the description of the actions and the alternative path of BUC *Consultation.*

  o **Operator:** it appears in the description of the actors, the precondition and the description of the actions of BUC *Consultation.*

  o **Client:** it appears in the description of the actors, the description of the actions and the postcondition of BUC *Consultation.*

  o **Form:** it appears in the description of the actions of BUC *Consultation.*

The rule BUCM.1 is not applied in this example, since any BUCAbstract has not been defined.

On the other hand, the rules number 2 and 3 of the BUCM either cannot be applied since a single BUC has been defined. The defined BA are Operator and Client, and no is related to itself, with which it is verified the rule BUCM.4 (see business use case diagram).

Respect to the rules of the BAM, the rule BAM.1 is verified since no BE is related to itself or to another BE (see class diagram of the domain model).

The artifacts BUCR, BW, and BEv have not been modeled in the example, by this, rule number 2 cannot be applied.

Finally, the BEs defined are *line*, *operator*, *client*, *reason*, *form* and *call*, which appear in the BG, with which verifies the rule BAM.3.

In this way, all it applicable rules in the case study have been verified.

Conclusion

This chapter shows the definition of a generic model of the business model, expressed by means of a UML class diagram, together with a set of rules expressed in natural language. This model and their rules are translated into a formal specification language like Object-Z through a translation mechanism defined.

This formalization of the generic model is now a well-formed reconstruction of the original model presented by RUP that allows to visualize and specify not only the artifacts that compose the business model in a complete and organized way but also the relationships holding among them. In addition to this, this formalization expresses precisely the restrictions associated to these artifacts that stem from the UML class diagram of the generic model as well as from the general rules of the model. Moreover, it provides a consistent association among the generic model (expressed in UML class diagram), its associated rules (expressed in natural language), and the translation of both into Object-Z.

In this way, the graphic representation of the business model by means of only one class diagram that shows every artifact that composes this model as well as the relationships among them, simplifies the problem of business modeling. Moreover, the formalization of the model allows one to verify its correctness precisely and rigorously during the construction process or during the process of revision of a previously built model.

References

Baum, G., Daniele, M., Martellotto, P., & Novaira, M. (2004). Un modelo genérico para el modelo de negocio. X *Congreso Argentino de Ciencias de la Computación,*

CACIC2004. Workshop de Ingeniería de Software y Base de Datos (WISBD) (pp. 509-519). Universidad Nacional de La Matanza.

Becker, V., & Pons, C. (2003). Definición formal de la semántica de UML-OCL a través de su traducción a Object-Z. *CACIC 2003. Workshop de Ingeniería de Software y Base de Datos (WISBD)* (pp. 977-989). Universidad Nacional de la Plata.

Booch, G., Rumbaugh, J., & Jacobson, I. (1999). *The unified modelinglanguage: User guide*. Addison Wesley.

Eriksson, H. E., & Penker, M. (2000). Business modeling with UML. In *Business patterns at work*. John Wiley & Sons.

Jacobson, I., Booch, G., & Rumbaugh, J. (1999). *The unified software development process*. Addison Wesley.

Kim, S. K., & Carrington, D. (1999). Formalising the UML class diagram using Object-Z. In *Proceedings of the 2ⁿᵈ International Conference on Unified Modelling Language (UML '99)* (LNCS 1732). Springer-Verlag.

Kim, S. K., & Carrington, D. (2000). A formal mapping between UML models and Object-Z specifications. In *Proceedings of ZB2000: International Conference of B and Z Users* (LNCS 1878).

Kim, S. K., & Carrington, D. (2004, April). A formal object-oriented approach to defining consistency constraints for UML models. In *Proceedings of the Australian Software Engineering Conference (ASWEC 2004)*, Melbourne, Australia: IEEE Computing Society.

Moura, P., Borges, R., & Mota, A. (2003, October 12-14). *Experimenting formal methods through UML*. Presented at the VI Brazilian Workshop on Formal Methods, Campina Grande, Brazil.

Object Management Group (OMG). (2001). *Unified Modeling Language specification, version 1.3, ad/00-03-01*.

Ortín, M., García Molina, J., Moros, B., & Nicolás J. (2001). El modelo del negocio como base del modelo de requisitos. In *Jornadas de Ingeniería de Requisitos Aplicada*. Spain: Facultad de Informática de Sevilla.

Rational unified process (RUP). (2000). Retrieved from http://www.rational.com/rup/

Roe, D., Broda, K., & Russo, A. (2003). Mapping UML models incorporating OCL constraints into Object-Z. (Tech. Rep. No. 2003/9). London: Imperial College.

Salm, J. F. (2003). *Extensões da UML para descrever processos de negócio*. Dissertação (Mestrado em Engenharia de Produção), Universidade Federal de Santa Catarina, Florianópolis.

Sinogas, P., Vasconcelos, A., Caetano, A., Neves, J., Mendes, R., & Tribolet, J. (2001, July 7-10). Business processes extensions to UML profile for business modeling. In *Proceedings of the 3ʳᵈ International Conference on Enterprise Information Systems,* Setubal, Portugal (Vol. 2).

Smith, G. (1992). *An object oriented approach to formal specification*. Thesis for the degree of Doctor of Philosophy. Australia: The Department of Computer Science, University of Queensland.

Smith, G. (2000a). *The Object-Z specification language: Advances in formal methods.* Kluwer Academic Publishers,.

Smith, G. (2000b). Recursive schema definitions in Object-Z. In J. P. Bowen, S. Dunne, A. Galloway, & S. King (Eds.), *1st International Conference of Z and B Users (ZB 2000)* (LNCS 1878, pp. 42-58). Springer-Verlag.

Spivey, J. M. (1992). *The Z notation: A reference manual* (2nd ed.). Prentice Hall.

UML 2.0. (2003). *OMG Adopted Specification, ptc/03-09-15.* Object Management Group.

Chapter XIII

Efficient Software Quality Assurance Approaches Oriented to UML Models in Real Life

Luis Fernández, Universidad Europea de Madrid, Spain

Pedro J. Lara, Universidad Europea de Madrid, Spain

Juan José Cuadrado, Universidad de Alcalá, Spain

Abstract

UML is accepted as the standard notation for object-oriented (OO) development. UML models have a widespread use in today's software practices. Any initiative to improve software quality assurance (SQA) should assume that a high percentage of deliverables to be controlled are currently based on the use of UML notation. However, real life projects are strongly influenced by the need of reaching tangible productivity and efficiency goals. SQA techniques should be customized to meet the balance between quality and budget supported by risk analysis. In this chapter, different strategies and techniques devised to follow the above philosophy of efficiency are presented, especially centred in automatic testing generation from specifications. Our proposal is mainly based on a recommended course of action as well as on integrated tool support for Eclipse environments.

Introduction

As defined by ISO (2000a), quality is defined as "the ability of a set of inherent characteristics of a product, system, or process to fulfil requirements of customers and other interested parties." In the case of software development and maintenance, quality can be promoted by actions in three different axes:

1. **Selection, recruiting, training, and motivation of the best human resources for the development team:** Good developers tend to produce good software and sometimes there are "Net negative producing programmers" who do not produce but also reduce productivity of the rest of the team (Schulmeyer, 1992). Models like PSP (Humphrey, 1996) and TSP help to set individual performance apart from other considerations of degree or educational curricula for IT professionals (Fernández & García, 2003).

2. **Best practices and organization for development processes acting as frameworks for exploiting the benefits of the two other axes:** Models like ISO 9001 (ISO, 2000a), CMMi (Chrissis, Konrad, & Shrum, 2003) or ISO 15504 SPICE (series of standards starting with ISO, (2004)) provide a framework for evaluating, improving, and certifying best practices related to software processes.

3. **Improvement of development methods, techniques, tools, and technology:** What it is assumed is that better resources lead to better characteristics of the produced software. This is not only applicable to development methods that prevent the insertion of defects and get better designs or code (e.g., use of new compilers, environments or even notations like UML, etc.) but also to all the activities for controlling results and detecting and fixing problems before customers begin to use the software (e.g., inspections, testing tools, etc.). Obviously, technology markets tend to use exaggerated expectations and promises to enhance capabilities of products that have been reported with interesting data in references like McConnell (1996) or Jones (1994).

In this chapter, we will explore different possibilities of improving and making more efficient the methods and techniques for preventing and detecting defects for real-life practitioners following a philosophy of SQA defined as a "planned and systematic pattern of all actions necessary to provide adequate confidence that the item or product conforms to established technical requirements" (IEEE, 1991).

One of the problems is that today's software development market rules do not favour a real competition between providers based on offering high quality as the primary reasoning of their strategy because projects are still mainly driven by schedule and budget stringent schemes. This market is not mature enough to have a customer culture

Figure 1. The triangle principle for software projects: for example, fewer budgets should be balanced by an increment in time and/or defects to preserve area size

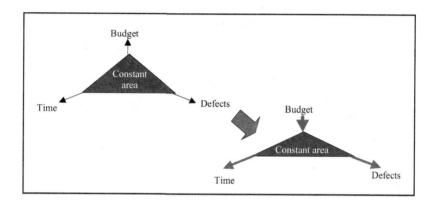

with a clear concept of what it is really software quality and how to evaluate it. Although the triangle principle is conceptually assumed for projects (see Figure 1), as McConnell (1996) explains there are still many occasions where it is not practised (at least 40% of times, simultaneous restrictions along the three axis are imposed).

In this market environment, managers need a dramatic improvement of efficiency and cost reduction in order to have enough arguments to bet on real implementation of SQA techniques in the projects. Obviously there are conspicuous initiatives to promote high level (organizational perspective) models for improving results following the above work line 2: executive staff is likely more interested in this top-down schemes than in more detailed actions simply because they are more understandable for them. It is clear that a huge amount of effort has been devoted to quality management systems (e.g., based on ISO 9001) but mainly due to marketing reasons (e.g., ISO certificates offer a good image of the organizations) or customer dispositions (e.g., ISO certificated organizations tend to demand certification of providers). As explained before, CMMi and SPICE offer a good number of studies that supports, at first sight, benefits of increasing productivity and reducing risks.

In this chapter, we are more concerned in offering more detailed ways to software practitioners (a guerrilla approach) to improve efficiency in SQA implementation with common techniques like testing, metrics and review processes like inspections. To understand all the implications of this approach, we should pay attention to the following facts:

- There are no techniques that enable developers or SQA personnel to verify the absence of defects in the software products. For example, no feasible testing procedure has been devised. As Dikjstra has stated: "Testing cannot guarantee the

Figure 2. SQA as a series of hurdles for the software "athlete"

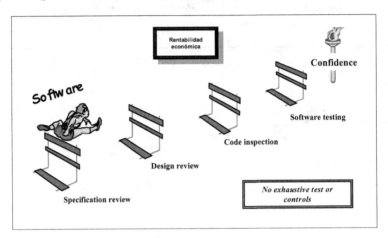

absence of defects; it can only demonstrate that they exist in the software." It is common to conceive SQA controls (following the definitions and philosophy of ISO (2000a) like the different hurdles of an athletics competition (see Figure 2). Each of them is not so high an obstacle that demonstrates the value of the software but the whole series of controls lets us have a good degree of confidence that software meets expectations.

- Any initiative to improve SQA should assume that a high percentage of deliverables to be controlled are currently based on the use of UML notation. If SQA methods force developers to have a dual set of models or documents, they will reject following the control procedures because they cannot (and do not like to) afford extra efforts. Efficient approaches try to integrate tools and models in the same environment to avoid additional management and translation activity. Trends like integration through the lifecycle of models (e.g., RUP, MDA, etc.) or tools (e.g., complete vendor solution integrating CASE-model tools with configuration management, metrics, and other complimentary facilities). Developers tend to be reluctant to follow methodology or notational guides (although their benefits have been proven repeatedly). They want to see that their effort in this area lead to additional benefits: for example, saving future efforts in quality control activities like, for example, testing design and execution or, especially, code generation like in the model-driven (MDA or MDSD) paradigm. Indeed, a high percentage of developers suffer from a deficient training on software testing and SQA techniques, and small- and medium-sized companies are not prepared for a correct implementation of SQA approaches. We have detected this in several surveys developed within the Software Quality Group of ATI (the National Spanish Professional Association, http://www.ati.es) and with 1994 data from QAI (http://www.qaiusa.com).

- A great variety of experiments and data collection experiences have revealed that best results in defect detection are achieved when a proper combination of techniques (both static and dynamic) is deployed throughout the life cycle. Different authors have observed how reviewing processes (e.g., inspections, formal technique reviews, etc.) are more appropriate to find out certain kinds of defects (that constitutes an specific percentage of the total number) and how testing are more suitable to detect other types of "bugs". Moreover, SQA should be established in a life cycle basis to allow an early detection scheme with clear economic benefits, for example, cost of defect repair rises exponentially as the project advances up to 1:60 rates from specification to system testing (a good compilation of these benefits could be found in Pressman (2003)).

- It is more difficult to reach highest levels of efficacy and efficiency of the main SQA techniques (e.g., the ones recommended by IEEE std. 730 (IEEE, 1998) and 1074 (IEEE, 1997) like testing, reviewing techniques, software measurement, etc.) if there is not a good definition and standardization of the project deliverables where they applied to. An adequate formalization and definition of documents and models to be produced in each project is as important as designing the best scheme of control activities. This is an implicit consequence of process improvement models like CMMi: certain control techniques are not feasible to be applied before processes have not reached a minimum degree of definition and formalization. One clear example is testing: it is impossible to have good results if there is not a proper requirements management because tests should be based on descriptions of what it is the expected behaviour of the program for each type of input action.

- Finally, nowadays conditions of actual development projects are so stringent in budget and schedule that productivity is necessary for software organisations. Obviously, processes, methodology, and notation are not feasible without the proper support of tools and integrated automation of activities. One important point is that requirements volatility and in-process modifications of software models during projects are a common issue, so developers need a change in UML models. This could be rapidly translated into changes in the SQA activities. Ffor example, techniques that can enable a change in the software requirements specification can be directly and easily inserted into the corresponding acceptance-test specification. Another important aspect is the need to establish a priority of software requirements and test cases because project leaders should have mechanisms to deal with delays and risks as they appear (e.g., it is not possible to complete the execution of the whole set of test cases before the ending date. Most important cases related to most important requirements and most frequent functions should be addressed first).

Background

As a starting point, we will present different recommendations related to SQA approach where the use of UML is intended under the perspective of the above assumptions.

Table 1. Scenario matrix

Scenario Name	Starting Flow	Alternative Flow
Scenario 1 — Successful registration	Basic Flow	
Scenario 2 — Unidentified user	Basic Flow	A1
Scenario 3 — User cancels	Basic Flow	A2
Scenario 4 — etc.	Basic Flow	A3

Table 2. Requirements and scenario analysis table

Test-case ID	Scenario	User ID	Password	Expected Result
RC 1	Scenario 1 — successful registration	Valid	Valid	User enter the system
RC2	Scenario 2 — Unidentified user	Invalid	N/A	Error: Back to login screen
RC3	Scenario 2 — Unidentified user	Valid	Invalid	Error: Back to login screen
RC4	Scenario 2 — Valid User Cancels	Valid	Valid	Login screen appears.

Considering the classical phases of software life cycle, first point to be considered is test-case generation from software specification based on use cases and complimentary diagrams. These diagrams are considered as a first milestone and a result of the requirements capture (or analysis and specification) phase. Obviously, one important previous point is to assure that use-case models and descriptions are verified and validated using different SQA techniques like inspections and checklists. These controls are designed to support traditional techniques like reviewing processes to allow a cheaper implementation of these V&V actions and will be treated in the second part of this section. Finally, a revision of tools combining risk analysis, testing-completion criteria, coverage analysis, and test environments will be briefly described.

Test-Case Generation from Use Cases

In a software-development project, use cases are normally used to define system software requirements. Use-case modelling begins with the first steps of the project so real use cases for key product functionality are available in early iterations of the lifecycle. According to UML, a use case " ... fully describes a sequence of actions performed by a system to provide an observable result of value to a person or another system using the product under development" (Booch, Rumbaugh, & Jacobson, 1998). Use cases tell the customer what to expect, the developer what to code, the technical writer what to document, and, the most important thing for us, the tester what to test.

Obviously, many approaches have been devised to diminish the impact of possible problems and to prevent errors and miscommunications during the initial phases of a project. Nowadays, it is generally accepted that good practices include the use of well-known notation guides such as UML (Booch, Rumbaugh, & Jacobson, 1998) and the application of modern software processes like unified process (Jacobson, Booch, & Rumbaugh, 1999). These and other best practices have enabled developers to abate traditional problems related to the functional requirements definition.

Software testing includes many interrelated tasks, each with its own artefacts and deliverables. Generation of test cases is the first fundamental step; test procedures are designed for those cases and, finally, test scripts are created to implement the procedures. Test cases are key products for the process because they identify and communicate the conditions that will be implemented for testing. They are necessary to verify and validate successful and acceptable implementation of the product requirements. Although few developers actually do it, project teams should create test cases as soon as use cases are available, no matter if any code is written (as agile methodologies like Extreme Programming also recommend to do). Different approaches are available for generating test cases from use cases, although, as discussed in the section "Generation from Nonformal Specifications of Use Cases", they present different shortcomings in our opinion so we present our own proposal for test design in the section "A SQA Process for Efficiency Supported by an integrated tool environment".

Generation from Nonformal Specifications of Use Cases

A test case is considered as a set of test inputs, execution conditions, and expected results developed for a particular objective: to exercise a particular program path or verify compliance, for example, with a specific requirement. From this definition, a typical method (Heumann, 2002) to develop test cases from a fully detailed use case is the following:

1. **For each use case, we should generate a full set of use-case scenarios:** Read the use-case textual description and identify each combination of main and alternate flows (scenarios). This is documented using a scenario matrix (Table 1 shows a partial scenario matrix for a sample registration use case with no nested alternate flows).

2. **Identification of test cases:** This can be done by analyzing the scenarios and reviewing the use-case textual description as well. There should be at least one test case for each scenario, but there will probably be more (see RC2-RC4 test cases). Boundary conditions should be added. Conditions or data elements required to execute the various scenarios should be identified (Table 2 shows the results for the explained registration use case: no data values have been actually entered).

3. **Identification of data values for tests:** Test cases should be reviewed and validated to ensure accuracy and to identify redundant or missing test cases. Finally, actual data values should be used to substitute Is and Vs.

Main advantage of this method is simplicity and direct application; absence of a formal representation of use cases reduces automation capability and efficiency of the process.

Scenario-Based Test Generation

SCENT, a method for SCENario-Based Validation and Test of Software (Ryser & Glinz, 2003) is similar to the previous method but based on scenarios of use cases and with a formal notation as basis for the process. It assumes that scenarios elicit and document requirements, functionality, and behaviour of a system so they help to discover ambiguities, contradictions, omissions and vagueness in natural language descriptions by formalizing narrative scenarios with state charts (Harel, 1988). If state charts (where necessary and helpful) with pre and postconditions, data ranges and values, and performance requirements, complement the information of use cases, we can systematically derive test cases for system test by traversing paths in the state charts, choosing an appropriate testing strategy.

The SCENT method includes the following phases: scenario creation, scenario formalization, and test-case derivation.

- **Scenario creation:** Table 3 shows the fifteen steps of this procedure.
- **Scenario formalization and annotation:** The process includes two steps that transform the scenario in a state-chart representation (formalization) and extends the diagram to include important information for testing, such as preconditions, data, and other nonfunctional requirements (annotation).
- **Test-case derivation:** Test-case derivation in the SCENT method comprises three substeps:

Table 3. Steps to create a scenario

#	Step Description
1.	Find all actors (roles played by persons/external systems) interacting with the system
2.	Find all (relevant system external) events
3.	Determine inputs, results and output of the system
4.	Determine system boundaries
5.	Create coarse overview scenarios (instance or type scenarios on business process or task level)
6.	Prioritize scenarios according to importance, assure that the scenarios cover system functionality
7.	Create a step-by-step description of events and actions for each scenario (task level)
8.	Create an overview diagram and a dependency chart (see "Integrated Tool Support for the Process")
9.	Have users review and comment on the scenarios and diagrams
10.	Extend scenarios by refining the scenario description, break down tasks to single working steps
11.	Model alternative flows of actions, specify exceptions and how to react to exceptions
12.	Factor out abstract scenarios (sequences of interactions appearing in more than one scenario)
13.	Include nonfunctional (performance) requirements and qualities in scenarios
14.	Revise the overview diagram and dependency chart
15.	Have users check and validate the scenarios (Formal reviews)

- o **Step 1 (mandatory):** Test-case derivation from statecharts.

- o **Step 2 (mandatory):** Testing dependencies among scenarios and additional tests (e.g., testing for specific characteristics).

- o **Step 3 (optional):** State-chart integration and test-case derivation from the integrated statechart.

In SCENT, test cases are derived by path traversal in state charts. First, the normal flow of actions represented in the state chart is followed, and then the paths representing the alternative flows of actions and the exceptions are covered. In the method, all nodes and all links in the graph should be "executed," that is, every state and every transition is covered by at least one test case.

Most states and many transitions are usually traversed more than once due to the use of the annotations to refine test cases. Preconditions to state charts define test preparation that has to be done before test cases derived from the state chart can be executed. The data specified in the scenarios and annotated in the state charts help develop boundary value tests. Domain-testing techniques and data-flow testing can be applied to derive further test cases (Beizer, 1990, 1995; Myers, 1979). Furthermore, as path traversal in state charts will only generate tests for valid sequences of events, the tester has to ensure inclusion of invalid event sequences in the test. These tests are constructed by evoking or generating events while the machine is in a state where it should not respond to the generated events. Thus, exception testing can be improved and systematized and a better test coverage can be achieved. Notes on performance and nonfunctional requirements in the scenarios help to generate test cases to test these properties.

A new diagram type called dependency charts (that include timing, logical and causal dependencies between scenarios) for supporting the second step of the method is defined in SCENT. Although the method has been yet applied with good results, the effort needed to implement it makes difficult a standard use.

Statistical-Based Test Generation

Based on usage or reliability tests, the main idea is to find those parts of the system that do not need to be tested so deeply because they are less important or frequent. Statistical tests try to identify the 10% of the code that consume the 90% of the runtime. The method allows the systematic transformation of a use-case model of a software system into a usage model (Walton, Poore, & Trammel, 1995). The usage model serves as input for automated statistical testing.

A software "usage model" characterizes intended use of the software in the intended environment, that is, the population from which a statistically correct sample of test cases will be drawn (Walton et al., 1995). Usage models resemble finite state machines with transitions weighted with probabilities. The resulting model typically is a Markov chain (although other notations, such as graphs and formal grammars, can be used alternatively) describing the state of usage rather than the state of the system.

Typically, the process proposed consists of five main steps:

1. **Use-case refinement**

2. **Use-case transformation into state diagrams:** The result of this step is a hierarchy of state diagrams and a higher degree of formalization. Separate usage models can be created per state diagram, allowing testing application at component rather than system level.

3. **State diagrams transformation into usage graphs:** A usage graph has a single start and a single final state. Transitions between states are labelled with the user action causing the transition to be taken.

4. **Usage graphs transformation into usage models:** There is no general systematic approach for deriving these models. The probability of some outgoing transition of a usage state may depend on previous execution of the system. This violates the usage model's Markov property: solution relies on the replication and connection of that state and its dependent states to assure that historic dependencies are solved and, eventually, all of the usage graph's states invocation probabilities depend only on the immediately preceding state of the diagram.

5. **Usage models transformation into test cases:** Random testing is applied assuring that minimal arrow coverage is reached before truly random test cases are generated.

State-Driven Test Generation

All software can be modelled as a state machine. Usually, this method has been applied to communication systems, but in OO development, the state machine is a natural way of describing the status of system or objects. State-driven test generation concentrates on validating the correct sequencing of program actions and intermediate states. Different actions and state combinations, that is, paths through the program, are tested (as a whole or partially). A fault in the program may result in a wrong action that leads it to a nonexpected program state. State-driven testing is also used to detect deadlocks.

Following this idea, Kangasluoma (2000) describes an algorithm based on selecting paths or segments to be tested within the state diagram and allocating a test case to each transition although this ignores how effects may depend on previous transitions. To overcome this shortage, other proposals, for example, Offutt and Abdurazik (1999), suggest covering all predicates in each transition's guard conditions to assure that they represent all the intended effects.

In the case of AGEDIS, the basis of the method is a model of the software application written in a modelling language, specifically designed to enable the automated test generation. The AGEDIS test methodology is based on an iterative process that can be divided into six steps:

1. A behavioural model of the system under test is built. Originally, it is based on class diagrams with a state chart of the behaviour of objects in each class and object diagrams that describe the initial state of the system under test. UML use cases can be used for this model because a state diagram of the use-case behaviour can be used for it.

2. Testing objectives (coverage goals, specific use cases, etc.) and testing architecture (deployment details) is translated into a set of test generation and test execution directives.

3. An automatic test generator generates a test suite, satisfying the testing objectives stated in the previous step.

4. The behavioural model, the test directives, and the test suites are reviewed by developers, architects, and final users using specific tools for visualizing and animating these artefacts.

5. Test suites are automatically executed and the test execution environment logs the results.

6. Steps 2 to 5 are iterated until the desired coverage and quality objectives have been reached.

Not all software may be treated by the AGEDIS tools; even for those applications that fit the AGEDIS profile, not all test cases can be generated and executed automatically.

Test Generation Based on Path Analysis Techniques

Each use-case path is derived from a possible combination of following use-case elements: basic flow, alternate flows, exception flows and extends and include relationships. Each path through a use case is a potential test case.

The path analysis process consists of following four major steps (Ahlowalia, 2002):

1. **Drawing a flow diagram (or activity diagram) for each use case**: Each node represents the point where flow diverges or converges: several branches (or connections between two nodes) are present. Each use case has only one start and can have multiple ending points. Normally people tend to begin to construct the diagram by drawing the basic (happy day) flow and extending it to represent the rest of the necessary behaviour.

2. **Determining all possible paths:** Beginning from the starting point each time, we should list all possible ways to reach an ending node, keeping the direction of flow in mind. In some complex use cases, especially when there are many feedback branches, there could potentially be a very large number of paths. The aim here is to list all these paths. Each path can be named with an id like P1, P2 and so on, with a sequence of numbers of branches traversed (e.g., 2,3,4,5,...) and a textual description of the complete sequence of user actions and system responses taking place along the path (in fact, a description of the test case itself).

3. Once a valid set of paths is generated, an **analysis process** leads to a priority allocation to each path based on frequency and risk of its execution.

4. **Most important paths are selected:** to discover as much defects as possible with a minimum cost of execution.

Review Processes

As stated, SQA experiences have revealed that defect detection rates are dramatically increased when testing and review processes are combined. Besides, early controls (at least, at the end of each development phase as recommended in process standards) avoid incurring additional costs when defects remain unfixed phase after phase. When no executable deliverables are available, defect detection should rely on review processes.

There is a huge amount of evidences of benefits obtained from the inclusion of reviewing controls, especially when inspections are the chosen technique. For example, Fagan (1986), Grady and Caswell (1987), and Wheeler, Brykczynski, and Meeson (1996) report important reduction in development effort (25-40%), interesting return of investment (ROI: 8:1 to 30:1), and decreasing number of defects (e.g., 38%). The bad news appears when we analyze the effort required to implement a successful inspection program: it could be high for standard organizations. Although ROI is interesting enough, the investment capacity needed to afford this kind of programs tend to frighten managers interested in this kind of initiatives.

To face this problem, organizations have developed different initiatives to reduce the cost and effort required. Basically, all the proposals have focus their attention on reducing the need of human resources without pushing the results of defect detection below the line risk analysis recommend for each project. There are a great number of studies that analyze the influence of different factors on inspections performance, efficiency, and efficacy, for example, Biffl and Halling (2002, 2003) or Boodoo, El-Emam, Laitenberger, and Madhavji (2000). Certainly, certain organizations reduce inspection team even to peer review. In our case, we prefer to concentrate on the use of metrics and tools as means for transferring tasks from humans to automated tools, especially if we consider that an integrated environment for supporting these activities could be devised as part of our proposal.

The first work line of organizations for efficient inspections is the customization of controls according to the risk profile of the project (what it is consistent with the approach for generating test cases included in this proposal). Following the idea of Pareto analysis, for almost all the projects, organizations cannot afford deep inspections of all the parts of the system so they have to prioritize where controls should be applied. Fortunately, different studies have demonstrated a clear relationship between certain software metrics and important external behaviour characteristics of software. Briand, Wuest, and Iconomovski (1998) showed how a high complexity leads to defect-prone parts or maintenance that is more difficult. Validation experiments for OO metrics have also revealed a relationship between them and the number of defects or the maintenance effort: for example, Abreu and Melo (1996) or Basili, Briand, and Melo (1996). Sometimes, organizations can determine a threshold value from historical data that determines when it is reasonable to establish deeper controls to detect more problems.

The second work line is based on the use of certain tools to check compliance (of products to be inspected) to important reasonable guides that enhance software quality. For example, style and documentation guidelines are better reinforced if there are available tools for developers to check by themselves if they follow the rules (Fernandez & Lara, 2004). In this case, compliance to style rules or successful syntactical checks is necessary to enter the inspection process: they are part of entry (just the same as requirement a clean compilation as entry requirement for code inspections). We do not want to dedicate expensive human resources to check aspects that can be easily analyzed by tools. This is the approach adopted in a major Spanish Telco company (Borrajo, 1994, 1995). In it, all the designs and code inspected had to demonstrate style compliance. They also applied the Pareto analysis to determine where intensive control effort had to be dedicated.

Risk Analysis to Improve Test Efficiency

As we have discussed before, one work line for enhancing efficiency of SQA controls is the customization of the intensity of techniques according to the risk profile of the software to be developed. Risk analysis can help us, for example, to rank test cases in order to help us to choose most important cases for risk abatement as the first test cases to be executed. Almost all the test generation techniques presented above use explicitly or implicitly some kind of risk analysis to select and determine an order of execution for test cases.

According to NASA (1997), risk is a function of the anticipated frequency of occurrence of an undesired event, the potential severity of resulting consequences, and the uncertainties associated with the frequency and severity. This standard defines several types of risk such as, for example, availability risk, acceptance risk, performance risk, cost risk, schedule risk, and so on. From the point of view of the test cases, the most important is reliability-based risk, which takes into account the probability that the software product will fail in the operational environment and the adversity of that failure. Hutcheson (2003) highlights the importance of previously determining the probability of occurrence of events that cause failures and the severity of the failure in terms of economic cost or even social or human consequences. Due to the inherent difficulty of this task, it is usual to estimate by qualitative analysis what are the factors associated to a risk and by quantitative analysis how this factor affect that risk.

Different approaches have been devised for risk analysis. One of them is historical analysis to guide testing activities. It uses defect analysis of software components to focus test intensity on parts of the software that have been revealed as fault-prone in earlier releases or earlier life cycle phases, such as development. For example, Stringfellow and Andrews (2002) adapted a reverse architecting technique using defect reports to derive fault architectures. A fault architecture determines and visualizes components that are fault-prone in their relationships with other components, as well as those that are locally fault-prone. Comparison across releases lets one know if some components are repeatedly included in fault-prone relationships. These results can be used to identify those parts of the software that need to be tested more.

This type of analysis can also exploit different metrics like a defect cohesion measure at the component level which is an indicator of problems local to the component and a defect coupling measure between two components as an indicator of relationship problems between components (Wohlin & Runeson, 1995). High values in these metrics are undesirable as a symptom of potential problems. Other methods (Ohlsson, Von Mayrhauser, McGuire, & Wohlin, 1999; Ohlsson & Wohlin, 1998; Von Mayrhauser, Wang, Ohlsson, & Wohlin, 1999) combine prediction of fault-prone components with code decay analysis. These techniques rank components based on the number of defects in which that component plays some role.

Another line of risk analysis is heuristic analysis. Heuristics are often presented as a checklist of open-ended questions, suggestions, or guidewords. Its purpose is not to control actions, but help us to consider more possibilities and interesting aspects of a problem. One of remarkable contribution to this type of risk analysis techniques for testing is the MIT (most important test) introduced by Hutcheson (2003). Two main tasks are included:

- **Establishing a test effort efficiency limit:** That is, a limit determined by the amount of available resources, for example, time to deliver or budget (see Figure 3).

- **Determination of a measure of risk for potential problems based on several criteria to assess risk:** Risk includes requirements, severity of problems, probability of occurrence, cost of failure, visibility, tolerance and human factor. An expert or a group of experts should assign a value from 1 to 5 (1 is the highest priority value) according to the answers to a set of predefined questions.

Different formulae are devised to combine the risk evaluation results to categorize the different test cases combining information of the most important no analytical tests (MINs), most important paths (MIPs), most important data (MIDs), and most important environments (MIEs). One of the results is a number of tests that can be used to negotiate the test effort in function of the risk assumed by the customer.

Figure 3. S-curve for effort vs. detected errors

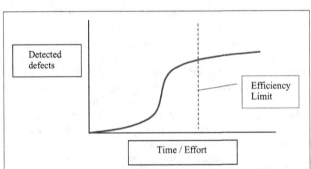

Finally, another trend in risk analysis for testing is statistical analysis using UML at architectural level. The method proposed in Goseva-Popstojonova (2003) describes two kinds of elements in any software architecture: components and connectors. For each of them a heuristic factor and a measure of the severity of a failure are determined and afterwards a Markov model is applied to get the different scenario related with the risk factors. Use cases and scenarios drive the process; component relationships are based on sequence diagrams for each scenario or use case (Rumbaugh, Jacobson, & Booch, 1998). For each scenario, the component (connector) risk factors are estimated as a product of the dynamic complexity (coupling) of the component (connector) behavioural specification measured from the UML sequence diagrams and the severity level assigned by the domain expert using hazard analysis and failure mode and effect analysis (FMEA). Then, a Markov model is constructed for each scenario based on the sequence diagram and a scenario risk factor is determined. Further, the use cases and overall system risk factors are estimated. The outcome of the above process is a list of critical scenarios in each use case, a list of critical use cases, and a list of critical components/connectors for each scenario and each use case.

This approach can be supplemented with risk mitigation strategies where developers can estimate the fault proneness of software components and connectors in the early design phase of the software life cycle. Different studies, for example, Munson & Khoshgoftaar (1996) has shown correlation between complexity of a software component and the number of faults found in it and dynamic complexity of state charts can be computed as a dynamic metric for components and also related to the fault proneness for connectors (Hassan, Abdelmoez, Elnaggar, & Ammar, 2001). Coupling between components provides important information for identifying possible sources of exporting errors, identifying tightly coupled components, and testing interactions between components.

Test Coverage for Risk Control

Test coverage analysis reveals the areas of software exercised by a set of test cases. Recommended test practices suggest a combination of black-box and white-box testing to achieve the best results (Myers, 1979). Test coverage act as a completeness criteria: if the planned coverage is reached, testing is completed; otherwise, we should create additional test cases to reach the desired level unless other factors in the project determine the need of a reducing the planned level of testing. In all cases, test coverage measure offers managers objective information of what exact risk level they are facing after a set of tests.

Obviously, different coverage levels are possible: statement, decision, condition, multiple conditions, path, DDP, and LCSAJ (McCabe, 1976; Myers, 1979; Ntafos, 1988; Roper, 1994; Woodward, 1980). In the case of the projects of the European Space Agency, statement coverage is necessary. Different contributions have been treated coverage analysis in several manners (Friedman, Hartman, & Shiran, 2002; Kosmatov, Legeard, Peureux, & Utting, 2004; Vincenzi, Maldonado, & Delamaro, 2005) and numerous tools have been developed to implement some of these techniques. One of these tools is Clover (http://www.cenqua.com/clover), which applied to Java projects gives measures for method, branch, and statement coverage. Other open source tools complete the spectrum of test analyzers (http://java-source.net/open-source/code-coverage).

Test Frameworks and Environments for Efficiency

A great variety of tools have been developed to support different activities of testing and improving efficiency and efficacy. The use of test frameworks or test environments is remarkable and is becoming increasingly frequent as time passes. Large organizations like IBM (Kan, 2002) have implemented efficient systems for reducing testing effort. Vendors like IBM Rational offers a suite of products oriented to cover a great variety of testing tasks: manual test execution (manual tester), automated functional and regression testing tool (functional tester) and products oriented to performance improvement (http://www-306.ibm.com/software/rational/offerings/testing.html). Other vendors also offer a variety of interesting testing tools. Even freeware or cheap tools (Crowther & Clark, 2005) are useful: tools like JUnit, JTest and Panorama for Java developments and csUnit and HarnessIt for C# programs are analyzed in this reference.

SQA Process for Efficiency Supported by an Integrated Tool Environment

Our proposal is based on devising a course of action of different SQA activities that follows the philosophy presented above. Focussing on test generation as part of a quality assurance process shown in Figure 4, the process could be divided in the phases described as follows. Notice that a set of controls and activities has been include in analysis and design phases to assure the whole set of control is coherent and successful. Activities specially related with test design are highlighted in Figure 4 using an orange-yellow area. Contributions of SQA complimentary techniques are depicted with dashed lines while direct relationships between test-related activities and documents are represented with continuous arrows and lines.

- **Analysis:** Oriented to generate the different use cases analyzing the point of view of the user. It does not only include the ATABUS methods to be described in subsequent sections but also a recommend course of action for the requirements specification process. The IRS process described in Fernandez et al. (2004) is aimed to offer a better integration of nonfunctional requirements than the current analysis practice and a convenient support of test generation and synchronization with use cases. The IRS Process consists of the following steps:
  - o Description of the right use cases with detailed information about the graphical user interface as recommended in the RUP requirement process (Jacobson et al., 1999).

- ○ Analysis of the usability of the interaction described in each use case changing the description or the structure of the use case if necessary.

- ○ Construction of a preliminary performance forecast for each case trying to suggest changes that improve the required processing workload to execute the represented functionality.

- ○ Generation of acceptance test cases to cover the use-cases definition using the method ATABUS described in "Test Case Generation from Use Cases."

- ○ This phase should be rely on a close collaboration between the analyst and the user representatives in order to document use-case descriptions that represent as close as possible the real needs of final users. The user will participate in the use-case selection and description as well as in the usability analysis of the software using not only the use-case analysis but also the interface diagrams associated with the use case and the activity diagrams built on design phase. Of course, as usual in iterative development processes, evolutionary prototypes (or draft versions of the system) should play a main role in the communication between analysts and users to validate models.

- **Design:** In addition to the typical results in OO design, such as class and collaboration diagrams, a test-case design and a traceability cube to describe the relationship between use cases, classes, and test cases should be done. Two additional main tasks are needed to complete the process when using this cube:

  - ○ Risk associated to each use cases scenario should be determined.

  - ○ Fault-proneness of classes and components should be evaluated using metrics as described in "Review Processes".

  - ○ **Code and test:** Before executing tests, they should be ranked according to associated risks using the traceability cube and analyzing:

    - ➢ The risk of the associated scenario

    - ➢ The fault proneness of the related classes

    - ➢ The probability of occurrence of an specific path

    Conventional coverage metrics (structural and functional) will contribute to complimentary analysis of testing effort, especially related to the next phase.

  - ○ **Regression testing and test iterations:** Developers should iterate test and design phases as many times as necessary to reach the desired level of testing.

All the process should be controlled using the correspondent review processes for the different deliverables involved.

Figure 4. Proposed process

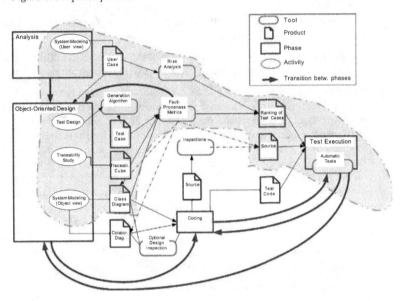

ATABUS: Test-Cases Generation Algorithm

Use cases are an essential part of UML notation to explain the external behavior of an information system. Use cases are even more useful when combined with activity diagrams (ADs). An AD is a special case of a state diagram: a model showing the set of different states of an object during its life and the conditions to change from one state to another. In ADs most of states are action states and most of transitions are activated when action related to the previous state finishes. Given a use-case description in a standard representation template (Schneider & Winters, 2001), the process for generating the AD is explained below using an example.

- **Use Case:** Deleting user data
- **Goal:** Remove all the information about one user in the data base.
- **Main event flow:**

Actor	System
1. Inits user drop process	2. Asks for User ID
3. Introduces User ID	4. Shows user data an asks for confirmation
5. Confirms user drop	6. Drop user and Show confirmation.

- **Alternative workflows:**
  - o   If the introduced ID does not match, a message is shown at step 4 and workflow return to step 3.
  - o   Any time, if the actor decides to cancel the action then no changes should be done and control return to the main menu.
    - ➢   **Preconditions:** The user to be deleted is stored in the system
    - ➢   **Postconditions:** No information about the deleted user may remain in the database
    - ➢   **Interface:** See Figure 5.

Based on this standard description we can generate an AD like the one shown in Figure 6 where each scenario of the use case can be determined by a specific path from the initial activity to the end one. Our proposal ATABUS (algorithm for test automation based on UML specification) for test generation from use cases (Fernandez & Lara, 2003) uses AD as the common information collector of the use-case behavior to address the generation and ranking of test cases and the operation time measurement of each scenario. Use cases and ADs is our reference model for requisite specification based on use case (in a format similar to what it is usual in development practice) and ADs to clarify the behavior of the system.

Considering a scenario to be each different path that could be traced across an activity diagram, the number of scenarios to be analyzed tend to be extremely high if we take into account two facts: (a) a path should be counted as a different one only due to the number of times that a loop is executed and (b) each input action of this path can generate itself one subpath for each combination of input values. This huge amount of possibilities make impossible to test all of them, so what people used to do is to select a few cases that could be considered as representative of many others (the rest) equivalent ones.

In ATABUS (Fernandez & Lara, 2003), the first proposed selection rule is a coverage criterion similar to the one established in Memon, Soffa, and Pollack (2001). Based on the graph theory of McCabe (1976), the minimum set of paths should ensure that the execution trace crosses, at least once, all the arrows and edges of the graph (Myers, 1979). It can be express as follows:

A use case (as described by its activity diagram) will be enough tested enough if the execution trace covers all the arrows or transitions in the diagram at least once.

According to this, five paths can be found in the diagram of the Figure 6 that can be condensed in four types of interaction between the users and the system:

- •   Init deletion, ask for ID an Cancel
- •   Init deletion, ask for ID, introduce an incorrect ID, introduce a correct ID, deletion is confirmed

Figure 5. User interface

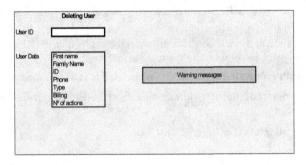

Figure 6. Activity diagram

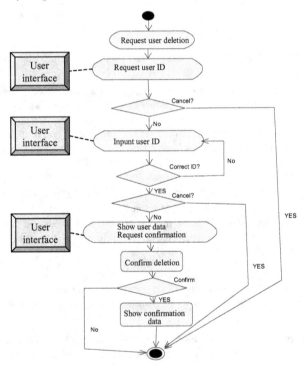

- Init deletion, ask for ID, introduce a correct ID, deletion is cancelled
- Init deletion, ask for ID, introduce a correct ID, deletion is not confirmed

Secondly, following the traditional recommendations about black-box-test design, an analysis of the domain of the input data values should be done to detect data groups or classes with homogeneous behavior. This technique is called equivalence classes (Myers, 1979). An equivalence class may include a group of valid data and a group of invalid values. For instance, if an input specification describes a range of values, we consider two classes of invalid data (values under and over the range limits) and a third one that groups all the valid values. Our second selection criterion can be described as follows:

For each input data action in a use case, every valid equivalence classes should be covered using the minimum number of test cases but each invalid class should be include in a separated test case to monitor all the limit values.

In order to construct an activity diagram with complete information about equivalence classes, we propose to introduce a subdiagram for every activity node where data input action is involved. In the drop user example, if we assume that a valid user id is any integer number with a maximum of six digits, the following data should be considered: 999999, 000000, A546B6, 1000000, -000001.

It is essential that this information appears in the activity diagram. UML hierarchical activity diagrams are implemented in all commercial tools (e.g., Rational Rose) so they can be used to develop the diagram shown in Figure 7.

Once these two criteria have been explained, the definition of our test-cases generation process is the following (Fernandez & Lara, 2003):

1. Generation of an activity diagram for each use case where the events flow paths are indicated (see Figure 6).

2. Identification of data input action concerning each possible path in the diagram, analyzing the equivalence classes, boundary values, and possible combined functioning ((Fernández, 2000) inspired on (Myers, 1979)).

3. Each input action should be considered an activity state containing a sub-diagram where each input option included (Figure 7), building the definitive diagram where decision nodes referred to correctness of input data disappear.

4. Execute both coverage criteria to cover each arrow or edge at least once.

One of the most important contributions of the process is the formalization of the algorithm and all the elements involved in it (Escribano, Lara, Fernandez, & Hilera, 2005). In the following section, this formal model will be described and the algorithm itself will be formalized.

Figure 7. Introduction of the user ID subdiagram

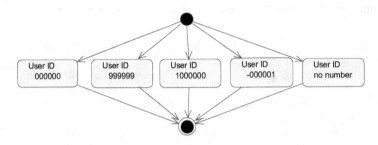

ATABUS: Formal Models and Algorithms for Test Generation

The following elements will be used as basis for defining an AD:

- **DA** = Activity diagram
- **Ca** = Path from the initial node to the final node.
- N_A = {graph nodes representing activities in the DA}
- N_D = {graph nodes representing decisions in the DA}
- N_F = {graph nodes representing forks in the DA}
- N_J = {graph nodes representing joins in the DA}
- **T** = Transitions in the DA, that is, every arrow between two different elements and the associated guard, if it exits.
- N_o = Origin of an arrow.
- N_d = Destination of an arrow.

Now, an AD can be seen as:

$$G = (N, T)$$

Where $N = N_A \cup N_D \cup N_F \cup N_J \cup$ *{start point, end point} and* $T = $ *(edge, guard)*
and
Guard $\in$ *{λ, condition} being λ the empty set*
condition $=$ *boolean expression*

$$edge \subseteq N_O^i \times N_d^j \quad i, j \in \mathbf{N}^+$$

where

$$i \cdot j = i \vee j$$

and if

a. $i > 1 \Leftrightarrow N_d \in N_J \wedge \forall k = 1..i \; N_o^k \notin N_F$

b. $j > 1 \Leftrightarrow N_o \in N_F \wedge \forall k = 1..j \; N_d^k \notin N_J$

For the ATABUS algorithm, an extended formal model of AD is required. Before proceeding with this extended model, it is necessary to establish these three restrictions:

- A well-balanced and verified AD (Object Management Group, 2001) should be used as starting point.
- We will use an acyclic AD because it is necessary to ensure that every node in the AD is visited at least once. Two types of loops can be found in an AD. Those where the probability of any number of cycles are the same and those where the probability of a new cycle is decreasing. First type of loops can be simplified as a new alternate path with a fixed probability. The probability of the second one should follow a Poisson distribution.
- The probability of executing a transition is independent from the previous one. Fault proneness study is omitted to simplify the algorithm.

The elements we have to change are the following:

N'_A = {graph nodes representing Activities in the DA plus the list of data to be considered}

In other words:

$N'_A = N_A \times data^*$
$data = (id, value^*)$

where "*" represent the Kleen closure used in regular expressions.

So, now:

$G = (N, T')$

where:

$N = N'_A \cup N_D \cup N_F \cup N_J \cup \{\text{start point, end point}\}$
$T' = (\text{edge, guard, P, C})$

$edge \subseteq N_O^i \times N_d^j \quad i, j \in N^+$

where:

$$i \cdot j = i \vee j$$

a. $i > 1 \Leftrightarrow N_d \in N_J \wedge \forall k = 1..i\ N_o^k \notin N_F$

b. $j > 1 \Leftrightarrow N_o \in N_F \wedge \forall k = 1..j\ N_d^k \notin N_J$

P = Probability of a transaction calculated as:

$if\ (n_o, m) \notin N_D x N^j \Rightarrow P = 1$

$if\ (n_o, m) \in N_D x N^j \Rightarrow 0 < P < 1$

$\sum_{i=1}^{n} P_i = 1\ si\ \{(n_o, m_{d_1})...(n_o, m_{d_n})\} \in edge$

$\wedge$

$(n_0, m_d) \in edge \Leftrightarrow \exists i \in \{1..n\},, d = d_i$

C = Cost of an error in the transition, calculated as:

$if\ (n_o, m) \notin N_D x N^j \Rightarrow C = 0$

$if\ (n_o, m) \in N_D x N^j \Rightarrow 0 \leq C \leq 5$

Based on this, it is possible to write two algorithms, one for generation and rank of paths in the AD (test cases) and another for operation time evaluation.

The final algorithm ATABUS is stated as follows:

- Generate an AD, restrictions compliant, for each use case.

$$\forall N' \in N'_A$$

where:

$$N' = N x (d_{1}, ...d_{n}) x\ OT$$

and:

$n \neq 0$

a. Assign values to attributes (P, C), using the techniques shown above.
b. Build a subdiagram where each input data value is included (Figure 7) and decision nodes referred to correctness of input data disappear. So:

$\forall (id, vi) \in data^*, create :$

a new node Ni

a new transition

$t = ((N, Ni), (id = vi), P, C)$

and

$\forall t = ((No_t, Nd_t), g_t, P_t, C_t) \in T\ where$

$g_t = (id = vi)\ and$

$(id, vi) \in data\ ^*$

deleted t

- Let S the set of different paths existing in the new AD.

$\forall\ p \in S$

> let T_p the set of transitions in p
>
> let $T_D \subseteq T_p$, such as
>
> $t = (N_{ot}, N_{dt}, g_t, P_t, C_t) \in T_D :\Leftrightarrow N_{ot} \in N_D$
>
> calculate the probability of p as

$$P(p) = \prod_{t \in T_D} P_t$$

> and calculate the cos t of p as

$$C(p) = \underset{t \in T_D}{Max}(C_t)$$

- Rank the paths (Test Cases) use the risk of every path as a function:

$$f(P(p), C(p)).$$

Integrated Tool Support for the Process

The ATABUS algorithm presented before is interesting for generating test cases form use cases but it is not useful if there is not appropriate tool support for assuring efficiency and comfortable process for developers. Following our philosophy, we have developed diverse utilities for supporting the different tasks of the process, sometimes using COTS software. Our choice for development was an open-source IDE with an extensible plug-in architecture to make easier to add new functionality. In that sense, Eclipse was chosen and a plug-in called AGAPE (in Spanish, Analysis & Automatic Generation of Test Cases with Eclipse) was developed as the first prototype of the tool to cover the ATABUS algorithm for test generation.

Fully integrated with Eclipse, the AGAPE plug-in lets developers draw activity diagrams for every use case defined on the system and fill out all the required information to transform the initial diagram into the extended one. AGAPE also generates automatically the test cases from the resulting diagram. Additionally, every test case will be associated a risk value that can be calculated from the information introduced by analyst about probability of occurrence and cost of failure (Figure 8) for every possible bifurcation and for every possible data value.

Figure 8. Snapshot of the AGAPE activity-diagram editor

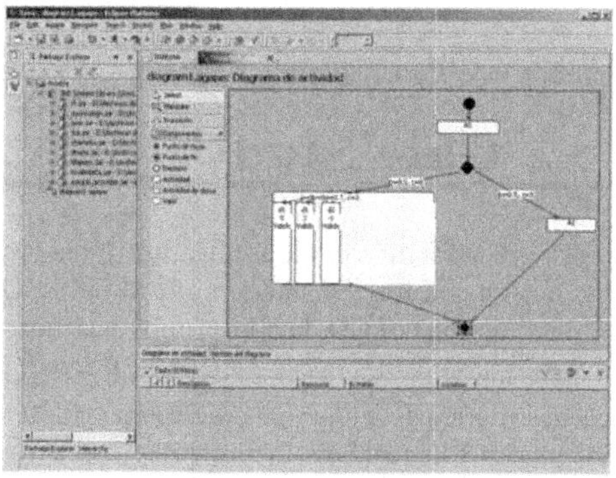

This first prototype provides the following functionalities:

- A graphical editor to create an activity diagram
- A graphical and textual editor to manage data activities, data, and values of this data.
- Generation of test cases from the information of the activity diagram. The test cases are generated in XML language.

However, the whole process also needs further support for the rest of activities. Several Eclipse plug-ins have been developed to help in quality assurance activities. Relating with OO metrics it is possible to find tools like TeamInABox that calculates various metrics for your code during build cycles and warns you, via the Task List, of 'range violations' for each metric. Another plug-in like Metrics 1.3.5 offers up to 25 different metrics of UML models and source code. These utilities help reviewers to adapt their effort to project conditions using Pareto analysis (as presented in "Review Processes").

Other plug-ins are more oriented to force programmers to write quality code, another key point for review processes. Jalopy, for example, is a source code formatter for the Sun Java programming language. It formats any valid Java source code according to some widely configurable rules to meet a certain coding style without putting a formatting burden on individual developers. CheckStyle is another java style checker but it does not change code, it just warns that the lines of code do not comply with SUN style . Of course, this is not new since vendor tools not integrated with Eclipse — for example, Logiscope — also helps to follow style guides with the Rule Checker module (it also has a module for test coverage named TestChecker).

Finally, a plug-in like Clover for controlling test coverage are also available and tools like JUnit or GJTester are widely used to accomplish the unit, regression and contract testing of Java programs or modules.

Case Study

In order to promote a deeper understanding of the application of the process in projects, a case study based on the design and implementation of a simple CD store system is presented. Users require the functions of CD data insertion, deletion, and information retrieval. Table 4 includes an example of one use-case description of the system.

During the project, different software development practitioners (software engineering students and professional experts like teachers, senior analysts and developers) where involved in the project to control the advantages of the proposed process. At the beginning of the project, different software engineering students and some experts analyze the requirements of the system to generate test cases.

Students received different amount and detail of information about the functionality of the systems: some of them with all the information about use cases (like the one shown in Table 4), others with less information, for example, without an activity diagram. In general, we can imagine that better information and use-case descriptions leads to better test cases and facts tend to confirm this. The group of students with less information generate up to 36% less of test cases that those one with more complete information. In addition, while more than a half of possible test cases were found for more than 50% of well-informed students, this percentage was reduced to a 27% in the case of the students who had only a brief textual description of the use cases. This reinforces an accepted idea in software engineering (e.g., in CMM model or testing references): quality of testing cannot be better than the quality of the requirements specification that acts as reference for it. Strong validation and verifications mechanisms (including reviews and inspections) for assuring quality of use-case descriptions with participation of user representatives should be implemented to have a solid basis for this SQA process. A series of references has addressed this activity (Bernardez, Durán, & Genero, 2004):

It is assumed that software experts should reach better results than students but what it is important for our proposal is to confirm all the test cases designed by the experts are included in the set of test cases produced by ATABUS. Combining the list of test cases designing by the students, they only covered 37 test cases for use cases of the CD management application with an average of 26,1 test per student. Just for the use-case number 1 (insert a new CD), only 11 test cases were found for at least 50% of students. In the case of experts, this amount increases up to 16. ATABUS found 34 test cases only for the use-case number 1 (Table 5) and more than 70 for the whole application. Obviously, these cases should be considered as equivalent of the well known linearly independent paths defined in (McCabe, 1976) for flowgraphs, that is, a real test execution (as we have checked using the coverage tools mentioned as part of the process in "A SQA Process for Efficiency Supported by an Integrated Tool Environment") could cover several of these paths.

Table 4. Use-case description example

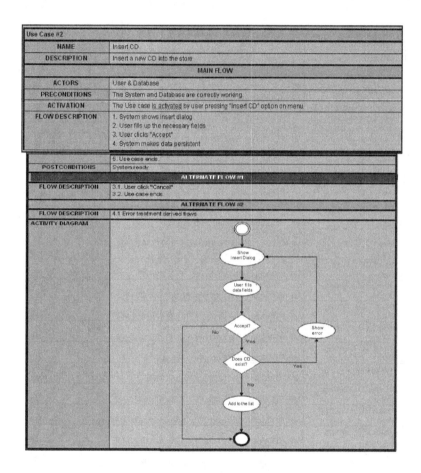

Use Case #2	
NAME	Insert CD
DESCRIPTION	Insert a new CD into the store
MAIN FLOW	
ACTORS	User & Database
PRECONDITIONS	The System and Database are correctly working.
ACTIVATION	The Use case is activated by user pressing "Insert CD" option on menu.
FLOW DESCRIPTION	1. System shows insert dialog 2. User fills up the necessary fields 3. User clicks "Accept" 4. System makes data persistent 5. Use case ends.
POSTCONDITIONS	System ready.
ALTERNATE FLOW #1	
FLOW DESCRIPTION	3.1. User click "Cancel" 3.2. Use case ends.
ALTERNATE FLOW #2	
FLOW DESCRIPTION	4.1 Error treatment derived flows
ACTIVITY DIAGRAM	

Table 5. Test cases for Insert CD use case

Test ID	Short Description	Path	Valid?
1	User cancels	MP-RD(Mclan, Sin Enchufe, 13,90, 1:05:20)-Fin	Si
2	Insert existent CD + cancel	MP-RD(Mclan, Sin Enchufe, 13,90, 1:05:20)-ME-MP-Fin	Si
3	Insert existent CD + Insert non-existent CD	MP-RD(Mclan, Sin Enchufe, 13,90, 1:05:20)-ME-MP-RD(Mclan, Sopa Fría, 13,90, 1:05:20)-AL-Fin	Si
4	Insert non-existent CD	MP-RD(m, Sin Enchufe, 13,90, 1:05:20)-AL-Fin	Si
5	Insert non-existent CD	MP-RD(01234567890123456789012345678, Sin Enchufe, 13,90, 1:05:20)-AL-Fin	Si
6	Insert non-existent CD	MP-RD(Mclan, s, 13,90, 1:05:20)-AL-Fin	Si
7	Insert non-existent CD	MP-RD(Mclan, 01234567890123456789012345678, 13,90, 1:05:20)-AL-Fin	Si
8	Insert non-existent CD	MP-RD(Mclan, Sin Enchufe, 13, 1:05:20)-AL-Fin	Si
9	Insert non-existent CD	MP-RD(Mclan, Sin Enchufe, 0, 1:05:20)-AL-Fin	Si
10	Insert non-existent CD	MP-RD(Mclan, Sin Enchufe, 13,90, 0:55:20)-AL-Fin	Si
11	Insert non-existent CD	MP-RD(Mclan, Sin Enchufe, 13,90, 1:0:20)-AL-Fin	Si
12	Insert non-existent CD	MP-RD(Mclan, Sin Enchufe, 13,90, 1:05:0)-AL-Fin	Si
13	Insert non-existent CD	MP-RD(Mclan, Sin Enchufe, 13,90, 25:05:0)-AL-Fin	Si
14	Insert non-existent CD	MP-RD(, Sin Enchufe, 13,90, 1:05:20)-ME	No
15	Insert CD – Wrong Data	MP-RD(MasDe30/01234567890123456789012345678, Sin Enchufe, 13,90, 1:05:20)-ME	No
16	Insert CD – Wrong Data	MP-RD(Mclan, , 13,90, 1:05:20)-ME	No
17	Insert CD – Wrong Data	MP-RD(Mclan, MasDe30/01234567890123456789012345678, 13,90, 1:05:20)-ME	No
18	Insert CD – Wrong Data	MP-RD(Mclan, Sin Enchufe, , 1:05:20)-ME	No
19	Insert CD – Wrong Data	MP-RD(Mclan, Sin Enchufe, aa,90, 1:05:20)-ME	No
20	Insert CD – Wrong Data	MP-RD(Mclan, Sin Enchufe, 13.90, 1:05:20)-ME	No
21	Insert CD – Wrong Data	MP-RD(Mclan, Sin Enchufe, -13,90, 1:05:20)-ME	No
22	Insert CD – Wrong Data	MP-RD(Mclan, Sin Enchufe, 2^64, 1:05:20)-ME	No
23	Insert CD – Wrong Data	MP-RD(Mclan, Sin Enchufe, 13,90,)-ME	No
24	Insert CD – Wrong Data	MP-RD(Mclan, Sin Enchufe, 13,90, 1:05)-ME	No
25	Insert CD – Wrong Data	MP-RD(Mclan, Sin Enchufe, 13,90, 1:05:20:50)-ME	No
26	Insert CD – Wrong Data	MP-RD(Mclan, Sin Enchufe, 13,90, aa:05:20)-ME	No
27	Insert CD – Wrong Data	MP-RD(Mclan, Sin Enchufe, 13,90, 1:aa:20)-ME	No
28	Insert CD – Wrong Data	MP-RD(Mclan, Sin Enchufe, 13,90, 1:05:aa)-ME	No
29	Insert CD – Wrong Data	MP-RD(Mclan, Sin Enchufe, 13,90, 25:05:20)-ME	No
30	Insert CD – Wrong Data	MP-RD(Mclan, Sin Enchufe, 13,90, -1:05:20)-ME	No
31	Insert CD – Wrong Data	MP-RD(Mclan, Sin Enchufe, 13,90, 1:100:20)-ME	No
32	Insert CD – Wrong Data	MP-RD(Mclan, Sin Enchufe, 13,90, 1:-05:20)-ME	No
33	Insert CD – Wrong Data	MP-RD(Mclan, Sin Enchufe, 13,90, 1:05:100)-ME	No
34	Insert CD – Wrong Data	MP-RD(Mclan, Sin Enchufe, 13,90, 1:05:-20)-ME	No

The comprehensive number of test cases initially generated by ATABUS is the seed that make necessary to rank them to get the maximum number of defects with the minimum number of executions of test. Unfortunately, the quality of results of testing using ATABUS depends on the quality of risk analysis: probability, severity, and fault proneness and, at least, the first two issues are expert dependent, so a big effort in improve skills and knowledge of project managers and analysts about metrics, risks, and so on, is essential.

After the initial generation of tests cases, a series of inspections and evaluations about important software metrics were performed to follow the process. Style and certain types of design defects were detected using Checkstyle and other metric tools like those mentioned in "Integrated Tool Support for the Process". Thus, preventive detection and fewer defects (not easily detectable with testing) were fixed before reaching the test execution phase. As an example of dangerous defects detected, the following pieces of code are presented.

```
for (Iterator i = getCDsIterator(); i.hasNext())
        CD cd = (CD) i.next();
        if (cd.getArtista().equals(artista)) {
                resultado += cd + "\n";
        }


for (Iterator i = getCDsIterator(); i.hasNext()) {
        CD cd = (CD) i.next();
        if (cd.getArtista().equals(artista)) {
                resultado += cd + "\n";
        }
}
```

The code on the top column does not accomplish the style rules of Sun for Java code: a "for" block should be always between braces. A developer could believe that the "if" block are inside the "for" block, but it is really outside the loop, making the code erroneous. The use of braces on the right column avoids this kind of errors. Table 6 and Figure 9 are example of metrics and audit reports provided by the tools integrated with Eclipse for this project.

Table 6. Metrics report automatically generated by TeamInABox Eclipse plug-ins

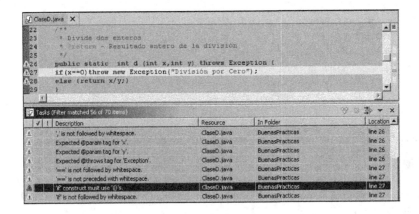

Short Name	Full Name
CC	Cyclomatic Complexity
LOCm	Lines of Code in Method
NOL	Number of Levels
NOP	Number of Parameters
NOS	Number of Statements
Ce	Efferent Couplings
LCOM-CK	Lack of Cohesion in Methods (Chidamber & Kemerer)
LCOM-HS %	Lack of Cohesion in Methods (Henderson-Sellers)
NOF	Number of Fields
WMC	Weighted Methods Per Class

CC (max)	LOCm (max)	NOL (max)	NOP (max)	NOS (max)	Ce (max)	LCOM-CK (max)	LCOM-HS % (max)	NOF (max)	WMC (max)	Package
1	4	1	1	3	5	3	100	3	6	UML
1	6	1	1	2	4	0	0	1	4	UML2

Figure 9. Warnings about code style generated by Checkstyle plug-in for Eclipse

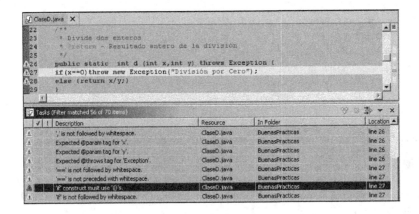

Future Trends

ATABUS provides a process to automate the generation of test cases from UML specification. A first tool to implement part of the process has been developed. However, as we have shown, what it is efficient is a framework to specify requirements, generate tests, and execute them and this is clearly much more than a set of isolated tools with different functionality and a common purpose. Vendors and researchers are now focusing their proposals not only in different methods and techniques but also especially in integration of tool support to avoid extra efforts to developers.

In fact, in the future we expect that construction of real integrated environments (by commercial proprietary vendors or in open environments like Eclipse) will allow, at least, the following features:

- **Use-case extended specification:** Activity diagrams include with all the necessary information to enable risk analysis.

- **Integration of more sophisticated metrics tools to evaluate models and design:** Even more, it is probable that tools will be able to give advice for using design patterns (Grand, 1999).

- **Traceability cube form:** This cube should allow the refinement of the risk analysis with information about fault-proneness ratios obtained from metrics tools and the guided replication of test when specification changes.

- **Redefinition of a test specification language**: To get executable scripts from it that make easier to execute the test cases generated using the algorithm.

- **Integration of GUI, unit, and regression testing tools:** To cover all these kind of tests with the same language and supporting with all the information collected during the process.

- **Coverage analysis of the final set of most important tests:** To ensure a good coverage percentage.

Conclusion

It is frequent to hear software managers to say that quality and productivity are not compatible. Sometimes this feeling is stimulated by the low perception of efficiency and capability of customization of SQA techniques. As we have presented in the introduction, there are several work lines to support the need of productivity, especially the inclusion of serious risk analysis and the transfer of task from humans to tools. We hope that the different methods, techniques and tools presented along the process for a minimum SQA activity could be enough to stimulate a more positive attitude to the inclusion of these techniques that has been proven very useful for developers and managers, with interesting ROI figures. Obviously, one important lesson for practitioners is the absence of silver bullets: each organisation should customize the use of tools and techniques to each project, depending on the risk level they can afford, available resources, and so on. Obviously, managers and developers should be well educated in disciplines like metrics and SQA to exploit the advantages of this process.

References

Abreu, F., & Melo, W. (1996). *Evaluating the impact of object oriented design on software quality*. Paper presented at the 3rd International Symposium on Software Metrics: From Measurement to Empirical Results, Berlin, Germany.

Ahlowalia, N. (2002). *Testing from use cases using path analysis technique*. Paper presented at Object System Group. International Conference On Software Testing Analysis & Review, Edimburg, Scotland.

Basili, V., Briand, L., & Melo, W. L. (1996) A validation of object-oriented design metrics as quality indicators. *IEEE Transactions on Software Engineering, 22*(10), 751-760.

Beizer, B. (1990). *Softwaretesting techniques*. New York: VanNostrand Reinhold.

Beizer, B. (1995). *Black-box testing*. New York: John Wiley & Sons.

Bernárdez, B., Durán, A., & Genero, M. (2004). Empirical evaluation and review of a metrics-based approach for use case verification. *Journal of Research and Practice in Information Technology, 36*(4), 247-257.

Biffl, S., & Halling, M. (2002). *Investigating the influence of inspector capability factors with four inspection techniques on inspection performance*. Paper presented at the Eighth IEEE Symposium on Software Metrics (METRICS'02), Ottawa, Canada.

Biffl, S., & Halling, M. (2003). Investigating the defect detection effectiveness and cost benefit of nominal inspection teams. *IEEE Transactions On Software Engineering, 29*(5), 385-397.

Booch, G., Rumbaugh, J., & Jacobson, I. (1998). *The Unified Modeling Language user guide*. MA: Addison-Wesley.

Boodoo, S., El-Emam, K., Laitenberger, O., & Madhavji, N. (2000), *The optimal team size for UML design inspections (NRC/ERB-1081)*. Ottawa: National Research Council of Canada, Institute for Information Technology.

Borrajo, J. (1994). *Automated metrics to measure the UK*.

Borrajo, J. (1995). *A tool and a set of metrics to support technical reviews*. Paper presented at Software Quality Management IV, Seville, Spain.

Briand, L., Wuest, J., & Iconomovski, S. (1998). *A comprehensive investigation of quality factors in object-oriented designs: An industrial case study* (Tech. Rep. No. ISERN-98-29). Los Angeles, CA: International Software Engineering Research Network.

Chrissis, M. B., Konrad, M., & Shrum, S. (2003). *CMMI®: Guidelines for process integration and product improvement*. Menlo Park: Addison-Wesley.

Crowther, D. C., & Clarke, P. J. (2005). Examining software testing tools. *Dr. Dobbs Journal, 18*(373), 26-33.

Escribano, J. J., Lara, P. J., Fernandez, L., & Hilera, J. R. (2005). *A study of the relationship between usability and test cases precedence based on a formal model for activity diagrams.* Paper presented at the International Conference on Software Engineering Research and Practice (SERP'05), Las Vegas, NV.

Fagan, M. E. (1986). Advances in software inspections. *IEEE Transactions on Software Engineering, 12*(7), 744-751.

Fernández, J. L. (2000). Utilización de casos de uso en las pruebas de aceptación.. In *Proceedings of the V Jornadas de Innovación y Calidad del Software,* San Sebastián, Spain (pp. 65-76).

Fernández, L., & García, M. J. (2003). Software engineering professionalism. *Upgrade, 4*(4), 42-46.

Fernandez, L., & Lara, P. J. (2003). Generación de casos de prueba a partir de especificaciones UML. In *Proceedings of the VIII Jornadas de Innovación y Calidad del Software,* Barcelona, Spain (pp. 48-58).

Fernandez, L., Lara, P. J., Escribano, J. J., & Villalba, M. T. (2004). *Use cases for enhancing IS requirements management.* Paper presented at the IADIS International Conference: e-Society, Ávila, Spain.

Friedman, G., Hartman, A., & Shiran, K. N. a. T. (2002). Projected state machine coverage for software testing. In *Proceedings of the 2002 ACM SIGSOFT International Symposium on Software Testing and Analysis* (pp. 134-143). Rome, Italy: ACM Press.

Grady, R., & Caswell, D. (1987). *Software metrics: Establishing a company-wide program.* Englewood Cliffs, NJ: Prentice-Hall.

Grand, M. (1999). *Patterns in Java: Aa catalog of reusable design patterns illustrated with UML.* New York: John Wiley & Sons.

Harel, D. (1988). On visual formalisms. *Communication of the ACM, 31*(5), 514-530.

Hassan, A., Abdelmoez, W., Elnaggar, R., & Ammar, H. (2001). *An approach to measure the quality of software designs from UML specifications.* Paper presented at the Fifth World Multi-Conf. Systems, Cybernetics and Informatics, Orlando, FL.

Heumann, J. (2001, June). Generating test cases from use cases. *The Rational Edge.*

Humphrey, W. S. (1996). *Introduction to the personal software process.* Boston: Addison-Wesley.

Hutcheson, M. L. (2003). *Software testing fundamentals.* Indianapolis, IN: Wiley Publishing, Inc.

IEEE Computer Society. (1991). *IEEE 610-1991 computer dictionary.* New York: author.

IEEE Computer Society. (1997). *IEEE 1074-1997 IEEE standard for developing software life cycle processes.* New York: author.

IEEE Computer Society. (1998). *IEEE 730-1998 standard for software quality assurance plans.* New York: author.

ISO. (2000a). *Quality management systems — Fundamentals and vocabulary.* Geneve, Italy.

ISO. (2000b). *Quality management systems — Requirements.* Geneve, Italy.

ISO. (2004). *Information technology. Process assessment. Part 1: Concepts and vocabulary*. Geneve, Italy.

Jacobson, I., Booch, G., & Rumbaugh, J. (1999). *The unified software development process*. Boston: Addison-Wesley

Jones, C. (1994). *Assessment and control of software risks*. Saddle River: Yourdon Press.

Kan, S. H. (2002). *Metrics and models in software quality engineering*. Reading, MA: Addison Wesley

Kangasluoma, M. (2000). *Test case generation from UML state chart*. Master thesis. Finland: Helsinky University of Technology.

Kosmatov, N., Legeard, B., Peureux, F., & Utting, M. (2004). Boundary coverage criteria for test generation from formal models. In *Proceedings of the 15th International Symposium on Software Reliability Engineering (ISSRE 2004)*, Saint-Malo, France (pp. 139-150).

Lara, P.J., & Fernández, L. (2004, April). ¿Cómo mejorar el estilo en desarrollos Java? *Dr Dobbs Journal España*, 54-59.

McCabe, T. (1976). A software complexity measure. *IEEE Transactions on Software Engineering, 2*(6), 308-320

McConnell, S. (1996). *Rapid development: Taming wild software schedules*. Redmond, WA: Microsoft Press.

Memon, A. M., Soffa, M. L., & Pollack, M. E. (2001). Coverage criteria for GUI testing. Paper presented at the *8th European Software Engineering Conference Held Jointly with 9th ACM SIGSOFT International Symposium on Foundations of Software Engineering*, Vienna, Austria (pp. 256-267).

Munson, J., & Khoshgoftaar, T. (1996). Software metrics for reliability assessment. In M. R. Lyu (Ed.), *Handbook of software reliability and system reliability*. Hightstown: McGraw-Hill.

Myers, G. J. (1979). *The art of software testing*. New York: John Wiley & Sons.

NASA (1997). *NASA technical standard 8719.13A, software safety*. Washington, DC.

Ntafos, S. (1988). A comparison of some structural testing strategies. *IEEE Transactions on Software Engineering, 14*(6), 868-874.

Object Management Group (OMG). (2001). *Unified Modeling Language* (Technical report of Object Management Group). Needham, MA.

Offutt, J., & Abdurazik, A. (1999). *Generating tests from UML specifications*. Paper presented at UML'99 — The Unified Modeling Language. Beyond the Standard. Second International Conference, Fort Collins, TX.

Ohlsson, M., & Wholin, C. (1998). Identification of green, yellow, and red legacy components. In *Proceedings of the International Conference on Software Maintenance, ICSM'98*, Bethesda, MD (pp. 6-15).

Ohlsson, M., Von Mayrhauser, A., McGuire, B., & Wohlin, C. (1999). *Code decay analysis of legacy software through successive releases*. Paper presented at IEEE Aerospace Conference, Aspen, CO.

Pressman, R. S. (2003), *Software engineering: A practitioners' approach*. Boston: McGraw-Hill.

Roper, M. (1994). *Software testing*. London: McGraw-Hill

Rumbaugh, J., Jacobson, I., & Booch, G. (1998). *The Unified Modeling Language reference manual*. Reading, MA: Addison-Wesley

Ryser, J. M., & Glintz, M. (2002/03). *SCENT: A method employing scenarios to systematically derive test cases for system test*. Zurich, Switzerland: Institut für Informatik.

Schneider, G., & Winters, J. P. (2001). *Applying use cases: A practical guide*. Reading, MA: Adisson-Wesley.

Schulmeyer, G. G. (1992). *Handbook of software quallity assurance*. Reinhold: Van Nost.

Stringfellow, C., & Andrews, A. (2002). Deriving a fault architecture to guide testing. *Software Quality Journal, 10*(4), 299-330.

Vincenzi, A., Maldonado, J., & Delamaro, W. W. a. M. (2005). Coverage testing of Java programs and components. *Science of Computer Programming, 56*(1-2), 211-230.

Von Mayrhauser, A., Wang, J., Ohlsson, M., & Wohlin, C. (1999). *Deriving a fault architecture from defect history*. Paper presented at International Conference on Software Reliability Engineering, Boca Ratón, Florida.

Walton, G., Poore, J., & Trammell, C. (1995). Statistical testing of software based on a usage model. *Software, Practice and Experience, 25*(1), 97-108.

Wheeler, D. A., Brykczynski, B., & Meeson, R. A. (Eds.). (1996). *Software inspection: An industry best practice*. Los Alamitos, CA: IEEE Computer Society Press.

Wohlin, C., & Runeson, P. (1995). Experimental evaluation of capture-recapture in software inspections. *Journal of Software Testing, Verification and Reliability, 5*(4), 213-232.

Woodward, M., Hedley, D., & Hennell, M. (1980). Experience with path analysis and testing of programs. *IEEE Transactions on Software Engineering, 6*(3), 278-286.

Chapter XIV

Safecharts Model Checking for the Verification of Safety-Critical Systems

Pao-Ann Hsiung, National Chung Cheng University, Taiwan

Yen-Hung Lin, National Chung Cheng University, Taiwan

Yean-Ru Chen, National Chung Cheng University, Taiwan

Abstract

Unintentional design faults in safety-critical systems might result in injury or even death to human beings. However, the safety verification of such systems is getting very difficult because designs are becoming very complex. To cope with high design complexity, model-driven architecture (MDA) design is becoming a well-accepted trend. However, conventional methods of code testing and hazard analysis do not fit very well with MDA. To bridge this gap, we propose a safecharts model-based formal verification technique for safety-critical systems. The safety constraints in safecharts are mapped to semantic equivalents in timed automata. The theory for safety verification is proved and implemented in the SGM model checker. Prioritized and urgent transitions are implemented in SGM to model the safechart risk semantics. Finally, it is shown that priority-based approach to mutual exclusion of resource usage in safecharts is unsafe and solutions are proposed. Application examples show the benefits of the proposed model-driven verification method.

Introduction

Safety-critical systems are systems whose failure most probably results in the tragic loss of human life or damage to human property. There are numerous examples of these mishaps. The accident at the Three Mile Island (TMI) nuclear power plant in Pennsylvania on March 28, 1979 is just one unfortunate example (Leveson, 1995). Moreover, as time goes on, there are more and more cars, airplanes, rapid transit systems, medical facilities, and consumer electronics, which are all safety-critical systems in our daily lives. When some of them malfunction or fault, a tragedy is inevitable. The natural question here is: Should we use these systems without a very high confidence in their safety? Obviously, the answer is no. That is why we need some methodology to exhaustively verify safety-critical systems.

Traditional verification methods such as simulation and testing can only prove the presence of faults and not their absence. Some methods such as fault-based testing and semiformal verification that integrates model checking and testing can prove the absence of prespecified faults. Simulation and testing (Sommerville, 2004) are both required before a system is deployed to the field. While simulation is performed on an abstract model of a system, testing is performed on the actual product. In the case of hardware circuits, simulation is performed on the design of the circuit, whereas testing is performed on the fabricated circuit itself. In both cases, these methods typically inject signals at certain points in the system and observe the resulting signals at other points. For software, simulation and testing usually involve providing certain inputs and observing the corresponding outputs. These methods can be a cost-efficient way to find many errors. However, checking all of the possible interactions and potential pitfalls using simulation and testing techniques is rarely possible. Conventionally, safety-critical systems are validated through standards conformance and code testing. Using such verification methods for safety-critical systems cannot provide the desired 100% confidence on system correctness.

In contrast to the traditional verification methods, formal verification is exhaustive. Further, unlike simulation, formal verification does not require any test benches or stimuli for triggering a system. More precisely, formal verification is a mathematical way of proving a system satisfies a set of properties. *Formal verification* methods such model checking (Clarke & Emerson, 1981; Clarke, Grumberg, & Peled, 1999; Queille & Sifakis, 1982) are being taken seriously in the recent few years by several large hardware and software design companies such as Intel, IBM, Motorola, and Microsoft, which goes to show the importance and practicality of such methods for real-time embedded systems and SoC designs. For the above reasons, we will thus employ a widely popular formal verification method called *model checking* for the verification of safety-critical systems that are formally modeled.

Model checking (Clarke & Emerson, 1981; Clarke et al., 1999; Queille & Sifakis, 1982) is a technique for verifying finite state concurrent systems. One benefit of this restriction is that verification can be performed automatically. The procedure normally uses an exhaustive search of the state space of a system to determine if some specification is true or not. Given sufficient resources, the procedure will always terminate with a *yes/no* answer. Moreover, algorithms can implement it with reasonable efficiency, which can be run on moderate-sized machines. The process of model checking includes three parts: modeling, specification, and verification. *Modeling* is to convert a design into a formalism accepted by a model-checking tool. Before verification, *specification*, which is usually given in some logical formalism, is necessary to state the properties that the design must satisfy. The *verification* is completely automated. However, in practice it often involves human assistance. One such manual activity is the analysis of the verification results. In case of a negative result, the user is often provided with an error trace. This can be used as a counterexample for the checked property and can help the designer in tracking down where the error occurred. In this case, analyzing the error trace may require a modification to the system and a reapplication of the model-checking algorithm.

A safety-critical system model and its model checking procedures are implemented in the *state-graph manipulators* (SGM) model checker (Wang & Hsiung, 2002), which is a high-level model checker for both real-time systems as well as systems-on-chip modeled by a set of timed automata.

The remaining portion is organized as follows. The current state-of-art in the verification of safety-critical systems, especially how formal verification has been integrated into conventional techniques, is described in the section on Related Work. Basic definitions used in our work are given in the section on System Model, Specification, and Model Checking, along with an illustrative railway signaling system example. The section on Model Checking Safecharts will formulate each of our solutions to solving the issues encountered in formally verifying safety-critical systems modeled by safecharts. Implementation details of the proposed method in the SGM model checker are given in the section on the Implementation in a Model Checker. Application examples are given in following section. The article is concluded and future research directions are given in the final section.

Related Work

Traditionally, safety-critical systems have been verified mainly using *hazard-analysis* techniques such as checklists; hazard indices; fault-tree analysis (FTA); management oversight and risk-tree analysis (MORT); event-tree analysis; cause-consequence analysis (CCA); hazards-and-operability analysis (HAZOP); interface analysis; failure modes and effects analysis (FMEA); failure modes, effects, and criticality analysis (FMECA); and fault-hazard analysis (FHA) (Leveson, 1995). Hazard analysis is a continual and iterative process, which generally includes the following steps: definitions of objectives and scope, system description, hazard identification, data collection, qualitative ranking of hazards, identification of causal factors, identification and evaluation of corrective measures, verification of control implementations, quantification of unresolved hazards and residual risks, and feedback and evaluation of operational experience. Hazard-analysis techniques have been successfully applied to several different real-world safety-critical systems. Nevertheless, a major limitation of hazard analysis is that phenomena unknown to the analysts are not covered in the analysis, and thus hazards related to the phenomena are not foreseen. This becomes a severe limitation when the system is complex and analysts may overlook some possible hazards. Safety-critical systems are getting increasingly complex, and there is a trend to use methods (Bozzano, 2003; Jacky, 2000) that are more automatic and exhaustive than hazard analysis — for example, model checking.

The verification of safety-critical systems using formal techniques is not something new (Leveson, 1995). This can be seen in methods such as state-machine hazard analysis that was based on Petri nets (Leveson & Stolzy, 1987) and the application of model checking to safety-critical system verification based on various formal models such as finite state machines (Bozanno, 2003), statecharts (Bozzano, 2003), process control event diagrams (Yang, Chung, Kowalewski, & Stursberg, 2000), Scade (Deneux & Akerlund, 2004), and Altarica (Bozzano, 2003). A common method for the application of model checking to safety-critical system verification is through the specification of safety-related properties using some temporal logic such as CTL or LTL and then checking for the satisfaction of the safety specification (Johnson, 2002). However, as noted by Leveson (1995), this approach is inadequate because in the system models we are assuming that all the components do not fail and the system is proved to be safe under this assumption. However, the assumption is not valid so transforming each hazard into a formal property for verification as in (Johnson) is not sufficient. Some work have also integrated traditional FTA techniques with model checking such as in the *Enhanced Safety Assessment for Complex Systems* (ESACS) project (Bozzano, 2003; European Union, 2003), which expressed the *minimal cut sets* (MCS), that is, the minimal combinations of component failures, generated by a model checker, using fault trees. Nevertheless, a safety engineer must still inject failure modes of components into the system model before model checking can be performed. Bieber, Castel, and Seguin (2002) used model checking as a means to check if all unexpected events have been eliminated by conventional FTA techniques. Yang et al. defined various fault modes for each component and used model checking in each fault mode to check for safety properties. In all the above models and methods, safety-related actions such as failure mode capturing, safety requirements capturing, and model analysis must all be performed separately from the model checking process. In this chapter, the work on using safecharts to verify safety-critical systems contributes to the state-of-art in formal verification of such systems in several ways as described in the following:

1.   The *unified modeling language* (UML) is an industry de-facto standard for model-driven architecture design. Safecharts, being an extension of the UML statecharts, blends naturally with the semantics of other UML diagrams for the design of safety-critical systems. The work described in this article automatically transforms safecharts into the timed automata model that can be accepted by conventional

model checkers. Thus, safecharts is suitable for both design and verification, thus acting as a bridge between the two, the link between which was seen as an "over the wall process" for a long time (Fenelon, McDermid, Nicholson, & Pumfrey, 1994).

2.   Safecharts allow and require the *explicit* modeling of component failures and repairs within the safety layer of its models. This is unique and is very helpful not only for the safety design engineer but also for the safety verification engineer. Further, using safecharts, there is no need to separately define failure modes and effects, thus preventing accidental omissions and inconsistent specifications.

3.   The work here shows how a *conventional* model checker can be extended to perform safety-critical system verification, without the need to integrate conventional methods. Safecharts play a major role in the feasibility of such a simple extension through its unique features of risk states, transition priorities, and component failure and repair modeling artifacts.

4.   Due to safecharts being a variant of the UML statecharts, automatic code generation is supported through model-driven development that is becoming a standard way of software code design. Safety requirements proved in the models can thus be preserved into the final software code through this automatic code generation process. This is out of scope here in this work, but is an added advantage that must be carefully proved.

System Model, Specification, and Model Checking

Before going into the details of how safecharts are used to model and verify safety-critical systems, some basic definitions and formalizations are required as given in this Section. Both safecharts and their translated ETA models will be defined. TCTL and model checking will also be formally described. A railway signaling system is used as a running example for illustration. Since safecharts is based on the UML statecharts, we first define statecharts in Definition 1 and then define safecharts in Definition 2.

- **Definition 1: Statecharts.** *Statecharts are a tuple $F = (S, T, E, \theta, V, \phi)$, where S is a set of all states, T is a set of all possible transitions, E is a set of all events, θ is the set of possible types of states in statecharts, that is, $\theta = \{AND, OR, BASIC\}$, V is a set of integer variables, and $\phi ::= v \sim c \mid \phi_1 \wedge \phi_2 \mid \neg\phi_1$, in which $v \in V, \sim \in \{<, \leq, =, \geq, >\}$, c is an integer, and ϕ_1 and ϕ_2 are predicates. Let F_i be an arbitrary state in S. It has the general form:*

  $F_i = (\theta_i, C_i, d_i, T_i, E_i, l_i)$ *where:*

  o θ_i : the type of the state F_i; $\theta_i \in \theta$

- o C_i : a finite set of direct substates of F_i, referred to as *child states* of F_i, $C_i \subseteq S$.

- o d_i : $d_i \in C_i$ and is referred to as the *default state* of F_i. It applies only to *OR* states.

- o T_i : a finite subset of $F \times F$, referred to as explicitly *specified transitions* in F_i.

- o E_i : the finite set of events relevant to the specified transitions in T_i; $E_i \subseteq E$.

- o l_i : a function $T_i \rightarrow E \times \phi \times 2^{Ei}$, labeling each and every specified transition in T_i with a triple, 2^{Ei} denoting the set of all finite subsets of E_i.

Given a transition $t \in T$, its label is denoted by $l(t) = (e, fcond, a)$, written conventionally as $e[fcond]/a$. $e, fcond$ and a in the latter, denoted also as $trg(t) = e$, $con(t) = fcond$, and $gen(t) = a$, represent respectively the triggering event, the guarding condition and the set of generated actions.

Safecharts (Dammag & Nissanke, 1999; Nissanke & Dammag, 2000, 2002; Lin & Hsiung, 2005) is a variant of statecharts intended exclusively for safety-critical systems design. With two separate representations for functional and safety requirements, safecharts brings the distinctions and dependencies between them into sharper focus, helping both designers and auditors alike in modeling and reviewing safety features. Figure 1 shows the *functional* and *safety* layers of a safecharts model for setting a route of a railway system. The functional layer specifies the normal functions of requesting and setting or rejecting a route. The safety layer enforces the safety restrictions for setting or unsetting a route. The notations ! and ! in the safety layer will be defined in Definition 2 and basically restricts setting a route or enforces the release of a route when any of the signals in that route is or becomes faulty.

Further, safecharts incorporates ways to represent equipment failures and failure handling mechanisms and uses a safety-oriented classification of transitions and a safety-oriented scheme for resolving any unpredictable nondeterministic pattern of behavior. It achieves these through an explicit representation of risks posed by hazardous states by means of an ordering of states and a concept called *risk band* (Lin & Hsiung, 2005). Recognizing the possibility of gaps and inaccuracies in safety analysis, safecharts do not permit transitions between states with unknown relative risk levels. However, in order to limit the number of transitions excluded in this manner, safecharts provides a default interpretation for relative risk levels between states not covered by the risk ordering relation, requiring the designer to clarify the risk levels in the event of a disagreement and thus improving the risk assessment process.

- **Definition 2: Safecharts.** *Safecharts* Z extends statecharts by adding a safety-layer. States are extended with a risk ordering relation and transitions are extended with safety conditions. Given two comparable states s_1 and s_2, a risk ordering relation $\preccurlyeq$ specifies their relative risk levels, that is $s_1 \preccurlyeq s_2$ specifies s_1 is safer then s_2. Transition labels in safecharts have an extended form: $e[fcond]/a[l, u) \psi[G]$ where $e, fcond$, and a are the same as in statecharts. The time interval $[l, u)$ is a real-time constraint on a transition t and imposes the condition that t does not execute until at least l time units have elapsed since it most recently became enabled and

Figure 1. Safechart for route[x] with functional and safety layers

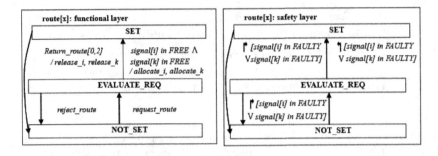

Figure 2. Routes and signals

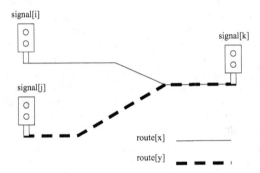

must execute strictly within *u* time units. The expression $\psi[G]$ is a safety enforcement on the transition execution and is determined by the safety clause *G*. The safety clause *G* is a predicate, which specifies the conditions under which a given transition *t* must, or must not, execute. ψ is a binary valued constant, signifying one of the following enforcement values:

o   **Prohibition** enforcement value, denoted by ⅂. Given a transition label of the form ⅂[*G*], it signifies that the transition is forbidden to execute as long as *G* holds.

o   **Mandatory** enforcement value, denoted by ⌐. Given a transition label of the form [*l*, *u*) ⌐[*G*], it indicates that whenever *G* holds the transition is forced to execute within the time interval [*l*, *u*), even in the absence of a triggering event.

A railway signaling system that sets and releases routes is given as an example for

Figure 3. Integrated safechart for route[x]

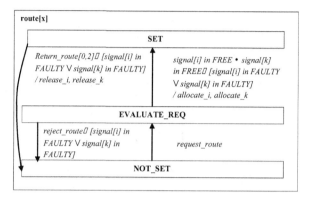

Figure 4. Integrated safechart for signal[i]

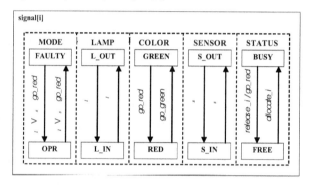

modeling using safecharts. In Figure 2, we can see there are two routes: route[x] and route[y] such that route[x] must have signal[i] and signal[k] allocated, while route[y] must have signal[j] and signal[k] allocated, where signal[k] is a resource shared between the two routes.

The safecharts model for route[x] was given in Figure 1 and that for route[y] will be similar. However, we can also express the two layers through an integrated model as in Figure 3. The integrated safecharts model for signal[i] is given in Figure 4.

The safecharts model is used for modeling safety-critical systems; however, the model checker SGM can understand only a flattened model called *Extended Timed Automata* (Hsiung & Wang, 1998), which was enhanced with priority and urgency, as defined in Definition 4.

Figure 5. ETA corresponding to MODE safecharts in signal[i]

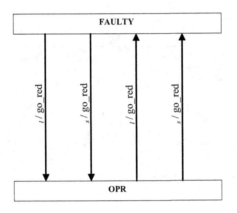

- **Definition 3: Mode predicate.** *Given a set C of clock variables and a set D of discrete variables, the syntax of a mode predicate η over C and D is defined as*: $\eta := false \mid x \sim c \mid x - y \sim c \mid d \sim c \mid \eta_1 \wedge \eta_2 \mid \neg\eta_1$, where $x, y \in C, \sim \in \{\leq, <, =, \geq, >\}, c \in N, d \in D$, and η_1, η_2 are mode predicates.

  Let B(C, D) be the set of all mode predicates over C and D.

- **Definition 4. Extended timed automaton:** *An extended timed automaton (ETA) is a tuple $A_i = (M_i, m_{i0}, C_i, D_i, L_i, \chi_i, T_i, \lambda_i, \pi_i, \mu_i, \tau_i, \rho_i)$ such that: M_i is a finite set of modes, $m_{i0} \in M$ is the initial mode, C_i is a set of clock variables, D_i is a set of discrete variables, L_i is a set of synchronization labels, and $\varepsilon \in L_i$ is a special label that represents asynchronous behavior (i.e., no need of synchronization), $\chi_i : M_i \to B(C_i, D_i)$ is an* invariance *function that labels each mode with a condition true in that mode, $T_i \subseteq M_i \times M_i$ is a set of transitions, $\lambda_i : T_i \to L_i$ associates a synchronization label with a transition, $\pi_i : T_i \to \mathbf{N}$ associates an integer priority with a transition, $\mu_i : T_i \to \{lazy, eager, delayable\}$ associates an urgency type with a transition, $\tau_i : T_i \to B(C_i, D_i)$ defines the transition triggering conditions, and $\rho_i : T_i \to 2^{Ci \cup (Di \times N)}$ is an* assignment *function that maps each transition to a set of assignments such as resetting some clock variables and setting some discrete variables to specific integer values.*

  Take as an example, the ETA that is semantically equivalent to the MODE safecharts in signal[i] of Figure 4 is illustrated in Figure 5.

A system state space is represented by a *system state graph* as defined in Definition 5.

- **Definition 5: System state graph.** *Given a system S with n components modeled by $A_i = (M_i, m_{i0}, C_i, D_i, L_i, \chi_i, T_i, \lambda_i, \pi_i, \mu_i, \tau_i, \rho_i)$, $1 \leq i \leq n$, the system model is defined as a state graph represented by $A_1 \times \ldots \times A_n = A_S = (M, m^0, C, D, L, c, T, l, \pi, \mu, \tau, \rho)$, where:*

  ○ *$M = M_1 \times M_2 \times \ldots \times M_n$ is a finite set of system modes, $m = m_1.m_2.\ldots.m_n \in M$,*

  ○ *$m^0 = m_1^0.m_2^0.\ldots.m_n^0 \in M$ is the initial system mode,*

  ○ *$C = \cup_i C_i$ is the union of all sets of clock variables in the system,*

  ○ *$D = \cup_i D_i$ is the union of all sets of discrete variables in the system,*

  ○ *$L = \cup_i L_i$ is the union of all sets of synchronization labels in the system,*

  ○ *$\chi: M \rightarrow B(\cup_i C_i, \cup_i D_i), \chi(m) = \wedge_i \chi_i(m_i)$, where $m = m_1.m_2.\ldots.m_n \in M$.*

  ○ *$T \subseteq M \times M$ is a set of system transitions which consists of two types of transitions:*

    ➤ **Asynchronous transitions:** *$\exists\, i, 1 \leq i \leq n, e_i \in T_i$ such that $e_i = e \in T$*

    ➤ **Synchronized transitions:** *$\exists\, i,j, 1 \leq i \neq j \leq n, e_i \in T_i, e_j \in T_j$ such that $\lambda_i(e_i) = (l, \text{in}), \lambda_j(e_j) = (l, \text{out}), l \in L_i \cap L_j \neq \emptyset, e \in T$ is synchronization of e_i and e_j with conjuncted triggering conditions and union of all transitions assignments (defined later in this definition)*

  ○ *$\lambda: T \rightarrow L$ associates a synchronization label with a transition, which represents a blocking signal that was synchronized, except for $\varepsilon \in L$, ε is a special label that represents asynchronous behavior (i.e., no need of synchronization),*

  ○ *$\pi: T \rightarrow \mathbb{N}$ associates an asynchronous transition with its original priority, and a synchronous transition with the maximum priority among all the synchronized transitions,*

  ○ *$\mu: T \rightarrow \{\text{lazy, eager, delayable}\}$ associates an asynchronous transition with its original urgency type and a synchronous transition with the eager type if there is one synchronized, or with the delayable type if there is one, otherwise with the lazy type,*

  ○ *$\tau: T \rightarrow B(\cup_i C_i, \cup_i D_i), \tau(e) = \tau_i(e_i)$ for an asynchronous transition and $\tau(e) = \tau_i(e_i) \wedge \tau_j(e_j)$ for a synchronous transition, and*

  ○ *$\rho: T \rightarrow 2^{\cup i\, Ci \cup (\cup i\, Di \times N)}, \rho(e) = \rho_i(e_i)$ for an asynchronous transition and $\rho(e) = \rho_i(e_i) \cup \rho_j(e_j)$ for a synchronous transition.*

- **Definition 6. Safety-critical system.** *A safety-critical system is defined as a set of resource components and consumer components. Each component is modeled by one or more safecharts. If a safety-critical system H has a set of resource components $\{R_1, R_2, \ldots, R_m\}$ and a set of consumer components $\{C_1, C_2, \ldots, C_n\}$, H is modeled by $\{Z_{R1}, Z_{R2}, \ldots, Z_{Rm}, Z_{C1}, Z_{C2}, \ldots, Z_{Cn}\}$, where Z_X is a safechart model for component X. Safecharts Z_{Ri} and Z_{Cj} are transformed into corresponding ETA A_{Ri} and A_{Cj}, respectively. Therefore, H is semantically modeled by the state graph $A_{R1} \times \ldots \times A_{Rm} \times A_{C1} \times \ldots \times A_{Cn}$ as defined in Definition 5.*

For our railway signal system, {signal[i], signal[j], signal[k]} is the set of resource components and {route[x], route[y]} is the set of consumer components. The system is thus modeled by the state graph $A_{signal[i]} \times A_{signal[j]} \times A_{signal[k]} \times A_{route[x]} \times A_{route[y]}$.

Timed computation tree logic (TCTL) (Henzinger, Nicollin, Sifakis, & Yovine 1992) is a *timed* extension of the well-known temporal logic called *computation tree logic* (CTL), which was proposed by Clarke and Emerson in 1981. We will use TCTL to specify the safety properties that are required to be satisfied by a safety-critical system modeled by safecharts. The SGM model checker also chooses TCTL as its logical formalism, which is defined as follows.

- **Definition 7. Timed computation tree logic (TCTL).** *A* timed computation tree logic *formula has the following syntax:*

$$\phi ::= \eta \mid EG\ \phi' \mid E\ \phi'U_{\sim c}\ \phi'' \mid \neg\phi' \mid \phi' \vee \phi'',$$

  where η is a mode predicate, ϕ' and ϕ'' are TCTL formulae, $\sim \in \{<, \leq, =, \geq, >\}$, and $c \in N$. EG ϕ' means there is a computation from the current state, along which ϕ' is always true. E $\phi'U_{\sim c}\ \phi''$ means there exists a computation from the current state, along which ϕ' is true until ϕ'' becomes true, within the time constraint of $\sim$ c. Shorthands like EF, AF, AG, AU, $\wedge$, and $\rightarrow$ can all be defined (Henzinger, et al., 1992).

For the railway signal system, we can specify that the following safety properties must be satisfied:

1.   AG($\neg$(route[x] in SET $\wedge$ route[y] in SET))
2.   AG(signal[i] in FAULTY $\rightarrow \neg$(route[x] in SET))
3.   AG(signal[j] in FAULTY $\rightarrow \neg$(route[y] in SET))
4.   AG(signal[k] in FAULTY $\rightarrow \neg$(route[x] in SET $\vee$ route[y] in SET))

The first property states that both routes should not be set at the same time since they share a common resource signal[k]. The other three properties state that a route should not be set if there is any of its resources (signals) is faulty.

- **Definition 8. Model checking.** *Given a safechart Z that represents a safety-critical system and a TCTL formula, ϕ, expressing some desired specification, model checking (Clarke & Emerson, 1981; Clarke et al., 1999; Queille & Sifakis, 1982) verifies if Z satisfies ϕ, denoted by $Z \models \phi$.*

Model checking can be either explicit using a labeling algorithm or symbolic using a fix-point algorithm. *Binary decision diagram* (BDD) and *difference bound matrices* (DBM) are data structures used for Boolean formulas and clock zones (Clarke et al., 1999), respectively. For our railway signal system, we must check if $A_{signal[i]} \times A_{signal[j]} \times A_{signal[k]} \times A_{route[x]} \times A_{route[y]} \models \phi$, where ϕ is each of the four properties described above.

Model Checking Safecharts

Safecharts have been used to model safety-critical systems, but the models have never been verified. In this work, we propose a method to verify safety-critical systems modeled by safecharts. Our target model checker is *state graph manipulators* (SGM) (Hsiung & Wang, 1998; Wang & Hsiung, 2002), which is a high-level model checker for both real-time systems, as well as, Systems-on-Chip modeled by a set of extended timed automata. There are several issues to be resolved in model checking safecharts.

In the course of developing a model-based verification method for safety-critical systems, several issues are encountered as detailed in the following. First, we need to decide how to model safety-critical systems. Our decision is to adopt safecharts (Dammag & Nissanke, 1999) as our models. Safecharts are a variant of statecharts, especially for use in the specification and the design of safety-critical systems. The objective of the model is to provide a sharper focus on safety issues and a systematic approach to deal with them. This is achieved in safecharts by making a clear *separation* between *functional* and *safety* requirements. Other issues encountered in designing the formal verification methodology for model-based safety-critical systems are as follows:

- How to transform safecharts into a semantically equivalent *Extended Timed Automata* (ETA) model that can be accepted by traditional model checkers? How can the transformation preserve the safety semantics in safecharts?

- What are the properties that must be specified for model checking safecharts?

- Basic states in safecharts have a risk relation with each other specifying the comparative risk/safety levels. Safety non-determinism allows only safe transitions between states with known risk levels in safecharts. How do we represent such information in ETA for model checking?

- The current semantics of safecharts states that mutual exclusion of resource usages can be achieved through priority. This is clearly insufficient, as priorities cannot ensure mutual exclusion.

Briefly, our solutions to the above-mentioned issues can be summarized as follows:

- **Flattening and safety semantics:** To transform safecharts into ETA one has to take care of two things, namely, flattening the hierarchy in safecharts and combining the functional and safety transitions of safecharts, while preserving equivalence to the safety semantics of safecharts. Urgent transitions are also implemented into our model checker for this transformation.

- **Functional property and safety constraint:** The specification of functional properties is the same as that in any conventional model checking such as using a temporal logic. However, properties corresponding to the safety constraints can be specified in two ways according to the types of safety constraint.

- **Risk band and transition priorities:** Risk bands are automatically constructed and risks associated with states. Nondeterminism in safecharts is resolved by prioritizing transitions such that transitions leading to safer states are given higher priorities. Risk levels and prioritization of transitions are implemented in our model checker using a novel clock zone subtraction operation.

- **Resource access mechanisms:** Resource allocation and de-allocation can be modeled in safecharts, however mutual exclusion between resource usages cannot be guaranteed in safecharts without importing modeling restrictions. In the section on Resource Access Mechanism, we will give an example to explain why this is important and describe modeling guidelines that designers need to follow for mutual exclusivity of resource usages.

A system designer models a safety-critical system using a set of safecharts. After accepting the safecharts, we transform them into ETA, while taking care of the safety characterizations in safecharts, and then automatically generate properties corresponding to the safety constraints. The SGM model checker is enhanced with transition priority and urgency types. Resource access mechanisms in safecharts are also checked for satisfaction of modeling restrictions that prevent violation of mutual exclusion. Finally, we input the translated ETA to SGM to verify the safety-critical system satisfies functional and safety properties. Each of the issues encountered during implementation and the corresponding solutions are detailed in the rest of this section.

Flattening Safecharts and Safety Semantics

Our primary goal is to model check safecharts, a variant of statecharts. However, safecharts cannot be accepted as system model input by most model checkers, which can accept only flat automata models such as the extended timed automata (ETA) accepted by SGM. As a result, the state hierarchy and concurrency in safecharts must be transformed into semantically equivalent constructs in ETA. Further, besides the functional layer, safecharts have an extra safety layer, which must be transformed into equivalent modeling constructs in ETA and specified as properties for verification.

There are three categories of states in safecharts: OR, AND, and BASIC. An OR-state, or an AND-state, consists generally of two or more substates. Being in an AND-state means being in all of its substates simultaneously, while being in an OR-state means being in exactly one of its substates. A BASIC-state is translated into an ETA *mode*. The translations for OR-states and AND-states are performed as described in Lavazza (2001). Some of the details are given in the sections on implementation.

Safety Semantics

The syntax for the triggering condition and action of a transition in safecharts is: $e\,[fcond]$ $/\,a\,[l, u)\,\psi\,[G]$, where e is the set of triggering events, $fcond$ is the set of guard conditions, a is the set of broadcast events, $[l, u)$ is the time interval specifying the time constraint, ψ means the execution conditions for safety constraints, and G is the set of safety-layer's guards. In safecharts, $e\,[fcond]\,/\,a$ appears in the *functional* layer, while $[l, u)\,\psi\,[G]$ may appear in the *safety* layer. The two layers of safecharts can be integrated into one in ETA as described in the following. However, we need to design three different types of transitions (Altisen, Gössler, & Sifakis, 2002):

- **Eager Evaluation (ε):** Execute the action as soon as possible, that is, as soon as a guard is enabled. Time cannot progress when a guard is enabled.
- **Delayable Evaluation (δ):** Can put off execution until the last moment the guard is true. Therefore, time cannot progress beyond a *falling edge* of guard.
- **Lazy Evaluation (λ):** You may or may not perform the action.

The transition condition and assignment $e[fcond]/a\,[l, u)\,\psi\,[G]$ can be classified into three types as follows:

Figure 6. Transformation of prohibition evaluation

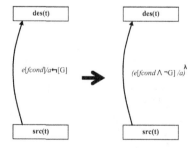

Figure 7. Transformation of mandatory evaluation

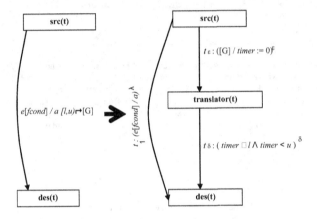

1. ***e[fcond]/a*** : There is no safety clause on a transition in safechart, thus we can simply transform it to the one in ETA. We give the translated transition a *lazy* evaluation λ.

2. ***e[fcond]/a ⌐[G]*** : There is *prohibition* enforcement value on a transition *t*. It signifies that the transition *t* is forbidden to execute as long as *G* holds. During translation, we combine them as $e[fcond \land \neg G]/a$. We give the translated transition a *lazy* evaluation λ. The transformation is shown in Figure 6.

3. ***e[fcond]/a [l, u)⌐[G]*** : There is *mandatory* enforcement value on a transition *t*. Given a transition label of the form $e[fcond]/a$ [*l, u*) ⌐ [*G*], it signifies that the transition is forced to execute within [*l, u*) whenever *G* holds. We translate functional and safety layers into a transition t_1 and a path t_2, respectively. t_1 represents $e[fcond]/a$, which means t_1 is enabled if the triggering event *e* occurs and its functional conditional *fcond* is true. We give t_1 a *lazy* evaluation λ. Path t_2 is combined by two transitions, t_ε and t_δ. Transition t_ε is labeled [*G*]/*timer*:=0, where *timer* is a clock variable used for the time constraint, and we give t_ε an *eager* evaluation ε. When *G* holds, t_ε executes as soon as possible, and t_ε's destination is a newly added mode, named *translator(t)*. t_δ's source is *translator(t)*, and its destination is *t*'s destination. t_δ's guard is [*timer* ≥ *l* ∧ *timer* < *u*]. However, we give t_δ a *delayable* evaluation (δ), which means it can put off execution until the last moment the guard is true. The procedure of translation is shown in Figure 7. Details of implementing the different types of urgent transitions are given later.

Property Specification for Safecharts

In the safety-layer of safecharts, there are two types of safety conditions on a transition, one is *prohibition* and the other is *mandatory*. After parsing the safechart models of a safety-critical system, corresponding properties are automatically generated without requiring the user to specify again. Such properties are used to verify if the safety-layers work or not. As described in the following, to ensure that the safety constraints are working, two categories of properties are generated automatically for model checking.

1. **AG (($src(t) \wedge$ G) $\rightarrow \neg$ EX($des(t)$)))** : If a transition t in safechart has prohibition condition $\lceil[G]$ in its safety-layer, it means that such transition is forbidden to execute as long as G holds. As shown in Figure 6, t's source is $src(t)$, and its destination is $des(t)$. Due to $\lceil[G]$, $src(t)$ is not allowed to transit to $des(t)$ as long as G holds. If such property is tenable in our system state graph, which means that there is no transition from $src(t)$ to $des(t)$ executing whenever G holds, then we can know that the safety-critical system will not become dangerous while G holds.

2. **AG ((src(t) $\wedge$ G $\rightarrow \neg$ EX ($\neg$ translator(t))) and AG(translator(t) $\wedge$ timer < u)** : If a transition t in safechart has $[l, u)$ $\lceil[G]$ in its safety-layer, it means that such transition is enabled and forced to execute within $[l, u)$ whenever G holds. As mentioned in former sections, we add two transitions for the safety-layer's behavior, namely t_ε and t_δ, and a mode, *translator(t)* between them. From Figure 7, when G holds, t_ε must be executed as soon as possible due to its eager evaluation and the next active mode must be *translator(t)*. Moreover, we know that if the mode *translator(t)* is active, then the next active state must be $des(t)$ within the time limit $timer \geq 1 \wedge timer < u$. If this constraint is violated, then the safety condition will not be satisfied.

By the first category, we can ensure that a safety-critical system will not be dangerous under certain prohibited conditions. By the second category described above, we can check if a safety-critical system with some faults or malfunctions will go to a safer situation that can deal with such faults or violates the time limits.

Transition Priority

When modeling safety-critical systems, it is important to eliminate any nondeterministic behavior patterns of the system. Nondeterminism arises if the triggering expressions of two transitions starting from a common state are simultaneously fulfilled. Because of its concern with safety-critical systems, safecharts remove non-determinism in all cases except when there is no safety implication. In the safechart model, we use a list of *risk relation* tuples to establish a *risk graph* (Nissanke & Dammag, 2000) of this safechart. Noncomparable conditions may still exist in a risk graph. An example is given in Figure 8, where, relative to other states, the state O may have received less attention in the risk assessment, resulting in it becoming non-comparable with other states in the graph, namely, the states *N* and *P*. Consequently, safecharts do not allow any transition between them, for instance, a transition such as *O→P*.

As solution to the above problem, the authors of safecharts proposed *risk band* (Nissanke, 2000), which can be used to enumerate all states in a risk graph to make precise their relative risk relations that were not explicitly described. To adopt this method, we implemented transition priorities based on the risk bands of a transition's source and destination modes. According to a list of risk relations, we can give modes different risk bands, as depicted in Figure 8, where the maximum risk band, max_{rb}, is 6. We assign each transition a priority as follows:

$$pri(t) = max_{rb} - (rb_{src(t)} - rb_{des(t)}),$$

where *pri(t)* is the priority assigned to transition *t*, $rb_{src(t)}$ is the risk band of transition *t*'s source mode, and $rb_{des(t)}$ is the risk band of transition *t*'s destination mode. Moreover, the smaller the value of *pri(t)* is, the higher is the priority of transition *t*. In Figure 8, *pri(t4)* is 4, and *pri(t6)* is 3. Obviously, when *t4* and *t6* are both enabled, *t6* will be executed in preference to *t4*. With risk bands, we can give a transition leading to a lower risk band state a higher priority.

By such method, we can remove most nondeterminisms that may lead the safety-critical system to a dangerous condition. However, if two transitions lead to modes in the same risk band how should we determine their priorities? According to the authors of safecharts (Nissanke & Dammag, 2000a, 2000b), to ensure the system will not become

Figure 8. Risk graph with risk band

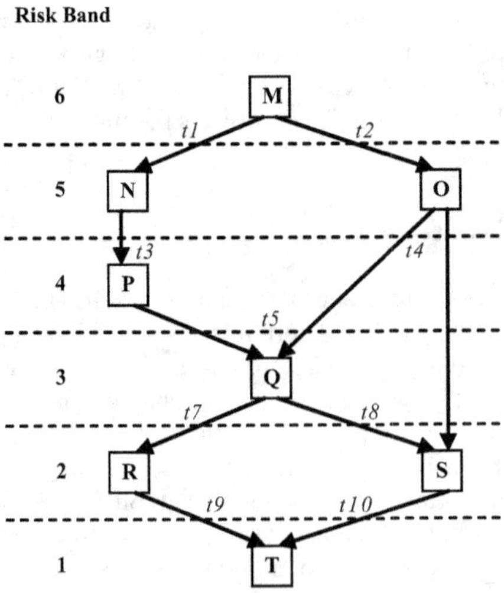

dangerous, one has to look for the risk bands of the two transitions' *future targets*. When the risk bands of their future targets are different, one should give the one leading to a lower risk band eventually higher priority and the other lower priority. In our implementation, when a state has two or more transitions with the same priority, we use a recursive call to modify the transitions' priorities by checking the risk bands of *future targets* if the risk bands of *future targets* are different. For example, in Figure 8, initially $t1$ and $t2$ are assigned the same priority, 5. After we find that M has two transitions with the same priority, we continue to check their future targets. As a result, we come to know that $t2$ will lead to a safer condition in the future, thus we give $t2$ a higher priority than $t1$. In Figure 8, Q has two transitions $t7$ and $t8$, both of which lead to T. Thus, we have no need to modify their original priority, 5.

For implementing transition priorities into the SGM model checker, the triggering guards of a transition are modified as follows (Altisen, 2002):

$$t'(t_i) = \wedge_{\pi(tj) > \pi(ti)} \neg \tau(t_j) \wedge \tau(t_i)$$

where $\tau(t_i)$ and $\tau(t_j)$ are the guard conditions of transitions t_i and t_j, $\pi(t_j) > \pi(t_i)$ means that the priority of t_j is higher than that of t_i, and $t'(t_i)$ is the modified guard condition of t_i. This application results in allowing t_i executed only if there is no enabled transition t_j that has priority over t_i.

Resource Access Mechanisms

Safecharts model both consumers and resources. However, when resources must be used in a mutually exclusive manner, a model designer may easily violate the mutual exclusion restriction by simultaneous checking and discovery of free resources, followed by their concurrent usages. A motivational example can be observed in the railway signaling system as illustrated in Figure 2, Figure 3, and Figure 4, where signal[k] must be shared in a mutually exclusive way between route[x] and route[y]. However, each route checks if signal[k] is free and finds it free, then both route will be SET, assuming G does not hold. This is a modeling trap that violates mutually exclusive usages of resources. A serious tragedy could happen in this application example as two intersecting routes are set resulting in perhaps a future train collision.

From above we know that when consumers try to acquire resources that cannot be used concurrently, it is not safe to check only the status of resources. We need some kind of model-based mutual exclusion mechanism. A very simple policy would be like Fischer's mutual exclusion protocol (Larsen, Steffen, & Weise, 1996). For each mutually exclusive resource, a variable is used to record the id of the consumer currently using the resource. Before the consumer uses the resource, it has to check if the variable is set to its id. Figure 9 is a corrected variant of the route safechart from Figure 3. When *route[id]* transits into EVALUATE_REQ, it sets variable *reg* to its id. When *route[x]* tries to transit into the SET mode to acquire the usage of *resource*, it needs to check if *reg* is still its id. If *reg* is still *x*, then *route[x]* acquires the usage of the resource. Other mechanisms such as atomic

Figure 9. Safechart for route[x] with mutual exclusion

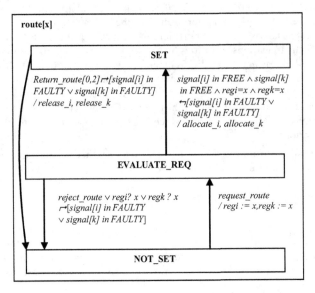

test-and-set performed on a single asynchronous transition can also achieve mutual exclusion.

Implementation in a Model Checker

The model checking of safecharts has been implemented in the *state-graph manipulators* (SGM), which is a TCTL model checker for real-time systems such as communication protocols, systems-on-chips, and embedded systems. SGM was a conventional model checker that could take only a set of ETA as the system model. We enhanced SGM in several ways to accommodate the verification of safecharts. First, we had to develop an input language that could allow recursive definitions of the hierarchical safecharts models. Second, we had to employ a flattening algorithm to remove all the hierarchies and obtain a set of ETA that was semantically equivalent to the originally specified set of safecharts. Third, the preservation of safety semantics from safecharts to ETA demanded the support for transition urgencies such as eager and delayable, besides the original lazy semantics. We implemented support for transition urgencies in SGM through a novel zone capping operation. Finally, we had to develop and implement algorithms for the construction of risk bands from the risk relations specified in safecharts and then use the risk levels as the risk associated with the ETA states. We had to also check if there are any transitions between states with unknown risk levels. For implementing safe nondeterminism we had to support prioritized transitions in SGM, which we accomplished using a clock zone subtraction operation. All the four parts of SGM enhancements are described in greater detail in the rest of this section.

Safecharts Input Syntax

We developed our input language for the specification of safecharts and a parser for the language. The language syntax is recursive because a safechart can have other safecharts in a lower hierarchy such as that for an AND or an OR state in a safechart. Each safecharts was required to be specified as one of the following: AND, OR, or BASIC. We made no distinction between a state and a safechart. Risk relations were specified for basic safecharts only. In the language, we allowed each outgoing transition from a safechart to have two layers: functional and safety. The safety version of a transition was to be specified only if required. A simple example can be seen from the following piece of input file for the railway signal system.

```
safechart signal[i] := AND[MODE, LAMP, COLOR, SENSOR, STATUS]
{
                safechart MODE := OR[]
                {
                        initially OPR;
                        safechart FAULTY := BASIC
                        {
                                functional:
                                        when sync repairL may goto OPR;
                                        when sync repairS may goto OPR;
                                safety:
                        }
                        Safechart OPR := BASIC
                        { ... }
                }
                ......
}
```

Flattening Safecharts into ETA

Safecharts, like UML statecharts, have three kinds of states: AND, OR, and BASIC. An AND state has two or more parallel safecharts and an OR state represents another safechart. Thus, there is concurrency and hierarchy embedded within a safechart, which must be represented into a flattened model such as ETA for model checking so that SGM can be used to verify safecharts.

Figure 10. Representing concurrency in ETA

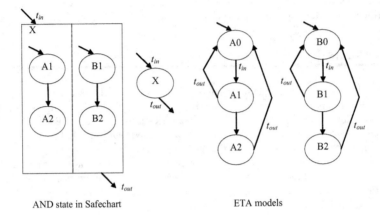

AND state in Safechart   ETA models

The flattening procedure that was implemented into SGM has been adapted from (Lavazza, 2001) for safecharts such that besides representing concurrency and hierarchy into ETA, safety semantics were also transformed and preserved from safecharts into ETA. We give a brief account of the representation of concurrency and hierarchy in this section and discuss safety semantics in the next section.

As shown in Figure 10, concurrency was represented as follows. Each safechart in an AND state was represented by an ETA. Except for a topmost level AND state, for all other AND states in the other levels, each generated ETA has an extra initial state and a transition from the initial state to the original initial state in the corresponding safechart. In Figure 10, A0 and B0 are the two newly introduced states in the corresponding ETA. The reason for introducing the new initial state is that any transition leading into an AND state must be such that all the safecharts in the AND state start from their original initial states simultaneously. In the ETA representing the parent safechart of an AND state, the transition leading into the AND state is synchronized with all the transitions outgoing from the new initial states of the corresponding ETA, for example, t_{in}. When an AND state is exited, all corresponding ETAs return to their respective newly introduced initial states to wait for the next transition into the AND state and simultaneous entries into respective original initial states. For each transition exiting from an AND state in a safechart, a set of transitions must be introduced from each state of each ETA to the ETA's new initial state. In the ETA representing the parent safechart of an AND state, the transition exiting from the AND state is synchronized with all the corresponding transitions in all the ETA representing the safecharts in the AND state, for example, t_{out}.

As shown in Figure 11, hierarchy was represented as follows. Rather than representing the safechart in an OR state by a separate ETA, we chose to embed the ETA into the ETA that represents the parent safechart. This approach reduces the number of ETA generated and the inherent parallelism of the generated set of ETA. However, we have

Figure 11. Representing hierarchy in ETA

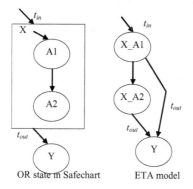

OR state in Safechart   ETA model

to carefully represent the transitions leading into and exiting from an OR state. For each transition leading into an OR state, an ETA transition must be introduced from the source state of the transition to the initial state of the embedded ETA representing the OR state, for example, t_{in}. For each transition exiting from an OR state, a set of ETA transitions must be introduced such that there is a transition from each state of the embedded ETA to the destination state of the transition, for example, t_{out}. This generates a large number of transitions; however, this is inevitable just as a system reset behavior can allow a system to transit from any state it is currently in to the initial state of the system. For all other transitions leading into or exiting from some specific state within the OR state, a corresponding ETA transition can be introduced between the two specific states in the final ETA generated. Currently, we do not support *history* states, that is, return to the state within an OR state from which the OR state was exited the last time. This is due to the limited expressiveness of ETA compared to safecharts.

Supporting Transition Urgencies

For enforcement of safety constraints such as the mandatory transitions represented by $[l, u)$ $t[G]$, it was described in Section 4.1 that we need to support transition urgencies in the SGM model checker. However, SGM takes timed automata as system models and timed automata assume a lazy semantics for transitions, that is, a transition *may* or *may not* be taken when its triggering condition is satisfied. To support urgency semantics, we need to force a transition to be taken by some deadline (as soon as an eager transition is enabled or before a delayable transition is disabled after being enabled). Given the expressiveness of ETA, we can only use state invariants to force transitions to be taken from a state. The transition deadline implies some time point in the future and time is usually represented by clock zones and implemented by *difference bound matrices* (DBM) (Clarke et al., 1999) in most model checkers. We propose a new *zone capping* operation ZCap that sets an upper bound (deadline) on the DBM in a state invariant. Given a zone z_1 represented by DBM D_1, it can be capped by another zone z_2 represented by DBM D_2, as defined in the following:

$$D_1(i,0) = \min(D_1(i,0), D_2(i,0)) \text{ and } D_1(i,j) = D_1(i,j), j \neq 0$$

For a state s with some eager and some delayable transitions, the DBM D_s in the state invariant is capped as follows:

$$D_s = \quad \text{ZCap}(D_s, \text{ESub}(D_s \cap D_t)) \quad \text{if } t_d \text{ is disabled no later than } t_e \text{ is enabled}$$
$$\text{undefined} \quad\quad\quad\quad\quad\quad\quad\quad\quad \text{otherwise}$$

where ESub is the earliest subzone of a zone that can be obtained by taking the lower bounds (first region) of each clock, t_d is the earliest disabled delayable transition, and t_e is the earliest enabled eager transition. It must be noted here that all timings are compared using region semantics, where a region is an equivalence class of states that give the same model checking results (Clarke et al., 1999). Intuitively, the above zone capping method sets the deadline as the earliest enabling time of all eager transitions and does not set the deadline if the earliest disabling time of all delayable transitions is earlier than the earliest enabling time of all eager transitions. The rationale for this deadline is that if we do not set it as we did, the urgency semantics of one or more transitions that are urgent will be violated.

Supporting Transition Priority

Though it was mentioned in Section 4.3 that the triggering condition of a transition t_i should be modified into $\tau'(t_i) = \wedge_{\pi(tj) > \pi(ti)} \neg\tau(t_j) \wedge \tau(t_i)$, where $\pi(t_i)$ is the priority of t_i. For Boolean predicates the conjunction of a negated predicate is straightforward, however for clock constraints that are expressed as clock zones and implemented by DBMs, it is more complex. The reason is that zones are not closed under negation. A clock zone when viewed geometrically is a convex polyhedron in the $\mathbf{R}^n$ space for a system with n clocks. When a clock zone is negated, the result may become a non-convex polyhedron. Thus, the set of zones is not closed under negation. We proposed an employed a partitioning method for dividing the possibly non-convex zone into a set of convex zones. The partitioning method is implemented a subtraction operation on two DBMs and generates the minimal number of partitioned zones. Details of the optimal subtraction operation can be found in Hsiung and Lin (2005) and Lin and Hsiung (2005). We give an algorithm here for DBM subtraction.

- **Algorithm 1: DBM subtraction z1 - z2.**

input : DBM: $z1, z2 \; // z2(i,j) = "\sim c"$

output: DBM*: $z \; //$set of DBMs

DBM*: $ztmp, zprev$

2 for *each* $z2(i,j); \; i \neq j$ do

3        $\text{init}(ztmp) \; // \; ztmp(i,j) = "<\infty", i \neq j \; \& \; ztmp(i,i) = "\leq 0"$

4        $ztmp(i,j) = \sim'c \; // \sim' \in \{>, \geq\}$ for $\sim \in \{\leq, <\}$, respectively

5        $ztmp = ztmp \cap z1$

6   if $zprev \neq NULL$ and mergeable($ztmp, zprev$) then

7                $ztmp = \text{merge}(ztmp, zprev)$

8                $z = z \backslash \{zprev\}$

9   end

10        $z = z \cup \{ztmp\}$

11   if $zprev \neq ztmp$ then

12                $zprev = ztmp$

13   end

14 end

15 return z

The complexity of the DBM subtraction algorithm is $O(n^4)$, where n is the number of clock variables. Since we work on each element of $z2$, it gives a $O(n^2)$ complexity. In each iteration, we need to perform zone intersection, which is also $O(n^2)$ complexity. Hence, the $O(n^4)$ complexity of the DBM subtraction algorithm. We can prove that a minimal number of partitions (zones) are generated after subtraction (Lin, 2005). We only give the theorem here.

- **Theorem 1:** *The number of zones generated by the DBM subtraction algorithm is minimal.*

Application Examples

The proposed model checking verification methodology was applied to several safety-critical systems, including several variants of the basic railway signaling system, which was illustrated in Figure 2, the hydraulic system in Airbus A320 airplane, and a nuclear reactor model of the TMI accident.

Figure 12. ETA for route[x]

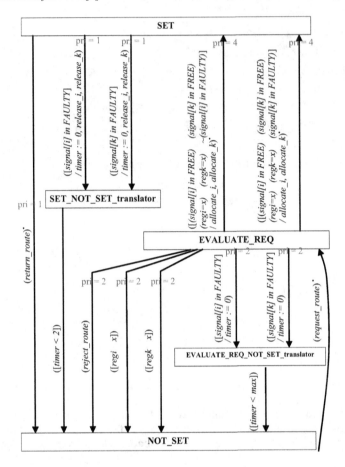

Railway Signaling System

The basic railway signaling system consists of two routes: route[x] and route[y], where route[x] requires signal[i] and signal[k], and route[y] requires signal[j] and signal[k]. The numbers and sizes of the safecharts and the generated ETA are given in Table 1. As illustrated in Figure 12 and Figure 13, for each route safechart, one ETA is obtained and for each signal safechart, five ETA are generated. Thus, in the full system consisting of 5 safecharts, 17 ETA are generated. It can be observed that the number of ETA modes,

Figure 13. Five ETA for each signal[i] safechart

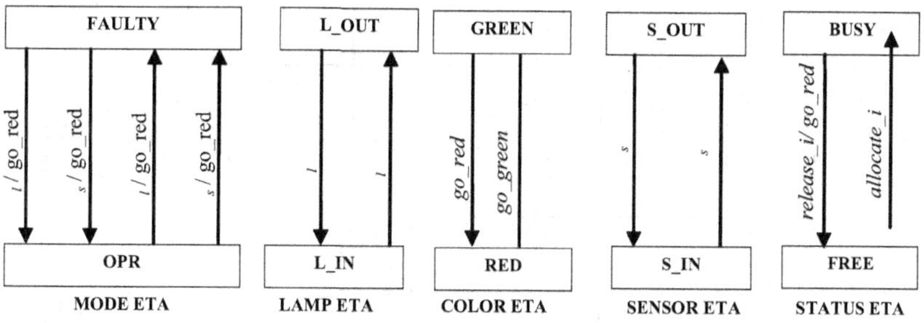

| MODE ETA | LAMP ETA | COLOR ETA | SENSOR ETA | STATUS ETA |

Table 1. Results of the railway signaling system

Component	Safecharts		ETA		
Name	$|S|$	$|T|$	#	$|M|$	$|T|$
route[x]	4	7	1	5	13
route[y]	4	7	1	5	13
signal[i]	16	16	5	10	16
signal[j]	16	16	5	10	16
signal[k]	16	16	5	10	16
full system	56	62	17	40	74

40, is lesser than the number of safecharts states, 56. The reason for this reduction is that hierarchical states do not exist in ETA. The mutual exclusion issues were both resolved for this railway system.

As illustrated in the figures given in the Appendix, a number of variants of the basic railway signaling system were used for validating the proposed method's scalability and efficiency. Varying the number of routes and the number of signals in each route increases the complexity and the concurrency of the system. However, we can observe from the verification results in Table 2 that the amount of time and memory expended for verification do not increase exponentially and are very well acceptable. The number of properties to be verified also increases and thus their automatic generation is a crucial step for successful and easily accessible verification of safety critical systems. The number of issues solved implies how the proposed solutions in this work are significant for the successful verification of complex systems modeled by safecharts. The safety properties that were verified for these railway-signaling systems are as given previously after TCTL was defined.

Table 2. Results of application examples

	System		safecharts			ETA			$|\phi|$	Issues Solved	Time	Mem
	$|R|$	$|S|$	#	$|S|$	$|T|$	#	$|M|$	$|T|$		ME	(μs)	(MB)
A	2	3(1)	5	56	62	17	40	74	20	1	230	0.12
B	2	4(1)	6	72	81	22	50	94	25	1	292	0.12
C	2	4(2)	6	72	84	22	50	98	30	2	337	0.13
D	3	4(1)	7	76	85	23	55	103	30	1	326	0.14
E	3	5(2)	8	92	110	28	65	131	45	2	515	0.14
F	4	5(1)	9	96	108	29	70	132	40	1	634	0.14

Airbus A320 Hydraulic System

The hydraulic system in an advanced airplane such as Airbus A320 supplies hydraulic power for aircraft control during flight and on-ground (Bieber, 2002). The safety requirements are as follows: (1) we need to ensure that we are not in a state of total loss of hydraulic power, which is classified as catastrophic; (2) we need to verify that a single failure does not result in total loss of power. As shown in Figure 14, there are three kinds of pumps: electric motor pump (EMP) powered by the electric system, engine driven pump (EDP) powered by the two aircraft engines, and one RAT pump powered by RAM air turbine. There are three power distribution channels: Green, Blue, and Yellow. The Blue channel is made up of one electric pump EMPb, one RAT pump, and a distribution line

Figure 14. A320 hydraulic system model

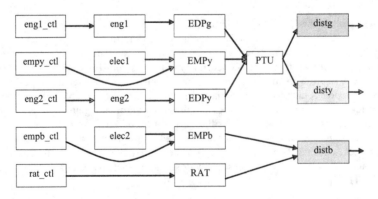

distb. The Green channel is made up of one pump driven by engine 1 EDPg and a distribution line distg. The Yellow channel is made up of one pump driven by engine 2 EDPy, one electric pump EMPy, and a distribution line disty. A power transfer unit PTU opens a transmission from green hydraulic power to yellow distribution line and vice versa as soon as the differential pressure between both channels is higher than a given threshold.

There are two types of models in this system, namely basic block and controller block. Each basic block was modeled by a safechart with a MODE OR state representing if it is working or faulty, a SENSOR OR state modeling its sensor, and an OUTPUT OR state showing if the basic block is providing hydraulic power. Each controller block, besides the MODE and SENSOR states, also has a STATUS OR state representing if the system is on ground or in flight, and an OUTPUT state representing if it is currently activated or not. As we can see, the failure modes for each component block are explicitly modeled into safecharts, thus eliminating the need to separately define the failure modes and effects. Figure 15 shows the generic model for a basic block and Figure 16 shows the generic model for a controller block.

Safecharts modeled each of the five pumps and their corresponding controllers, along with the three distribution lines. However, since the blue system is independent of the other two systems, we verified the blue system separately. To check for total loss of hydraulic power, we had to check if the blue system does not supply power (i.e., EF (EG (powerB = 0))) and if the rest of the system (green and yellow systems) also does not supply power (i.e., EF (EG(powerG = 0 & powerY = 0))). It was easy to check the second safety requirement, that is, if a single failure results in total loss of hydraulic power, which expressed in TCTL is EF(EG(MODE in fail => powerB=0 & powerG=0 & powerY=0)).

In this A320 hydraulic system model, there were 13 safecharts with 145 states and 105 transitions, which were automatically transformed into 44 ETA models with 98 modes and 125 transitions.

Nuclear-Reactor System

The Three Mile Island 2 Nuclear Reactor was also modeled to see if we could verify the failure that occurred during the accident on 28th March, 1979. As shown in Figure 17, there are two circuits: a primary circuit and a secondary circuit. The primary circuit (Nissanke, 2002) generated steam due to the reactor heat and was confined in a containment building to avoid the leakage of radiation. A pressurizer valve and some control rods controlled the nuclear reaction. The secondary circuit fed water to the primary circuit for cooling and heat exchange and used the steam generated from the primary circuit to drive a turbine.

We summarize the events that led to the TMI accident as follows. Due to some manual errors, the feedwater valve in the secondary circuit was closed; heat exchange was thus stopped, resulting in a temperature increase in the primary circuit. As expected, the pressure relief valve (PRV) was opened and the control rods were dropped to slow down the nuclear fission. This is the *loss of coolant accident* (LOCA). When the pressure and temperature dropped, the PRV should have closed and control rods lifted. However, the

Figure 15. Integrated safecharts model for basic block in A320

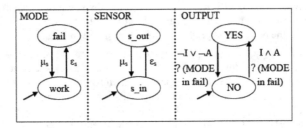

Figure 16. Integrated safecharts model for controller block in A320

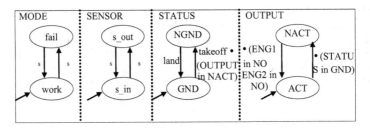

PRV was stuck open and this was not detected by the solenoid (sensor). As a result, the coolant from the primary circuit kept draining, thus endangering its environment with possible radiation.

Safecharts can be used to model the components in the TMI nuclear reactor and since safecharts can explicitly model all the failure modes of a component such as the stuck-open failure more of the PRV we can use safecharts to check for such safety violations in the model itself. Figure 18 illustrates the safechart model for PRV, where we can see that the sensor in the model detects PRV stuck-open failure, however, in the actual TMI reactor, during the accident, the PRV-close transition was taken, and thus the sensor could not detect the failure of the PRV to close. Figure 19 illustrates the safechart model for the primary circuit in the TMI nuclear reactor along with LOCA. The hazard that was checked for this model is EF (status in stuck-opened & sensor in prv-closed & flow in stopped). Any witness to the satisfaction of this TCTL property generated by the SGM model checker was evidence that the hazard could happen in this model. There were two safecharts with 27 states and 28 transitions, which were transformed into 6 ETA models with 19 modes and 30 transitions.

Figure 17. Three Mile Island 2 nuclear reactor

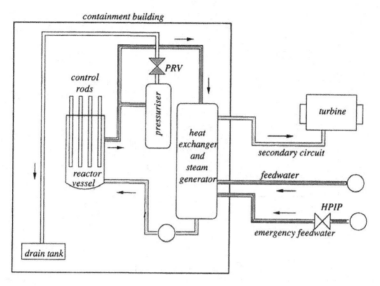

Figure 18. Safechart model of pressure relief valve at TMI

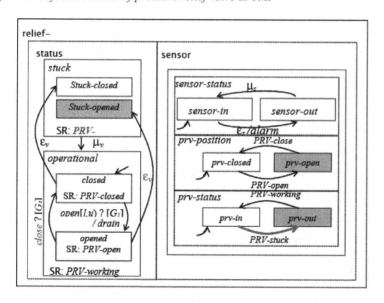

Figure 19. Safechart model of primary circuit at TMI

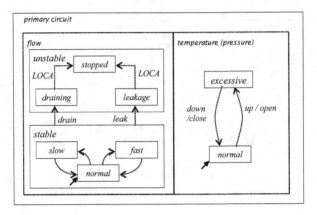

Conclusion

Nowadays, safety-critical systems are becoming increasingly pervasive in our daily lives. To reduce the probability of tragedy, we must have a formal and accurate methodology to verify if a safety-critical system is safe or not. We have proposed a formal method to verify safety-critical systems based on the safecharts model and model-checking paradigm. Our methodology can be applied widely to safety-critical systems with a model-driven architecture. Through several examples, we have shown the benefits of the proposed verification method and system model. We hope our methodology can have some real contribution such as making the world a safer place along with the development of science and technology.

References

Altisen, K., Gössler, G., & Sifakis, J. (2002). Scheduler modeling based on the controller synthesis paradigm. *Real-Time Systems, 23,* 55-84.

Bieber, P., Castel, C., & Seguin, C. (2002). Combination of fault tree analysis and model checking for safety assessment of complex system. In *Proceedings of the 4th European Dependable Computing Conference* (LNCS 2485, pp. 19-31). Springer-Verlag.

Bozzano, M., Cavallo, A., Cifaldi, M., Valacca, L., & Villafiorita, A. (2003). Improving safety assessment of complex systems: An industrial case study. In *Proceedings of the International Formal Methods Europe Symposium* (LNCS 2805, pp. 208-222). Springer-Verlag.

Bozzano, M., & Villafiorita, A. (2003). Improving system reliability via model checking: the FSAP/NuSMV-SA safety analysis platform. In *Proceedings of the International Conferece on Computer Safety, Reliability and Security* (LNCS 2788, pp. 49-62). Springer-Verlag.

Clarke, E. M., & Emerson, E. A. (1981). Design and synthesis of synchronization skeletons using branching time temporal logic. In *Proceedings of the Logics of Programs Workshop* (LNCS 131, pp. 52-71). Springer Verlag.

Clarke, E. M., Grumberg, O., & Peled, D. A. (1999). *Model checking*. MIT Press.

Dammag, H., & Nissanke, N. (1999). Safecharts for specifying and designing safety critical systems. In *Proceedings of the 18th IEEE Symposium on Reliable Distributed Systems* (pp. 78-87).

Deneux, J., & Akerlund, O. (2004). A common framework for design and safety analyses using formal methods. In *Proceedings of the International Conference on Probabilistic Safety Assurance and Management (PSAM) and European Safety and Reliability Conference.* Springer.

European Union. (2003). *Enhanced Safety Assessment for Complex Systems* (ESACS) Project, Retrieved from http://www.esacs.org

Fenelon, P., McDermid, J. A., Nicholson, M., & Pumfrey, D. J. (1994). Towards integrated safety analysis and design. *Applied Computing Review, 2,* 21-32.

Henzinger, T. A., Nicollin, X., Sifakis, J., & Yovine, S. (1992). Symbolic model checking for real-time systems. In *Proceedings of the IEEE International Conference on Logics in Computer Science* (pp. 394-406).

Hsiung, P. A., & Lin, S. W. (2005). Model checking timed systems with priorities. In *Proceedings of the International Conference on Real-Time and Embedded Computing Systems and Applications* (pp. 539-544). IEEE CS Press.

Hsiung, P. A., & Wang, F. (1998). A state-graph manipulator tool for real-time system specification and verification. In *Proceedings of the 5th International Conference on Real-Time Computing Systems and Applications* (pp. 181-188).

Jacky, J. (2000). Formal safety analysis of the control program for a radiation therapy machine. In *Proceedings of the 13th International Conference on the Use of Computers in Radiation Therapy* (pp. 68-70). Springer.

Johnson, M. E. (2002). Model checking safety properties of servo-loop control systems. In *Proceedings of the International Conference on Dependable Systems and Networks* (pp. 45-50). IEEE CS Press.

Larsen, K. G., Steffen, B., & Weise, C. (1996). Fischer's protocol revisited: A simple proof using model constraints. In *Hybrid System III* (LNCS 1066, pp. 604-615).

Lavazza, L. (Ed.). (2001). A methodology for formalizing concepts underlying the DESS notation. *ITEA.*

Leveson, N. G. (1995). *Safeware: System safety and computers.* Addison Wesley.

Leveson, N. G., & Stolzy, J. L. (1987). Safety analysis using Petri nets. *IEEE Transactions on Software Engineering, SE-13(3),* 386-397.

Lin, S. W., & Hsiung, P. A. (2005). Model checking prioritized timed automata. In *Proceedings of the International Symposium on Automated Technology for Verification and Analysis* (LNCS 3707, pp. 370-384). Springer Verlag.

Nissanke, N., & Dammag, H. (2000a). Risk bands — A novel feature of safecharts. In *Proceedings of the 11ᵗʰ International Symposium on Software Reliability Engineering* (pp. 293-301).

Nissanke, N., & Dammag, H. (2000b). Risk ordering of states in safecharts. In *Proceedings of the 19ᵗʰ International Conference on Computer Safety, Reliability, and Security* (LNCS 1943, pp. 395-405). Springer Verlag.

Nissanke, N., & Dammag, H. (2002). Design for safety in safecharts with risk ordering of states. *Safety Science, 40*(9), 753-763.

Queille, J. P., & Sifakis, J. (1982). Specification and verification of concurrent systems in CESAR. In *Proceedings of the International Symposium on Programming* (LNCS 137, pp. 337-351). Springer Verlag.

Sommerville, I. (2004). *Software engineering* (7ᵗʰ ed.). Addison Wesley.

Wang, F., & Hsiung, P. A. (2002). Efficient and user-friendly verification. *IEEE Transactions on Computers, 51*(1), 61-83.

Yang, S. H., Chung, P. W. H., Kowalewski, S., & Stursberg, O. (2000). Automatic safety analysis of computer controlled plants using model checking. In *Proceedings of the 10ᵗʰ Symposium on Computer-Aided Process Engineering (ESCAPE 10)*.

Appendix

These are the ETA models for the variants of the railway signaling system.

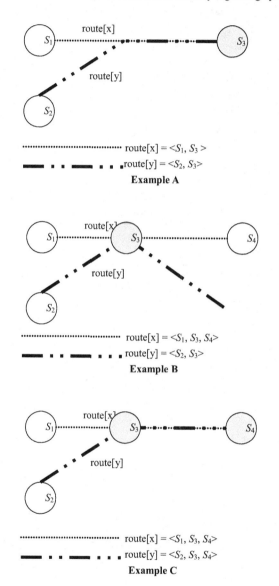

route[x]

route[y]

S_1 S_3

S_2

route[x] = $<S_1, S_3>$

route[y] = $<S_2, S_3>$

Example A

route[x]

route[y]

S_1 S_3 S_4

S_2

route[x] = $<S_1, S_3, S_4>$

route[y] = $<S_2, S_3>$

Example B

route[x]

route[y]

S_1 S_3 S_4

S_2

route[x] = $<S_1, S_3, S_4>$

route[y] = $<S_2, S_3, S_4>$

Example C

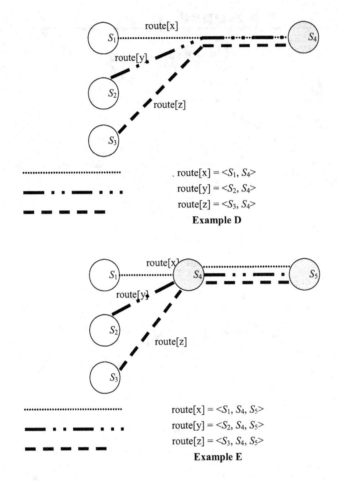

Example D

route[x] = <S_1, S_4>
route[y] = <S_2, S_4>
route[z] = <S_3, S_4>

Example E

route[x] = <S_1, S_4, S_5>
route[y] = <S_2, S_4, S_5>
route[z] = <S_3, S_4, S_5>

About the Authors

Aristides Dasso is an associate professor at the Departmento de Informática at Universidad Nacional de San Luis, Argentina. He has published more than 50 articles in international conferences and journals and has presented several papers in international conferences on software engineering and information systems, both areas of research that he is currently pursuing, with special emphasis in the area of formal methods. He has studied political science in Argentina and computer science in Argentina and France and has been a fellow at the International Institute for Software Technologies of the United Nations University, Macao. He is a member of both ACM and IEEE.

Ana Funes is an assistant professor at the Departamento de Informática at the Universidad Nacional de San Luis, Argentina. She holds a master's degree in software engineering from that university. She is a researcher at the SEG (Software Engineering Group) of the Universidad Nacional de San Luis. Her main research interests are focused on formal and semiformal specification techniques, and testing.

* * * * *

Evon M. O. Abu-Taieh an assistant professor in The Arab Academy for Banking & Financial Sciences, Jordan. She worked for 10 years as IT department head in the Ministry of Transport and has many research papers in simulation, simulation & software engineering, GIS, artificial intelligence, and ciphering systems. Her main interests in research are: simulation, AI, and ciphering systems. She was posted track chair in IRMA conference in 2006 and track cochair in IRMA Conference 2005. She holds a BSc and MS in computer science from St. Martin's College and Pacific Lutheran University, respectively. She earned her PhD from The Arab Academy for Banking & Financial Sciences.

Hyggo Oliveira de Almeida received an MSc in informatics from the Federal University of Campina Grande, in 2004, and a BS in computer science from the Federal University of Alagoas, at Maceió, Brazil, in 2002. Currently, he is a PhD student, since 2004, in electrical engineering at the Federal University of Campina Grande. He has authored or co-authored over 50 research papers, including conferences, journals, and book chapters. His research is on the fields of component and multiagent-based dynamic-software composition, software engineering for embedded systems, and pervasive computing.

Liane Bandeira graduated with a degree in computer science from the State University of Ceará – Uece. For a year and a half, she acted as a test analyst, performing activities of planning, projection, and execution of software tests, both manual and automated. She has also participated in the implantation of functional-system automated tests and carries on expanding it to other projects. She has participated in the process of implementation and certification ISO 9001:2000, defining and formalizing processes and methodologies of software development based on RUP, ISO, CMM, and CMMI. Beforehand, she was analyst of the Laboratory of Patterns and Quality in Software Engineering in Uece, where she implanted and audited a development process based on RUP.

Gabriel Baum is co-director of LIFIA (Laboratorio de Investigación y Formación en Informática) at the University of La Plata, Argentina. He is also president of SADIO (Argentinean Society of Computer Science). He is a professor of theoretical computer science, functional programming and formal languages at the University of La Plata and the University of Rio Cuarto. He coauthored books and published numerous technical papers. His research interests comprise formal methods including specification and derivation of programs, calculus of program construction based on fork algebras and generic programs, computability, abstract and concrete complexity, logics, and algebra.

Sami Beydeda studied computer science at the University of Dortmund. After studying computer science, he was a research associate at the Universities of Dortmund and Leipzig (1999-2003). In 2003, he finished his PhD thesis on "The self-testing COTS components (STECC) method." Currently, Beydeda is at the Federal Finance Office (Bundesamt fuer Finance), which is part of the Federal Finance Ministry of Germany. Research interests include testing and analysis, component-based development, model-driven development, and aspect-oriented programming.

David Cabrero is an associate professor at the Department of Computer Science, University of A Coruña, Spain. He received his PhD in Computer Science in 2002 (University of A Coruña) for his work on tabular parsing. His research interest includes accessibility in information systems, distributed programming as well as the use of formal methods on software engineering, in particular formal verification with theorem provers like PVS.

Yean-Ru Chen received a BS in computer science and information engineering from the National Chiao Tung University, Hsinchu, Taiwan, ROC in 2002. From 2002 to 2003, she was employed as an engineer in the SoC Technology Center, Industrial Technology Research Institute, Hsinchu, Taiwan, ROC. She is currently working toward an MS at the National Chung Cheng University. Her current research interest is formal verification.

Juan José Cuadrado received a BSc in 1994 from Universidad Complutense de Madrid, Spain and a PhD in 2001 from Universidad Carlos III de Madrid, Spain. He lectures at the School of Computer Sciences at the University of Alcalá (Spain). His research interests include software measurement and experimentation in software engineering. He is author of several research papers in scientific journals and books.

Paula Luciana da Cunha is a specialist in e-strategic information management and graduated in informatics from the University of Fortaleza (UNIFOR). She has worked in the Instituto Atlântico (software development company, certified in CMM level 2 and ISO), for two years as a test analyst. Her main activities are elaboration of institutional procedure and processing of software tests; planning of software tests; elaboration and modeling of test cases; analysis and execution of software tests and test-analysis automation (with tools Rational Administrator, Rational Test Manager and Rational Robot). She is also a team member of the project *Functional Systemic Test Automation*, part of the 2005 cycle of the Brazilian Program of Software Quality and Productivity (PBQP Software). She also participated in the following trainings: *Rational TeamTest Fundamentals for Performance Testing*, *Rational TeamTest Fundamentals for Functional Testing* and *CMMi Level 2 – PA of Verification and Validation*.

Marcela Daniele has a BS in systems engineering and is currently working on her master's thesis project on software engineering under the supervision of Gabriel Baum. She is a professor and researcher in the Department of Computer Science at the National University of Río Cuarto, Argentina. She lectures on system analysis and design and software engineering. Her research interests are software engineering, in particular object-oriented software modeling. She has published papers involving UML, development processes, UML extensions, formal methods, and business modelling.

Paula Donegan has been a test analyst at a Brazilian research and development institution (Instituto Atlântico) for almost 2 years. She has managed test activities, test-case design, and performed manual and automated software tests for various systems. She has experience in automation of software tests using rational test tools (Rational TestStudio). She has an MS in computer science from the State University of Ceará (Uece). She has published papers at national and international events, receiving a prize from a renowned Brazilian symposium in 2005. She also presented a project of test automation for the Brazilian Product Quality Program from the Science and Technology Ministry.

Anne Eerola teaches software engineering in the Department of Computer Science at the University of Kuopio, Finland. Her research emphasizes requirements management and architectures, software modelling and design, and software testing. She has a research group that strives to improve software-engineering methods in healthcare and energy domains.

Luis Fernández received a BSc in 1989 from Universidad Politécnica de Madrid (Spain) and a PhD from Universidad del Pais Vasco in 1997 (his thesis won the extraordinary award for doctoral students). He worked as a lecturer at Universidad Politécnica de Madrid for 8 years. He is with the Universidad Europea de Madrid (Spain) as a professor and head of the Department of Computer Systems. His research interests include software quality, testing and software development processes and methodologies. He is author of research papers in scientific journals and books.

Glauber Ferreira is an MSc student at the Federal University of Campina Grande. He received a BS in computer science from the Federal University of Alagoas, Maceió, Brazil (2004). His research areas include multiagent-systems interaction protocols, pervasive computing, and software components for building mobile virtual communities applications.

Elizabeth Furtado is a doctor in computer science and a professor at the University of Fortaleza -UNIFOR in the computer science undergraduate course and in the master's program. She is a consultant in the improvement of software-development processes and in usability of software products. She is part of the national and international program committees in the area of human-computer interaction (HCI) and she is the chair of the ACM BR-CHI organizing committee. Her most relevant and recent publications are in a workshop in ICSE 2005, in the Latin-American Conference in HCI (CLIHC 2005) and in the workshop Task Model and Diagrams for User Interface Design (TAMODIA 2005) concerning the areas of semiotic engineering, software engineering, and usability engineering.

Víctor M. Gulías is an associate professor at the Department of Computer Science, University of A Coruña, Spain. He received his PhD in computer science in 2000 (University of A Coruña) for his work on distributed functional programming. His research interest includes functional and object-oriented design and programming as well as the use of formal methods in the software-development cycle. In the last years, he has been leading the VoDKA project, an industrial-strength distributed video-on-demand server developed using the functional language Erlang.

Pao-Ann Hsiung received a BS degree in mathematics and a PhD degree in electrical engineering from the National Taiwan University (1991 and 1996, respectively). From February 2001 to July 2002, he was an assistant professor in the Department of Computer Science and Information Engineering, National Chung Cheng University, where he is currently an associate professor. He was the recipient of the 2001 ACM Kuo-Ting Li Young Researcher Award and a recipient of the 2004 Young Scholar Research Award given by National Chung Cheng University. He is a member of the IEEE, ACM, and IICM. He has published more than 100 papers in international journals and conferences. His main research interests include: formal verification, system-on-chip and embedded-system design and verification, hardware-software co-design, and software engineering.

J. Santiago Jorge is an assistant professor at the Department of Computer Science at the University of A Coruña, Spain. He received his PhD in computer science in 2004 from the University of A Coruña for his work on software verification. His research interests include functional and object-oriented programming, and formal methods of software engineering, in particular formal verification with theorem provers.

Pedro J. Lara received a BSc in 1995 from Universidad Politécnica de Madrid, Spain. He has been software developer during four years and worked as a Web services and middleware consultant in HP Spain for the next two years. Since 2000, he is with the High Technical School at Universidad Europea de Madrid (Spain) as lecturer. He is now developing his PhD thesis at Universidad de Alcalá (Spain). His research interests include software processes, test automation and object-oriented modelling. He is author of several research papers about these topics.

Yen-Hung Lin received a BS in computer science and information engineering from the National Chung Cheng University, Chiayi, Taiwan, ROC (2005). He is currently working toward an MS at the National Chiao Tung University. His current research interests include VLSI CAD, safety-critical systems, and formal verification.

Pablo E. Martínez López (better known in the academy as Fidel) earned a doctorate of computer science from the National University of Buenos Aires (UBA), Argentina, Magister on Informatics from Pedeciba, University of the Republic, Montevideo, Uruguay, and Licenciate on Informatics from the National University of La Plata (UNLP) and from Latin-American Superior School on Informatics (ESLAI) as part of National University of Luján (UNLu), both in Argentina. His teaching and working experience covers more than 13 years. Currently he is working as a teacher and researcher in the National University of La Plata (UNLP), at LIFIA, from the Computer Science Faculty. Before, he has taught at diverse national universities, such as those of Río IV (UNRC), La Matanza (UNLM), Buenos Aires (UBA), and Rosario (UNR), and has been part of several groups of software development. His main interests in research are functional programming and programming-languages theory, specializing in techniques for automatic production of programs, domain-specific languages, and systems for the static analysis of programs.

Emerson Loureiro is an MSc student at the Federal University of Campina Grande, Brazil. He received a BS in computer science from the Federal University of Alagoas, Maceió, Brazil (2004). His current research fields are pervasive computing, mainly on middleware development and software engineering for pervasive computing systems, and service-oriented architectures, focused on service composition and provision for pervasive computing environments.

Camila Maia is analyst of systems in the Atlantic Institute, which develops products of technology with high value added for its customers, in Fortaleza - CE-Brazil. She acts in the area of software testing, including automation of functional-system tests, planning of activities of test and elaboration of statistics over encountered defects. Before this, she worked in some companies as Web developer. In 1999, she formed techniques in industrial computers in the Centro Federal de Educação Técnológica - CEFET. In 2004, she was graduated in Computation in the Universidade Federal do Ceará - UFC. In 2005, she concluded the specialization in information technologies with emphasis in Web development, also in the Universidade Federal do Ceará.

Paola Martellotto has a BS in computer science from the National University of Río Cuarto, Argentina. She is an advance student of a master's in software engineering. She is a teaching assistant in the Computer Science Department at the National University of Río Cuarto, Argentina. She also is programmer in computer center at the National University of Río Cuarto. Her research focus is in system verification and software engineering. She has published papers on type theory, functional and imperative programming, UML extensions, and business modelling.

Cristina Matos is an undergraduate in computer science and postgraduate (specialist) in information strategic management from UNIFOR - University of Fortaleza. Working as a test analyst, she has been busy developing planning activities and performing software tests, modeling test cases and automation by using rational tools (e.g., rational administrator, rational test manager and rational robot) for almost three years. She is a member of the support institutional group for the CMM and ISO development and setup process at Instituto Atlântico, participating in the definition of processes and methodologies of software development based on RUP (rational unified process) and CMM. She is also a consultant of the MPS.BR model - Brazilian Software Process Improvement.

Pedro Fernandes Ribeiro Neto received an MSc in electrical engineering from the Federal University of Paraíba, Campina Grande, Brazil (2001), and received a BSc in computer science from State University of Ceará in 1997. Since 1998, he has been an assistant professor of software engineering at the State University of Rio Grande do Norte, Mossoró, Brazil. He is currently a PhD student in electrical engineering in Federal University of Campina Grande, Brazil. His research is in the fields of real-time systems, real-time databases, quality of service, formal methods, and colored Petri nets.

Angelo Perkusich received a PhD and MSc in electrical engineering from Federal University of Paraíba, Campina Grande, Brazil (1994 and 1987, respectively), and received his BSc in electrical engineering from the engineering faculty of Barretos in 1982. From 1988 to 1990, he was an assistant professor of electronics and systems at the Federal

University of Pernambuco. From 1992 to 1993, he was a visiting research professor at the University of Pittsburgh, Pennsylvania. From 1991 to 1994, he was an assistant professor of electrical engineering at the Federal University of Paraíba, Campina Grande, Brazil. Since 1994, he has been an adjunct professor in that department. He is a project leader/ consultant at the affiliated Nokia project for the development of embedded systems applications for mobile devices.

Maria Lígia Barbosa Perkusich received a PhD in electrical engineering in 2000, an MSc in computer science in 1989, and a bachelor's degree in informatics in 1985, all from Federal University of Paraíba, Campina Grande, Brazil. From 1994 to 1997, she was an assistant professor of State University of Paraíba. In 2001, she joined the Department of Informatics and Statistics, Catholic University of Pernambuco, where she is currently an assistant professor. Her main research interest areas are real-time databases and mobile databases.

Mario Piattini has an MSc and a PhD in computer science (Politechnical University of Madrid) and an MSc in psychology (UNED). He is also a certified information system auditor and a certified information system manager through ISACA (Information System Audit and Control Association) as well as a full professor in the Department of Computer Science at the University of Castilla - La Mancha, Ciudad Real, Spain. Furthermore, he is the author of several books and papers on databases, software engineering, and information systems. He leads the ALARCOS research group of the Department of Information Systems and Technologies at the University of Castilla - La Mancha, Ciudad Real, Spain. His research interests are: software metrics, IS security and audit, software maintenance, and testing.

Macario Polo is an associate professor at the University of Castilla - La Mancha, where he got a PhD in computer science. He is a member of the ALARCOS research group, in the Department of Information Systems and Technologies. His main research areas fall into the automation of software maintenance tasks, especially reengineering and testing.

Marisa Analía Sánchez received a PhD in computer science from Universidad Nacional del Sur in Bahía Blanca, Argentina. She is currently a professor of graduate and postgraduate courses at Department of Management Sciences at Universidad Nacional del Sur. From 1994 to 2004, she had been on the faculty of the Departments of Computer Science and Electrical Engineering. Her research interests are in software engineering, particularly software testing. She is also interested in business modeling.

Albert Schilling graduated in computer science from the University of Fortaleza - UNIFOR. He is currently a student at the specialization course for information strategic management at UNIFOR and he is also a researcher and UI designer at the Laboratory of Software Usability and Quality. He has published the results of his works at the lab concerning the application of a test strategy in a project for the Brazilian Digital Television System in international conferences, such as a Workshop on Advances in

Model-Based Software Testing at ICSE 2005 and also in Brazilian workshops focused on Digital TV.

Asim Abdel Rahman El Sheikh is a graduate of the London School of Economics & Political Science, University of London. His major areas of interest are simulation and modeling. He worked as a consultant and teaching professor in many organizations and was also a researcher in the computer-aided simulation modeling (CASM) research group in London. Currently he is the dean of information systems & technology faculty in The Arab Academy for Banking & Financial Sciences, Jordan. He also enjoys system analysis and software engineering in addition to simulation and modeling.

Leandro Silva received his BS in computer science from the Federal University of Alagoas, Maceió, Brazil (2000) and his MSc in electrical engineering from the Federal University of Campina Grande, Campina Grande, Brazil (2002). Currently, he is a PhD student in electrical engineering at the Federal University of Campina Grande. His research is on the fields of formal software verification, model checking, coloured Petri nets, component-based software systems, and embedded systems. Leandro has spent a year at the University of California, Santa Cruz, working as visiting researcher in the timed interfaces project with Professor Luca de Alfaro.

Kenia Sousa graduated in computer science from the University of Fortaleza (UNIFOR) and is a graduate student in applied computer science at UNIFOR, Brazil. She is vice-chair of the ACM BR-CHI organizing committee. She has been working with human-computer interaction (HCI), more specifically on processes, methods, and models of UI design and evaluation. Her most relevant publications were in TAMODIA 2002 and 2004, CADUI 2002, INTERACT 2003, HCI INTERNATIONAL 2003 and 2005, two workshops (integration of HCI and SE, and A-MOST) in ICSE 2003, 2004, and 2005, and DSVIS 2005. At UNIFOR, she is currently working on a research project for the definition of the Brazilian Digital Television System, financed by the Brazilian government.

Tanja Toroi (MSc) is a researcher and PhD student at the University of Kuopio, Finland, where she received her master's degree in 1999. She has worked in different positions, such as assistant, senior assistant, lecturer, and researcher, at the university since 1998. Her main research interests are software-component testing and conformance testing of open interfaces. At the moment, she is working in the OpenTE (open integration testing environment) research project, which studies interfaces and their conformance to specifications especially in health information systems.

Index

A

absolute validity interval 99, 100, 107
abstract model 221, 255
acceptance test 174
ACID (see atomicity, consistency, isolation, and durability) 101
activity diagram 358
adaptive techniques 175
admission control 102
AHL net (see algebraic high-level net) 43
algebraic high-level (AHL) net 43
algebraic type 287, 291
alpha testing 174
anonymous function 271, 283, 291
aperiodic 98-100
application
    73, 74, 76, 78, 79, 80, 81, 85,
    222, 241, 260, 271, 274, 277, 283,
    288, 291, 308
application integration 119
architecture 125
argument
    231, 232, 237, 251, 271, 274, 277,
    283, 290, 291, 298, 301, 308
arrival pattern 100

artifact 318, 320, 322, 324, 325, 326
assertion checking 169
ATLM (see automate testing life-cycle methodology) 93
atomicity, consistency, isolation, and durabiliity (ACID) 101
Australian Healthcare Messaging Laboratory 122
automate testing life-cycle methodology (ATLM) 93
automated software testing 73
automated testing 74
automatic code generation 382
automating software test 72
automation management 91
automation tool 82
axiom 229, 230, 274, 283

B

b-reduction 249, 250
basis-path testing 166
beta-program 73
binary search-based test case generation (BINTEST) 187, 200
binder 274, 290
black-box testing 170

black-boxing 162
BMC software 92
Boolean 274, 283, 291, 301, 309
bottom-up testing 162, 169
bound variable 271, 301, 308
boundary value analysis 168
branch testing 171
Brazilian System for the Digital Television 48
bug 91
bug tracking 87
business model 318, 329
business process 318, 321
business use-case model 322
business-analysis model 322, 333

C

capture/playback tool 83
CA (see client application) 35
cause-effect graphing 162, 172
checklist 60
client application (CA) 35
code-coverage analyzer 86
code-instrumentors tools 86
coloured Petri nets 25, 31, 113
commercial-off-the-shelf (COTS) 191
compatibility function 101
completeness
     281, 283, 286, 291, 315
component
     185, 186, 187, 191, 192, 193
component object model 189
component type 189
component-based development
     186, 187
composition 273, 274, 283
computation tree logic 40
concrete business model 319, 333
condition testing 171
conditional 274, 283
conformance 118, 121, 123
conformance clause 121, 125
conformance testing
     118, 119, 120, 124, 130, 133
consistency 101
constructor 283, 301

conventional database system 97
conventional technique 175
Coq
     220, 221, 229, 230, 232, 233, 248
correctness
     274, 283, 286, 291, 308, 315
correctness proof 165
currification 277, 278, 283

D

data access type 100
data analysis 165
data input (see also input domain) 76, 79
data-flow testing 171
database management systems 97
DBM subtraction 400, 401
DC (see duration calculus) 6, 8
deadline 98, 100, 102, 110, 115
debug 162
decidability 274, 290, 291
defect 76, 83, 85, 86, 87
defect (see also bug) 73
defect tracking 87
delayable evaluation 391
derivation
     274, 283, 291, 293, 301, 308, 310, 315
design/CPN 26, 31, 32
desk checking 163
digital 61
discrete event simulation 154, 157
durability 101
duration calculus (DC) 6, 8
dynamic VV&T technique 162

E

eager evaluation 391
EAI (see external authoring interface) 27
effects 306, 308
EFSM (see extended finite state machine) 17
Enterprise JavaBeans 189, 190
entity bean 190
environment 274, 283, 291, 308
equivalence partitioning 167

Erlang 222, 253
execution monitoring 162, 167
execution profiling 162, 167
execution testing 167
execution tracing 162, 167
expansion 302, 308
expression
    274, 283, 291, 301, 303, 308, 315
expressiveness 269, 274, 298, 301
extended finite state machines (EFSM)
    17
extended timed automaton (ETA) 386
extensible 3D graphics (X3D) 28
extensible markup language (XML) 28
external authoring interface (EAI) 27,
    33

F

face validity 163
failure mode and effect analysis (FMEA)
    355
false 274, 299, 301, 308
fault injection 4
fault-based symbolic testing 4
fault-based testing 2, 3, 20
fault-tree 7, 13, 20
fault/failure analysis 173
field testing 162, 170
finite state machine (FSM) 21
firm deadline 100
fix 274, 283, 302, 308
fixpoint 271, 283, 302
flattening safechart 397
formal language 127, 132
formal method 221, 253
formal specification 317
formal specification language 327
formal system 274,
    285, 291, 306, 315
formal verification 379
formal VV&T technique 162
free variable 271, 274, 283, 301, 310
FSM (see finite state machine) 21
FSMWeb technique 21
function
    271, 274, 283, 291, 301, 308

function space 273, 283
function type 273
functional 274, 283, 291
functional configuration audit 163
functional language 274, 287, 291
functional program 222
functional programming 270, 274
functional testing 170
functional-testing tool 83
functionality 72, 73, 75, 77, 86
fusion places 103, 104

G

generalization 295, 301
generic instance 293
generic model 317, 324
global state 291, 297, 301
grammar 274, 305, 308
graph modeling 317, 319
graph-based testing method 166
graphical comparison 162, 173
graphical user interface (GUI) 19
GUI-testing tool 83, 85

H

hard deadline 99
hardware operations test 74
Haskell 274, 305, 308
hazard analysis 380
HCI (see human-computer interaction)
    47, 50, 55, 62
HCPN (see hierarchical coloured Petri
    net) 26
Health Level 7 (HL7)
    122, 123, 130, 132
healthcare 126
heuristic evaluation 56
hierarchical coloured Petri net (HCPN)
    26, 31, 98, 103, 107, 116
higher order logic 180
hook method 291
HTML 20
human-computer interaction (HCI) 47,
    50, 55, 62

I

identity function 276, 283, 291
identity substitution
    282, 283, 291, 301
if-then-else 271, 299, 301
imprecision 101, 102, 103, 110
input domain 75, 76
input variation 80
inspection 342, 368
instance 283, 304, 308
instance variable 287, 291
integrating the healthcare enterprise
    (IHE) 122
integration 119
interface analysis technique 172
interface specification 120, 124
interface-driven modeling 93
internal consistency 101
interoperability
    118, 119, 121, 126, 128
isolation 101
isomorphic 302

J

Java 281, 283
Java 3D 28, 42
Java language 27
JavaScript 38
JavaScript language 27
judgement
    274, 283, 285, 290, 291, 315

K

key word 126

L

lack of information
    186, 187, 194, 195, 212
lambda calculus 173
lazy evaluation 391
let 271, 274, 283, 291, 301
let-bounded polymorphism 290, 291
letrec 272, 274
list 273, 315

load, performance, and stress testing
    86
local definition 274, 275
logical consistency 97, 99
logical constraint 111
loop test 171

M

mandatory enforcement 392
manual proof 221
manual proving 228
manual software testing 73
manual test 75
mapping 102, 112, 278, 291
Markov model 355
mean time to failure (MTTF) 5
memory-leak detection tools 85
message sequence chart (MSC) 105,
    108, 114
message-driven bean 190
metacommunication 50
metamorphic testing 4
metrics 367
metrics reporting tool 86
minimal cut set (MCS) 381
mode predicate 386
model checking
    32, 40, 221, 379, 380, 388
model reduction (see slicing) 13
model testing 156
model validation 155
model verification 156
monitoring 102, 112
monomorphic 290, 291, 308
monotype 290, 291, 308
most general unifier 282, 283
most important data (MID) 354
most important environment (MIE) 354
most important no analytical test (MIN)
    354
most important path (MIP) 354
most important test (MIT) 354
MSC (see message sequence chart)
    105, 108, 114
MTTF (see mean time to failure) 5
mutation operator 140, 141, 150

mutation testing 3
mutual exclusion 395

N

National Institute of Standards and
      Technology 122
natural language 128
negotiation 102, 111, 112
network-testing tools 86
new variable 285, 291
non-computable 274
notation 290, 291

O

object oriented 291, 352, 357
object-oriented simulation 174
Object-Z 317
observation 60
occurrence graph 107
OpenTE project
      118, 119, 120, 132, 133
oracle 4, 20
overloaded type 270, 274
overloading 274, 301, 308

P

paper sketch 63
parametric polymorphism
      286, 291, 308
parse tree (see also syntax tree) 10
parser 269, 274
partial evaluation 315
path analysis 162
path testing 171
performance metric 102, 112
performance test 77
periodic 98, 114, 115
periodicity 115
Petri net 26, 43, 103
Petri net kernel (PNK) 42
Petri net model 43
physical configuration audit 163
polymorphic type system
      274, 291, 301, 308
polymorphism 283, 291, 308

predicate 308
predictive validation 162
principal type 308
process integration 119
program 72, 73, 74, 77, 78, 79, 80
program slicing 9
prohibition 392
projection 274, 301
proof obligation 231, 241, 242
propagation, infection, and execution
      (PIE) 5
PVS 220, 222, 255, 260, 264

Q

QoS management 112
QoS parameters 102
qualified type 296, 301, 308
quantification 291
quantified variable 291, 301
questionnaires 60

R

radiotherapy 127
real-time database
      96, 97, 98, 99, 100
record 301
recursion 274, 301, 308, 315
recursive call 283, 291
recursive definition 274, 308
recursive expression 283
recursive type 274, 283, 301, 308
recursive-descent parsing (see also
      parse tree) 10
referential transparency 222
region 308
register 308
register allocation 274, 308, 315
regression fault 167
regression test
      73, 74, 76, 77, 81, 92, 162, 167
relative validity interval 100
RELAY model 4
reliability theory 2, 4
remote home interface 198
remote interface 198
renaming 283

requirement-driven model-based test automation 93
requirements 71, 73, 76, 77, 83, 89
requirements state machine language 9
resource reservation 102
retest (see also regression test) 72
revealing subdomain 4
review 165
risk analysis 346, 352
risk band 394
risk graph 393
risk relation 393
rule 274, 283, 291, 301, 315, 332

S

safechart 381, 383, 393
safety semantics 391
safety-critical system 378, 387
scope 274, 301
script 74, 75, 77, 78, 79, 80, 82, 85, 87
scripting language 87
SDCT 122
SDP (see software development process) 48
SE (see software engineering) 47
security function specification (SFS) 93
seed 291, 301
self-testability 185, 195, 196, 200, 210
semantic-lock technique 101
semiformal language 127, 132
semiotic engineering 48, 50
sensitivity analysis 162, 171
sensor network 96, 97, 98, 109
session bean 198
SFS (see security function specification) 93
shelfware 83
simulation 156, 157, 379
simulation model 97
simulation-development process 156
slicing 9, 10, 12
soft deadline 99
software component 188

software development 73, 82
software development process (SDP) 48
software engineering (SE) 47, 49
software implementation 50
software product 73, 87
software quality assurance (SQA) 341
software testability 5
software testing 119, 120
software-development life cycle 107
software-engineering practices 155
soundness 274
specific business model 328
specific technique 176
specification 102, 108, 112, 221, 274, 283, 291, 301, 310, 315
specification-based testing 2, 11
specified requirements 80
sporadic 99
stakeholder 89
state graph manipulator (SGM) 380, 389
statechart 11, 381, 382
statemate semantics 18
statement testing 171
static analysis 274, 283
static type system 274
statistical technique 162
STECC 185, 192, 200
stereotype 325
stress test 77, 162, 170
structured walkthrough 163
submodel testing 162, 172
substitution 281, 283, 291
substitution transition 103, 104
sum type 299, 301, 315
sums 301, 308
symbolic debugging 162, 172
symbolic execution 162
symbolic VV&T technique 162
syntactic category 274, 283, 291, 301
syntax analysis 164
syntax directed 291, 301
syntax tree (see also parse tree) 10
system 88, 89, 90, 91, 92, 93

system communicability analysis 50
system requirement 318
system state graph 387

T

tag 301
tagged type 301
target architecture 125
TCP/IP network 35
TD (see timing diagram) 109
temporal restriction 97
temporal restriction (see also timing
     constraint) 97
term 274, 283, 291, 301, 308, 315
term variable 274, 281, 283
test automation 75
test case
     73, 77, 79, 81, 83, 85, 90, 92, 93,
     136, 137, 138, 139, 140, 141, 143,
     144, 145, 147, 150, 151
test class (see also test script, script)
     73
test engineer 73, 82, 85, 86, 87
test environment 346
test execution tool 83
test procedure (see also test case)
     74, 78, 83, 85
test scenario 85
test script (see also script)
     73, 79, 80, 82, 85, 87
test stage 72, 82, 83
test support tool 83
test template 139, 140, 149
test-case 136
test-case generation 137
test-case mutant 140
test-case mutation 136
test-cases generation algorithm 358
test-data extraction tool 85
test-data generator 85
test-development tool 83
test-management tool 86
test-procedure generator 83
testability
     120, 123, 124, 125, 127, 133
testable beans approach 211

testing 2, 154, 220, 255, 379
testing-completion criteria 346
theorem prover 221, 228, 229, 260
timed computation tree logic (TCTL)
     388
timestamp 99, 110
timing constraint 99, 105
timing diagram (TD) 109
top-down testing 162, 169
traceability assessment 173
transition priority 393, 400
transition urgencies 399
translation mechanism 328, 329
tree 283, 308
true 274, 283, 291, 299, 301, 308
tuple 274, 290, 291, 296, 298, 301
turing test 165
type 274, 283, 291, 298, 299, 301,
     308, 315
type checker 274
type equivalence 301
type inference
     274, 283, 291, 301, 308, 315
type language 283, 291, 301
type scheme 291
type specialization 274, 301, 315
type system
     274, 283, 291, 301, 308, 315
type variable 283, 291, 308
type-correctness condition (TCC)
     231, 241
typechecking 274, 283, 301
typing judgement 274, 308, 315

U

UI (see user interface) 47
UI design alternatives 48
UI design patterns 64
UI evaluation 51
UML (see unified modeling language)
     98, 318, 341, 344, 381
unification 283, 291
unified modeling language (UML)
     98, 318, 341, 344, 381
unified software development process
     318

unify 283, 291
unit 299, 301
unit testing 80, 85
universal quantification 291, 304, 308
UPi-Test 51, 53, 61
usability engineering 48, 50, 55
usability inspections method 49
usability test 77
usability-measurement tool 87
use case 72
use cases (see also requirements) 76
user interface (UI) 47
user-interface evaluation 48

V

valid judgement 283, 315
validation 154, 155, 156, 172
validation and verification (V&V) 155
validation technique 25
validity interval 99, 100, 107, 111
variable 274, 283, 291, 301
variant 274, 301
verification 24, 32, 154, 156, 172,
    176
video-on-demand 222, 253
video-on-demand kernel architecture
    (VoDKA) 253
virtual chat 61
virtual reality modeling language 25, 33
visualization 162, 170
void 287, 301
VV&T 162

W

white-box testing 162
World Wide Web Consortium (W3C)
    122

X

X3D (see extensible 3D graphics) 28
XML (see extensible markup language)
    28, 132

Z

zone capping 400

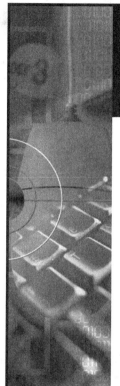

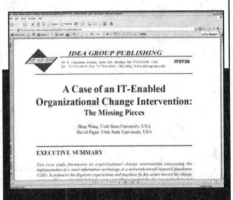